NAMING THE WORLD

ANDREW COWELL

NAMING THE WORLD

*Language and Power Among
the Northern Arapaho*

THE UNIVERSITY OF
ARIZONA PRESS
TUCSON

The University of Arizona Press
www.uapress.arizona.edu

We respectfully acknowledge the University of Arizona is on the land and territories of Indigenous peoples. Today, Arizona is home to twenty-two federally recognized tribes, with Tucson being home to the O'odham and the Yaqui. Committed to diversity and inclusion, the University strives to build sustainable relationships with sovereign Native Nations and Indigenous communities through education offerings, partnerships, and community service.

© 2018 by The Arizona Board of Regents
All rights reserved. Published 2018
First paperback edition published 2025

ISBN-13: 978-0-8165-3855-3 (cloth)
ISBN-13: 978-0-8165-5536-9 (paper)
ISBN-13: 978-0-8165-3906-2 (ebook)

Cover design by Carrie House, HOUSEdesign llc
Cover photo: *The Name Giving* by Sara Wiles

Library of Congress Cataloging-in-Publication Data are available at the Library of Congress.

Printed in the United States of America
♾ This paper meets the requirements of ANSI/NISO Z39.48-1992 (Permanence of Paper).

CONTENTS

Acknowledgments vii
Abbreviations and Symbols ix

Introduction. An Ethnography of Language Shift Among the Northern Arapaho   3

1. Northern Arapaho History and Communities of Practice   15
2. Cultural Metaphors and the Indigenous Discourse of Language Endangerment   48
3. Ethnogeography Through Time: Names and Power in the Landscape   82
4. Personal Names and Naming   127
5. Folk Etymology and Language Purism   168
6. Neologisms and the Politics of Language Maintenance   201

Conclusion. Communities of Practice: A Linguistic Summary   242

Notes 271
References 285
Index 297

ACKNOWLEDGMENTS

I WOULD OF COURSE FIRST like to thank the people of the Northern Arapaho Tribe who have hosted me over the years, especially adopted family members. Many thanks to those who have spent time helping me learn about the Arapaho language as well as the world of Wind River, and special thanks for their willingness to be audiotaped and videotaped, which has greatly enriched my understanding as well as the completeness of this book. Secondly, I would like to thank Sara Wiles for many interesting conversations about the society of Wind River, and she and her husband Steve for hospitality over the years, which has greatly decreased the cost of my fieldwork. Speaking of costs, I note that this research was funded in part by a sabbatical year fellowship from the American Council of Learned Societies, a fellowship from the University of Colorado Council on Research and Creative Work, a Major Documentation Project grant from the Hans Rausing Endangered Languages Documentation Programme, and a grant from the National Endowment for the Humanities/National Science Foundation Documenting Endangered Languages program, plus two sabbatical semesters from the University of Colorado. Earlier versions of parts of chapters 3 and 4 have been published in *Anthropological Linguistics* (Cowell and Moss 2003) and the *Papers of the Algonquian Conference* (Cowell and Moss 2004b), respectively. Finally, many thanks to my wife, Puahau Aki, and son, Kawena Cowell, for putting up with all my absences during fieldwork as well as providing their own indigenous inspiration for my work. Mahalo!

ABBREVIATIONS AND SYMBOLS

*	unattested proto form (Proto-Algonquian)
<	derives from
>	changes into
=	has meaning of
1	first person
2	second person
3	third person
0	third person inanimate
AC	Arapaho Culture
AI	animate subject intransitive verb
BIA	Bureau of Indian Affairs
COP	community of practice
ELAR	Endangered Languages Archive
excl.	exclusive
II	inanimate subject intransitive verb
incl.	inclusive
lit.	literally
MTH	more-than-human
NA	noun, animate
NALCC	Northern Arapaho Language and Culture Commission
NI	noun, inanimate

P	(in Arapaho transcriptions) indicates midword pause or break by speaker
PA	Proto-Algonquian
PL	plural
p.n.	personal name
s/b	should be
SG	singular
s.o.	someone
s.t.	something
TA	transitive verb, animate object
TI	transitive verb, inanimate object
XXX	segment of a recording not clearly audible

NAMING THE WORLD

INTRODUCTION

AN ETHNOGRAPHY OF LANGUAGE SHIFT AMONG THE NORTHERN ARAPAHO

LANGUAGE SHIFT, CONTINUITY, AND DISCONTINUITY

BILL[1] WAS A NORTHERN ARAPAHO MAN born in 1933, with whom I worked closely in my early days on the Wind River Reservation. He once told me that, in the old days, the St. Stephens Mission on the reservation would show cowboy and Indian movies on Saturday nights for the community for free. I asked him who the Arapahos cheered for when watching those movies, and he said, "The cowboys!" He also noted that when he was child, he and his friends would play cowboys and Indians down by the Little Wind River. He said, "Nobody wanted to be the Indians." Then I asked him what language the kids used as they played: "Arapaho!" he said.

Anyone watching those children play during the 1930s would have assumed that the Arapaho language had a good future. In fact, it was the only language most of them knew. Yet appearances can be deceiving. As the community's cheers and the children's play preferences show, linguistic and social perceptions about the Arapaho language and Arapahoness were already in place that would soon contribute to a major language shift. More theoretically, there was a fundamental discontinuity already in place between the language practices of the community and its language ideologies—its beliefs about language, languages, and language behaviors.

Such discontinuities are common in all societies, but especially so in situations of language shift.[2] Bourdieu talks of "the distance between the order of practice and the order of discourse" (1991:133), while Margaret Field notes the "tension between cultural practice and discursive beliefs" (Field 2009:40, with many additional references; cf. Meek 2010:39). This book is an ethnography of both language behavior and language shift among the Northern Arapaho, expanding on earlier studies (Gross 1951; Salzmann 1951; Anderson 1998; Anderson 2009), and a study of continuity, discontinuity, and the subtle and often surprising forms these take in the context of language shift (see Meek 2010:x, where she uses the term *disjuncture* in a way very similar to my *discontinuity*). Most broadly I am interested in what Marshall Sahlins calls "structure[s] of conjunction" (1985:125; see also Kulick 1992:18–20 for a language-specific discussion).

The concept of continuity and discontinuity is problematic, however, as it supposes some clearly identifiable past and present practices and ideologies and thus a basic continuity as the grounds for comparison: the idea of a "Northern Arapaho culture" must be continuous at least, in order for statements about changes in its practices or ideology to be meaningful. I want to argue, however, that this is not the case. Instead, we must think more loosely about cultural and specifically linguistic *resources*[3]—the Arapaho language in particular, and certain common language behaviors such as place naming, personal naming, creation of new words over time as new objects and concepts arise, and use of narrative and metaphor to make sense of the world—which are continuous. Bill recognized this himself. In his old age, he was often asked to provide personal names for young people. He would think carefully about the names as he believed they carried great power and history. But he noted that "a lot of times [the young people] just, they just want a name, you know (laughs). 'Can you give me [an] Indian name?' you know, like that (laughs). I said, 'Wait a minute . . . there's more to it . . . But you kids here, you probably don't know that. You just want an Indian name'" (Wiles 2002:8). Bill recognized the discontinuity between himself and many younger people in their cavalier attitude toward names—and the name giver. Most importantly, his use of the term *Indian* suggests that the young people in question are no longer engaged in Arapaho-specific linguistic and identity practices, but perhaps more oriented toward Pan-Indian goals.

Deborah House, in a study of language shift among the Navajo, notes that examinations of endangered languages and language shift often take an implicit or explicit culturalist perspective: "a" community has "a" language and "a" culture, and then shifts to another language (2002:xxv, 19–21; see also Muehlmann 2014:586–87). Here, I propose an alternative perspective, drawing specifically on practice theory (Bourdieu 1977; Ortner 2006) and the concept of a *community of practice*. At the broad level, there exist societies, such as the Northern Arapaho society on and around the Wind River Reservation. Societies seek prosperity (on their own terms—not necessarily narrowly economic) and continuity (as long as prosperity on their own terms remains viable). These societies then contain or are traversed by multiple communities of practice (henceforth COP): "an aggregate of people who come together around mutual engagement in an endeavor. Ways of doing things, ways of talking, beliefs, values, power relations—in short, practices—emerge in the course of this mutual endeavor." (Eckert and McConnell-Ginet 1992:464).

Any society is always partially overlapping and in collaboration with, and partially in rivalry with, adjacent societies. Likewise within a single society, multiple COPs arise, which offer partially overlapping and partially competing solutions for achieving the prosperity and continuity of the society, while also drawing in part on solutions proposed by COPs in adjacent societies (since COPs are not necessarily coterminous with societies). Within Northern Arapaho society, there are several different COPs that offer alternative visions for the future of that society. My reliance on the notion of a COP is thus part of a larger claim that there is no unitary Arapaho "culture" per se (see Wickwire 2007; House 2002:xv on Navajo; Collins 1998b:7 on Tolowa; Abu-Lughod 1991; Clifford 1988:21–54).

My turn to the concept of COPs is also meant to situate the Arapaho language in a specific way. The definition of a COP does not contain any necessary reference to language. I want to insist that the real focus of the sociocultural diversity and contestation examined in this book is not the Arapaho language or even language generally. Rather the diversity and contestation are fundamentally about identities and social reproduction, with the language community(ies) being what Michael Silverstein calls a "precipitate of social-cultural processes" (1998:402). The very interesting and important question that many Arapaho people are currently asking, however—and that I examine in this book—is what is the place of the Arapaho language within the issues of identity, social reproduction, and competing COPs at Wind River?[4]

Virtually all the COPs at Wind River draw on the resource of the Arapaho language and various Arapaho language behaviors as they seek legitimacy in the larger society and among their own practitioners, and as they seek powerful symbolic elements around which the COP can coalesce. In the words of Jane Hill, people "attempt to shape heteroglossia into 'voices' that will constitute a community identity and permit engagement with others on the most favourable possible grounds" (1993:70). Yet the particular linguistic practices and ideologies related to Arapaho language, while sharing some elements in common between any two or more COPs, are also quite different from COP to COP in many ways. In other words, Arapaho personal naming may exist in multiple COPs, but the exact practices and their underlying ideologies may be quite different from one COP to another. Thus the question of continuity and discontinuity is necessarily a synchronic as well as a diachronic problem: not only do practices and ideologies within a COP change over time, but differing COPs emerge or dissipate over time within Arapaho or any other society. The internal diversity of even small Native American societies is a key point of much recent literature (Gal 1998:319–23; Kroskrity and Field 2009:7–9, 11; Field 2009:31–32; House 2002; Collins 2003; M. Nevins 2013), as is the need to focus more on this diversity (Irvine and Gal 2000:76), yet I find that often the diversity is treated either only diachronically or only synchronically and that an implicit notion of a single tribal "culture" undergirds many of the analyses, despite the appreciation of internal complexity.

To summarize, my claims at this point are as follows:

1. There is a Northern Arapaho society in and around Wind River Reservation, Wyoming, whose members seek continuity and social reproduction over time.
2. That society shows continuities, but also striking discontinuities, in language practices and/or ideologies, both at present and over time.
3. Practices and ideologies need not be unified with each other, diachronically or synchronically.
    3a. The discontinuities can best be understood, both synchronically and diachronically, as the product of competing COPs within a changing socioeconomic matrix rather than as variations or changes in a unitary "culture."
    3b. The Arapaho language and various subsets of specific language behaviors (personal naming) are symbolic resources (rather than narrower "practices") available within Northern Arapaho society. These resources are variably adapted and used by the competing COPs as part of broader strategies of competition (or coalition building).

Thus personal naming in Arapaho may be motivated by competing ideologies in different COPs, which belie an initial appearance of continuity in practice. Conversely, the specific details of the practice of place naming may have changed over time within a single COP. These changes can be understood, however, as motivated by a continued respect for a deeper ideology of the power of place names, with the specific changes coming in response to language shift and a changing socioeconomic matrix. In all cases, the practices and ideologies are part of larger efforts by the members of the COPs to maintain symbolic prestige, power, and legitimacy within the society as they compete to influence the pathways of social reproduction.

Up to this point, I have focused especially on real or apparent discontinuities. Situations of language shift typically involve especially large changes in sociopolitical and language ecologies. They thus offer rich opportunities for understanding the dynamics of continuity and discontinuity, as demonstrated in studies by Meek (2010), House (2002), Collins (1998b), Perley (2011), M. Nevins (2013), and Kulick (1992). Due to the obvious discontinuity of language shift, however, one may be tempted to see only discontinuity. This is a pervasive tendency in the larger literature on language shift; the shift is often associated with near total loss of identity, traditional knowledge, or community (Harrison 2007). As a person heavily involved in language maintenance, I do not wish to diminish the consequences of language shift. But a bias toward discontinuity can be exacerbated by failure to recognize fully the presence of multiple COPs and discourses in a society, due to a mistaken assumption that there is one operative "culture." A similar problem arises when one attempts to analyze a society based on categories such as age or gender without accounting for differences between COPs. Language shift, due to its generational nature (and often its differential results across gender lines), tends to exaggerate this tendency or temptation. Put simply, when Bill was criticizing some young people for "just" wanting an Indian name, we should not assume that this included all young people or that he was representative of all older people. I contend that neither age nor gender per se are adequate categories for understanding Arapaho society, though they certainly do have some correlates with different COPs. The crucial factor is an understanding of the different COPs and a recognition that they all contain individuals of different ages, genders, and other categories. Despite obvious examples of contestation, I believe there is more continuity and coherence within Northern Arapaho society than is often realized by most elders or young people within that society (or many outside observers). But it must be sought within COPs, not across them, and it must be sought in a careful understanding of the continuities in either practice or ideology that often underlie seeming discontinuities in the opposite member of the pair.

For this reason, I take an ethnographic and particularist perspective in this book, inspired by the work of Jane Hill and Kenneth Hill (1986), Kulick (1992), Meek (2010), M. Nevins (2013), and others (see also Gal 1998:318). I use a multiscalar approach, examining daily linguistic practice and shifts in practice at the microlevel, while linking those details to the macrolevel changes occurring in Arapaho society over the last 150-plus years.[5] I rely on and cite as much as possible natural Arapaho discourse, much of it recorded on video, including a great deal of interaction between native speakers. Much of the video has been deposited with transcription, translation, and linguistic analysis at the Endangered Languages Archive (ELAR), housed at SOAS University of London. I cite those sources by file number in many of the examples used in this book, so a good deal of the data used here is open for public scrutiny in a way unusual for anthropology generally and linguistic anthropology in particular.[6] I have tried to include large amounts of language data in the original language. I have also tried to include large numbers of examples of specific interactions between Arapaho speakers and to provide the larger context for the cited interactions. When I quote individual remarks, I provide the context that produced them whenever possible. Such remarks always accomplish social work in a specific context and within a specific COP, and failure to appreciate these contexts can exacerbate an exaggerated impression of discontinuity. There are no context-free language ideologies. Ideologies are discursive structures and stances that are deployed in moments of interaction to accomplish social work. People do not just have "beliefs" about language. Rather, they have awareness of many different metadiscourses about language; they are selectively influenced by these, and they deploy them selectively in interaction to achieve social and communicative goals (cf. Debenport 2015:40).

SACREDNESS, POWER, AND NAMING

A final question that naturally arises is why certain specific language practices or ideologies become especially salient cultural resources, such that they are worthy of a place in a COP or a chapter in a book. The number of language practices and ideologies in a given community is theoretically infinite, and not all of them are created equal (see Kroskrity and Field 2009:6–7, with additional references).

Most fly below the radar, unnamed or unrecognized in public consciousness. Yet some rise to prominence and become the objects of debate and contestation. Kroskrity distinguishes in this regard between *discursive* and *practical* consciousness (Kroskrity 1998). Bourdieu argues that the process of "symbolization . . . gives the objectivity of public discourse and exemplary practice to a way of seeing or of experiencing the social world that was previously relegated to the state of a practical disposition of a tacit and often confused experience" (1991:130). Thus we can talk about symbolic practices and ideologies, which have special prominence in and across COPs.

One symbolic ideology in particular will dominate this book: the idea that the Arapaho language is sacred.[7] In Arapaho, the term *sacred* (*beeteenoo'* 'it is sacred')[8] is intimately linked to ideas of power. If something is sacred, it has more-than-human (henceforth MTH) power.[9] The word used to describe this in Arapaho is *nono'o3oo'* ('it is powerful'; also 'it is intense, terrifying'). The same concepts can be expressed with regard to humans: *beeteet* 's/he is sacred', *nono'oteihit* 's/he is powerful' and possesses *no'otehiit* 'sacred power'. A person is sacred and powerful because that person literally has within them—or has access to—power derived either from the natural world or from ancestors—both of whom mediate the general MTH power of the Creator, which is immanent in the world.

Although the idea of one's indigenous language being sacred and powerful is widespread (J. Hill 2002; House 2002; Watahomigie 1998; McCarty 2008; Adley-SantaMaria 1999), there is not a great amount of detailed ethnographic study of what this means in practice *outside* of narrowly ceremonial contexts. And equally importantly, when a community shifts from an indigenous language to a global one such as English, how does this shift affect concepts and practices related to power within the community? The ideology of the sacredness of one's language is especially common in situations of language endangerment, or it at least takes on more and more salience in this context (J. Hill 1993, 2002) and can do so in initial revitalization as well (Grenoble and Whaley 2006:66–67). As Native American languages become more endangered, many are increasingly used in primarily sacro-ceremonial settings; they are increasingly used only by older individuals who are often seen as prestigious and powerful in their communities; and they become quite similar to forms of special, restricted knowledge, such as sacred ceremonial knowledge.

The belief in the sacredness of one's language is certainly not simply a product of language shift or endangerment, however. At its most basic, Northern

Arapaho ideology about the sacredness of the language reflects what Silverstein (1979) calls a performative, as opposed to a reflectionist, view of language. Arapaho people have long had a well-developed theory of power (*no'otehiit*) and its functions in their society—indeed, several well-developed, partially competing theories. The Arapaho viewpoint in its broad outlines is similar to that found in many other Plains Indian tribes, and studies of Plains Indian religions provide a useful framework for thinking about power from an indigenous perspective (see Harrod 1987; Irwin 1994; Sullivan 2000:introduction; Griffin-Pierce 2000; Powers 2000; Grim 2000). One of the best descriptions I have found is in the book *Blackfoot Ways of Knowing* by Blackfoot elder Betty Bastien (2004). She speaks of the "spiritual energies [that] permeate the cosmic universe" (3) and that derive from *Ihtsipaitapiiyopa* (3), which the Blackfeet consider the source of life. Bastien evokes "the spiritual nature of the sun, constellations, birds, animals, waterfowl, etc. and their ability to communicate some of their sacred knowledge to humans" (11). She states that "the focus of human development is premised on experiences, which connect the individual to the transformational powers of the universe" (84). Animals in particular "mediate a number of transformational powers for humans" (92). All humans should seek "an identity founded upon transformational experiences with the sacred" (93–94).[10] Crucially, the knowledge and relationships she discusses are based on reciprocity with sacred power: she talks of "reciprocal relationships with the sacred and the ancestors" (75) and says that "all knowledge and wisdom comes through alliances with insects, animals and plants" (82). This is all true for the Arapaho religion as well (see Kroeber [1902–7] 1983:418–54; Anderson 2001a:240, 257, 259–61, 273 [and 240–73 generally]), though we could add that the land itself, especially certain very powerful places, can also mediate transformational power, as can ceremonies, including the specific material components of those ceremonies such as the sweat lodge or the Sun Dance lodge. An additional source of such power, though not a focus of this book, would have been from other tribes, or from Whites (see Anderson 1998:55–56).[11]

All the preceding will sound generally familiar to anyone who has experience with "traditional" Plains Indian religious and ceremonial practice. This idea of power draws directly on Blackfoot—and Arapaho, and Cheyenne, and Gros Ventre, and Lakota—discourse. These studies of religion are in the main quite sensitive to indigenous perspectives on MTH power as sought and enacted in ceremonial contexts. On the other hand, the theoretical tools used by anthropology for thinking about power in social relations are quite different from indigenous Arapaho perspectives on this matter. The Arapaho individuals with whom I have worked largely understand social relationships as forms of reciprocity with contemporary humans, with ancestors, and with the land and natural world, all of which involve some degree of transfer or management of MTH power. Thus their theory of social relations relies on a notion of MTH power, similar to *mana*, as the motivator and goal of relationships—in a certain sense, all of life partakes of ceremonialism and, as the idea of ceremonialism implies, all life is about collective goodness. MTH power is the controlling goal and mechanism through which all human relationships are finally conceptualized, even if MTH power is not overtly at stake in the vast majority of daily interactions. This viewpoint is quite similar to ones elucidated by recent theorists of gift culture, who see all horizontal exchanges of gifts in human society as ultimately understandable in reference to a concept of the sacred and a desire for access to and vertical exchanges with the sacred (J. Weiner 1991; Godbout 1998; Godelier 1999). One gives in order to keep, or keep access to, or gain access to, items of a sacred order.

The notion of *symbolic capital* is also key to the anthropological theories of power I will be using (Bourdieu 1991:72–6). Bourdieu argues that "relations of communication are always . . . power relations which, in form and content, depend on the material of symbolic power accumulated by agents . . . involved in these relations and which, like the gift or potlatch, can enable symbolic power to be accumulated" (1991:167). The word *capital*, of course, evokes a strongly socioeconomic and sociopolitical perspective on human relations, in which societies are ultimately markets. In its richer meaning, *power* includes the idea of larger-scale structural coupling between actors, institutions, and ideologies in such a marketplace (see Bourdieu 1991:37–40). Individuals engage with and use social institutions (schools, ceremonies) to accomplish personal and collective goals, thereby reinforcing these institutions. Institutions are undergirded by ideologies that reinforce their legitimacy and therefore their efficacy. Without general collective consent to the ideologies and structures of these institutions, social organization and individual exercise of power cannot be maintained. Power involves the assent and cooperation of the many, even though the marketplace is an arena of competition and contestation at a more immediate level: without the agreed-on terms of the market, the competition and contestation cannot occur in a socially organized manner. In a Foucauldian perspective, cooperation even includes resistance, since engaging in resistance involves being interpolated by that which one resists.[12] In this book, I seek to use both the Arapaho concept of *no'otehiit* 'sacred power' and the anthropological concepts of reciprocity and symbolic capital to understand power relations within Arapaho society, as they are mediated by language ideologies and practices.

While the Arapaho language was and is one key means of tapping into MTH power, not every word, phrase, sentence, or discourse is equally powerful. Instead, both MTH power and symbolic capital are especially located in certain language practices. Obvious, widely studied examples include ceremonial song, prayer, ritual oration, and traditional narrative. But special power is also located in personal names. These, we will see, are small forms of prayer, with their pronunciation carrying MTH power. It is located in many place names, which index sites of power in the natural world. It is found through the process of folk etymology, which seeks out hidden nexuses of power in sound correspondences. It is found by referencing cultural metaphors, which link contextual discourse back to deeper understanding, wisdom, and authority. It is even found in neologizing, which works to assimilate the alien to the familiar, to conquer the strange and harmonize it with existing frameworks of linguistic power.

All these practices are in a sense *naming*. In all languages, we tend to privilege names (prototypically, of persons or places) as special kinds of words that refer to things in the world in a way that "ordinary" words do not. As Bodenhorn and vom Bruck say in *The Anthropology of Names and Naming*, names are "the vehicle for crossing boundaries between life and death, past and future, humans and non-humans" (2006:4). From a traditional Arapaho perspective, one could say that names directly link not just to the world, but to power (*no'otehiit*) in the world. In *Native American Religions*, Sam D. Gill writes of Pueblo stories of creation that feature Thought-Woman: "The world was literally formed as she thought what form it should take. Her partners in creation followed her act of creative thinking by naming those things given form by Thought-Woman. Thus her acts of creation became humanly meaningful through language" (Gill 1982:39).[13] The greatest power of all is the transformative power of creation, and names and naming allow humans to have connection to and understanding of that power. "Naming the world" could be thought of more literally for the Arapaho as using language to touch, connect with, and access the MTH power of the world, including both the power of the land and the power of ancestors. In this sense my use of the term *naming* overlaps with Bourdieu's remarks:

> The social sciences must take as their object of study the social operations of naming and the rites of institution through which they are accomplished. But on

a deeper level, they must examine the part played by words in the construction of social reality and the contribution which the struggle over classifications . . . makes to the constitution of classes—classes defined in terms of age, sex, social position, but also clans, tribes, ethnic groups or nations. (Bourdieu 1991:105)

Thus when Arapaho speakers talk *about* their language, they tend to talk about personal names and place names or about conceptual metaphors, and folk etymology is the genre par excellence of talking *about* language. Neologizing is also a key point of reflection about the English and Arapaho languages. These are all domains of the language where individual words have not only uses and meanings but actual stories about them and how they came to be. The words have overt histories, in the oral tradition. As such, all these domains of language use could be seen as partaking in the practice of reported speech—which itself is intimately linked to constructing authority (see Gal 1998:322)—as well as in the practices of decontextualization and recontextualization as understood in performance theory (Bauman and Briggs 1990). This book is very much about language ideology and its relation to political practice and ideology, and the domains of language usage just mentioned are where ideology is most highly developed and overtly expressed. Taking Woolard and Schieffelin's understanding of language ideology as "a process involving struggles among multiple conceptualizations and demanding the recognition of variation and contestation within a community as well as contradictions within individuals" (1994:71), then the topics of this book are privileged sites for such struggles and contestation.

As with the ideology of the sacredness of the language, practices of naming also typically become increasingly salient in the context of language shift and loss. The language is used less and less for everyday communication, by fewer and fewer people, but the high-saliency linguistic practices continue as much as possible. In the extreme case, the language can become largely a series of names: nouns, words with translatable meanings, often in reified forms such as recordings, print, signs, emblems, and the like. In the broader sense of *naming* suggested above, the language can lose more and more everyday uses, while retaining those that allow access to MTH power. This tendency toward "nominalization" as well as "disembodiment" of the language is something many scholars have noted in endangered language settings (Perley 2011:174; Anderson 2009:69; Field 2009:45; Bender 2009:137, 145; Errington 2003; Meek 2010:130) as well as in revitalization settings (Grenoble and Whaley 2006:66–67). Thus the title of this book is simultaneously a reference to Arapaho linguistic practices and ideologies that predate language shift and a nod to the way in which language shift produces fundamental changes in—and increasing saliency for—those practices and ideologies over time.

The central claim of this book is therefore that Arapaho views of MTH power fundamentally determine ideologies of knowledge in the society, as well as the form that human relationships take, since these relationships are about mediating the flow of knowledge. Competing ideologies of knowledge and proper relationships are then the basis for understanding the differing COPs that exist in Arapaho society, as well as the different language ideologies and practices within those COPs. The Arapaho idea that "the language is sacred" is a direct outgrowth of the traditional views of MTH power since the language mediates the transfer of that power. The importance of "naming practices" as described above is likewise an outgrowth of traditional views of MTH power since naming occurs at the times and places where this power and its transfer is most intense or overt. And finally, the sacrality of the language and the naming practices are intimately embedded in reciprocal relationships involving prestige and respect. The context of language shift has now heightened the saliency of all these ideas and practices, and of the Arapaho language more generally, even as many other everyday language practices—and the everyday use of the language generally—have fallen away. I also argue that beyond Northern Arapaho society, the phenomena to be discussed here are relevant to many indigenous societies undergoing language shift, especially where traditional religion, ceremonies, and concepts of MTH power remain influential.

1

NORTHERN ARAPAHO HISTORY AND COMMUNITIES OF PRACTICE

THIS CHAPTER PROVIDES A SURVEY of the Wind River Reservation of Wyoming and its vicinity over the last 150 years. I focus especially on family and kinship, band and tribe, ceremonialism, and certain key performative domains, as they provide roles and identities to Arapaho individuals. I examine in particular how changes in these domains have affected roles and ideologies in terms of age, gender, and knowledge. I then provide a brief description of Arapaho language shift since World War II, and I conclude with a discussion of the various COPs on the reservation.

THE PRE-RESERVATION ERA

KINSHIP, PERFORMANCE, CEREMONY, AND TRIBE

The 1851 Treaty of Fort Laramie recognized the lands of the Arapaho people as extending from the Arkansas River to the North Platte River and from western Kansas and Nebraska to the Continental Divide. By 1878, however, the Northern Arapaho had been forced onto the Wind River Reservation, which they share with the Eastern Shoshone (see Fowler 1982 and Trenholm 1986 for more on pre-reservation history).

Prior to 1878, Arapahos understood their identity within the tribe in relation to a large number of institutionalized roles and relationships. Family and kinship roles were complex and extensive, with sets of expectations attached to each role (Eggan 1955). Extended networks of kin were the central organizing feature of Arapaho life. These networks, and associations with other kinship groups, were the basis of band affiliations. These bands were led by chiefs whose authority was largely based on personal example and influence.

Although an ethnic and linguistic identity as 'Arapaho' was recognized, there was no formal political structure for the tribe. Instead Arapaho identity found its fundamental expression in a set of ceremonial structures, which crosscut the ties of family, kin, and band with organizations based on age and gender. All men in the tribe were members of a set of age-graded ceremonial lodges, with both religious and social functions, and their wives had allied functions. These lodges represented and served the entire tribe. There were also ceremonial organizations specifically for women, such as the women's Buffalo Lodge and the quillwork society (see Anderson 2013). As with the men's groups, these fulfilled social and religious functions for the entire tribe (see Dorsey 1903; Kroeber [1902–7] 1983; Eggan 1955; Hilger 1952; Fowler 1982, 2010; and Anderson 2001a for more on pre-reservation social and ceremonial life).

At the summit of this ceremonial organization was (and is) the *hoseihoowu'* (lit. 'offerings lodge' but commonly referred to as the Sun Dance in English). Associated with this are a number of sacred objects (the Sacred Flat Pipe, the Sacred Wheel) and offices (the Pipe Keeper, the Wheel Keeper, the Sun Dance priest), as well as ancillary ceremonies. The Sun Dance complex has a pervasive, virtually year-round influence on tribal life. Young men participate, helped by a ceremonial "grandfather," and supported by young female relatives who fast and pray outside the Sun Dance lodge. The families of the young men and the grandfathers provide food, cooking, gifts, and other support to each other. The relationship between the "grandfather" and the "grandson" lasts year-round, with sets of mutual obligations—to take a modern-day example, a grandson is not supposed to pass a grandfather on the road if he approaches him from behind.

In summary, a young Arapaho man would have understood his identity and status based on classificatory kinship categories such as *hiisoh'o* 'older same-sex brother' of a younger brother, *hiih'o* 'son' of a father and also of the father's brothers and their wives, *hi3e'e3o* 'nephew' of his mother's brothers and their wives, and so forth. He would also be a member of a band. In addition, he would be a member of an age-graded lodge, which itself had internal rank gradations and offices. And he would likely have a relationship with a particular Sun Dance grandfather. There were also distinctions obtainable through performance: success in hunting, raiding other tribes, obtaining horses, performing well in combat, obtaining and using special "medicine" powers, either through vision quests or apprenticeships to older experts, and showing conspicuous generosity.

The same set of relationships and criteria would have been in place for a young woman, with two distinctions. First, the areas of performance were different (domestic accomplishments such as beadwork or quillwork), and somewhat fewer cross tribal roles existed for younger women, with a relatively stronger focus on family and kinship circles. Nevertheless, women were indispensable supporters and helpers of their husbands as the latter pursued tribal roles, and with increasing age, women increasingly exercised independent authority inside and outside kinship circles and had access to independent tribal ceremonial roles comparable to those of men. Loretta Fowler (2010) underlines just how important strong marriage *partnerships* were to the achievements of either or both members of a couple.

THE IMPORTANCE OF AGE, AND THE IDEOLOGY OF KNOWLEDGE

The preceding suggests two important points for the rest of this study. The first is the importance of age and the controlling role of older individuals in the lives of the young, both inside and outside the kin group. If a young woman wanted to make quillwork ornaments, she had to receive permission and instruction from the seven old women of the quillwork society (Anderson 2013). If a young man wants to participate in the Sun Dance, he has to find an older man who will agree to be his grandfather. Advancement through the age-graded lodges depended on finding sponsors in higher-level lodges who would provide instruction to the younger cohort. Hunting might offer success to a young man, but failure to respect the guidance of older Dog Lodge men on tribal hunts could result in severe punishment. Raids and warfare were another potential avenue to status, but success was believed to be highly dependent on access to holy, "medicinal" powers for aid, and this access was typically controlled by older men. Many forms of status were specifically tied to age and available only to the more elderly, and potential avenues to status that were available to younger individuals depended crucially on the control of elders, who could give or withhold permission to pursue the activity and who held privileged access to the information and special power needed for the pursuit.[1]

Such control is of course present in all societies, but the degree of control exercised by elders in traditional Arapaho society was very strong and highly institutionalized, especially for a society that was quite egalitarian in other areas. It was also very widespread in the domains to which it extended. It is important to recognize, however, that this control was almost never authoritarian but rather depended on social consensus built around an ideology of elder respect (*heeteenebetiit*), to which most members of the society seem to have readily (though no doubt in some cases more grudgingly) consented, at least as long as prosperity reigned. Of course the controls and ideology could be challenged, and a number of traditional myths and historical narratives focus on just this situation. Indeed, some myths and historical narratives explicitly recognize the potential of the young to surprise their elders and provide valuable social contributions—sometimes even by directly disobeying customs or commands (see Cowell, C'Hair, and Moss 2014:"Tangled Hair and Found-in-the-Grass"). Others recognize the potential tyranny that could be exercised by older individuals on younger ones (Cowell, C'Hair, and Moss 2014:"Lime Crazy"). Thus the ideology of elder respect was not unquestioned, and it was clearly recognized as potentially problematic if allowed to become a tyranny lacking in a sense of mutual responsibility across the generations.

The second important point for this study is the issue of information and knowledge. A tendency to control information and restrict it to certain subgroups is a universal feature of society. But among the Arapaho, such restrictions were especially powerful and pervasive, especially in the ceremonial realm. The full creation story was only told in the Rabbit Lodge and thus fully known only to the handful of members of that lodge. It was and is believed that a ceremony will not have efficacy if it is not performed according to the proper procedures, so ceremonial knowledge is highly valued but therefore also closely guarded. Medicinal knowledge is treated similarly. This ideology of knowledge is most commonly expressed in Arapaho discourse through the concept of *danger* (*neestoonoo'* 'it is dangerous', *neestoonoo3oo'* 'it acts dangerously/has dangerous characteristics', *neenebeenoo'* 'it is taboo, forbidden, restricted, dangerous'). High-level ceremonial and medicinal knowledge in particular are considered dangerous for two reasons. First, knowledge of this sort is quite literally power: Arapaho ceremonies are generally conceived not simply as prayers asking for help or changes in the world but as ways of directly acting on the world or directly obtaining access to this help, so to be able to perform the ceremony and speak the proper prayers and rituals is to literally act powerfully. Second, these powers can potentially be misused by those who are not qualified to have them. Similarly, mistakes can be made in the performance of a ceremony that will harm the person at fault and also his or her family and kin and even the entire tribe; rather than the ceremony simply "not working" due to the mistake, it does produce effects—but wrong or unintended ones. Thus after the Arapaho women's quillwork society ceased to function, the Northern Arapaho turned down an offer from women of another tribe to teach them the skills because of a fear that without full knowledge and proper procedure, negative consequences could result. More prosaically, Arapahos say about this kind of knowledge and practice *ciibehcou'utii* 'don't mess with it/don't bother it' or 'leave it alone'. It is also suggested that if knowledge and the power associated with it are abused, it can cease to work. This ideology of danger provides a strong basis for the restriction of knowledge—and a strong support for the ideology of elder respect.

This ideology of knowledge meant that when questions were asked of an older person, the questions and responses would often be filtered through younger intermediary speakers. Jeffrey D. Anderson gives an old example (2009:58–59), but the practice continues today. In the early 2000s, a group of Arapaho speakers was presenting to a largely White audience at the public library in Lander. At the end of the presentation, the audience began asking questions. Four Arapaho speakers were sitting side by side: an older woman in her seventies (Susan) and her somewhat younger husband (Henry), and a younger couple both in their sixties. Once the first White audience member asked a question, the younger woman, Helen, leaned over to her husband, Chris, and said to him,

HELEN: He3ebei'towuuninee, ne'P nehe' heetcesisitoot.
Tell her about [the question]; this one [pointing toward the older woman] will start.[2]

CHRIS: Yeah.

HELEN: Uhm!

The intention here was for her husband to translate the question from English into Arapaho for the older woman, as a sign of respect. This is a standard procedure in such situations. However, the command was ambiguous, as it could mean "address your response to the White woman's question to the older Arapaho woman." Confused, the husband then asked his wife,

CHRIS:	Koonenei'towuunoo?
	Do I tell it to [the older Arapaho woman]?
HELEN:	Hiiko, neh'eeno heetne'cesisitoot.
	No, her, she's the one who will start [answering the questions].

The wife thus clarifies here that the older speaker will be the one to answer the questions—or at least take the first crack at them—but through the linguistic and social mediation of Chris. But when Helen points for Chris, it is unclear to Susan and her husband, Henry, toward which of them Helen is pointing:

CHRIS:	Wohei.
	Okay.
HENRY:	Me? her?
HELEN:	Neh'eeno.
	This one [pointing specifically at Susan].
HENRY:	Okay.

As Susan prepares to start, Chris then asks on her behalf whether she should speak in Arapaho or English, to which the recorder (me) answers, and then Susan finally gets underway with her response (which will eventually be translated into English for the audience by her husband, Henry):

SUSAN:	Wohoe'etniisiini . . .
	I wonder what . . .
CHRIS:	Koohinono'eiyeitiit wo'ei3 nih'oo3ouniihi'?
	In Arapaho or English?
ANDY:	Uhh, hinono'eitiit.
	Uhh, Arapaho.
CHRIS:	Wohei.
	Okay.
ANDY:	Wohei.
	Okay.
SUSAN:	Well . . . teecxo' hu'un nihii . . . nuhu' heeteihinoo, hinono'eiteen, nih'ee3neebixoo3eti3i', teecxo'. . .
	Well . . . long ago that well . . . the [tribe] that I'm from, the Arapaho tribe, they really loved each other, long ago . . .

(ELAR 14a)

This long and complicated negotiation shows the care with which Arapaho speakers seek to defer to the oldest person present, both in allowing her to speak first and in allowing her to be addressed in Arapaho if possible (though she is fluent in English). Susan clearly takes Chris to be speaking for her when he asks me what language to use, and she clearly takes the exchange between Chris and me as relevant to her as well, but she is a listener in this entire exchange, never an interactant, even though everything is being said for her benefit or to or about her. Helen arranges the entire interaction, but she has her husband, Chris, who is younger than her, directly mediate between Susan (the oldest Arapaho speaker) on the one hand, and the White audience and me on the other, while the role of translator is reserved for Henry (who is older than Chris). There is a clear hierarchy:

1. Susan [speaks Arapaho to the audience, speaks first]
2. Helen [arranges for Susan to speak, gives clarifying instructions to Henry and Chris]
3. Henry [translates what Susan says for the audience into English]
4. Chris [directly interacts with audience and recorder as well as Susan, translates questions and commands into Arapaho]
5. White audience and recorder

The same process can be seen throughout the session. When it comes to a conclusion, Chris mediates this as well (ELAR 14h), first asking me in Arapaho if it is time to quit. When I nod, Helen says the same thing to Susan (in Arapaho), to which Susan responds (in Arapaho) in agreement. Then Chris, having heard all this, announces the same thing in Arapaho for the benefit of the audience (switching to exclusive "we") and then concludes in English with "Are there any more questions?" with a tone and rapidity that suggest there clearly should not be any:

CHRIS [to me]: Wohei koo[woow]?
     Okay are we done?
[I nod]
HELEN: Yeah.
SUSAN: Uhm!
HELEN [to Susan]: Heetce'P . . . woow benee3toono'.
     We [incl.] will . . . now we are through.

SUSAN [to Helen]: Nooxeihi' heetwoniini bee3P . . .
    Maybe we will finish . . .
CHRIS [to aud.]: Woow benee3tooni'. Koohen[tou]P . . . Any more questions?
    Now we [excl.] are done. Are there. . . . Any more questions?

Although all the Arapaho speakers understand all of this, an intricate hierarchy of relationships is performed and maintained, by which higher-ranked speakers are often addressed indirectly and, when directly, by the next-ranking speaker in the hierarchy. Of course this is a formal setting, and not every conversation works this way, but these examples illustrate what is meant by the idea of mediated transfers of knowledge based on an age-graded hierarchy. Clearly the transfers involve not just sacred or ceremonial knowledge but cultural commentary of any sort (such as Susan's stories about Arapaho history and values). The pathways of interaction are modeled—and explicitly ideologized by native speakers—on prototypical sacred knowledge transfers, such as medicinal or ceremonial knowledge. In the Sun Dance, a ceremonial grandfather addresses the head of the Sun Dance on behalf of the young man ("grandson") participating in the ceremony and conveys responses from that head person to the grandson. The grandson does not normally speak directly to the head of the Sun Dance. This can be compared to the way that kiva speech is the *dominant ideology* model for much of what one sees linguistically in Tewa society more generally (Kroskrity 1998). In addition to the special interaction features of such encounters and relationships, there are numerous specific linguistic features as well, including use of indirect questions (Cowell and Moss 2008:297–98); delayed, suggestive, and indirect imperatives (Cowell and Moss 2008:271–83; Cowell 2007); impersonal verbs (Cowell and Moss 2008:194–95, 279–80); and other features that generally fall under the rubric of "politeness" or "negative face" in Arapaho.

THE RESERVATION ERA

The social system just described has undergone radical challenges and changes since the beginning of the reservation period (see Fowler 1982, 2002, 2010; and Anderson 2001a for more on reservation-era history. The topic of the old times versus the present is pervasive in the database of Arapaho conversation as well.)[3]

KINSHIP AND FAMILY

Family and extended kinship structures and relationships remained strong for many decades after settlement on the reservation. These included respect for one's opposite-sex sibling—talking to that person only when necessary and avoiding joking and various topics such as references to sexuality—and conversely, joking with one's brother-in-law and sister-in-law and constantly seeking to tease them, very often about sexual topics. The ideologies and practices around kinship involve not just language but expectations regarding who punishes or scolds children, who gives advice to them, and who is expected to be primarily a comforter; or, among older relatives, who is expected to provide material support to those in need, who directs family discussion and decision making, who does the cooking, and so forth. In a somewhat attenuated form, this system remains active, especially among many older Arapahos, and to some extent among most people in the Wind River community, providing an important sense of individual roles and identity and an avenue for attaining status within the family.

I would suggest as an aside that one reason for the continuation of many kinship practices has been the continuing relevance of "irregularly pulsed resources" (cf. J. Hill and K. Hill 1986:21–37 on unstable resources and reciprocity as a safety net in response to this; Harrod 1987:5–17). In a nomadic hunting culture, small groups of people would often obtain large amounts of game at irregular intervals—far more than could be processed and consumed. Large, intricate, and closely connected kinship networks were a way of distributing this resource more widely to avoid waste, with the knowledge that beneficiaries would reciprocate at a later time. Thus irregular pulses in resource availability were smoothed out. Similarly, income and wage labor have been scarce and often functioned as pulsed resources for many Arapaho families throughout much of the twentieth century, as tribal members have suffered economic hardship while working in seasonal or unstable jobs.[4] Contemporary elders, when talking about their childhood, constantly stress that people no longer visit each other (*ceitoonetiitooni'*) and that they no longer invite each other over (*noh'oubetiitooni'*). While one may be tempted to look at such talk as merely an example of nostalgia (see J. Hill 1998:68–70), these actions are clearly grounded in Arapaho social relationships: the visiting keeps the extended kin networks alive so that the inviting can occur when pulsed resources become available.

Traditionally, the family roles with the most prestige and status have been grandmother and grandfather, and that remains the case today. This is an arena where elder respect continues to play a prominent role, and many older individuals see their current social role overwhelmingly as a grandparent in the Arapaho sense: the family member ultimately responsible for the health, education, care, and prosperity of the entire family. Thus many elders continue to work at salaried jobs as long as they are physically able, sharing their salaries widely through gifts and loans, taking in younger family members, and raising grandchildren and great-grandchildren, while also offering ceremonial leadership, knowledge, prayers, and general community advice and wisdom. As available jobs and subsistence needs have shifted from relatively hard manual labor in the first two-thirds of the twentieth century to white-collar or at least nonmanual-labor positions more recently (accountants, secretaries, teachers, tribal bureaucrats and officers, teacher's aids, casino workers), the ability of older Arapahos—women in particular—to continue working at salaried positions has increased.[5] For this reason, the economic influence of the grandparent and great-grandparent generation has remained strong or even increased in many families over the last fifty years. On the other hand, within a number of families, the growing availability of jobs for young people in the hotel, casino, and related new areas has worked in the opposite direction over the last ten to fifteen years.

Despite the importance of grandparents, there are numerous complaints today that children do not respect their elders enough. Interestingly however, it tends to be especially children outside their own family whom elders complain about. While this is partly no doubt just a general human bias, it does suggest that *tribal-level* ideologies of elder respect, independent of economic or familial helpfulness, may be the issue, rather than family-internal respect relationships (though there are certainly complaints about these as well from some people). A key claim of Jeffrey D. Anderson's 2001 ethnography of the Northern Arapaho is that family-centric organization has largely replaced cross tribal ceremonial organization (2001a:208–11, 217–18, 223–26). Helen, an elder woman with ceremonial duties, said explicitly in May 2009 at a public presentation that in the old days there used to be much more community discipline of children, but now there is only parental discipline. She said that whereas in the old days the elders controlled the young people, now only the family does so:

> As I was growing up, ahm, in, in our home . . . discipline was taught . . . we could not talk back to our parents . . . and then, if we went to a social function, and if

any of us misbehaved, if we misbehaved, anyone, there was someone older there, that was there, a lady, or a man, and he would tell us to quit. He would tell us to behave. There were times that he would have to raise, or she would have to raise her voice at, uh, different children. And it was accepted at that time. A mother and father were happy. They would say, "I'm glad you disciplined my child. I'm glad you got after my child for doing something wrong." But you know, today it's not like that. If you holler at another person's child, the mother or father get mad at you. They say, "that's not your child." "You had no business getting after this child." And then I always say that we, we have lost one generation in our culture, and in our language. And we are trying to regain that now. We're teaching our people, our young children the Arapaho language, but we still have to teach 'em respect. We have to get that back, before our children can learn the language and can learn the culture. Respect has to be brought back in. (ELAR 14a)

Her use of *respect* is very much in line with the understanding of intergenerational reciprocity outlined in the introduction. She is suggesting that the Arapaho language (and implicitly, the MTH power embedded in the language) cannot flow successfully without such relationships, and more particularly that the younger generations of parents and children are primarily responsible for impeding this flow. At the same time, the impedance is not just a matter of age but also of differing horizontal relationships with regard to either extended kinship or cross kin recognition of authority.[6]

In summary, over the last 150 years, Northern Arapaho elders and younger people have passed through several stages of economic status and relationship within the family: elders were pre-reservation holders of ceremonial knowledge and access to sacred powers that allowed and enhanced hunting success, and they were also distributors of communally hunted game and others foods supplied by younger people; elders were then relatively disempowered in early reservation days (1878–1900), as reservation agents took over the supply and distribution of both goods and jobs; elders remained somewhat disempowered as hard manual labor formed the basis of family income for two-thirds of the twentieth century; elders then were increasingly empowered as relatively scarce but less strenuous job options increased their ability to make economic contributions, beginning in the 1960s and more so in the 1970s and 1980s; and now elders are again potentially less empowered in some families in that more and more young people have access to wage jobs, primarily through the casinos.

The relative economic influence of women, on the other hand, has increased in virtually every family on the reservation over the last fifty years as a result of the increase in nonmanual-labor jobs. This is the case for both older and younger women. Conversely, with the rise of per capita payments beginning in the 1950s, and then more reliable wage labor for at least some people in recent decades, the importance of irregularly pulsed resources and the more extended kinship networks that existed around them has declined significantly, though they are still an important part of Arapaho life.

BAND AND TRIBE

Band structures continued to exist in early reservation days, but BIA authorities worked hard to undermine these, especially through practices such as allotment and the imposition of tribal council forms of government, though Arapaho leaders creatively resisted these pressures in various ways (see Fowler 1982:67–127). The authorities also commonly distributed crucial wage jobs to younger people. This was a direct challenge to Arapaho social organization, to the ideology of elder respect, and to the economic and political practices of distribution of goods through elders, which helped maintain this ideology. At present, though older individuals at Wind River can often name the band with which they were affiliated if directly asked, bands are functionally defunct.

Despite the changes, current political structures are actually somewhat more consonant with traditional models than might first appear. The chiefs-and-bands political structure has been replaced by a unified tribal council, but election to the tribal council is often crucially determined by the candidate's connection to both direct kin and a range of other associates. Thus the different tribal councilpersons depend on a somewhat bandlike model of support to attain their positions. Tribal councilpersons tend to funnel jobs and other benefits back to supporters in a way not radically different from the way that more traditional chiefs once did. A key difference from the past is that the resources that the councilperson distributes were not necessarily generated by the recipients, so rather than individual bands being largely self-sufficient economically, there is intense competition for access to council seats and tribal resources. Related to this is a strong sense of inequity on the part of those families excluded from the benefits. For these reasons, political leadership offers less prestige and status cross tribally than it did traditionally. Thus many elders are not attracted to this role, preferring lower-visibility but more stable jobs or ceremonial roles.

CEREMONIALISM AND TRIBALISM

During the initial reservation period, new ceremonial movements arose, such as the Ghost Dance and later the associated Crow Dance (see Mooney 1896), as well as the Peyote Lodge/Native American Church. As Loretta Fowler's work shows (2010), these new ceremonial/religious movements were often initiated and most heavily patronized by younger members of the society, and they constituted challenges both to the structure of traditional age-graded lodges and the Sun Dance and to the roles of elders more generally. The ceremonies (including Native American Church and the Pan-Indian sweat lodge) also tend to provide more similar roles for men and women, though specific gender roles still occur in both instances. While Fowler's work focuses on Oklahoma, this same situation developed in Wyoming. The age-graded lodges gradually fell into disuse. Meanwhile numerous Christian denominations have established a presence among the Northern Arapaho, first the Catholic and Episcopal churches via early missionaries, and more recently Evangelical groups and Mormons. The women's quillwork society has ceased to exist, while the highest of the age-graded lodges ("The Seven Water-Sprinkling Old Men") has morphed into a separate group called "The Four Old Men."

The result of all of these ceremonial changes is that the Sun Dance continues to be practiced and is promoted as a key unifying ceremony for the tribe. Allied practices (Sacred Flat Pipe, Pipe Keeper, renewing the Pipe, the Rabbit Lodge, ceremonial grandfather/grandson relationships) also continue. Nevertheless, there is no longer an automatic linkage between Arapaho ethnic identity and the Sun Dance complex, as existed during pre-reservation times: some Arapahos do not attend the ceremony and, more importantly, do not adhere to the ideology surrounding it. Thus even the Sun Dance is now one more affiliative choice among others: one hears people describe themselves as "I'm a Sun Dance man" as opposed to claiming some other ceremonial/religious affiliation. The Native American Church ("Peyote men") continues, as does the Crow Dance, along with various Christian religious denominations. Ceremonial sweating is another available affiliation ("I'm a sweat man"). But overall, ceremonialism functions as a much less unifying tribal force than it once did.

Ceremonialism also now offers fewer avenues to high-status participation for younger men and women, since the loss of the age-graded societies left a major void at the lower age levels of the society. The relative opportunities and roles for elders in the various forms of ceremonialism are quite variable. The

Sun Dance is the place where they are most pronounced and numerous. They occur in an attenuated form in more Pan-Indian practices such as the Native American Church and sweat ceremonies. Both of these activities occur widely, but each tends to have cohorts of regular participants linked to certain families or neighborhoods. They are most often put on or led by an older individual, but this is not a necessity, and there is no higher-level organization. Positions of status for elders are least available within Christian denominations, though they are certainly not absent there. All the newer forms of ceremonialism tend to have relatively equal participation by men and women, unlike the age-graded and Sun Dance ceremonies. Men typically lead a sweat ceremony, but women often participate with the men, and the same is true for the Native American Church and Christian denominations.

VENUES FOR PERFORMANCE

Finally, we can consider the various arenas of Plains Indian culture where status can be gained through social performance, outside of political, ceremonial, or kin networks. Among the most common and prominent of these are: (1) sports performance, especially in basketball (Wiles 2011:196–99); (2) military duty (Wiles 2011:58–61); (3) powwow competitions (Wiles 2011:76–79); (4) wage labor, in support of the family; and (5) higher education and degrees, which provide access to key positions in the tribal government and economy. As with pre-reservation society, many of these are more available to younger people (though wage labor, as we have seen, is increasingly engaged in by the elders, and some dance powwow into their eighties). One could even draw rough parallels between older and newer forms of performance (the military aspect as equivalent to traditional raiding, wage labor as equivalent to hunting, or higher education as roughly similar to medicinal knowledge and power). But a key difference is that the practitioners are much less dependent on approval of the older generation for access to privileged information in order to pursue these avenues toward status. Of course there are coaches to please, commanders to obey, powwow judges to impress, bosses, and so forth as in any society and economy, but a good deal of these activities occur outside the Wind River community and, other than those involving sports coaches, do not create Arapaho-internal youth-elder relationships of authority and reciprocity. Another key difference from pre-reservation times is that these performative venues are all equally open to both genders, and the prestige available at Wind River is roughly equal for both genders. In other words, these pathways offer greater freedom to younger people of both genders than pre-reservation options would have offered, and they involve much less monitoring and control—and thus authority—by the elder generation.

LANGUAGE TRANSFORMED

Today the Northern Arapaho Tribe has around ten thousand enrolled members. Of those living in and around the reservation, the majority work for the tribal government, the local tribally controlled school districts, or the casinos and hotel. Most tribal revenue derives from either the casinos and the connected hotel and conference center, from royalties paid for oil and gas mining on the reservation, or from federal-level grants and funding. Some of this is paid out in monthly per capita payments, but the yearly amounts per person are not huge (they are in the hundreds currently). As recently as the 1940s, most individuals lived in tents and used horses and wagons for transportation, but since the 1950s, single-family homes and cars have become the norm. Television also arrived in the 1950s, as did both (larger than at present) per capita payments and more extensive year-round employment, though the unemployment rate remains high. Most students attend schools on the reservation, though the last of the local boarding schools closed down long ago; many others attend White-majority schools in Lander and Riverton. The tribe is acting assertively to repurchase lands within reservation boundaries, suing to protect air and water quality, taking control of its own health-care system, diversifying economic opportunities, and asserting its sovereignty generally (see Anderson 2001a:199–332 for a much more detailed study of these transformations at Wind River, up to the late 1990s).

All these changes have been accompanied by language shift. This began in the years following World War II; currently the youngest fluent native speakers of the language are mostly age sixty-five or older.[7] The shift was relatively rapid, with a number of families having older siblings who are productive speakers but younger siblings who are not. Northern Arapaho Language and Culture Commission cochair Ron told me he attributed the shift especially to the influence of returning World War II veterans, who had seen the outside world in a way young people before them had not and thus decided to start using their newly acquired fluency in English with their children (see Anderson 1998:80); his cochair Joe points especially to the influence of rising prosperity on the reservation in the same era, leading to cars, jobs in town, televisions, and the sudden pervasive influence of the outside, English-speaking world (see Anderson 1998:80). In fact, the causes are quite complex, and many additional explanations are offered by other Arapahos (see Anderson 1998:70–82; as well as Perley 2011:31–62 for a parallel investigation of Maliseet, another Algonquian language, at a roughly similar stage for very similar reasons). My focus in this book is less on what *caused* this shift however, and much more on *responses* to it.

The shift proceeded apace, apparently largely unnoticed, into the 1970s. Many Northern Arapahos today say that they never intended to switch from Arapaho to English (see Anderson 1998:56)—they simply wanted to make sure their children knew English and therefore spoke English to them at home, assuming they would pick up Arapaho "eventually," in a way similar to that described for the shift in Gapun village, New Guinea, from Taiap to Tok Pisin (Kulick 1992:13–14).[8] The goal was therefore stable bilingualism.[9] The result, however, was a situation where, for the generation born in the 1950s and 1960s, English was linked to educational and career success, "progress," and "modernity," while Arapaho was broadly linked to "tradition" and "the past." Most important for the future of the language, there were now virtually no spatiotemporal frames wherein Arapaho could be spoken for those of this younger generation (see Anderson 2009), as "Arapaho-only" language ideologies now applied only to ceremonial contexts, in which the vast majority of speech production came from older individuals. Note that Arapaho speakers do not show a strong ideology of language purism in relation to everyday contexts, and they readily engage in code-switching—though they are highly purist in relation to formal genres such as traditional narrative, song, prayer, speeches, and the like, where English is strongly avoided if possible. This selective purism has been a key factor in the increasing tendency to view the language as sacred, similarly to in other Native American communities (Gómez de García, Axelrod, and Lachler 2009:107).

Only in the 1970s did the community collectively come to the realization that the children of the 1950s and 1960s, while able to understand Arapaho, could mostly not speak it, and that the children of the 1970s were no longer even able to understand it in many cases. They instituted efforts at language revitalization that continue to this day. While those efforts have produced large amounts of documentation and curriculum and exposed many children to basic levels of the language, they have produced no fluent speakers and only a handful of younger second-language learners who are partially productive speakers. The primary reason for this failure is that the language ecology that produced the shift to English remains intact: very few people are committed to using Arapaho in the home as a primary language, and English continues to be seen as the language of education and career success and prosperity. The desire to speak Arapaho is primarily a desire to have "knowledge" of the language (in the way that older bilingual individuals have this knowledge today) without for the most part a desire to use it regularly, though there are certainly some younger people who do seek communicative competence for everyday usage (primarily with older relatives). Today probably around one hundred people speak Arapaho well. I have been involved with the Northern Arapaho in the role of outside academic since 1999, and I have witnessed the end stages of this language shift, while also contributing advice, curriculum, training, and documentation to try and forestall its full effects.

NORTHERN ARAPAHO COMMUNITIES OF PRACTICE

The preceding sections provide the groundwork necessary for understanding the various COPs that currently exist at Wind River. As we will see, initially here and then in much more detail in the rest of the book, differing COPs have different perspectives on age, gender, knowledge, kinship, tribe, ceremony, and performance, as well as language. Although I avoid the term *culture* in this book as an analytical tool, Northern Arapaho individuals from across many COPs talk pervasively about *Arapaho Culture*. Yet the number of individuals in the community who actually speak Arapaho more or less fluently has fallen from somewhat less than 10 percent of the population when I arrived in 2000 to a little more than 1 percent as I finished this book in 2016 (out of a total enrolled population of roughly ten thousand, not all of whom reside in the reservation area).

While many Northern Arapaho individuals use the term *Arapaho Culture*, they recognize that not all Arapaho individuals (as defined by political membership in the Northern Arapaho Tribe) take part in Arapaho Culture. Effectively, they recognize the ones who do as members of a specific COP, which I will call the Arapaho Culture (henceforth AC) COP, in deference to community usage. The AC COP is a political and ideological position that exists on and around the Wind River Reservation. It offers one model of social relations, group coherence, access to resources, and pursuit of individual and collective interests, among several other competing positions. The others include most prominently Politico-Tribalism (which focuses on a specifically Arapaho identity but does not necessarily rely heavily on such things as the Arapaho language or traditional Sun Dance religion for iconicity), Evangelical Christianity, Assimilationism to Euro-American Society, and Pan-Indianism.

The AC COP is the primary focus of this book, but it cannot be understood outside the context of these others, so I discuss them a good deal. Whereas *Arapaho* is in part a legal and blood quantum category, participation in AC is a matter of degree, time, and place. Virtually all individuals at Wind River participate in multiple COPs and move between them according to contexts and needs. Sara Wiles's biographies of specific Northern Arapaho individuals nicely illustrate this point (see Wiles 2011:37–41 and 128–31 for two good examples).[10] Many Arapahos are considered not "Arapaho" at all from the perspective of AC, especially by Arapaho-speaking elders, and some Whites are labeled as "more Arapaho" than many blood quantum/legal Arapaho individuals (see Anderson 1998:74). AC is thus a prototype category. Notably, many younger people who do not actually speak Arapaho are widely considered to be part of AC, while a few elders who do speak the language, but who do not use it and do not associate with those who do, are not considered to be part of the COP.

The focus on the AC COP is in part because, as a linguistic anthropologist, I am especially interested in the Arapaho language, and the AC COP is where the practice of the language is now located for the most part. In addition, the AC COP almost certainly represents the most overall continuity with what could loosely be called "traditional Arapaho culture" of the pre-reservation era. Arapaho society of that time certainly had competing COPs, just as Arapaho society at present does—it was not a homogeneous and self-contained group any more than any other society is. However, we largely lack access to the details of those COPs now—though we can note that, in relation to the encounter with non-Indians in the nineteenth century, there was clearly a resistance wing of the tribe and a collaborationist wing. In addition, it is clear that Arapaho practice had important broader links to Northern Plains Native American language and practices more generally, as I point out explicitly several times in the book. Nevertheless, our view of the nineteenth-century Arapaho tends to look artificially homogeneous. This is exacerbated by the fact that most early consultants were from an older generation heavily affiliated with an earlier AC COP,[11] though from Fowler's work in particular, we can see that competing COPs were clearly present during early reservation days, including emergent ceremonial/religious movements such as the Ghost Dance, Crow Dance, and Native American Church, and collaborationist versus resistance positions in relation to the pressures of reservation life. Most generally, as Michael Silverstein notes about many studies of the transformations of small language groups, "there lurks a recuperative diachrony that implies its own—generally mythic—horizon of purity and isolation of systems" (1998:409).[12]

Nevertheless, to talk about change over time as well as diversity in the present, one must start from somewhere, and certain issues and complexities, as well as certain mediating relationships between present and past, must always be bracketed off (Kockelman 2014:618). With these limitations in mind, I have tried to provide a reconstruction of Arapaho linguistic and sociocultural practices from the pre-reservation and early reservation time periods, in order to have a basis for understanding the competing positions of the current COPs and the relationship of the current AC COP to the past of the larger tribe and society. At the risk of caricature (insert the words "to at least some extent" for each point below), prototypical contemporary AC could be described as:

1a. belief that "power" exists in the natural world and that this power is accessible to Arapaho individuals through certain socioculturally mediated channels. This power is sought primarily for the benefit of the tribe as a whole, but social prestige and capital also accrue to those individuals who are able to obtain, manage, and use it properly.
1b. belief that this power is held by humans in the form of "knowledge" (of how to access and use the power), and it is desirable that this type of knowledge be restricted along age and gender lines and transmitted in careful, formalized ways.
2. belief in the value of the Arapaho language (though this does not exclude profound ambivalence on this subject), including personal and place naming practices and folk etymology, and an automatic respect for those who speak it as having special "knowledge."
2a. use of the Arapaho language whenever possible, and a belief in the greater efficacy of the Arapaho language in comparison to English, at least in some situations (notably ceremonies).
3. use of Arapaho English when speaking English.
4. commitment to long-term intergroup reciprocity, in terms of exchange of money, goods, personal and ceremonial service and support, and knowledge (though this does not exclude attempting to use that system in an unbalanced way primarily for one's own benefit).
5. belief in the legitimacy and efficacy of the various traditional Arapaho ceremonial activities—Sun Dance, sweat lodges, vision quests, cedaring/

smudging, ceremonial painting, prayer, medicinal practices, and song—and in the authority of ceremonial offices such as Pipe Keeper, Wheel Keeper, and Four Old Men (now also included, but with lesser symbolic value, are the Native American Church and powwow).

6a. acceptance of the principle of age hierarchy, implying automatic respect for someone due to age alone, including recognizing social authority due to this factor alone.

6b. acceptance of a principle of gender distinctiveness (not necessarily asymmetry), where certain social and ceremonial responsibilities are clearly divided along gender lines.

7. commitment to practicing traditional Arapaho kinship relationships (father's brothers equivalent to father, mother's sisters equivalent to mother, children of father's brothers and mother's sisters equivalent to biological sisters and brothers, etc.), including accepting the social authority and reciprocal obligations embedded in these relationships.

8. commitment to principles of humility and egalitarianism in interpersonal relationships: a wariness of self-promotion, of "showing off" in behavior, speech, dress, or possessions, or of making demands or impositions on others other than through culturally sanctioned mechanisms; modest, non-revealing attire; quietness and restrained expression of emotion in larger public settings.

9. a critical attitude toward "White" culture (though this does not exclude profound ambivalence toward this culture or willing participation in it).

10. commitment to remaining on or (when absent from) returning to the Wind River Reservation as one's true home, and also going to a reservation-located K–12 school.

11. belief in the preferability of the Arapaho to other tribes.

12. commitment to traditional hunting and food-gathering practices; ceremonial foods; and practice of some subset of traditional artistic or entertainment activities, such as drumming and singing, beadwork, leatherwork, tipi maintenance, and handgame.

(*Belief* here should be taken as a combination of explicitly stated verbal opinions and associated participation and actions.) The above is a description of a roughly typical understanding of AC by someone in their sixties or seventies. Several elements of it might be more or less strongly contested, especially by younger people. (I am talking here specifically of *internal* contestation—by those who also identify with and participate in AC.) Moreover, there are a number of potential or actual tensions and even contradictions within the definition given above, which can be exploited by individuals within AC for competing aims. One example is the tension that often occurs between family relationships and respect for ceremonial authority. Within ceremonies, there are competing understandings of the status and meaning of various ceremonial practices. I do not want to suggest that AC constitutes a completely harmonious, coherent unity. Rather it is made up of a set of sociocultural practices and related identity positions with some greater or lesser degree of political and ideological coherence in relation to competing COPs and identities.

The other COPs can be described more briefly for the moment. Assimilationism does not necessarily involve a rejection of AC but rather a neglect of it and an active engagement in the Euro-American COPs that are pervasive on and around the reservation. The term *assimilationist* itself is admittedly problematic. As James Collins has noted, indigenous people are in many ways "conscripts to civilization" whose "alternatives were slowly eroded" (1998b:54), and thus people in this position are rarely unambivalent. Thus verbal support is paid to many of the elements of AC by Assimilationists, but the critique offered by AC members of their behavior—"s/he is too busy being a White man"—nicely captures the dynamic of this COP. A basic distinction between AC and Assimilationism is similar to what Jane Hill and Kenneth Hill find for Mexicano speakers— access to reciprocity within AC, access to capitalism within Assimilationism (J. Hill and K. Hill 1986:3).[13] Pan-Indianism tends to focus more value on intertribal cultural institutions and practices such as powwows, the Native American Church, the tribal college movement, basketball, and generalized informal sweating ("cowboy sweats" in Arapaho English) as opposed to Arapaho-specific ceremonial sweating in AC COP. It typically shares some practice of elements numbered 1, 3, 4, 6, 7, 8, 9, and 12 with AC, though often with less commitment, and it shows a positive attitude toward—and some practice of—number 2 and especially number 5. Evangelical Christianity (see Wiles 2011:80–83) tends to neglect or even in some cases strongly reject numbers 1, 2, and 5, not surprisingly, and show a weakened commitment to numbers 4, 6, 7, and sometimes 9 and 12, while also strongly embracing small, often family-oriented churches, which are reservation-based and usually entirely Native American in membership. The church membership replaces more traditional kinship lines (to the extent these are separable) in relation to numbers 4, 6, and 7. More loosely, this COP includes other mainline Christian practitioners (primarily Catholic and Episcopal), some with an Assimilationist orientation. Many mainline Christian practitioners at Wind River are highly syncretic, however, and they participate in the AC and/or Politico-Tribal and/or Pan-Indian COPs (see Anderson 2001a:211–18). This distinction between Evangelical and more syncretic Christians echoes that found by M. Nevins (2010) for the Western Apache and includes some of the same tensions. The Politico-Tribal COP[14] is oriented toward Arapaho-specific identity but tends to focus more on land and history, as opposed to just language and culture, as iconic of Arapaho identity, as well as on concepts of shared experience that resonate with concepts of indigeneity and aboriginality (see Perley 2011:151, 156, 178, 182 on Maliseet for similar observations). It could be thought of as the tribal response to the concept of nationalism. Members of this COP have positive attitudes toward virtually all values of the AC COP, but their practice of these is often greatly attenuated. They most often see the language as iconic of tribal sovereignty, and they are heavily oriented to legalistic views of Native American and Arapaho identity and sovereignty, especially in relation to "White" identity (see Kroskrity and Field 2009:24; Kroskrity 2009; and Bunte 2009 for similar observations about the linkage of language to political sovereignty). As James Collins has noted, an increasing engagement with mainstream legal and political domains is virtually a necessity for indigenous peoples, as their "rights" are often defined in relation to those domains (1998b:7, 57, 104; see also M. Nevins 2013:25–37). These are the people who most overtly view "Arapaho" as a political and even economic/corporate identity, in relation to other tribes as well as the U.S. government, with whom they are in competitive relationships. Their own goals within the tribe are often political as well, oriented toward controlling certain offices or institutions.[15] Note also that among the Arapaho, politics and traditional religion are much more separate than is the case for Pueblo groups, for example (Debenport 2015:8–18). This leads to a more pronounced potential division between the AC and the Politico-Tribal COPs than is the case in the Southwest.

While only 1 percent of Northern Arapaho people speak the language today as a first language, perhaps another 10 percent or more in their forties, fifties, and sixties are fluent or near-fluent passive understanders of the language, and many of these can produce individual words or fixed phrases. Many younger individuals have had exposure to the language in school classes. Thus the language has much more saliency in the community than the figure of 1 percent would suggest. It would be extremely difficult to say how many people are in some degree affiliated to or practitioners of the AC COP, but the number is likely around half the enrolled members of the tribe, though the core membership may be 25 percent or less.

Note that my description pays less attention to certain kinds of highly salient symbolic practices (orientation toward traditional ceremonial foods) and focuses instead more on a set of socioeconomic relationships and acceptance of certain types of social authority, as well as on models of personal agency and interpersonal interaction. This is the sense in which I understand AC as fundamentally a political position, since authority, agency, and distribution of socioeconomic resources are fundamentally political. Within AC, power is weakly institutionalized and heavily dependent on individual assent and adherence. This is even truer today than in the past, as AC has shifted from the dominant position within Northern Arapaho society to one of several competing alternatives, and as certain key institutional components of AC (the age-graded society lodges and women's ceremonial organizations) have disappeared. Likely few people ever had the feeling of being "oppressed" within Arapaho society of the eighteenth and nineteenth centuries, and certainly in the current era power within AC is largely a matter of maintaining voluntary adherence. For this reason, power is best thought of in terms of individual prestige and shifting alliances of prestigious individuals. Prestige derives from both perceived access to *no'otehiit* and the successful use of it for the community good. Finally, *no'otehiit* is normally conveyed or shared within the community—and converted to tangible goods, services, and money—via small-scale structures of reciprocity.

LANGUAGE, POWER, AND RELATIONSHIPS IN ARAPAHO COPS

At this point, we can see more clearly how the AC concept of power and the analytic terms *power* and *symbolic capital* are closely related. Returning to Bastien's *Blackfoot Ways of Knowing*, we find a clear integration of the two concepts of power. She states that "relationships are reciprocal by nature" (4) and that people "generate knowledge by renewing these relationships" (4). On the one hand, this means that people maintain relationships with plants, animals, places, and the land, in which they care for and honor these sources of power and in return receive benefits from them, including sacred knowledge. On the other hand, human relationships are also reciprocal by nature, and these relationships are intimately based on the transmission of knowledge and power. The statements can be understood as referring to both the sacred and the human realms together, not just the two realms in parallel. Humans "generate knowledge" of the sacred by "renewing relationships" with fellow individuals, and conversely humans "generate knowledge" within their own society by "renewing relationships" with sources of sacred power. She says that knowledge is generated for the purpose of "maintaining relationships" (2). This can mean that sacred knowledge is sought and generated, so that it can be shared with other humans and used to benefit them, thus maintaining social relationships. And it can mean that social knowledge is sought out from others who have wisdom and power in order to allow an individual to maintain and renew his or her relationship with sacred power. And again: traditional learning is an "interactive process" that involves a "network of relationships" (119). The two senses of power, sacred—or what I am calling MTH—and social, are completely fused in this statement (see also Harrod 1987:67, 89–93).[16]

AC-affiliated individuals report the same ideas quite explicitly. Henry explained to me that ancestor spirits (*cei3wooono'*) are powerful sources of aid for those who possess them, and these can be transferred from one person to another—from stepfather to stepson in the particular case he recounted. However, he stressed that the spirits are not simply possessed by humans but can have a will of their own, and they will only submit to transmission if the proper ritual procedure is followed by both transferer and transferee in their interpersonal relationship.

On one occasion, a woman I know decided to have a "sing" at her house for the ceremonial Eagle Drum—a typical part of getting ready for the Sun Dance that gives the singers an opportunity to practice, while also receiving blessings for oneself and one's neighbors. The specific occasion for the sing was the fact that several people in the immediate area had died recently. The Arapaho idiom for the practice in question is that one "feeds the drum," and in return the resonant booming of the drum heals the surrounding area from illness and death, bringing life and strength to the area. "Feeding" the drum gives it strength and keeps it healthy, the woman explained. The drum returns this strength to the area where it is fed. More literally, one feeds the drummers (who in Arapaho are called "the drum" as a group—there is no distinction in the language between the drum and the drummers) and gives them strength. Normally, neighboring relatives contribute to the feast or "feed" as well—and take leftovers home with them. And of course the drummers are the ones who play the drum and enable it to give forth its strength. The drum, the drummers, the host of the feast, and the relatives who contribute to it are all bound up in reciprocal relationships with each other involving power, in all senses of the word, with all MTH power and blessings mediated by human social relationships, and the power of the MTH givers is sustained by these human relationships as well.

As the preceding statements show, social power resides in one's prestige and in voluntary adherence by those around one. This prestige and adherence is derived from maintaining strong social networks of reciprocity, including providing benefits to those around one and receiving their adherence and admiration in return. The basis of providing benefits ultimately lies in access to (i.e., a reciprocal relationship with) MTH power, which provides the ability to accomplish all truly challenging tasks and to obtain the benefits one shares with and distributes to others. MTH power that is not distributed—or the lack of a strong social network through which to distribute it—is of little use. The benefits of this MTH power are received, by less prestigious (and younger) individuals, via actions and exchanges from (older) individuals with whom one maintains strong social relationships. Eventual access to this MTH power will normally be mediated for less prestigious individuals by the MTH knowledge shared with them by more prestigious individuals as part of strong social relationships. This is the system that forms the model on which the elders' exchanges at the public library event were based, even though MTH power was certainly not directly at stake in that setting, and this model allows us to better appreciate that series of exchanges in a broader context.

In other words, less prestigious individuals generate and maintain social relationships in order to gain MTH knowledge and power—and benefits— while more-prestigious individuals generate and maintain MTH knowledge and power in order to gain social relationships (i.e., prestige and social power), and they generate and maintain these social relationships in order to have mechanisms through which to distribute MTH power and knowledge. This model contrasts with the overtly political or bureaucratic model of Tribalism, in which fiscal resources (jobs, grants, loans, etc.) are the key focus of relationships, and political positions and key jobs within the tribal governance and economic structure (especially schools and the hotel and casinos) are the basis of prestige and power. It also contrasts with Evangelical Christian models, which conceive of MTH power as directly accessible through a personal relationship with God and use the small, local, often extended-family-based churches as the nexus for distribution and exchange of resources. Pan-Indian models focus more on relationships external to the tribe, as developed through the powwow circuit, the tribal college movement, the National Indian Education Association and similar organizations, the Native American Church/peyote ceremony (see Wiles

2011:120–23; Fowler 1982:124–25), and other venues. This model provides a potentially wider network of reciprocity for those with a more "cultural" orientation, and a wider network of bureaucratic and political links for those looking to extend these modes of interaction beyond the tribal level. It also focuses more on shared identity through behavioral associations (education, government, sports), as compared to the kin- and age-based focus of the AC model.

None of these COPs is exclusive, of course, and individuals move between them freely, while nevertheless maintaining predominant orientations (though these too can shift over time). One can operate within one COP at one time and place, and within another on a different occasion. In some cases, which COP is "in force" may actually be unclear or contested, and multiple COPs can be "in force" simultaneously in certain situations. There is a tension in my analysis between a focus on specific times and places where the AC COP is most operational, and the tendency of AC members themselves to identify specific individuals as "more" or "less" "Arapaho" (more or less part of AC), as part of an identity that partially transcends local interaction. The longer I have worked within Northern Arapaho society, the more I have come to appreciate not just the diversity of viewpoints but also the way in which AC is a highly abstract and emergent entity, coming and going in unexpected times, places, and ways. In contrast, specific cultural resources such as personal names or place names have a concreteness and seeming continuity that belie the ever-changing networks of ideology and practice that incorporate and make use of them in competing ways.

The Arapaho language certainly plays a role in the other COPs, though in most cases that role is symbolic in nature and not actually linked to the sacred or MTH power—a key point to which we will return later in the book. The powwow, sweat lodge, and peyote ceremony are key points of tension, in that they engage with Pan-Indianism yet also with ideas of power, and AC members may seek to appropriate them ideologically to AC, while others resist this. In contrast other settings lack this focus on MTH power. In March 2009, William, a key educational leader in the tribe, stated at a meeting with other Arapaho supporters of the Wind River Tribal College, "When we quit practicing our sovereignty, when we quit speaking our language, we're conquered." This is a powerful—and common—statement of the importance of the language, but it evokes, at least overtly, a context of political and bureaucratic power (Politico-Tribalism) rather than MTH power. In reality, the educator and his family are key participants in the AC COP (see citations from him in chapter 5 that are much more oriented toward MTH power, as well as those below), but the statement illustrates the way in which the symbolic capital of the Arapaho language works differently in different "markets" or COPs. It also shows how a single individual can invoke different or even competing perspectives and ideologies as he or she shifts between markets.

CONTESTED AND EMERGENT RELATIONSHIPS

Just as individuals can move among COPs and political positions, the Arapaho English term *Arapaho Culture* is internally complex and can index one or several of the particular parts of the prototypical definition offered previously, depending on context. In everyday usage, it often pays a good deal more explicit attention to the symbolic activities I allude to above—both very salient ones, such as the participating in the ceremonies, and more mundane everyday interactional routines, such as not looking someone in the eye constantly when they are speaking, or pointing with one's lips, or not throwing or tossing food, or driving a "rez car." Some of these practices are simply accidents of social habit— such as lip pointing—which, because they are done by (most) Arapahos but not Whites, are available to take on iconic significance within AC; others, such as not throwing or tossing food, can be linked quite clearly to deeper underlying attitudes toward resources and resource distribution; while some, such as driving a rez car, are the secondary effect of living out the realities of AC in an economically disadvantaged community. The term *Arapaho Culture* is thus used on the reservation as a *symbolic resource* as defined in the introduction, deployed in relation to the shared experience of Politico-Tribalism in the cases above, oriented toward AC language and ceremonialism in others, and in some cases used as a term that can appeal to multiple COPs simultaneously.

Affiliates of AC sometimes use this term specifically to refer to the AC COP. But often it is used more broadly, presenting Arapaho Culture as the ideal "natural" attribute of any Arapaho person, and as a timeless, unchanging, and coherent set of values inherited from the past. As such, it functions as a term of erasure that seeks to impose AC values and perspectives broadly across the tribe, including on other COPs, serves to deny internal contestation within AC, and seeks to deny historical discontinuities over time between AC and the Arapaho past. In reality, while some of the elements of AC of the early twenty-first century closely correspond to descriptions of Arapaho practice in the nineteenth century, some are quite different—notably the idea that the ability to speak Arapaho constitutes a special form of knowledge and authority. This perspective is a result of language shift and loss, and it was not present when Arapaho was simply the language of all in the community. Arapaho has now taken on second-order indexical and iconic functions in a way similar to what Bunte describes for San Juan Paiute: "Speaking has become revalorized as emblematic of a distinct social and moral character of a person who behaves in morally appropriate ways"—that is, as indicating AC affiliation—as opposed to "simply indexing . . . identity" (Bunte 2009:183). Likewise, the idea that one can be part of AC by showing adherence to the language, by believing in its importance (and knowing and using a few symbolic terms) without actually speaking it, is a newer component of AC, which is strongly contested by some older, fluent speakers. The loss of cross family tribal institutions such as the old age-graded societies also means that age alone as a criterion of authority is now often much less functional than kin-based criteria, and similar things could be said about specifically gender-based authority. Thus the invocation of the Arapaho language and the use of the term *Arapaho Culture* vacillate between moments that seek broad social cohesion and erasure of differences and discontinuities and moments that highlight heterogeneity and enhance prestige in relation to those around one.

I would like to close this chapter with a specific example that illustrates the way in which different practices and ideologies around Arapaho language are negotiated both within and across some of the COPs I have discussed above. The "Northern Arapaho Experience" is a program put on several days a week during the summer by the Wind River Casino, largely for tourists, as part of the casino's cultural tourism efforts. Tribal members present dances, songs, stories, and information about the tribe. While this is mostly done in English due to the audience, some Arapaho language is included as well, which is then translated. Many of the users of the language in the performance are younger students, who introduce themselves in Arapaho and tell a little about themselves in the language. This is a context in which the language has a heavily symbolic significance since none of the tourists understand it, and some of the speakers themselves have a tenuous grasp of exactly what they are saying, word by word. The Arapaho participants in this case could be understood as acting as members of the Politico-Tribal COP, in that they enact the language as a symbol of Arapaho sovereignty for tourists who are politically non-Arapaho, but whose goodwill (and political and economic support) is being sought. In listening to the exact contents of the presentations, however, one realizes that at least some of the performers could be understood as acting as members of the Pan-Indian COP. In particular, their personal introductions in Arapaho, which provide their names, their tribal memberships, and information on their relations (and sometimes clans), are performances of a practice that has become common at national tribal college gatherings and that seems based ultimately on Navajo practices of personal introduction. Many of the performers are associated with the Wind River Tribal College and regularly attend such gatherings. One introduces oneself in one's native language and then moves on to English for the remainder of one's talk. While the tourists are unaware of this, and no tribal college audience is available at the "Northern Arapaho Experience," the performers themselves perform for each other as members of this COP, and since all their (often memorized) personal introductions are similar, they are able to judge the linguistic quality of each other's statements. They do not, of course, expect fluent Arapaho from each other, and they are primarily supportive of each other's efforts to simply try and use the language.

One native speaker elder involved with the performance criticized the students' use of the language in this context, however. He suggested that they not use it, due to mistakes in pronunciation and grammar that they made. He said that "what I do, I do well, and I've been working with the language a long time." The younger Arapaho learners who were part of the performance argued, on the other hand, that the language needed to remain a part of the event. The overall coordinator of the performance, from the casino, ultimately agreed that the language could remain, though in reduced amounts.

The elder's criticism was a result of the fact that he was treating the Arapaho language performance in terms of AC norms and expectations. For him, the COP in operation was the AC COP, since he was present and was evaluating the spoken Arapaho as fully meaningful and potentially "powerful"—that is, as subject to evaluation by AC standards. Public, official speaking of Arapaho is often limited to recognized, knowledgeable elders, and even native speakers may be reluctant to speak at formal public occasions for fear of making mistakes either in the content and knowledge expressed or in pronunciation and grammar. At a funeral in July 2012, for example, a fluent native speaker of the language was asked by the family of the deceased to pray. After standing up in front of the gathering and saying what an honor this was, she then apologized for praying in Arapaho in front of other elders (who were older and generally recognized by the community as somewhat more knowledgeable in the language than she was). This apology invoked an AC language ideology that holds that making formal public pronouncements is a privilege that should be restricted to qualified, preselected individuals.

This ideology is represented in its most powerful form through the institution of the official tribal announcer, a ceremonial office that has evolved from the camp crier of older times (see Wiles 2011:50–53). There is a verb for public announcing (*noooxunee-*) and a name for the announcer (*noooxuneihii*). Both in the past and in the present, the crier or announcer is selected by elders and then formally presented to the rest of the tribe at a public event. There is an official "announcer's song" (*noooxun(een)oot*), which is used at these events to honor the announcer. The announcer uses a special cadence and intonation in the announcements, along with repetitions and parallelisms, and generally strives for eloquence and precision (see ELAR 77a–b for two examples). These announcements are closely evaluated by speakers for their performative qualities, and any mistake can become the basis for decades-long oral traditions.

Announcements are a very restricted type of speech. Prayers are less restricted in that potentially anyone can pray, but in reality only the best speakers of Arapaho are normally asked (or willing to accept), and there are once again decades-old stories in the oral tradition about people who made mistakes in praying or in other formal speech settings such as war stories or speeches to the tribal general council. Other forms of public speech are less formal and less restricted. In some contexts, public speech by learners, complete with potential errors, is in fact encouraged: demonstrations of learning at graduation ceremonies or parents' days, for example. The question at stake in the dispute between the elder and the language students regarding the "Northern Arapaho Experience" really involved the question of who the performance was for, and by what standards it should be judged—or in more theoretical terms, which COP was emergent in the setting, and what the goals of that COP are. The students saw the performance as externally oriented, for non-Arapahos, and primarily symbolic in importance, with grammatical and lexical issues of content being less salient. For them, the AC-internal issues of language competence and authority were less important. The elder, on the other hand, clearly invoked exactly these issues, with his statement about competence and long work on the language. Most generally, he was attempting to control and restrict language usage in such a way that the language could be understood as symbolic capital held by the elder in relation to other Arapahos, while the students saw the language as symbolic capital held by any Arapaho learners in relation to outsiders.

A final comment by the lead student renders the analysis more complex, however. The student complained privately to me that the learners needed practice with the language in order to be good at it. Thus the student saw the occasion as having implications not only for the Pan-Indian COP mentioned earlier but potentially for the AC COP as well. The student went on to note that if the elders have been working on the language and teaching it for so many years and the young people were still not up to their standards, perhaps it was the elders' fault. These complaints suggest that the student does accept the AC linguistic performance standards that are part of the AC language ideology and wishes to eventually meet those standards or at least continue to pursue them. The student is clearly a strong adherent to the AC COP. At the same time, the comments suggest a resentment from the student toward the elders and, in particular, a perception that the elders are, at best, unable to effectively transfer the symbolic capital of the Arapaho language to the younger generation and, at worst, attempting to restrict access to this symbolic capital. Thus the student suggests that the elder is violating the norms of social relations in the AC COP by inappropriately restricting the flow of knowledge and ultimately that of power—exactly the contrary of what Helen said in the comments above about trying to correct younger people. The student suggested implicitly that if the elders cannot convey the language effectively, then the students must acquire it on their own. In so doing, they may no longer be bound by the forms of linguistic authority that have been embedded in the older modes of Arapaho language acquisition, in the home in particular.

At its deepest level, the dispute focuses on the changes in modes of language acquisition among the Arapaho and the kinds of linguistic authority that are embedded in different modes of acquisition. The public dispute, mediated by the casino producer, focused on externalist issues of intended audiences for the performance and the types of standards that should be invoked for judging the performance. The issue that most concerned the student, however, but which the student was unwilling to state publicly, was an issue of AC-internal rivalry over the Arapaho language as symbolic capital, in which neither elder nor student questioned the basic ideological premise of AC that the language is both desirable and powerful, in a potentially MTH way, and each invoked differing aspects of AC language and social ideology to defend their positions.

Language shift is the reason for the changes in modes of language acquisition. Barbra Meek (2010) has shown how this process can lead to changes in language ideology as well: the language changes from a community property with little symbolic capital, since it is known and used by everyone, to a form of "knowledge" similar to ceremonial and MTH knowledge, which is seen as restricted and the special privilege of elders (see Anderson 1998:69, 73 for an early recognition of this same issue in Arapaho). Both student and elder accept this new ideology, but the student then implicitly proposes a new model of acquisition whereby students, in acquiring the language on their own through classes, websites, and so forth, would bypass elder authority. Yet the same student is a strong member of AC, and a strong respecter of elder authority generally as this is a key component of AC. And the elder, despite his misgivings in this situation, is more generally a strong advocate of sharing traditional forms of restricted knowledge, such as sacred narratives, more openly, so that they will not be lost entirely to the tribe and AC—as long as the narratives are performed and recorded properly by elders and their collaborators.

Language shift led to this dispute between student and elder precisely because they both care so passionately about the language and, more deeply, because they both accept so fully that the language carries power within it, which is central to the survival of AC. Thus we see, for the first but certainly not the last time in this book, how a discontinuity in language practice is embedded in a deeper continuity in language ideology. We also see how the very depth of the continuity in ideology has the potential to open up a gap—a discontinuity—in social relations in the context of language shift, as the maintenance of the ideology by the younger student leads that student to contemplate and even practice altered forms of respect—linguistic respect in particular—in relation to the elder. An intricate dance of continuity and change, of ideology and practice, within and between communities of practice, is played out across generations, as AC seeks its path into the future.

Certainly among the Northern Arapaho today, knowledge is now less and less of the MTH variety, and more and more located outside of Arapaho tribal domains generally. It is in schools, colleges, churches, the military, and Pan-Indian organizations, and it is openly available to men and women, young and old (see Anderson 1998:91–102; 2001a:206–7). These are the domains of knowledge that dominate the various non-AC COPs: Pan-Indian, Evangelical Christian, Politico-Tribal, and Euro-American Assimilationist.

Yet AC remains a strong identity position and focus of group organization. The AC model of (much) knowledge as properly restricted to or managed by older individuals, channeled through reciprocal interpersonal relationships, remains operational. Hunting, powwow dancing, sweat ceremonies, the Sun Dance, peyote ceremonies, beadwork and other traditional arts (Wiles 2011:127, 206–11), participation in ceremonial or social drum groups, handgame (Wiles 2011:216–19), hand-drum contests, and numerous other activities that are seen as both "Arapaho" and "traditional" are widely practiced, and all to some degree depend on knowledge mediated by elders as well as direct support from those elders in the form of regalia, feasts, implements, and so forth. William, the educator mentioned earlier, addressed a gathering of students one day about a cultural project they were doing, telling them, "If someone asks you what you're doing, you tell them to go to Felix." He was referring to an elder who was very involved with the tribal college. The college, and the educator in particular, has sought to involve elders heavily in the curriculum, not just because they know many things, but because the college seeks to transmit knowledge within an AC framework. His statement to the students recognizes the authorizing power of specific, named elders in relation to younger peoples' practice.

Conversely, the same person who criticized younger speakers at the "Northern Arapaho Experience" explained to me in May 2015 that he often sees young people engaging in questionable ceremonial activities (in the sense that they do not fully understand what they are doing, or they make mistakes). He said they claim they have the right to do the activity because an elder authorized it, but when asked to name a specific elder, they cannot do so, or if they do name someone, that person says upon further inquiry that he or she never gave such permission. In other words, the ideology of knowledge within the AC COP is being violated.

All the preceding examples show potential or actual tension across generations. But the participants all accept—or at least appeal to—the ideology of knowledge within AC. The AC ideology conceives of knowledge as specifically Arapaho in nature; as held by elders, separate from younger people; and as partially divided along gender lines. It conceives of the transmission of this knowledge in the context of intergenerational relationships of respect and reciprocity strongly guided by elders. The ordered flow of MTH knowledge is the basis of Arapaho social order and continuity, while the latter is what allows continued access to the former. We will look in the remainder of this book at the specific linguistic forms of social order and continuity and MTH knowledge within the AC COP, as well as at the status of the Arapaho language within competing COPs.

2

CULTURAL METAPHORS AND THE INDIGENOUS DISCOURSE OF LANGUAGE ENDANGERMENT

INTRODUCTION: THE CONCEPT OF CULTURAL METAPHORS

IN AN ARTICLE ON HOPI METAPHOR, Emory Sekaquaptewa and Dorothy Washburn show that certain key metaphors are "the vehicle for the transmission of cosmological ideas" among the Hopi (2004:459). They find these metaphors repeated in kiva murals, on pottery, and in song and ritual phrases, as part of a set of unitary cultural symbols. This is a theme that will be explored in great detail in chapter 3, where we will see that Arapaho place names, myths, and visual design elements echo each other as part of a single system of expression. Studies of metaphor and cultural expression of this type often focus on highly salient forms of cultural performance across multiple oral/aural and visual media and tend to emphasize the cultural continuity and even unity of such metaphors (see J. Weiner 1991). Elsewhere, Keith Basso's examination of Western Apache metaphor treats metaphor as quite salient within the culture, though it demonstrates that it need not necessarily be grounded in ritual and cosmology narrowly defined (1990:53–79). His presentation emphasizes the more individually creative and performative aspects of metaphor. On the other hand, the work of George Lakoff on cognitive metaphors tends to focus on everyday language and behavior (Lakoff and Kövecses 1987; Lakoff and Johnson [1980] 2003). It shares with Sekaquaptewa and Washburn's work a focus on metaphors that are part of the general culture and language, though certainly allowing room for individual play and variation. But unlike the previous two studies, it also examines forms of metaphor that are relatively nonsalient in conscious everyday life, in the sense that they are so deeply embedded in language and thought that they may rarely rise to the level of consciousness. In addition, while people certainly appropriate and use the conceptual models underlying these metaphors in creative ways, the use of the metaphors per se is not necessarily a part of any performance, and in fact most commonly is not. When someone describes another person as "boiling over with anger," this certainly marks a creative and colorful use of language, but it does not invoke ritual contexts or cosmological principles in the way that expressions such as "flocks," "shepherds," and "Lamb of God" and similar phrases work within the Christian tradition. Thus in some sense a distinction must be made between the generalized cognitive metaphors that pervade everyday thought and language and a select subset of such metaphors that rise to sociocultural prominence through ritual and performance, either of the more individualized variety described in Basso or the more institutionalized variety described in Sekaquaptewa and Washburn—what Quinn and Holland call "compelling" as opposed to "at will" metaphors (1987:11).

Arapaho speakers invoke numerous metaphorical conceptions in their speech, including both overt, ritual ones and covert, cognitive ones. This distinction itself is somewhat "metaphorical" in nature, however, and is best considered a heuristic device. Deeply embedded ritual eventually becomes a pattern of thought, and patterns of thoughts are appealed to by ritual. In this chapter, I want to illustrate some important metaphors that often occur in Arapaho speech and consider further their potential effects on thought and behavior. I am interested particularly in metaphors with strong moral content that connect directly with ideas of MTH power—the kinds of metaphors recognized in Native American communities as very closely tied to culture and morality, including reciprocal relationships.[1] We will see in chapters 5 and 6 that this practice of metaphor is intimately connected to both folk etymology and neologisms: it seeks to find deep connections of MTH power between different realms of life and experience, based on hidden correspondences, and it seeks to creatively extend known understandings of MTH power to new realms so as to effectively appropriate them.[2] In this chapter I am especially interested in the continuities and discontinuities that occur as cultural metaphors are extended to new sociocultural conceptual realms and dilemmas. Cultural metaphors are an especially interesting way to initiate this study, since they are in theory the least linguistically bound language feature that is explored in this book. Personal and place names, as well as neologisms and folk etymologies, are deeply embedded in the phonology, morphology, and syntax of Arapaho, while cultural metaphors would seem to be more about cognition. They should thus potentially be more available and translatable—into Arapaho English—as a cultural and linguistic resource for all COPs among the Northern Arapaho. In the chapter, I will explore several common cultural metaphors that occur in the Arapaho language and their extension to the domain of language endangerment.

CENTER AND PERIPHERY

One prominent Arapaho language metaphor involves a fundamental distinction between center and periphery. The two key linguistic roots involved in this pairing are *wotee-* 'to/at the center' and *nooo'-* (colloquially *no'o'-*) 'away/far from the center, at the periphery'. It should be noted that these are not abstract deictic forms indicating merely direction to or from a speaker. (These do also exist in Arapaho: *cih-* 'toward the speaker', *(n)eh-* and *(he)3eb-* 'away from the speaker'.) Rather, in their oldest meanings, they refer to the notion of 'to/at the center of the camp circle, to the front (of the crowd), in social presence' (*wotee-*) and 'out away from the camp circle, far from human presence' (*no'o'-*). More loosely, the latter form is also expressed in Arapaho English or Arapaho translations as "out in the hills" or "out on the prairie." This is a metaphor that is found more generally among Plains Indians. Lee Irwin notes, "Outside the camp circle is not a wilderness, but an open horizon where encounters with mysterious beings are more likely.... Movement from the socially known and nomadically defined encampment into the less secure and potentially mysterious world of the unknown is a movement into liminality" (1994:83–84).[3]

The concepts expressed in these roots are not necessarily metaphorical but rather quite literal in some senses. Yet the forms must be understood as part of a general Arapaho conceptualization of life in terms of not just literal but metaphorical centers and peripheries. Jeffrey D. Anderson (2001a) has analyzed Arapaho "life movement" in terms of the notions of centrality and periphery as complementary spheres of Arapaho conception, with the center associated with Arapaho and more generally human society, and the periphery associated with connections to the mediating sources of MTH power (plants, animals, weather phenomena, etc.) and with that power itself. One goes out into the hills for a vision quest, for example. In fact, in chapter 3 we will see this center-periphery metaphorical model echoed in an elevational model expressed through place names, with more permanent human presence associated with valleys and lower areas, and power (and vision questing) more closely associated with higher elevation areas. There are certainly other Arapaho models for understanding MTH power and access to it, especially in the context of group ceremonial activity; one of these is the idea of "going through" a narrow and difficult passage (the root *kohk-* carries this meaning and is used to describe going through a tunnel, as well as passing through ceremonial suffering, as in the Sun Dance). In contrast, the models of center/periphery and lowland/upland can be understood more specifically in relation to individualized access to power, such as through vision questing. Socioceremonial modes of access to power are intimately associated with ceremonial activities that occur at the "center" of Arapaho society, both literally and figuratively. This works in contrast to the idea of power as located at peripheries. Of course, the Sun Dance also assumes that power is high above (symbolized by the Thunderbird), so there is no way to completely separate the various metaphors for power sources in Arapaho society. Nevertheless, in contrast to the 'center' (*woteeniihi'*, to use the particle based on the root), *no'o'uuhu'* (again using the particle form) tends to mean most generally something on the order of 'out in the wilds' and is often closely associated with spirits, ghosts, traditional burial sites, game animals and birds, and a realm away from (current) human social presence. An excellent example of the use of this metaphor in traditional narrative (though with slightly different specific terms) is Paul Moss's Arapaho story "The Forks" (Cowell and Moss 2005a:313–33; see especially the introduction to the story). In this story, an Arapaho camp faces a famine. An elder directs two young men to ride out radially from the camp in different directions, then to ride toward each other on the arc of a circle. Their riding path thus forms a large pie-shaped portion of a circle, extended out from camp. They then ride inward to camp. As they return, all the animals within the pie-shaped area outlined by their initial path are forced (by MTH power) to run in toward the center of the camp, where they can be taken by the starving Arapaho people.

This metaphor has taken an interesting twist in more modern Arapaho language. The root *wotee-* has come to mean 'to/at town', as towns and cities are seen metaphorically as a variety of a camp circle. (Note that the independent word for 'town' or 'city' is *howoh'oowu'* 'many houses', so the form *wotee-* is used as a directional/locational prefix rather than as a noun.) Thus one can say *heet-wotee-koohu-noo* 'I am going to drive to town' or *heh-won-bii3ihi-n wotee-niihi'* 'let's go eat in town'. This metaphorical extension of the basic meaning is easily comprehensible. However, it produces a conundrum. A root that formerly referred to the 'center of the camp circle' and thus to Arapaho social life now also refers to (overwhelmingly White) 'town' (i.e., Lander or Riverton, Wyoming) as opposed to 'the reservation', which is of course the seat of current Arapaho social life. This new usage in fact metaphorically marginalizes the Arapaho themselves in relation to White society (though the reservation is not described as *no'o'uuhu'* in relation to town).

By a further metaphorical extension, since towns and cities tend to be White dominated, *wotee-* has now also come to mean 'to/at a place of Whiteness'. Thus *woteesee-*, originally 'walk (in)to the center of the camp circle, to the front of the group', now means in a metaphorical sense 'to assimilate to White society'.[4] Thus in a reflection on Arapaho history in 2003 for students in an Arapaho language and culture high-school class, Bill said:

'oh hooyei nehe' 3owo3nenitee, 'oh nihnei'eihit nuhu' nih'iisiine'etiit.
And most of the Indians were very attached to how they used to live.
'oh heihii ne'cihwooniini **woteesee**t.
But more recently they have assimilated [into White society].
Heeneito'oowuuni3i', heeneibiito'owuuwu3i'.
They all have houses, and they all own property.
. . .
Hiiwoonhehe' ceencei'soo', hiiwoonhehe' heesiine'etiit nehe' 3owo3nenitee,
Now it is very different, the way the Indian lives now,
hei'**woteesee**t nuhu' nih'oo3ouniini hiine'etiit.
once he has assimilated to this White Man way of life.
. . .
Heeneeesineyei3eiheino' nehe' nih'oo3oo.
Those are the things that this White Man has taught us.
'oh hi'in nenee': 3eb**woteesee**no'.
And we have assimilated to that [way of life].
'oh hiiwoonhehe', hiiwoonhehe' ne'niiteekuuwoono' nehe' nih'oo3oo.
And now, now we stand together with the White Man.

(Cowell and Moss 2006:131–39)

As a result of this extension of the metaphor, Arapaho society more generally is implicitly presented as marginalized, with White society seen as central.

And in this particular metaphorical frame, there is no complementary power associated with *no'o'uuhu'* for the Arapahos; as noted, this term is not used in complementary relation to the city/White society term *woteeniihi'*. It is as if the metaphorical relationship to White centrality has erased the Arapaho position entirely, in the sense of Irvine and Gal's (2000) term *erasure*.

Thus while the metaphorical extension of the meaning from 'camp circle' to 'town' makes perfect sense *semantically* and represents a continuity of conception in terms of clustered human dwelling, the *ideological* result completely reverses the deeper metaphorical connection between camp circle and the Arapaho social center. We will see very often in this study that continuity on one level is not matched on another. Even more perversely, efforts at continuity in one realm can actually produce discontinuities at more fundamental levels; we will see, for example, in chapter 4 that efforts at maintaining the exact phonological form of personal names lead to loss of meaning and of connection to language and history.

Of course Arapaho people are capable of creative responses to such situations and often resist the kinds of colonized relationships that others attempt to impose on them. Indeed, the very same Bill just cited also told and wrote out a story that he called "The Two Sons." The story (a reworking of the Biblical story of Jacob and Esau) tells of a man with two sons, one with white skin and one with brown skin. The man tells the two sons that he is hungry for meat, and whoever can get it for him will receive the gift of power (*no'otehiit*). The white-skinned son then goes out in the backyard, kills one of their goats, and presents it to his father. He receives the power. Meanwhile the dark-skinned son goes far out in the hills to procure deer, elk, moose, and antelope meat, which he brings back, but he is too late to receive the power. When he discovers the subterfuge of the white-skinned son, he points it out to his father and, in the written version of the story, says, *beebei'on no'o' nee['ee]tiinoo'einoo* 'I went way out in the hills to hunt for it'. The father, chagrined at being tricked, decides to give the dark-skinned son something "even better" than what he gave the white-skinned one. In particular, when he (and thus all Indians) dies, he will go "straight home" (i.e., to the afterlife). In contrast, the White Man will have "power" in the form of electricity, cars, planes, television, and so forth—that is, technology. But he will not be able to go "home" until his soul is pure.

In this story, the Indian is explicitly associated with *no'o'* as opposed to the *wotee-niihi'* of White civilization, and *no'o'* is a place of power again. The earlier speech from Bill hinged on the dual meanings of *wotee-*, with the morpheme finally falling into line with the modern metaphorical extension to White civilization, which decenters the Arapaho. In contrast, the story of the two sons hinges on the dual meanings of *no'otehiit* 'power', whose original meaning is MTH power (so often sought for *no'o'*), and whose metaphorical extension is to electricity and technology (prototypically found *woteeniihi'* 'in town'). Here, it is the White notion of power (or the metaphorically extended Arapaho meaning, if one wishes) that is decentered in favor of a much more traditional Arapaho conception of power, which, though located *no'o'*, is suggested as central and fundamental to Arapaho life, in a revalorization of the periphery.

Most abstractly, the accounts by Bill recognize that there are now at least two center-periphery models in play in Arapaho language and cognition, whose centers do not overlap. They share the same vocabulary of *no'o'* and *woteeniihi'*, as well as *no'otehiit* (which is tied to the larger notion of center-periphery). But the continuity in the use of the lexical items masks two different ideological frameworks, with two different semantic systems. While historically speaking we may describe the newer model and lexical meanings (Whites in town, at the center, having technological power) as metaphorical "extensions" of the older one, this is not really true ideologically or semantically. Rather we must recognize two different structural systems. When we try to align these systems, we find fundamental contradictions (in the meaning of *woteeniihi'*, most obviously), not continuity. The genius of Bill's larger body of storytelling, lectures, and thought (Cowell and Moss 2006), of which we have examined just two examples, is to operate with both systems simultaneously, playing with now one and now the other, in order to explore and bring to light the contradictions and discontinuities and make sense of them for his listeners and readers. In "The Two Sons," in particular, the *no'o'* referred to is the traditional power source of the Arapaho, but it is simultaneously a marginalized position in relation to the White boy who remains at the "center" of the story and the settlement. Bill seeks to revalue the new periphery (now symbolic of Arapaho identity and culture) in relation to the new center (White town life), by appealing to older traditional versions of the power of the periphery. In so doing, however, he implicitly suggests that "the sacred" is not just a part of Arapaho life, as in the "old days" when it was available out in the hills, but now virtually coterminous with Arapaho life. The reward for the Arapaho of being socially marginalized is now to occupy a *permanently* and *pervasively* sacred position in relation to White society. Thus the notion that the Arapaho language is sacred, which we will see so often in this book, especially in very modern contexts, finds a parallel in the fundamental sacredness of the

Arapaho people in relation to Whites. The quality of sacredness achieves greater salience specifically in the context of threats to language and culture.

The larger ideological import of the Bill's story of "The Two Sons" is underlined by the fact that the father, in addressing the son at the end, switches to second-person plural (*-nee*, iterative *-nei'i*) to make clear that he is addressing all Indians: *cee3ei'oo-nei'i, heetniixouuweeckoohu-nee* 'When you set off [for the next life], you will go straight home'. This line actually invokes another completely different but equally rich metaphor of Arapaho language, which I will argue is a cognitive metaphor in the sense used by Lakoff. In particular, this is the metaphor of the journey and the path, evoked in the expression *xouuweeckoohu-* 'go **straight** home'. While Arapaho social life is often conceived of as a circle of people camped around a central point, both individual life and history are most often conceived of in terms of the metaphor of journey and path. As with the previous model, however, this one can and has been extended to new domains. In the remainder of this chapter, I would like to explore more fully this metaphor in Arapaho language, life, and visual design motifs, as well as the surprising twists and turns it has taken through time.

PATHWAYS

Since the Arapaho were traditionally a nomadic people, it is not surprising that they placed special emphasis on images of travel, movement, and pathways—in song, in narratives, in artistic motifs,[5] or in the imagery and metaphors employed in everyday speech. Indeed, the general cognitive metaphor of "life is a journey" occurs in English as well (Lakoff and Johnson [1980] 2003). The metaphor also occurs widely within Native American languages but is often much more developed there than in English, and it takes on specific cultural valences and linguistic expressions that are absent in English.[6] To better understand this, we need to first discuss Arapaho motion verbs in general.

In Arapaho, there are two extremely general verbs for 'to go' (*yihoo-*) and 'to come' (*coo-*). Yet neither of these occurs especially commonly in actual discourse. Instead, most motion verbs consist of two parts—an initial element that indicates direction or location, usually very specifically, and a second, more general element that indicates the manner of motion. An example of a single specific initial element, combined with multiple general final elements, is:

no'(u)-	reach, arrive at destination
no'ukoohu-	arrive by running, arrive by driving
no'usee-	arrive by walking
no'uukoh-	arrive by horseback

Conversely, one can change the initial element:

-isee	walk [note vowel harmony often produces a change to -usee]
hoowusee-	walk downward, downhill
heeneinisee-	walk around aimlessly
ce'isee-	walk back, return by walking

Many of the manner-of-motion verb finals are unsurprising—'run', 'walk', 'swim', 'fly', 'climb', and 'fall'. There is also the final 'by horseback', which underlines the importance of horses for traditional Arapaho life. More striking is the existence of the verb final *-iihi-/-uuhu-* 'to move and camp as a group or community' (and now extended to mean 'change residence' or 'move to a new house'). Thus there are Arapaho verbs such as,

wo'wuuhu-	to move camp farther along, as a community
heeneiniihi-	to wander about nomadically as a group, camp all about
no'uuhu-	to arrive as a travelling community, arrive to make camp

Similarly, there is a verb final *-koni-* 'to move as a group, as a band'. The *-iihi-* final implies movement, but its most literal meaning is 'camp as a group', while *-koni-* explicitly refers to movement only, not camping:

cebkoni-	to move on along, past as a band
nih'eikoni-	to scatter as bands, bands scatter apart
hoowukoni-	to move downhill as a band

These two interesting verb finals—both of which address specifically group or community movement, not individual movement—suggest the importance of the notion of movement and pathway for traditional Arapaho culture. They are far from the only evidence for this fact, however. The idea of travel and paths must really be understood as a—perhaps *the*—central conceptual metaphor of traditional Arapaho life: life itself is a journey; it is movement. This metaphor—if such a conception can even be called "metaphorical" for a nomadic society—appears pervasively in Arapaho speeches, prayers, narratives, and other formal genres as recorded in the nineteenth through twenty-first centuries. In addition, many other actions and activities are conceptualized specifically in relation to movement and traveling.

It is not the terms for moving camp as a group, however, that are the most widely used in the metaphor of path and journey. Instead, those terms seem to largely remain concrete in traditional usage. Rather, another verb final, which serves as the default motion final, without any specification of manner of motion, is used. This final occurs as -*o'oo*- with intransitive verbs and as -*o'on*- with transitive verbs. Since it is the most abstract of all motion finals, it is of course not surprising that this final should be generalized and widely extended metaphorically.

Examples of this form in both concrete and abstract meanings include:

beeto'oo-	to finish a movement or journey; to pass on, die
cowo'oo-	to move along, past; to "get along" in life, "get by"
nohco'oo-	to move with, in company; to participate in an activity
towo'on-	to break into someone's path; to interrupt s.o., to disrespect s.o.
ce3eso'on-	to drive animals away; to force people from a territory, to defeat and expel them
heco'on-	to block s.o.'s path; to quarantine s.o.

In summary, the Arapaho verbal system is rich in final verbal elements that function as movement classifiers. Some of these elements, such as -*iihi*- and -*koni*-, are especially interesting due to their lexical specificity and close connection to the nomadic lifestyle. On the other hand, the element -*o'oo*- is interesting because its very lack of lexical specificity has allowed it to be widely used in metaphorical extensions in which abstract processes, including life itself, are conceptualized as movement along a path.

Such metaphorical extensions are certainly not limited to this final verb element, however. Many other verbs of motion are used in this way, notably -*isee*- 'walk' and -*koohu*- 'run', among others, sometimes with additional derivational elements (for example, -*isee*- is used with animate objects, but -*iseenoo*- is used with inanimates):

3ookutii-	to follow, trail; to obey rules, behave
ciixootee-	located far away; ancient, from a long time ago
hosei3iihi'	behind, backward; in the past (particle)
ce3ei'oo-	to depart/go away; to die
no'eeckoohu-	to go home; to die/go to heaven
xouuweeckoohu-	to go straight home; to go straight/right to heaven
kooko'eikoohu-	to run in circles; to party
xouuwusee-	to walk straight; to live correctly, morally
hiiyootisee-	to walk cleanly; to live properly, purely
cebiseenoo-	to go along; to happen, occur, as an extended event
kohkusee-	to walk through s.t. (as a hole or tunnel); to complete a ceremonial trial or test
hoseitisee-	to walk backward; to "step back" or retire from active participation in ceremonies, community affairs, etc., as commonly is done by elders
niicibisee-	to talk to the back of a location, or crowd; to remain on the margins observing, in a humble manner
ceibisee-	to walk crookedly, astray; to go astray morally, make a mistake
cebkoohuutii-	to run s.t. along to a place, deliver it; to manage an enterprise
ko'use-	to fall and land on the ground; to occur, as a sudden event
seese'ise-	to be all flat and smooth; things are going well in life
nousine-	to be stuck, mired; to be stuck in a difficult situation, to be unable to find a word in speaking

This system is further enriched by the fact that the Arapaho language allows for the formation of transitive verbs from the intransitive manner-of-motion finals listed above. Thus *cebisee-* 'to walk (along/past)' becomes *cebxoot-* 'to walk (along/past) something', and *tei'koohu-* 'to run strongly' becomes *tei'koohuut-* 'to run strongly in relation to something'. Interestingly, in actual discourse, these transitive verbs tend to be used most often in quite abstract and metaphorical ways. Indeed, one of the most common uses of these verbs is with the object "life" itself:

Nehe' honoh'oe beeyoo yenii3e'eekuut,
This young man standing facing in that direction [eastward],

beebeet heetihnee'eenih'inee-**cebixoot**-o' hiine'etiit.
we ask simply that he be helped to walk firmly and steadily in his life.
                    (Cowell, C'Hair, and Moss 2014:"Name Changing Prayer")

Noh heetniineyeihP neyeih-**tei'koohuut**-owuno'.
And we will try to, we will try to run strong in relation to [our new life].
                    (Cowell and Moss 2006:"Splitting of the Tribes")

The use of these types of metaphorical extensions, especially in their more complex transitive forms, is a key element of eloquent expression in traditional Arapaho discourse. But especially in their intransitive forms, the words are pervasive parts of everyday Arapaho speech and can be considered cognitive metaphors in the sense proposed by Lakoff and Johnson: they are ways of understanding abstract phenomena in terms of concrete experiences of the human body in its environment. As we have already seen, one such metaphor is that the human collective or "society" can be understood as oriented around a central point, in a series of circles, much like a traditional Arapaho campsite. Another is that individual and collective life is a journey, and more specifically, it is the physical act of proceeding along a path. The extreme concreteness of this idea of path can be seen in the usage and metaphorical extensions of the verb final *-ooxeihi-* 'to leave tracks'. Examples of this verb include:

cow-ooxeihi-	to leave tracks along in a path
no'-ooxeihi-	to leave tracks up to a point or place
ce3-ooxeihi-	to leave tracks departing from a place

While not all verbs involving tracks commonly have metaphorical extensions, many do:

n-ooxeihi-	to leave or make tracks; to live; to start walking (away), as in avoiding a bad situation
nosoun-ooxeihi-	to still/continue make tracks; to survive a trial or test, to be still living
beet-ooxeihi-	tracks come to an end; to die

Indeed, even the verb *to live* can, and often does, take directional markers in Arapaho, giving it a literal sense of pathway:

Noh nuhu' **hee3e'ein**-iine'etiino', heetihbeexo'uu3eti', heetihtei'eekuu' hetiine'etiitoonin.
And this path our life is following (lit. 'this direction in which we are living'), let it be only good, let us endure firmly in our life.

(Cowell and Moss 2006:131–39)

Hei'inou'u **hee3e'ein**-iine'etiino'.
[The Sacred Ones] know where our life/culture is heading.

(ELAR 15sppt2)

This specific pattern of language usage corresponds with Arapaho design motifs that we will explore in chapter 3: images of tracks and paths will be a very common feature. More generally in that chapter, we will see how many Arapaho place names can also be understood from a utilitarian standpoint as guides and markers for travel. Most generally, we will see that the process of homelanding among nomadic peoples often revolves around pathways between specific locations rather than just a vague notion of "territoriality"; and that Arapaho design motifs, like place names on the landscape, are heavily oriented toward geographical representations of the landscape in terms of place features and pathways connecting them.

Much more could be said on this topic of travel. The importance of streams for travel, in both nomadic times and on the current Wind River Reservation, is one example, to be examined in more detail in chapter 3. Settlement patterns—and thus roadways—largely follow stream valleys on the relatively arid reservation. Interestingly, however, waterways as travel corridors, or images of "flowing," seem to be rarely if ever extended metaphorically in the way that land pathways are in order to talk about life processes through time, though water has powerful symbolic connotations in other contexts. One exception to this is the fact that Trickster stories in Arapaho traditionally start out with the line *Nih'oo3oo he'ih'oowuniihisee* . . . 'Trickster was walking downstream . . .' The Trickster is of course emblematic of wandering, nonstraight living. He lacks the discipline to "follow the straight and narrow," as we might say in English. Thus streams and their pathways in Arapaho traditional narratives are often emblematic of problematic or inadequate agency—the Trickster sometimes ends up floating downstream aimlessly, in fact. Conversely, straight paths across the land can be understood as images and enactment of strong agency for individuals or groups.

In summary, the general Arapaho pathway/journey metaphor is as follows:

Life is a journey, walked with others.
One follows some other people (including ancestors), and one leads those behind one.
The journey should be straight.
The journey should continue as long as possible.
Going astray means error and danger.
Walking in a straight line requires effort and embodies human agency.
Walking/living involves doing something to things, acting on things, transitively.
One's path can become broader or narrower or even tunnellike at different times.
One can be blocked or stuck in following one's path at times.
One should not block others' paths or interrupt their progress.
The path leads to and from a series of camps, with centers and peripheries.

It is important to note that the metaphors and vocabulary discussed above can be found in other Plains languages and cultures, and in fact they have been suggested as a fundamental semantic process in polysynthetic incorporating languages as well, where the cultural and cognitive components of metaphor merge virtually completely (Bonvillain 1989). For Plains languages, this metaphor is most easily seen in religious, ceremonial, and ethnographic discourse, as in Bruce Ingham's publication of *Five Lakota Oral Discourses* (2009). Although Lakota is unrelated to Arapaho linguistically, it too has a lexical item indicating the camp circle (the noun *hočoka*) and another indicating directionality away from the circle and human presence (the adverb *manil*), and this imagery is commonly used metaphorically or symbolically (Ingham 2009:54–55, 59, 77, 87, 98; Powers 1986:35). In Blackfoot, the term *aakokatssin* is a key lexical item that refers to the Sun Dance, as well as the camp circle, as well as the motion of "moving to the center" (Bastien 2004:114). And like in Arapaho, in Lakota the verb *to walk* (*máni*) and the idea of the road or path—especially a "straight" one (the adverb *owothaŋla*)—is used pervasively in the metaphorical sense of "to live" or "to move through life" (Ingham 2009:17, 38, 40, 49, 52–53, 56–57, 68, 97–98, 105, 107). Similarly, central to Blackfoot philosophy is the idea of *niitsipapi*, which Betty Bastien (2004:49) translates as "a state of being in connection with the purpose of life" or "journeying with the nature of life." Life is then thought of in terms of *niitsitapiipaitapiiyssinni*, a "spiritual journey—coming home to the heart of niitsipapi's knowing" (Bastien 2004:74). Images of stumbling or going astray are used as contrastive metaphors in Lakota (Ingham 2009:39n, 45–46). In this context, the idea of "turning around" takes on a moral aspect (Ingham 2009:53). Another pervasive Lakota metaporical usage—which we will see below in relation to Arapaho as well—is that of "standing" as a strong moral action or stance: living in a certain way, taking part in a certain activity or lifestyle, or upholding certain values (Ingham 2009:46, 48–49, 57, 59, 68, 94, 97–98, 107). At least in the Lakota discourses Ingham examines, one stands almost always with the positive values, not with negative ones. Instead one wanders astray toward the negative values.[7]

The widespread occurrence of these metaphors among at least Northern Plains languages and tribes makes them especially attractive to Pan-Indian COPs, as well as to Arapaho-specific COPs. There are a number of Lakota individuals at Wind River, and some have relatively prominent places in local life. I have often heard metaphors of the camp circle or the pathway invoked by both Arapaho and Lakota people, in English, during speeches, prayers, funeral orations, and on other occasions. People speaking Arapaho English often talk about "making tracks" when they see someone they do not want to meet, and the use of pathway metaphors in particular is pervasive in Arapaho English as well as on other reservations that I have visited multiple times (Northern Cheyenne, Fort Belknap). Use of such metaphors, at least in their more traditional forms—as opposed to the innovative extensions to be seen shortly in Arapaho-specific discourse—is virtually indexical of Native American identity on the Northern Plains.

EXTENDING CULTURAL METAPHORS: THE DISCOURSE OF LANGUAGE ENDANGERMENT

Returning to the Northern Arapaho, we find that as with the idea of center and periphery, the idea of the pathway has been extended to new uses in the contemporary language. The extension of metaphors, including cognitive metaphors, into new domains as part of the creation of neologisms or the adoption of entirely new technologies has been discussed for several languages (see Ahlers 1997 on Hupa; Basso 1990 on Western Apache). In this case, I would like to look at a very salient domain in relation to the topic of this book: Arapaho language descriptions of language endangerment and loss. Surprisingly little work has been done on the ways in which indigenous people talk about the issues of language loss, maintenance, and revival in their own languages. As we will see next, for Arapaho speakers, the idea of pathways is key for their metaphorical understandings and overt discussions of language endangerment.

STANDING THE LANGUAGE BACK UP

There is certainly more than one way to talk about this topic among Arapahos, but virtually all of them seem connected to pathways in some form. One metaphor—already partially familiar from the Lakota examples—is that the language has "fallen over" and that it needs to be "stood back up." The verb *3owoten-* can be used in this context. It means 'stand something upright' and is normally used for inanimate objects, such as a tipi or tent. More commonly however, the verb *koheisen-* is used. While this verb is also used with grammatically inanimate objects, it is derived from the verb *kohei'i-*, which is used for people who stand up from a sitting position. Especially in this second case, the overall image is of someone who has been resting or not moving, who is arising to go into action, such as moving forward again. In another case, an inanimate intransitive (II) verb (*koheinoo-*) is derived directly from the animate intransitive (AI) verb *kohei'i-*, with the meaning of 'it arises [to get going again]'. Thus Roy, a key Arapaho ceremonial leader, in a discussion with Richard, who is also an important ceremonial leader, said,

> Woow, woow noonoohootowoo:
> *Now, now I see it*:
> nuhu', wootii woow heetcesiskoheinoo' heteenetiitoon[in].
> *this, it looks like now our language will start standing [back] up.*
>
> (ELAR 20nc)

Note that *koheisen-* implicitly treats the language as an object of human action, while *koheinoo-* treats it as an independent actor.[8] This is an important distinction that reappears often in Arapaho endangered language metaphors: is the language acted on by people, or does it have some kind of independent existence and even ability to act?

THE LANGUAGE ON A JOURNEY

A second metaphor that captures the notion of pathway more clearly is the idea that the language is on a journey or is being carried along on a journey. One woman, talking about the value of the language, said, *niiwoo3iheenoo* 'I have been given [the language] to carry along with me'. Another said that the Arapaho *ceebixotii3i'* 'take/carry it along' the language. There are also other expressions that rely on the notion of the language as a reified object but that do not explicitly evoke the idea of a journey, although they could be part of such an understanding. These include the use of the verb *hiisiiten-* (lit. 'seize, grab' but metaphorically 'catch on to'). People "catch on to" the language; the same verb is used for someone who catches on to or learns a new song. The verb *nii-3inowoo-* 'to possess permanently' is also used in relation to the language. One can also "pass along" (*ceben-*) the language from one person to another, and one can "bring it back" to a place (*ce'no'uxotii-*). It can also "return to a place" on its own (*ce'no'useenoo-*).

Language shift then means either that the language has been left behind on the journey, and the Arapaho people need to "turn back around" (AI *ce'iineesee-*)—again we have already seen Lakota equivalents—and go get it again, or that the language itself has gone astray and/or is going backward and needs to "turn back around" (II *ce'iineeseenoo-*) to get back on the right path with the people, or be "turned back around" by the people (transitive [TI] *ce'iineex-*). Thus in a 2003 speech, the retired language teacher Bill said,

Hosei3iihi' heneinootee'.
[The language] is laying back there behind us/in the past.
Hiiwo' **ce'iineesee**'! wo'tenowu'! ce'tonounowu'!
Hey, turn back around! pick it up! use it again!
Niiyou nih'oo3ouyeitiit: hee3ebniito'e'inowu'.
Here's the English language: we learn it first now as we move into the future.
Hii3e' hosei3iihi' heneinootee' neteenetiitoonin.
Our own language is laying back there behind us/in the past.

(Cowell and Moss 2006:131–39)[9]

Another current language teacher, Dave, said during a conversation with his sister-in-law Sandra (who also has worked at immersion schools),

DAVE: Hoo3oo'o' hoowkohtowu3ecootowuu;
Other people didn't give [the language] a thought;
SANDRA: Uhm-hmm.
DAVE: Nihnootou'u.
They left it behind.
SANDRA: uhm-hmm.

(ELAR 25c)

Likewise the ceremonial leader Richard says in the same conversation with Roy cited previously,

Nenee' notiihi', toonheetniis**ce'iineeseenoo**' hinee heteenetiitoonin.
This is what is being sought, whatever way that our language can turn back around.

(ELAR 20n)

He also said to the student recording the conversation,

Howoo neneenin, hee3ei'neeniihi' neyeiP, bii'iihi' heetniis**ce'iineex**ow hinee heenetiit.
You too, try as much as you can, [so that] a way can be found for you to turn that language back around.

(ELAR 20n)

Note that except in the last example, the two ceremonial leaders use II verb forms *koheinoo-* and *ce'iineeseenoo-*, which imply that the language itself is doing the action, while the language teachers who use TI *koheisen-* (i.e., people are acting on the language) also use AI *ce'iineesee-* to address humans who are supposed to act on the language. They also use several other TI verbs indicating action on an object. Thus some speakers often give the language independent life and agency, while others—notably teachers—treat it more commonly as the object of human action.

THE END OF THE PATH

A third metaphor involving pathways suggests that the language is coming to the end of its path, finishing its journey. This is a very common image and uses the AI verb *beetisee-* 'finish walking' or more commonly the derived II verb *beetiseenoo-*. Joe, a leading language activist (but not a teacher), in a conversation with another native speaker who is not involved in the revitalization process, noted that,

> Niiyou nuhu' heeneecxooyeihino', tohbee3iine'etiino', nooxeihi' heetne'nii'3e**beetiseenoo**'.
> *The ones of our age, when we finish living, maybe that's when [the language] will come to the end of its path.*
>
> (ELAR 49a)

He goes on to note that some people will know about the language and be able to write it, but he says that they "will not be able to carry on their lives with it." He thus underlines their lack of agency with the language, which is in concord with the view of the language as an independent agent here.

In a conversation between two teachers at the Arapahoe Immersion School, one of them, Dave, reported that his grandfather had told him as far back as the 1940s or 1950s that the language would need saving. The grandfather was aware of Sequoyah's system for writing Cherokee:

> "Wohei toonhei'iihi' neneenin heetniiwo3onohow nuhu' heesP heeseenetino'," nih'ii3einoo.
> *"Well sometime you are going to write it, the way we speak/our language," he said to me.*
> "Heetwo3onoheihiinoo'."
> *"It will be written."*
> "Hiiwoonhehe' woow heetP, he'ne'cesisbee**beetiseenoo**'," nih'ii3einoo.
> *"Now today it will . . . then it's starting to come to the end of its path," he said to me.*
>
> (ELAR 22a)

The grandfather here uses the independent agent ideology for the language, although he grants his grandson future agency to write and thus preserve the language in that way.

In the same conversation cited above between Dave and his sister-in-law Sandra, we find the metaphor used again, with the language and culture treated as independent agents:

DAVE: Hinono'eitiit heenoo heetnosou**cebiseenoo**'.
Arapaho language just has to keep going.
SANDRA: Uhm!
DAVE: Tonoo**beetiseenoo**'.
It is almost coming to an end.

(ELAR 25a)

The use of the independent agent ideology here occurs right after the speakers have been talking about their grandchildren and where they go to school. The speaker then mentions that he is trying to teach Arapaho language and culture in the schools. The lines cited above occur, and then Dave begins a discussion of how many older knowledgeable individuals have passed away. The general lament about loss of elders—about which he is obviously powerless to do anything—perhaps helps explain the use of the independent agent ideology for the language in this example.

The converse of this metaphor is of course to keep walking. As Dave says in ELAR 25a, it "just has to keep going" (*cebiseenoo-*). The two ceremonial leaders already cited say,

ROY: Ceniini'oo' niihookohuusciiteinoo'.
Something bad always has to get into things [such as revitalization efforts].
Heenoo heetno'P. Heetbi'ceibenou'u.
Necessarily something [comes up]. [But the students] will just push that aside.
Beebeet heetne'P. . . .
Then they will just. . . .
RICHARD: Uhm!
ROY: Ceeneeyohwo'oono'.
We keep plugging along tenaciously.

(ELAR 20nc)

Here the negative obstacle on the path is the independent agent, while first the students about whom they have just been talking, then they themselves as well, become active agents in continuing to pursue the path (note the *-o'oo-* general motion verb final in the last line). Interestingly, throughout their conversation, the two brothers grant the students and teachers greater agency in relation to the language, while portraying it much more often as an independent agent in relation to themselves:

ROY: Heetneyei3ei'i3i', neeneti3i'.
Where they are going to school, they are speaking it.

RICHARD: Uhm!

ROY: Nooxeihi' niiniini'itoot [personal name in English, teacher].
Maybe [p.n.] is doing good [at the school].

RICHARD: Hee.
Yes.

ROY: Yeah, hii3eti'.
Yeah, it's good.

(ELAR 20nc)

In summary, when the language is being taught or learned or transmitted, then agency is often expressed for those involved. For fluent speakers, however, the language is often presented as having independent agency.[10] In some cases, such as for ceremonial leaders, this is because they see the language as a truly powerful agent in ceremonies, with which they interact. In other cases, especially for native-speaking teachers, this same ideology is invoked more out of a sense of frustration about their own lack of agency in being able to successfully transmit the language to students as well as they would like, and the more general loss of the language.

LANGUAGE IS WHAT WE TRAVEL BY

A fourth metaphor is a variant of the second one, but with the language as an agentive helper on the journey.[11] In this case, it is not just carried along on the journey but is the means by which one accomplishes that journey. In some cases, the comitative prefix *nohk-* 'with, in conjunction with' is used to express this idea. Bill said of the Arapaho language and culture that *Cih-nokh-uusiii'oonoo* 'I grew up in conjunction with it'. This is a very common expression. In other cases, the more "powerful" instrumental prefix *hi-* 'with, by means of' is used, as in this statement from a ceremonial leader, Richard:

Noosouniini, noosouniini hitowoo'ootiininoo wo'ei3 howoo hiteenetiitooninoo, noosouniini **hi'**-eeneine'etii3i'.

Still, still, their ceremonies and also their language, [the Arapahos] are still living with the aid of that.

(ELAR 20n)

This particular version of the metaphor is very similar to that used for other actual sacred possessions of the tribe, such as the Sacred Flat Pipe and Sacred Wheel. These are talked about as going along on a journey with the Arapaho through time and place, literally as accompanying them as animate agents:

Ci'nihnii3neniibeino' nuhu' cesisiihi' no'uuhu' hiiwoonhehe'.
[The Sacred Pipe] has been with us since the beginning right up to the present.
Nono'o3oo' nihceneisee'; niitowo'o boo3etiitooni'.
It was very hard for us to make it to this point; at first we had to go to war [to preserve our life].
Hiit nenee', heeneesnosounii3neniibeit, noosouneeteniiheino'.
Here it is, [the Sacred Pipe] is still with us through all this, it is still caring for us.

(ELAR 15sppt2)

Bill explicitly combines these two ideas:

Heihii, howoo woow hooyei heeyeineenoniseenoo' nuhu' nono'eitiit.
Soon, and now too most of the Arapaho language has almost gone to oblivion.
Nih'oo3ou'u nih'neeyii3ni'iihino,' nihoo3ouyeitiit, noh hookoh nee'eesoo'.
Whites, we are really pulled toward that way of life, English, and because that's how it is [today] [i.e., that's what we have to use now].
[but the old men said:] "Nei'iitiibi' niiyou henii3iyoonin!
"Hold on tight to our possessions!
N-**i'**-iihoonowoo'oono' yii3e'einiihi' hinee beeheeteihit.
We pray to that Creator by means of [our language].
Nenii3inowuno'; howoo hinee beh'eihehi'; heniicooniit;
It's ours; and also that Old Man [i.e., Sacred Pipe]; he is the pipe;
hinee hotii, nii'eihii, hoonoo3oo'o', neniinii3inowuno'.
that [Sacred] Wheel, the eagle, other things, they are all ours.
Nei'iitiibi'! tonounowu'!
Hold on tight to it! use it!
Heetneh-**i'**-iine'etiinee."
You will live from this time forth by means of it."

He'ne'nih'iisinihii3i'.
That's what they said.

(Cowell and Moss 2006:131–39)

We have very little access to Arapaho conceptualizations of the Arapaho language prior to the period of endangerment. While the language must certainly have had symbolic importance in relation to Arapaho identity, it seems unlikely that it was conceptualized as a reified sacred object in the same way as the Pipe, the Wheel, or other objects such as medicine bundles. Certainly nothing in the linguistic or ethnographic record from prior to World War II suggests that such a reified view existed. In discussing the extension of the center-periphery metaphor, we noted how it is used in part to elevate and render more salient the idea of the Arapaho people as being sacred—a key corollary to the idea of the sacredness of the language. In the case of extensions of the pathway and journey metaphor, we find the Arapaho language reified in a way similar to the "nominalization" processes associated with naming that are another central theme of this book: the language becomes akin to the Sacred Flat Pipe. Thus native speakers can be seen extending the meanings of traditional Arapaho metaphors, within Arapaho-specific language discourse, in ways that further enhance the concept of both the people and the language as sacred, and the concept of the language as a series of names and words linked to the MTH power that—like ceremonial objects—sustains Arapaho society in their eyes.

STUDENT DISCOURSE ON THE ARAPAHO LANGUAGE

Now that we have looked at how first-language speakers of Arapaho talk about language shift and loss, within the domain of AC specifically, we need to look at how younger learners and students conceptualize the issue—again specifically within the domain of AC, since few other affiliates of the other COPs are interested in the language. I want to look in particular at responses provided by Arapaho students at Wind River Tribal College to the prompt "Why I want to learn Arapaho." These responses were done for a class and then included in a reader to be used by later students. The responses obviously are public discourse, so there is a bias toward saying what the students think they *should* say about the language, as opposed to what they might say in a completely private setting among only close friends, but they still offer interesting perspectives.

The responses are also elder mediated to an extent: the students composed their answers to the prompt largely in English, and then elders helped them shape their ideas into grammatical Arapaho. This process of translation no doubt introduced a degree of elder perspective, as opposed to reproducing exactly what the students might have said if they were fluent speakers themselves. For this very reason, however, the process is a perfect example of how elder mediation of the language and its practices and ideologies actually works today at Wind River, within AC. Rather than just mediating knowledge and power, elders mediate the language itself, in a reciprocal relationship with students.

I will begin by citing one response in its entirely. I have corrected spelling to match the community standard. I give both the English translation offered by the student and a more literal translation in brackets where needed, which more closely reflects the Arapaho language provided or shaped by the elder with whom the student worked.

> Neneeninoo hinono'ei.
> *I am Arapaho.*
> Nuhu' hinono'eitiit beeteenoo'.
> *Our language is sacred. [The Arapaho language is sacred]*
> Nuhu' nenee' hetiine'etiitoonin.
> *It is the Arapaho way of life. [This language is our life]*
> Noosoutonounowuno' nuhu' hinono'eitiit.
> *We need the language for our ceremonies. [We still use the Arapaho language]*
> Tei'yoonoh'o', heetih'ee3oobei'inou'u nuhu' hinono'eitiit.
> *Our children and grandchildren need to learn to speak our language. [I ask that the children truly know the Arapaho language]*
> Noosoucebeneihiinoo' nuhu' hinono'eitiit, toh'e'inowuno' nuhu' hinono'eitiit, tohce'eenetini'.
> *Our language has been passed on from generation to generation and we need to continue the process. [The Arapaho language is still being passed on because we know the Arapaho language, because we are speaking it again.]*

Note here that the student does not use the metaphor of a path or journey, or of an object carried on the journey. The language is treated as a reified object, but rather than being carried, it is passed along (*ceben-* 'pass along', *cebeneihiinoo-* 'passed along') in the way that an item at the table would be during dinner (*cih-ceben-oo niisiscoo'* 'pass the sugar to me'). This conception is reinforced by the reference to the language being sacred. Note that the student grants high agency to the Arapaho people, based on the English original, while the elder translator/helper has made this idea even stronger: the Arapahos "use" the language, "know" it, "pass it on" and "speak it."

In general, this passage as understood so far seems much closer to a Euro-American conception of language than the ones we examined from native Arapaho speakers—a language is an object one acquires, uses, and conveys to others via teaching. There is enough difference from the earlier passages to convince me that the elder translator has not simply imposed an Arapaho discourse onto the student but has largely respected his or her original conception. However, the student does indirectly evoke the idea of the language as "the thing we travel by" in saying that the language is equivalent to the Arapaho way of life and is crucially instrumental in ceremonies. In addition, the last two lines evoke the idea of social reproduction and suggest that the language is crucial to this process. The language is thus at minimum an instrumental coagent in Arapaho life, and perhaps a truly independent agent that empowers social reproduction. This view of the power of the language is fairly close to that seen from the native speakers, and the frequent use of "we" rather than "I" reinforces the idea of a community (of practice) engaged in a mutual endeavor.

In summary, the language ideologies of the elders are generally reinforced in this passage, but without the use of the cultural metaphor of the journey. A second example shows largely the same features:

Nuhu' neteenetiit henee3eeneetowoo, [toh]'unono'eininoo.
My Arapaho language is important to me. [I consider my language very important, because I am Arapaho]
Hinee neheiho' noh nesiho', niicihwoteesee3i'.
It brings my family together. [My aunts and my uncles, they come into the circle (with us)]
Niibeetnosounee'inowoo nuhu' neeneistootiini' nuhu' hinono'einiihi', neeneisbetee3i', neenei3owoo'oo3i'.
I want to carry on our culture, language, and traditions to my children. [I want to continue to know how things are done in the Arapaho way, how they have holy power, how they pray/conduct ceremonies]
Nuhu' toh'unono'eitino', nenee' nuhu' heteenetiitoonin, ne'niisei'inou'u.
The Arapaho Language is our Arapaho people's identity, that's the way they will know this identity. [Because we speak Arapaho, this is our language, that is how they know (their identity)]

Heetnosounii3inowuno'.
We are to keep it. [We will continue to possess it]
Heetnosoutonounowuno', toh'ee3neebeteenoo'.
We are to use it because it is very sacred. [We will continue to use it because it is very sacred]
Hiinono'eininoo.
I am Arapaho.

This example is more explicit about the idea of power in the language. It also evokes the idea of the camp circle (*woteesee-*), thus drawing on a cultural metaphor, though this seems to have been supplied by the elder, rather than directly conceived of by the student. Unlike the first one, it mentions the idea of identity, which I would argue is a horizontal or lateral positioning in relation to Pan-Indian and Euro-American COPs, rather than an AC-centric perspective.

There are five more responses in the collection, which I will not present in detail. They largely continue the same patterns. The third one invokes pride in one's heritage (another lateral positioning), the sacredness of the language (a modern AC ideology), and connections to ancestors (a more traditionalist focus on vertical power relations and transfers). The fourth one focuses on vertical relationships, the sacredness of the language, and the power of the language in ceremonies, but also on identity. The fifth one focuses on communication with relatives. The sixth one focuses on sacredness, vertical relations to the Creator, and the power of prayer. The seventh one focuses on identity but also on social reproduction and the power of the language as a tool to live by. None of the others, however, make use of a cultural metaphor of either center/periphery or path/journey.

I have often heard younger Arapaho individuals use the journey metaphor in various forms, in Arapaho English. This cultural metaphor has not been lost from AC, although the statements here certainly do not apply the metaphor to language loss and revitalization. The students' discourse about the language, from a strictly rhetorical perspective, is largely discontinuous from that of the elders, and the elder translators/mediators have clearly not attempted to impose their discourse on the students' conceptions via their own translations. This reflects a broader finding of this chapter: the more "traditional" uses of cultural metaphors, such as the center-periphery and pathway metaphor, have been widely passed on to younger people, in English, at Wind River and elsewhere on the Northern Plains, both within AC and among other COPs. However, the more recent, innovative uses of these metaphors—to talk about towns, Whites, and technology, or about language loss and revitalization—do not seem to have made it from the Arapaho speakers to the English-speaking members of AC. This seems like a great loss to the younger people, as they have missed the opportunity to see the language problems in a locally specific way deeply embedded in older Northern Arapaho cultural practices and resources. If, as Sekaquaptewa and Washburn (2004:366) suggest for Hopi, these types of metaphors are central to the maintenance of reciprocal relationships, then the relationships themselves seem at risk in this case—not surprisingly, since the failure of language transmission necessarily bespeaks a shift in the nature of those relationships. Instead, my general observation and experience is that the vocabulary of language endangerment, maintenance, and revitalization in Arapaho English often reflects the technocratic vocabulary of academic linguistics and governmental bureaucracy, for both older and younger individuals.

From a conceptual perspective, however, things are more complex. Several of the statements evoke the idea of identity—and the language as iconic of Arapaho identity—in a way that rarely appears in statements from AC elders when they are speaking about Arapaho in Arapaho. On the other hand, the students' statements all grant high agency to human actors in relation to the language: this fits with the tendencies of fluent teachers, if not with ceremonial leaders, and fits their role as students. Finally, almost all the statements focus on the ideas of MTH power and the social relations that manage that power, which seems very close to elder views within AC. The language is understood as crucial to proper social relations and as containing or transferring MTH power through vertical relations with the sacred. In summary, the students' rhetoric and metaphors, and their conception of language generally as an object obtained, possessed, and passed around among stationary actors, looks fairly Euro-American. But their conception of the Arapaho language specifically as having—or making possible one's access to—power, which they imply is not present in English, looks more AC in nature, as does their sense that this power can be transferred between generations or from ancestors. In other words, though the students do not use traditional metaphors, they express the gist of the ideas contained in those metaphors.

The question I am often led to reflect on, however, is whether the students truly *understand* (or believe) what they are saying about the language. I know from my own experience that it has taken me many years to understand the real implications of statements about the power and sacredness of the language—implications that will be developed in their fullest richness in the following chapters. The same can be said about the idea of "respect" for elders. In fact, this understanding comes largely from the *operational usage* of personal names, place names, folk etymologies, metaphors, and neologisms in the context of relationships, I would say, and this is something the students have largely not had the opportunity to experience. The students of course have a huge advantage over me, in that they have grown up as part of AC, even if they are not fully competent users of the language. On the other hand, they do not seem to have managed to carry on actual relationships with AC elders, in either Arapaho or Arapaho English, which would give them access to those elders' actual discursive framing of the questions of language loss, maintenance, and revitalization. Thus the claims about the role of the Arapaho language in mediating interpersonal relationships and power transfers may in many cases be based not on personal knowledge and experience but rather on repeating fragments of discourse from elders in the same way that graduate students in academia enunciate theoretical claims without really understanding what those claims mean and how they can be applied to specific situations. Sometimes those academic students may just be saying what professors want to hear. Others may be grasping more seriously toward the truth of the rhetoric they employ. For the best of the students, the mere claim is finally filled one day with true understanding. The role of teachers is in part to provide the students with the theoretical vessel (or rhetoric, or metaphor) into which understanding can eventually flow. The Arapaho students, in their statements, are perhaps in a similar position to students everywhere. Fortunately they have the benefit of elder mediators who can provide access to at least the broader ideologies of AC language and society and who are also helping them grasp toward a more fulfilling understanding of the words they speak, even as the students also explore new ideological positions. In summary, the daily process of interacting with elders in order to *produce* statements such as those above is likely much more important than the statements themselves, as it offers the opportunity to engage in language practice on a more mundane level and to achieve the relationships that will allow the students to "live their way into" the reality of the ideologies they express, and even eventually to access the cultural metaphors of the fluent speakers.

Returning to the lessons of the introduction about continuities and discontinuities, we could note that discontinuities seem to be everywhere in the preceding discussion: between the practice and the ideology of the students; between the practice of the students and that of the elders; and between some of the concepts and ideologies of the students and elders. There seems to be some continuity in some of the ideologies expressed by the students and those seen previously among the elders (i.e., "the language is sacred and holds power"), yet even here the implications of this ideology are perhaps different for the two groups. Despite this, the symbolic value of the concept of MTH power and the interpersonal relationships that mediate it serve as a ground on which young and old can come together, in an attempt to maintain the continuity of the AC COP. Most literally, they engage in Arapaho language work with each other. In doing so, they also work to arrive at new and emergent meanings for the ideology that they share in name, if not necessarily yet in practice, and thus seek to overcome discontinuities and forge a new understanding of AC. These collaboratively created statements have much to say indirectly about social relations in AC. They reveal continued elder commitment but an avoidance of elder dictation; and they show significant agency on the part of the students, or at least a meta-agentive discourse that projects a strong sense of agency. The relationship between student and elder is perhaps less asymmetrical than some elders have been used to in the past, or would prefer, but this is likely the type of relationship that has the best chance of future success at Wind River.

CONCLUSION

Returning for a moment to the discourse of the native speakers, we also see an interesting mix of continuity and discontinuity. In terms of conceptualization and vocabulary, Arapaho speakers have largely transferred some of their key traditional metaphors of moral discourse to this new situation of language endangerment. In so doing, they have also framed the issue of language survival as a moral issue, but more specifically as a human survival issue—in the form of a straight walk on a path. In this chapter, one can see the richness and diversity of the development of that metaphor, however, into four (and almost certainly more) varieties, each of which then contains additional nuanced reflection on the relative agency of human actors and the Arapaho language itself. Like the English-language anger metaphor described by Lakoff and Johnson, the various components of the path/journey metaphor for language can be used strategically and innovatively by speakers in different contexts to accomplish different social goals; just in the examples above, we have seen individual speakers use multiple variants of the metaphor, as well as multiple approaches to the agency question, in differing contexts, much as we will see with folk etymologies in chapter 5, for example.

Despite the continuity of metaphorical usage, the actual object to which the metaphor complex is being applied—the language—is seen in ways clearly discontinuous from the past. The Arapaho language is now often treated as something similar to the Sacred Pipe or some other ceremonial item. It is reified in a way that it most certainly was not in the past. The analogy to the Sacred Pipe also perhaps helps explain the vacillation between treating the language as an object and treating it as an independent entity. The Sacred Pipe, while clearly an object that must be carried by its keeper, is treated grammatically as animate in Arapaho and is considered to have the ability to act independently. It is prayed to in ceremonies, and it can respond to the prayers. While the Arapaho language is treated grammatically as inanimate by all speakers, we have seen it presented as "arising (again)" on its own or "turning back around" on its own by some, even as others talk about "picking it up" or "leaving it behind." The fact that it is now often called *beeteenoo'* 'sacred' further reinforces the connection to ceremonial items. Thus the extensions of the path metaphor—particularly in relation to the conceptual model of the Sacred Pipe—to the language are central to its enhanced sacredness within the current ideologies of AC. It is worth pointing out as well that the three language ideologies discussed here—reification, sacralization, and restricted guardianship—are very common in the Great Plains region of Native America generally, and also in the Southwest (i.e., in areas where traditional religions maintain a strong influence). Note that these ideas could be restated as objectification and hyperbolic valuation (see J. Hill 2002), and in such terms, they are often argued to be language ideologies imported from the outside, particularly from academia. Yet here we can clearly see the indigenous bases for such ideologies, via an extension of the Sacred Pipe concept.

This shift in the view of the language is somewhat similar to what Barbra Meek (201) describes for Kaska: as this Athabaskan language has become endangered, it too has become increasingly reified. Moreover, through its increasing association with elderhood, it has come to be seen as a special form of knowledge and power, much like ceremonial or medicinal knowledge or traditional narratives. Thus the language as a whole is increasingly labeled as "sacred," as opposed to just certain language practices being labeled as such. All of this is closely linked to the language's increasing saliency as an identity marker in a multilingual, language-endangerment context, and to its reification (Meek

2007, 2010). In the Kaska case, like the Arapaho one, there is cultural continuity in terms of metaphorical expression, elder respect, ceremonial practice and attitudes, and other features. But the view of the language itself is definitely discontinuous with past views, as it was not formally included qua language in the realm of special knowledge. This new inclusion has resulted in a situation where, due to the "sacredness" and "elderness" of the Kaska language, younger people are increasingly reluctant to use it. The highly counterintuitive result is that the "sacred" language is being lost due to language shift, and the ideology of sacredness is actually reinforcing this shift and loss in the everyday world.

The finding about Kaska is somewhat similar to what we will see for Arapaho in relation to folk etymology (chapter 5) and neologism practices (chapter 6). Certainly in the AC case, the same discontinuity in the view of the language now occurs, with the language often elevated to sacred status. The strict association of the language with elders, and consequent avoidance of usage for this reason, does not seem to have occurred, however, at least to the degree that Meek describes for Kaska. As noted in chapter 1, there are cases where elders feel that the language should not be used by students and learners unless they can use it well. However, this does not seem to impact behavior in informal settings, and even in the formal ones, students are willing to resist this pressure in most cases. Certainly when fluent elders are present, AC students do not attempt to speak in place of the elders, and they show respect for the elders' language abilities. However, they do not seem to self-limit their use of the language out of elder respect. Indeed, the complaint at Wind River is often the opposite of the Kaska one—the elders often complain that the students do not respect the elders *enough* or self-limit their language usage *enough*. Some younger people clearly see that knowledge of Arapaho itself is in fact *not* the same thing as ceremonial knowledge automatically worthy of respect: in June 2000, for example, one younger woman told me that she resents elders who use the language as a tool for forcing respect, for appearing wise and having authority based only on this, without really having deeper sources of authority.

Among more traditionalist master-apprentice pairings, there is in fact an active limiting of the use of Arapaho—but it comes from elders, not younger learners. At one of the immersion schools, an apprentice student is working with two older women who are native speakers. In helping out the older women with the children, she is also learning the language. The teachers work regularly with her and strongly encourage her interest in Arapaho. However, they have refused to let her speak in Arapaho "in public"—that is, in a formal setting—until her pronunciation and overall language skills improve, as they feel that her mistakes would reflect badly on them. This is a common situation where ceremonial, musical, medicinal, or other special knowledge is involved, and it thus makes perfect sense from an AC perspective, though it is certainly a new ideology in relation to language acquisition and clearly a product of language endangerment.[12] This is, by the way, the same school where teachers have been resistant to using provisional Arapaho names with students who lack an actual Arapaho name, so a consistent pattern of conservatism can be seen—expressed in a tendency to *not* use or allow the speaking of Arapaho in certain domains. This is a situation that looks like the Kaska situation that Meek describes in terms of traditionalism, respect, and the sacredness of the language, except that the restrictions come from above rather than below.

In fact, however, the most striking discontinuity in general Arapaho society is between the ideology that the language is sacred and the actual social relations with the elders that would mediate that sacredness. While many people in many different COPs invoke the notion of the sacredness of the language, many of those in the non-AC COPs strongly contest or even refuse the notion of elder mediation of language practices and flows of power—most particularly in the area of personal names, but also in the area of place names, and in many other nonlinguistic areas as well, including the conduct of ceremonies. For most people in non-AC COPs, the ideology that the Arapaho language is sacred seems to be primarily a symbolic statement that does indexical work, as a signpost for identity claims. There is often very little in their language practices or linguistic relationships that suggests that the ideology influences those practices—unlike the Kaska case. Rather, the ideology—or the statement of the ideology—indexes more general affiliation with Pan-Indian or Politico-Tribal COPs and can also be part of a general effort at maintaining social reproduction and coherence via invocation of this highly symbolic ideology. In this case, the literal content of the statement has little relevance to language practice, but as with all indexical forms, the social work done in making the statement is significant. The statement per se does not necessarily index affiliation with the AC COP, however—only with Arapaho identity generally. Of course, in AC context, and combined with various AC language practices and modes of relationship, the ideology can be an important feature of AC identity specifically. The key is to understand from the broader context the intended indexee(s) and, more generally, to appreciate that these can be multiple and emergent. Although this seems obvious now, I must admit that for quite a while I thought that this statement "meant" roughly the same thing for each person from whom I heard it at Wind River, when in fact it does not "mean" anything at all in the literal sense in some cases.

Within AC more specifically, many younger affiliates of this COP are in fact quite willing, broadly speaking, to accept elder mediation of power and practice in the areas we will be examining in this book. When it comes to the details of the practices, however, even they show a marked tendency to innovate or reorient specific language behaviors and ideologies—often using Arapaho English. These changes look and seem unfamiliar and uncomfortable to elders, even though they often help maintain more traditional practices in at least modified form. The innovators often desire to maintain certain traditional language ideologies as well—though not necessarily the ones that involve heavy elder mediation of the language and of the social and MTH power associated with it.

Thus to a certain degree the more purist AC elders are right in their complaints about lack of respect from younger people. But to some extent they fall victim to the same errors that linguists (myself included) often make when looking at situations of language shift: the most obvious thing one sees is the shift and associated discontinuities in practice in relation to the language code used. It is often much harder to immediately see the at least partial continuities in language ideology and the ways in which "new" practices have arisen out of older cultural resources, in modified form, to fulfill needs and functions often similar to the older practices. The fact that many linguists work primarily with older speakers in endangered language contexts tends to exacerbate the tendency to see things like many of the elders do, in terms of radical discontinuity, and the fact that linguists tend to focus especially on language (at the expense of other social processes) also tends to bias them toward seeing discontinuities, as noted in the introduction.

The AC elders who collaborate closely with students at Wind River Tribal College, such as in the responses to "Why I want to learn Arapaho," seem to be important exceptions to this tendency, as are some elders in immersion preschools. The tribal college, which has a heavy AC focus, is the site of some of the most productive elder/youth social relationships on the reservation outside family settings, for at least a limited number of students and elders. Indeed, it is so heavily AC-oriented that it faces criticism for not meeting the more "mainstream" educational needs of students looking for Euro-American-style education, and as a result it faces major enrollment pressures and concerns. The college is also the place where younger people seem to have the most freedom to use the Arapaho language. Notably, all the advanced students there have composed "introductions" in Arapaho about themselves. These introductions seem modeled on Navajo practice in terms of giving one's Indian name, and often one's relatives and clans, and so forth: they are widely seen among AC tribal college students, who have had extensive exposure to Navajo and other Native American students, but I have never seen them among older Arapaho speakers, and the students themselves note that they are modeled on introductions done by other tribes at tribal college conventions.[13] The introductions are worked out in collaboration with native speakers and then memorized, though some more advanced students can vary the presentation according to the audience. Most notably, they are often given in highly formal settings, including in front of native speakers. The presentations often contain small—and sometimes large—errors in pronunciation, grammar, or vocabulary. Some native speakers are highly critical of these introductions, both in the details of the errors and in the general idea of the practice, similar to the criticisms discussed in chapter 1 of the "Northern Arapaho Experience." The practice clearly violates an older norm wherein only the best speakers would speak in public in formal settings—typically meaning the oldest individuals.

The willingness and even insistence of some Arapaho students to stand up in formal public situations and make mistakes in Arapaho—and the willingness of some elders to help them do so, and to applaud their efforts—is thus highly significant.[14] It is of course highly complex, since such behavior can index AC affiliation but also tribal-college-oriented Pan-Indian affiliation, as well as Arapaho Politico-Tribal affiliation. In the latter cases, the use of the introductions may be largely symbolic, as few or no listeners understand them (cf. Debenport 2015:42 for similar practices in New Mexico). The introductions and the elders' support of them underline the great differences that exist even within the AC COP, much less among differing COPs at Wind River, even as the practice also serves as a symbolic resource that can work across COPs to create greater degrees of coherence and build coalitions. It also shows the degree to which some Arapaho-speaking elders are willing to rethink both ideology and practice in order to attempt to maintain continuity of language, in the face of daunting odds.

3

ETHNOGEOGRAPHY THROUGH TIME

Names and Power in the Landscape

INTRODUCTION: HOMELANDING

AMONG THE MANY STORIES TOLD BY Northern Arapaho storyteller Paul Moss is one about an attack by a band of Utes on some Arapaho scouts (Cowell and Moss 2005a:101–35). In the story, the scouts are conducting a sweat lodge ceremony. A lookout lets them know that the Utes have appeared and are about to attack. Despite this, the Arapahos make sure to finish the ceremony, with four rounds of singing. They get done just in time to race to the cover of a depression in a stream. From there, one brave scout runs out and attacks the Utes three times on his own. Then he is joined by his comrades for a fourth and final attack, which drives off the Utes and brings Arapaho victory.

There is clearly a moral lesson in the story about the need for proper ceremonial procedure, including the idea that following this procedure will bring rewards—power—that may literally save lives. The parallel between the four rounds of singing and the four rounds of battle, both leading to successful conclusions, underlines this moral lesson. But if we look at the details of the Arapaho-language description, we find that just as the Arapaho "pour" (*hiitookuutii-*) water onto hot rocks during a sweat lodge ceremony from a bucket, the Utes are described as "pouring" (*hiitoo'oo-*) over the ridge as they swarm down to attack in great numbers. And just as the water then becomes steam that infuses the entire space of the circular sweat lodge, bringing power and healing to those inside, the refuge spot in the river bed as Moss describes it is a "circular depression" (*ko'eitonoti-*), "dug out by water" (*nooxookoonee-*). In other words, the place of refuge in the riverbed is an inverse sweat lodge in shape, and the power of water has infused this location with protection just as it does inside the sweat lodge. The entire battle is described as a kind of inverse sweat lodge ceremony, with its four rounds. In the conclusion of the story, Moss uses *betee-* 'holy' and *no'oteihi-* 'powerful' in his summary (Cowell and Moss 2005a:128–29): *Wohei nenee', nehe'nih'ii3ei'neeno'otehehkoni', tihbeteehekoni'* 'Well that was how tough [powerful] they were, back when they had sacred power'.

This story is a masterpiece of reading events on the landscape in an analogical fashion as they unfold through time. The events are read in analogy to a key component of Arapaho ceremonial culture, which provides access to MTH power. It is also a wonderful example of the way the landscape itself can be read through the lens of analogy by a skilled Arapaho narrator. Most importantly, the "reading," narrating, and discovery of points of analogy between the riverbed and the sweat lodge are oriented toward locating power in the landscape. Analogies point to and locate this power. Of course, that power has been embedded in the landscape, the narrator suggests, by proper Arapaho ceremonial practice, of which the sweat lodge ceremony that occupies the entire first half of this story is just one example—had the ceremony not been done, the landscape would not have offered its power to the Arapahos, even if there still was a gouged-out area in the riverbed. The story offers us an understanding of power in the landscape as the result of reciprocal relationships between the land itself and its Arapaho occupants, each of which empowers the other, provided that reciprocity is respected. This story offers us in effect a theoretical description of traditional Arapaho ethnogeographic perspectives: the ways they see and describe the landscape, interact with it, and make it "home."

Ethnogeography is the attempt to understand the relationship between a community and the landscape it occupies. One key part of this project is the understanding of places and their names. Although the Arapaho story just described does not give place names, many Arapaho stories do, and the story offers a good example of the ideology that guides not just the viewing but also the naming of the landscape. It is well known that patterns of place naming in Native America are closely linked to the languages and cultures of the people who currently occupy or formerly occupied the landscapes (Hickerson 1978; Basso 1990; Afable and Beeler 1996; Collins 1998b; Schreyer 2006; M. Nevins 2008; Meadows 2008). Names reflect, reinforce, and help construct attitudes toward the landscape, and they actively form that landscape into a unique culturescape with meaning for the specific occupants. There are certain types of place names that are or are not used by some groups (Afable and Beeler 1996; Smith 1996), as well as different types of places that are characteristically named or not named (Guilliford 2000), so the practice reflects group specificities, and place naming has its own language ideologies associated with it. The ways in which place names are used in discourse are also group specific, though there is general recognition that places in the landscape, through the accretions of legend, history, and narrative that attach to their names, often acquire important moral significance (Hickerson 1978; Basso 1996; Collins 1998b; Schreyer 2006). Indeed, certain places are imbued with great power and become seen as "(geo)sacred sites" (Guilliford 2000). The different sites typically cannot be understood, however, as single, piecemeal locations: they are part of broader interrelationships among multiple sites, and they draw their meaning from their place in a larger landscape. Keith Basso's (1996) work with the Western Apache is a classic study of the way in which Apache language, culture, and landscape meld together into a cultural and discursive whole, imbued with great moral and spiritual significance.

As the study of ethnogeography has advanced, there has been increasing recognition of the dynamic nature of the relationship between people and places (J. Weiner 1991; Kelley and Francis 1994; Collins 1998b; Meadows 2008): there is no single cultural landscape shared by everyone in a group, and the relationships can change rapidly over time as well. The process that I will call *homelanding* can be understood as the effort by social groups to lay claim to "tenure" (Ingold 1987) over certain components of a landscape, and more broadly over certain territories, by imagining and mapping that landscape in terms of cultural patterns of belief and behavior unique to the group. Place names in the language of the group, motivated by the place-naming ideologies of that group, are a crucial part of this mapping process that leads to homelanding.

While the dynamics of language shift are well understood in linguistics and anthropology, the dynamics of cultural landscape shift in the same context have received less attention. Certainly it is clear that economic development and other landscape changes have major effects on local indigenous cultures (Kelley and Francis 1994; Collins 1998b; Meadows 2008), but what are the linguistic effects of such changes, in relation to individual place names, the larger naming system, the relationship of names to COPs, and the use of the names in discourse? Conversely, how do changing linguistic practices of assigning and using place names construct alternative cultural landscapes, even in the absence of intrusive disruptions on the land itself? The focus of this chapter will be on understanding how the process of homelanding can be understood as having a crucial linguistic component, down to the finest detail of the structure and content of individual place names, on how the process itself has changed over time in Arapaho society, and on how competing Arapaho COPs engage in alternative homelanding practices.

THE LINGUISTIC EXPRESSION OF "HOMELAND" FOR THE NINETEENTH-CENTURY ARAPAHO

In the homeland of the Northern Arapaho, ethnogeography was especially complex due to nomadism. Tribal groups came to know vast areas of the landscape, many parts of which were known (and named) by neighboring tribes. Studies in Native American ethnogeography for this area (see esp. Meadows 2008) show that at a minimum, one can recognize three different modes of relationship to the land, visible in three layers of place names: a supratribal, regional one; a tribal one; and a reservation-era, hybrid one, which incorporates features of Euro-American systems (which I save for the end of this chapter).

The first layer, particularly on the Great Plains and in the Rocky Mountains, involves joint use and occupancy of land, or at the least, joint familiarity with landscapes. As much as any one tribe might consider an area a "homeland" (Meadows 2008), allies would make common use of an area, enemies would intrude on raids, and some other tribe might have considered the area their homeland in the recent past (Meadows 2008; Albers and Kay 1987:72). This complex interweaving of relationships to the land among multiple tribes led to a broad sharing of place names (see Afable and Beeler 1996:190 for comparable situations). The Arapaho used the same name ("shell river") for the North Platte as the Cheyenne, the Gros Ventre, and the Kiowa, among others, and their name for the South Platte ("fat/tallow river") was shared with the Cheyenne and the Kiowa, though not the more distant Gros Ventre. In fact, a study of the Gros Ventre core area as it existed in the later nineteenth and twentieth centuries (Cowell, Taylor, and Brockie 2016) suggests that the immediately neighboring tribe (the Blackfoot) had names for many of the exact same geographical features as the Gros Ventre, and moreover, that the content of the names themselves overlapped to quite an extent. As one moves progressively further away from that core area (first to the Northern Cheyenne, then the Northern Arapaho, then finally the Kiowa), the number of features that have names in both Gros Ventre and another language declines regularly, as does the number of actual shared names. For the Gros Ventre themselves, conversely, the farther one moves from the center of the homeland, the lesser the density of places and features with Gros Ventre names—as is the trend for nomadic groups (Hanks and Winter 1986:273; Kelley and Francis 1994:81–90; Schreyer 2006; Meadows 2008:253). Thus one could say that the Gros Ventre were the primary occupants of their "homeland" in north-central Montana, but the homeland must be understood as nested within an overlapping set of circles of occupation, each radiating out from some more-core homeland of another tribe or subgroup. Not only did circles overlap, but the "weight" or "place-name density" of the circle varied depending on the tribe and how far its core homeland was from the Gros Ventre: the Blackfoot circle lay heavily over the Gros Ventre one, while the Kiowa circle was weak and diffuse at its outer edges in Gros Ventre country.

As a result of this pattern, place names were shared between tribes, in the sense that the meaning of a river's name would be the same in multiple languages, even though each tribe used its own language to express that meaning. Due to the existence of Plains Sign Language, this sharing was especially easy, despite language differences. The pattern of decline in shared-name features and shared names is, at least in the Gros Ventre study, independent of the degree of language relationship, suggesting that Plains Sign Language (along with some bilingualism) was very effective in disseminating place names. Thus on the broadest level, one can talk not about "Gros Ventre" or "Arapaho" place names or ethnogeography but rather about Arapaho-language versions of a generalized Plains Indian place-naming system (which certainly deserves further study, perhaps from a computational perspective, as a unified system with regional, dialect-like variations occurring name by name). Numerous Arapaho place names are representative of this first level of names. The majority are for rivers. They include, for the sake of illustration:

beesniicii	'big river'	Mississippi River
bei'i'einiicii	'shell river'	North Platte River
hiwoxuuniicii	'elk river'	Yellowstone River
niineniiniicii	'fat/tallow river'	South Platte River
woxniiinon	'bear's lodge'	Bear Butte, S.Dak.

The second layer of place names are tribal-specific names, which are most dense in the core homeland area of the tribe, and which often tend to be applied to small-scale features unnamed by other tribes. Even when such a feature is named by another tribe, the names themselves are much less likely to be shared. The boundary between these layers is certainly not discrete, it must be noted: there are certain well-known features of the Plains and Rocky Mountains, named by likely every tribe, but with Arapaho names that are distinctive from other known names. For example, the celebrated Medicine Wheel in the Bighorn Mountains of Wyoming (see Guilliford 2000:135–44) is known in Arapaho as *hii3einoonotii* 'buffalo wheel'. It is not possible to know at this date whether the Arapaho name represents a shift from an original regional, supra-tribal one that earlier existed in Arapaho, or whether the current name was the only one ever used by the Arapaho. But the Arapaho-specific name can be seen as part of a strategy of homelanding, in which tribal uniqueness is imposed on a feature in order to increase affinity with and claims to that feature—a process that has also been called "tenure" as opposed to a looser "territoriality" (Ingold 1987:130–64).

This strategy is particularly clear in this case due to the existence of a long traditional narrative in Arapaho about the Buffalo Wheel (Cowell and Moss 2005a:251–87). The narrative relates in detail the way in which the wheel was used for ceremonial vision questing by the Arapaho and, in particular, how the spokes-and-wheel pattern is related to the form of the Arapaho Sun Dance lodge. It serves to indicate the great age of the Sun Dance lodge and that ceremony's close ties to the landscape. Various details of practice at the Buffalo Wheel—calling on Eagle/the Thunderbird for blessing, using ceremonial whistles—are closely parallel to the Arapaho Sun Dance. But most important for this discussion, the narrator is at pains on multiple occasions to stress that the Arapaho name is not "Medicine Wheel" but "Buffalo Wheel." In part, the common name results from Euro-American imposition. But that imposition is itself the secondary extension of the common Plains Indian name. The narrator Paul Moss notes:

Wohei 3ebno'uuhu' hii3e', nih'oo3ou'u niiceyotowuuni ni[h]'ii3i';
Well up there, the White People call it in a false way;
"Medicine wheel," ni'iitou'u.
"Medicine Wheel," they call it.

'oh 3owo3nenitee, hinono'ei, heene'ino'.
But the Indians, the Arapahos, they [really] know all about it.

(section 26)

. . .

Wohei nuhu' nee'eesinihiinoo, buffalo wheel, he'ne'nih'iisih'iito'.
Well what I'm calling it, Buffalo Wheel, that is what [the Arapahos] named it.

(section 41)

Moss also is at pains to indicate that the Arapaho had intimate knowledge of this location and the surrounding area, as well as knowledge and stories about the origins of other place names in the region. In fact, as important as a place name is for claiming a place, it is the narrative of the meaning of the name that is crucial, in Moss's eyes:

Howoo nuhu' buffalo wheel, hii3einoon, hihcebee, ne'nih'iitcih'inowusee3i'.
And in addition [to] the Buffalo Wheel, the buffalo herds, nearby, that was where [the buffalo] disappeared under the earth.
Ce3eso'owuuneino' nih'oo3ou'u.
The White People chased them away from us.
Wohei neneee' Buffalo Creek, Buffalo Creek, wohei ne'nih'iitcihbisinoo'oo'.
Well it was Buffalo Creek, Buffalo Creek, well that area was where [water] appeared from under the ground.
He'ihceniiheih buffalo; ne'cesinoo'oo' water;
The buffalo was slaughtered; then water started coming [out of the ground];
Buffalo niisih'eihiinoo' hinee howoh'oowu';
Buffalo is how that town was named;
Buffalo Creek, Buffalo River, Powder River, hiisoho' 3ebiisiihi': ce'i3eeniiciihehe'.
Buffalo Creek, Buffalo River, Powder River, like that over that way direction: Powder River, [that's where that took place].

(section 44)

The narrative is referring to the idea that the buffalo originated from under the earth in ancient times and that the Whites have now chased them back under the earth. The narrative is likely a reference to a traditional myth, such as "The

White Crow" (see Cowell, C'Hair, and Moss 2014), which relates when the Arapaho first encountered the buffalo inside a mountain and then drove them out into the larger world. It argues that the Buffalo Wheel is so called by the Arapahos because it lies above the location where the buffalo appeared and disappeared. Moss goes on to explicitly stress the centrality of this location for the Arapaho:

'oh neeyou teesi', hinee ho3o', cenih'esoohooto'.
And there on top, that [North] star, you can see it from here.
Wohei 3ebiisiihi', 'oh Southern Cross, niitoh'uni . . .
Well in that [other] direction, [there is] the Southern Cross, where . . .
3oowohou'u, nee'eetoono'.
Right in the middle is where we are.

(section 91)

Throughout the story, Moss links the wheel itself and its center, where the spokes coalesce, to the centrality of its geographical and cosmological location for the Arapaho, at the site near where the buffalo arrived and departed.[1] The narrative about this place name and others in the associated area is a classic example of the process of homelanding in action, through the processes of centering (oneself in the landscape), naming (the central points of that landscape), and telling (the underlying reasons and order behind the names). It imposes culturally specific symbolic meanings onto a landscape.[2]

Unfortunately, without greater availability of this kind of specific narrative, it is hard to say which other Arapaho-specific place names were involved in a similar process of homelanding. But certainly there are other names for widely known places (Yellowstone region = *heetihco'oo'* 'where it [water] goes up'; Rocky Mountains in general and Medicine Bow Mountains in particular = *3ooxone'* 'jagged area') that do not match the names used by other tribes in the area so far as is known.

The prototypical second layer of names are specifically tribal names on specifically tribal geographic features. It is at this layer that tribal-specific patterns of ethnogeography are to be sought (cf. Goodman 1992). One difficulty in understanding local cultural patterns written onto landscapes in past times— and conversely, the way landscapes guide the evolution of cultural patterns—is the lack of adequate documentation of local Plains Indian place names. This is especially the case for nomadic groups of the Great Plains: once a community was forced onto a reservation, place names for all but the most prominent distant locations eventually fell out of use. Thus while the Arapaho names for major rivers such as the Arkansas, South Platte, and North Platte have been preserved, there is little current knowledge of less prominent place names of Colorado. Without access to the full range and density of names in an area, it is impossible to have access to an Arapaho-specific landscape perspective.

Fortunately we do have an excellent sample of such names from the Northern Arapaho for one concentrated region. In 1914, two Arapaho elders, Sherman Sage and Gun Griswold, along with an interpreter, Tom Crispin, were invited to the area of soon-to-be Rocky Mountain National Park by park supporters to provide information on Arapaho place names (see Cowell and Moss 2004a for more on this trip and the way the names were eventually used in helping to establish the park). This trip resulted in the documentation of 123 names for the area in and around the park—certainly one of the densest concentrations of documented nineteenth-century names for the Plains or Rocky Mountain areas. The names were published in 1962 by one of the original 1914 park supporters and have since been retranscribed and retranslated based on original wax cylinder recordings (see Cowell and Moss 2003 for the complete list, with discussion of all forms in detail).

Based on a combination of their origin and their linguistic structure and content, the names can be divided into a number of subsets. At first, this may seem like a fairly pedantic exercise, but in fact it reveals some extremely interesting correlations that are key to understanding traditional Arapaho ethnogeography. The first thing to note is that all the Arapaho place names are transparently analyzable, with the exception of just two or three forms. Second, all the forms are descriptive in the broadest sense, as is typical for many Native American communities, particularly those using polysynthetic languages (Basso 1990; Afable and Beeler 1996; Schreyer 2006). Following is a classification of the types of description used, with examples of each type.

Type 1: Names that describe the landscape and its features:
1a. descriptive names based on landscape-level features:

benii3oonoo'	'it is deep/steep sided'	Frasier River, Grand County, Colo.
heebe3ni'ec	'big lake'	Grand Lake, Grand County, Colo.
beniixoteyou'u	'they are bare mountains'	ridge in Rocky Mountain NP

1b. descriptive names based on association with animals or plants:

bih'ihii3esoo'	'mule deer pass'	Milner Pass, Rocky Mountain NP
nookhoosei'ikoh'owu'	'sage creek'	creek in Ball Park, Grand County, Colo.

1c. names based on description of absolute or relative location:

neeneb3i'eiitei'i	'they face to the north'	Mt. Olympus and two other peaks, east of Estes Park, Larimer County, Colo.
neneehii3ei'otoyoo'	'it is the middle mountain'	Mt. Baldy, Rocky Mountain NP

Type 2: Names based on "analogical resemblance" to some other item:

ce'eiinoonoohoet	'rawhide dish'	Boulder Creek area, north slope of Longs Peak, Colo.
tecenoo	'door'	area in Wyoming on the North Platte, near Saratoga and Encampment
heeniiyoowuu	'ant hills'	Grays and Torreys Peaks, Front Range, Colo.
woxotonou'u	'bear ears'	Strawberry Peak and another one nearby, SW area, Rocky Mountain NP

Type 3: Names based on human use of, or human and sacred events in, the landscape:

woo'teeneihi3' niih'eikuhnee3i'	'Utes were chased/ fled and scattered'	a park/meadow on West Creek below Bullfrog Peak, Rocky Mountain NP
beteesibiit	'fasting'	spur of land between Michigan and Illinois Rivers, North Park, Jackson County, Colo.

All the preceding classifications are based on informant information about the origin of the names, plus their linguistic content. Of special note is the close correlation between the classifications above and the linguistic structure of the names. The descriptive names of types 1a, 1b, and 1c are almost all either inanimate subject intransitive (II) verbs with geographic-reference medials (*beniix-ote-you'u* bare-mountain-II.PL), descriptive inanimate subject intransitive (II) verbs without geographic-reference medials (*benii3oo-noo'* steep/deep-II.SG), or geographic-reference inanimate nominal (NI) forms with a descriptive modifier (*heebe3-ni'ec* big-lake). All three of these structures are either rare or completely absent from the other two main categories of place names. Overall, of the 123 names in the sample, fifty can be included in this descriptive category. Thus there is a high degree of congruency between structure (descriptive intransitive verbs with or without geographic reference terms, or descriptive inanimate nouns with geographic reference terms), content, and source of origin.

The twenty-six analyzable "analogical resemblance" names can be seen as a specific case of the use of metaphors, similar to the discussion in chapter 2. They can be divided into two subcategories: nouns, most typically unmodified, that refer to human products or body parts ("door"); and nouns, typically modified, that refer to animal body parts or products ("bear paw," "ant hills"). Note that none of the names in this category includes a reference to a geographical feature via nominal or verbal means. Most interestingly, names that involve animals but that do *not* directly refer to a geographical feature all refer to some particular body *part* of an animal or a modified form of the animal ("*flying* bug"). On the other hand, whenever an animal's name is explicitly connected to a geographical feature, then it is *always* simply the species as a whole that is named. In other words, there are no "deer's head creek"-type names, only "deer creek," nor are there any physical features simply called "bear" or "elk" or "deer" if one translates the Arapaho correctly—it is always "bear's paw" or "elk's horn." Thus resemblance-type names focus on specific body parts or actions or products, while landscape description based on animal presence focuses on the species. Once again we find a strong congruence between source of origin and semantic content on the one hand, and linguistic structure on the other, as well as a strict distinction between names of types 1 and 2 where animals are concerned. This makes it clear that these Arapaho place names can be divided in an emic sense into separable categories.

There are forty-four analyzable names in the third overall category. Structurally, the great majority of these are intransitive action verbs with animate subjects (AI verbs), often passivized ("Utes were chased"), or participles based on these verbs ("fasting"). They refer to onetime or regular human activities, human events and actions, or mythological/sacred events. Among the rest, a few are nouns referring to resources obtained in an area, and others are names of trails, which all include the noun *booo* 'trail, road', as well as some modifying, associational element (six names). As before, there is a high degree of congruency between source of origin, semantic content, and linguistic structure. Indeed, this is an example of what place-name scholar James F. Weiner would call "second-order iconism" (1991:85) and an example of something else he notes, "the iconic properties of syntax" (1991:87). In other words, the specific syntactic features of the different types of names become representative—*independently* of the specific content of the name—of a certain type of name. Note, however, that due to its polysynthetic and agglutinating nature, the "syntax" of Arapaho shows up here internally to the structure of its complex verbs. Only with rigorous distinctions between place-name types can this second-order iconism be sustained.

The following table summarizes the name types:[3]

TABLE 1 Types of Arapaho Place Names

	ORIGIN	STRUCTURE
Type 1	Description: literal	Unmodified descriptor noun + geo term noun (descriptor noun is modifier of the geo term head noun); Descriptive verb + geo term verb medial; Descriptive verb
Type 2	Description: analogical	Modified noun: human or animal part or product (noun is the head of a noun phrase)
Type 3	Association: events or activities	Action verb (sometimes passivized or a participle)

Based on these correlations and restrictions, there seems to have been a very specific cognitive framework underlying Northern Arapaho place names of the nineteenth century.[4] Note in this regard that although many of the place names of type 3 are action verbs, only one transitive verb occurs, and that verb has an inverse direction of action marker (similar to a passive). Otherwise, all the verbs are either intransitive, referring to generalized actions *done by* the Arapaho grammatical subjects, or else intransitive middle voice and passive forms, with the subject being something or someone *acted on by* the Arapaho (as in the examples given above). In other words, in place names non-Arapahos and nonhumans typically do not act but rather are acted on or forced to act—they are "chased," "scattered," and so on. Thus constructions of agency and power are literally embedded into the place-naming system in type-3 names, which recall not just events and activities but the action of the Arapaho on the landscape and the animals and peoples that they encounter in it. This literal embedding of agency is not a feature of place names that I have seen mentioned elsewhere for Native America, though it must surely be present.[5]

Beyond the structural congruencies, the descriptive associations made between landscape and plants and animals not unexpectedly reflect traditional Arapaho practices and needs: game species such as elk, deer, and buffalo are the most prominently mentioned animals, and important food, utility, or medicinal species (buffalo berries, willows, white turnips) dominate the plant list. Where no species is named, many of the names can be understood as potential signposts for travel: "there is thick brush," "it is steep sided/deep," "drowning river," "where the land is flat." One of the names ("two mountains" = Longs Peak and Mount Meeker, Colo.) is translated by the Arapaho interpreter as "twin guides," and he explains that the mountains were used as a landmark for travel because of their clear visibility and unique profile from the plains (Toll 1962)—a common component of Kiowa place names (Meadows 2008) and for hunter-gatherer groups more generally (Schreyer 2006). Thus type-1 names can be understood as fundamentally utilitarian in nature, as well as descriptive. We could also say that they *enable* agency on the landscape—recall that the straight path metaphor seen in chapter 2 specifically includes a focus on human agency expressed in passage through the landscape.

The preceding explains much of the rationale and ethnogeographic perspective behind the first and third set of names, but what of the second set, based on analogical resemblance? It turns out that these names as well are far from random. Indeed, they are likely the most deeply embedded of all in Arapaho ethnogeographic and cultural perspectives. In particular, I have found in reviewing older sources that virtually all these names can be linked to Arapaho design motifs and/or myth and narrative. Alfred Kroeber collected many items of Arapaho material culture in 1899 and 1900 in Oklahoma and Wyoming. Fortunately, he obtained detailed descriptions from the owners of the symbolic motifs on the items, fashioned through painting, quillwork, or beadwork. He gives an extensive listing of these motifs ([1902–7] 1983:138–43). As it turns out, at least seventeen of the twenty-six "analogical resemblance" place names can be linked to the motifs Kroeber documented.

It is important to clarify the nature of the motifs. Arapaho design practice featured few motifs with universally fixed meanings, though these did exist, particularly in quillwork (Anderson 2013:14, 74). Even objects like the sacred medicine wheel could be "read" symbolically in multiple and even contradictory ways at times (see Dorsey 1903:12–15). In the case of beadwork and painting, one person could explain a beaded, pointed shape on her moccasin as a mountain, while another could explain the same shape on her legging as a tipi. However, the motifs tended to be abstracted from some natural resemblance, as the tipi/mountain example illustrates, and different people's versions of a tipi motif or a mountain motif all look similar.

Different individuals could also favor different motifs, for various reasons. Kroeber did not obtain information from his consultants about *why* they chose to use certain motifs, or how combinations of them might be related symbolically or even narratively—he only documented what each individual motif represented. Based on a general understanding of Arapaho culture, it is likely that some motifs could be connected to individual spirit visions, actual life occasions, or wishes and prayers. Of course pure whim or individual aesthetic taste could also influence choices. But despite the potential for individual variation, the range of motifs used is certainly not unlimited, and many recur quite a number (i.e., dozens) of times in Kroeber's documentation. Thus it is clear that individual users were choosing broadly from a cultural stock of symbolic motifs. Kroeber states that "there seems to be a conventional system of symbolism, a fairly distinct and characteristic tribal manner of viewing and thinking about decoration" ([1902–7] 1983:146). Jeffrey D. Anderson's recent study of Arapaho women's quillwork (2013) reinforces Kroeber's conclusions about general tendencies in tribally specific symbolism, with ample room for individual variation, and this is a more general pattern of Plains Indian iconography (Irwin 1994:163–236). Kroeber finds that certain overall patterns are recurrent, and Anderson's work shows that many abstract design motifs had specific names. Most importantly, he shows that women's quillwork was intimately linked to more general Arapaho culture, myth, and cosmology, all translated into material culture terms through the quillwork. Kroeber says that "the closeness of connection between symbolism and the religious life of the Indians cannot well be overestimated by a white man" ([1902–7] 1983:150). Anderson also notes that "among Plains cultures, the Arapaho are unique in the emphasis they place on the religious content and ritual boundaries of artistic production" (2001a:183, see also 266–67).

Thus if "analogical resemblance" place names can be so closely associated with artistic motifs, they would likely also be closely associated with myth, ceremonial practice, and the sacred. And indeed, among the motifs that occur in animal-related resemblance place names, the "bear's ears" and the "bear's paw" were associated with Whirlwind Woman, a mythological being present at the creation of the world and a source of MTH power. "Anthills" and ants are often connected to sacredness even today in Arapaho culture, and a virtual fixed expression that can be heard is "even the ants are/were sacred" (see also Irwin 1994:95; Powers 1986:113). Ants are among the creatures who inhabit two realms, surface and subsurface, and subsurface creatures are often associated with medicinal root plants. Moreover, several other analogical resemblance names, which do not correspond to symbolic motifs noted by Kroeber, can nevertheless be linked to Arapaho mythology: the "rawhide dish" is a key element in the myth of "Tangled Hair and Found in the Grass": a woman tries to serve the monster Tangled Hair a meal, but he refuses the food when it is offered on the standard rawhide dish, symbolizing his asociality and leading to the woman's death as her own body becomes the dish and is cut into (Cowell, C'Hair, and Moss 2014); the name "bone pipes" involves the same archaic word used to refer to the magical thigh bone of a bear, which cannot be burned and allows the bear to return to life and chase his killers, until they leap into the sky to escape, spending eternity as the Pleiades (Salzmann 1956:267–70); the name "white owls" may well recall the mythological unending struggle between the White Owl and the Thunderbird, representing night and day, winter and summer (Dorsey and Kroeber [1903] 1997:231).

Altogether, at least twenty of the twenty-six analogical resemblance names can be linked to symbolic motifs and/or mythological narratives by comparison with Kroeber's work. Unfortunately, the informant commentary recorded by Oliver Toll for the 1914 trip to document the place names does not make these links for us. Instead, the "bear's paw" is explained as simply as being due to the occurrence of many bears in the area, for example. Today, knowledge of the meanings of the motifs, as recorded by Kroeber, has been lost, as has much of the more global understanding of patterns of names of the landscape. A few traces remain: while visiting Rocky Mountain National Park with a group of consultants, we were in the Estes Park area. This is another "centering" location for the Arapahos, similar to Buffalo Wheel, and it is known as *heetko'einoo'* 'where it is round/the circle'. One of the consultants noted that Hiram Armajo [real name] had told her that there were four sacred mountains surrounding Estes Park. The association of wheels (including the ceremonial Sacred Wheel) with four directions in this way is a common feature of Arapaho thought, and of course this whole conceptual domain is related to the Arapaho center-periphery cultural metaphor discussed in chapter 2. Unfortunately the consultant could not identify the mountains, though a mountain to the east is known as "faces to the north" and another one to the west is a documented fasting site, so these could easily be two of the four. These kinds of tantalizing details suggest the former ethnogeographic richness of this landscape. Unfortunately there is no way at present to verify with certainty the connections between the place names, the material culture motifs, and the mythological and sacred concepts. The circumstantial connections are at the least powerfully suggestive, however. One suspects that Toll simply did not get the full story. He remarks on several occasions in his 1914 typescript that the two older Arapahos were somewhat reticent about supplying information to him, especially when tired or hungry or at the end of the trip when they were eager to return home. He himself knew no Arapaho and had had no previous contact with the Arapaho, so he was not someone with whom Arapaho elders were likely to willingly share information, especially of a sacred or mythological character, or of a complex, multilayered nature. In addition, Toll was communicating through a much younger interpreter who was boarding-school educated and might not have been privy to sacred forms of knowledge held by the elders. Basso (1996) offers multiple examples of how complex the narratives surroundings place names can become. James Kari, writing on Athabaskan names in Alaska, notes that religious associations in names are typically "covert" and that religious meanings were rarely communicated to him even by longtime informants; rather, he inferred these connections from other cultural knowledge (Kari 1989:143; see Kelley and Francis 1994:3 on the related Navajo). This tendency toward reticence regarding the sacred has always been strong among the Arapaho as well (see Anderson 2001a:250–54; Hilger 1952:4, 11, and esp. 143).

Even if we cannot absolutely verify the specifics of the myth/place/motif connections name by name, it is clear that the "analogical resemblances" noted by the Arapaho in nineteenth-century Colorado were not just random. Rather, resemblances were selected via comparison with a limited set of preexisting symbolic motifs of deep cultural significance, linked to power and sacredness. The names were no more randomly chosen than the plant names, descriptions of travel conditions, or animal names. Rather than looking at the landscape and then seeing "something," the Arapahos looked at the landscape through the lens of symbolic culture, and they looked for "meeting points" where landscape features and symbolic culture coincided. As Lee Irwin notes with regard to Plains Indian visioning, "A memorable feature of the landscape is recognized by the medicine man to be a potential ally for healing" (1994:36). In fact, the area in Rocky Mountain National Park called "bear's paw" actually looks very much like the design *motif* called "bear paw": the motif has three upright prongs/claws, while the area of Rocky Mountain National Park has two peaks on either side and a central, spikelike peak/ridge in the middle, with two deep valleys on either side. Likely resemblance worked in tandem with the symbolic function of a name to evoke powerful and sacred forces and to associate a particular place with those forces. As William Meadows has noted (2008:62), recognition of especially "powerful" or "sacred" landscapes is a common habit of viewing among Plains Indians. A key component of this ethnogeograpic perspective is the search for powerful places—locations that, as Andrew Guilliford describes it (2000:68), allow for the regeneration of the people, giving them power, and also facilitate communication with the spirits by the living—exactly the process that Paul Moss describes in his story about Buffalo Wheel, which focuses primarily on vision questing (see also Kelley and Francis 1994:46 on the Navajo). For the Arapaho, another key component of the same general tendency seems to have been the application of an already powerful name/motif to such a powerful place. To the extent that one can talk of an Arapaho quest for knowledge, much of that quest lies in seeking out hidden resemblances, which can reveal powerful connections. Alfred Kroeber documents an extensive series of such shamanistic-type resemblances in Arapaho ritual and healing: holding a smooth and slippery shell brings a smooth delivery to a mother in labor, for example (Kroeber [1902–7] 1983:450–54). Thus the process of homelanding and placing names on the landscape was neither about an already-powerful landscape nor about already-powerful stories, beliefs, and symbolic motifs, but seems rather to have been about looking for places in the landscape whose features (or events) in some way matched or recalled some narrative or motif. These places of connection seem to have been a key focus of Arapaho homelanding, and homelanding itself could be understood as a process of further "empowering" both the landscape and the motifs through names that commemorated and reinforced *connections* (see Kelley and Francis 1994:10 on the Navajo for a very similar claim). Tim Ingold (1987:130–64) has compared the process of land tenure to relationships of reciprocity and gift giving, in which the power of the land "grows the people who hold it" (1987:139), but in which the people also sustain and care for the land, both literally and spiritually. The way in which symbolic motifs and the landscape mutually reinforce and empower each other in and around Rocky Mountain National Park seems to be a linguistic expression—through place names—of this reciprocal relationship. The type-3 human use and presence names, with their focus on Arapaho agency, most powerfully represent the Arapaho act of "holding," while the type-2 resemblance names represent the power that "grows" the people occupying the land.[6]

PLACE NAMES AND LANDSCAPE AS ELEMENTS OF A MULTIMODAL SYSTEM

While we have focused on how material culture motifs show up on the land, it is important to note that the land itself also shows up on the material culture items. The motifs tended to "map" landscapes and narratives onto bags, parfleches, and other items. Many components of the place names given here—trails, rocks, passes, mountains, rivers, animal tracks ("deer road," "buffalo road")—also appear as motifs of Arapaho material arts. The motifs on the items also seem to have been especially concerned with movement and pathways through the landscape, just as many of the place names were, which resonates with the path metaphors discussed in chapter 2. Of the many design motifs that Kroeber discusses for the material items, one finds mountains (seventy-one occurrences—the most common motif), rocks (twenty), rivers (thirty-three), lakes (fourteen), springs (three), and paths (thirty-nine)—along with the earth (sixteen), stars (thirteen), and the morning star (twenty-five)—which of course would have been present in or above the Colorado mountain landscape. In extreme cases, items could take on a literally "quasi-map-like nature" (Kroeber [1902–7] 1983:93), as in the case of a small bag featuring a short yellow stripe representing "Yellow Canyon" (*niihoonouute'* 'yellow landform', Wind River Reservation), two rectangles representing the "House Mountains," and two red *A* shapes representing "Fox-Tent Creek" (*nouuhoowu'* 'swift fox lodge', east of Wind River Reservation) (Kroeber [1902–7] 1983:91). Such bags and other works of art could also carry either explicit or implicit narrative content.[7] Such explicit mapping was apparently uncommon, but even in more typical cases where an item is not literally a map, one finds, for example, a single toilet pouch with designs representing the morning star (not present in the place names here, but overhead, of course), bear claws, tipis, trails, mountain ranges, meat-drying racks (see 'elk meat' among the names), and lakes (Kroeber [1902–7] 1983:95). Every motif on this pouch is also on the landscape around Rocky Mountain National Park. It is as if the bag recalls a random slice of the Arapaho map of the area of the future park (see also Kroeber [1902–7] 1983:105 for the description of another bag that offers a very similar example).

Moreover, the most common decorative motifs are to a great extent in accord with the most common geographical features named by the Arapaho around northern Colorado. One could even go so far as to point out that the ratios of mountains and rocks, rivers, lakes, and springs among the decorative motifs roughly correspond to the ratios of the geographical features in the place names. There is one spring as well as five lakes and twelve rivers, for example, among the named geographical features, and the 1/5/12 ratio roughly matches the 3/14/33 ratio of documented occurrences of these items as design motifs. Clearly the number of motifs suggests that the Arapaho were especially interested in mountains, and the place names suggest the same thing. Most interestingly of all, perhaps, is that names of the symbolic/resemblance type (type 2) tend to be applied overwhelmingly to mountains and rocks (twenty of twenty-six names). While mountains are prevalent as named objects in all types of place names, they seem to have especially attracted the Arapahos' symbolic interest, both in the arena of place naming and in the arena of material arts. There are good reasons for this: mountains and high areas in general were often considered especially sacred and powerful and were the preferred location for fasting and vision quests. Height in general is intimately associated with sacredness, and the word *co'ouute-* 'to be high' is often a virtual synonym for "it is sacred," applied to the flight of eagles as well as to mountains, to ritual and ceremonial language ("high words"), and to the respect owed ceremonial elders (*co'ouut-eenow-* 'to think of someone in a high way'). Buffalo Wheel, discussed earlier, is described as *coo'ouu3i'* 'it is high' by Paul Moss as well (Cowell and Moss 2005a:270), as are the eagles that visited the fasters (Cowell and Moss 2005a:264, 276). Not surprisingly, there are a number of fasting sites among the locations in and around Rocky Mountain National Park, including a bluff in the middle of North Park, Colorado ("vision questing"), a mountain on the east side of the park, a mountain on the west side of the park, and a site in the Medicine Bow Mountains (also "vision questing"). There is also a reference to use of Grand Lake ("holy lake") as a fasting site.

In summary, the Arapaho of the nineteenth century seem to have had three prototypical types of place names, corresponding roughly to (1) landscape description or plant/animal association, (2) symbolic or sacred vision, and (3) human usage or history of the landscape. All three types could be seen as linked to power and agency in different ways. Most prosaically, the first type of names provided signposts to move through the landscape successfully and to find resources in it. The second type evoked MTH power, which the Arapahos might hope to access in order to be more successful in the landscape. The third type emphasized the Arapahos' power as historical and contemporary agents on the landscape, acting on both it and other peoples they might encounter there. And similarly, all three types of names appear as types of design motifs: ones that depict the landscape and especially focus on the idea of pathways through it (paths, rivers, passes, tracks)—a feature common to hunter-gatherer tenure of landscapes more generally (Ingold 1987:147–48); ones that evoke the MTH power needed to help negotiate that landscape; and ones that depict successful human life on the landscape (tipis, meat drying racks, etc.).

Thus rather than look at the place names in isolation, we must appreciate them as part of a larger naming system, with each type of name complementing the others (see J. Weiner 1991:31–32; Kelley and Francis 1994:2, 40–42; Stoffe, Halmo, and Austin 1997:231–32; Meadows 2008). In fact, the interrelationship of certain names in Rocky Mountain National Park is intriguing. For example, the White Owls and the Thunderbird are perennially at war in Arapaho cosmology, representing night and day, winter and summer. In the park, the Mummy Range ("White Owls") is directly adjacent to Lulu Pass ("thunder pass") and Sawtooth Mountain ("eagle's nest"—the Eagle and Thunderbird are closely associated), and on the other side of the pass are the Never Summer Mountains. Although it is purely speculative, one could suggest that the landscape and names evoke the general cosmological conflict described in Arapaho narratives—all centered on a key pass on the Continental Divide. But certainly the more general system of names must be understood as a complete landscape system rather than a series of isolated, random points. Indeed, one could go so far as to point out that the landscape shows a degree of vertical ordering: type-2 names as we saw are especially connected with rocks, cliffs, and mountains—high points closest to power, but normally little frequented by people. Type-3 names, in contrast, are especially connected to valleys, where most human activity occurred. In one sense, this is just a predictable "accident" of the geography of the Rocky Mountain National Park area. But in a deeper sense, it shows how sets of place names as integrated systems could serve to classify the landscape as part of a cultural perspective. This system also recalls the center-periphery model (in the form of valley/mountains) discussed in chapter 2.

In a more indirect sense, the material culture items discussed above also serve as human actions in and on the landscape and the natural world, embodying human agency, just as Anderson argues for Arapaho quillwork (2013:115–66). The same is of course true for the act of naming places: no matter what the category of name applied to the place, all names represent action in and on the land. As James F. Weiner writes, "Language and place are a unity. The manner in which human action and purposive appropriation inscribe itself upon the earth is an iconography of human intentions" (1991:50). Most importantly, one must be impressed by the care with which Arapaho people managed the practice of quillwork as documented by Anderson in order to sustain an ordered relationship with each other as well as with power and the sacred, and a similar process must have occurred with the items Kroeber documented. One must be equally impressed by the way in which the practice of place naming was similarly "managed" to produce a highly ordered ethnogeographic culturescape expressing the concept of reciprocity with land and power. The integration of all these complex domains of place names, narratives, ritual, cosmological belief, material culture, and physical movement through the landscape into interdependent systems testifies to a pervasive urge to seek connections across domains of practice—connections that must be understood as nexuses of power.[8] The three basic types of names isolated here echo some other findings on nomadic hunter-gatherer cultures of the plains and southwest. Hilger (1952:87) notes that pictographic representations on buffalo robes could be divided into three categories featuring records of outstanding natural events through time (similar to type-1 place names), records of people's own actions and lives (similar to type 3), and records of visions, which were often highly symbolic (similar to type 2). Though the pictograph records were temporal rather than spatial, they show the same distribution of interest between natural phenomena, human actions and events, and human symbolic relationships to nature, myth, and the sacred that Arapaho place names document. Kroeber also noted the similarities between Arapaho decorative symbols and pictographs ([1902–7] 1983:149). Keith Basso (1996:29–30) offers for the Western Apache an indigenous explanation of landscape organization that combines name types and temporal sequencing: for that group, descriptive names "came first . . . when [the] ancestors were exploring the land and deciding to make it their home." Clan-based place names, which were highly symbolic ways of linking humans to both animals and the landscape, were the second category, spatially and temporally. "Commemorative names were awarded last, after the Apaches had made the land their own." The same three categories of natural features, symbolic mediation, and human use and action occur once again—or, more basically, we find indexes of knowledge (type-1 place names) and power (obtained via type-2 place names, exercised in type-3 place names).[9]

The Arapaho system of narratives, motifs, and place names as part of a larger multimodal complex also has correlates among other indigenous societies in North America and elsewhere. Sekaquaptewa and Washburn report on the same phenomenon among the Hopi, where certain cultural metaphors (i.e., specific images and ideas) are repeated in multiple forms and locations, including in kiva murals, on pottery, and in song and ritual. The result is "unified cultural principles across media" (2004:460). Similarly, in talking about Plains Indian visionary experiences, Irwin writes that "the mythic structures of thought and experience are not best represented by a textual corpus, but rather by a fluid, dynamic field of interactive events and meanings embedded in a sacred topos. This field is constituted by its coherence and integration with the visual and tactile world. Yet it embodies a totality of visible and invisible beings, places, signs, and symbols" (Irwin 1994:187).[10] What this means is that the Arapaho place names recorded from Rocky Mountain National Park were not a closed system of knowledge. Nor was the larger multimodal complex of associations a closed system. Rather, it constituted a way of looking at the world and interacting with the landscape, which could be applied anew as new landscapes and events were encountered. The place names of the park are (some) records of that dynamic interactive process, and it is the process that is of fundamental interest.

TO THE PRESENT: CONTINUITY AND CHANGE

Arapaho-language place names continue in use today. However, their distribution and function in discourse appears to be markedly different from several decades ago. The first thing one notices is that the unmarked procedure in discourse is to refer to places in English, even when otherwise speaking Arapaho, except among the oldest speakers. This is a pattern we will see in chapter 4 with personal names as well. Moreover, new locations often have not even received Arapaho-language place names, so that examples such as the following are common in discourse. In this example, the Arapaho native speaker tribal college secretary is informing me about graduation and inviting me to come. She casually uses the English name for the location of the ceremony, then seems to want to find an Arapaho equivalent (given that she normally tried to talk to me only in Arapaho), but realizes there is no Arapaho name:

HELEN: And on the twenty second, heetne'beetouu3ei'i3i'.
And on the twenty-second, then they will graduate.

ANDY: Oh.

HELEN: Hiit, Blue Sky Hall, beetouu3ei'i3i', yeah.
Here, in Blue Sky Hall they graduate, yeah.
Yeah, heetBlueP heetP uhh beetouu3ei'i3i'.
Yeah, at Blue [Sky Hall] they will uhh graduate.
Noh heetbii3ihi3i'.
And they will eat/have a feast.
Noh uhh, heetP uhh beteee3i'.
And uhh, they will uhh dance/do a powwow.
Yeah, the twenty second, heetnehtiiP, heetihcih'entoon.
Yeah, the twenty-second, they will recognize [the graduates], you should come.

(ELAR 28g)

In contrast to this decline in processual usage in discourse, place names in Arapaho are often talked *about*, and knowledge of them (if not necessarily much usage) is a key form of cultural capital, again similar to what we will see in chapter 4 regarding personal names. Later in the same conversation at the front desk of the tribal college, the secretary told me that some old cassette tapes had been found in storage, with elders talking in Arapaho about history and culture. She continues:

HELEN: NihP nihceh'e3towoo.
I listened to them.
Yeah, Wes Shakespeare, Ben Friday, just different things, talking about religion, talking about, kee'in?
Yeah, Wes Shakespeare, Ben Friday, just different things talking about religion, talking about, you know?

ANDY: Okay, okay.

HELEN: Like there's one that's uhm, I had to listen to it real close, uhm . . . talking about these rivers, like that Popo Agie River, that's where that boo'oowu' ['it flows red'; name for Hudson, Wyo.] comes from, from the Popo Agie.

ANDY: Uhm-hmm. Right, yeah, red.

HELEN: There were asking him about that Wind River, nehe' [this] Wes, and there he said ceeneetoowoo' or ceP like blue river, ceeneeP; yeah, that's what he said, that's what they called it.
ANDY: Oh, okay.
HELEN: And you know it's just, it's different from way back.

(ELAR 28g)

Here, we find the opposite pattern to the previous: the secretary code-switches into English but talks about the places, focusing on their Arapaho names. Notice that this is the first detail she gives of the tape, suggesting the high capital and saliency associated with Arapaho-language place names as objects of knowledge. The same pattern of talking *about* place names occurs between Arapahos as well. One elder, Bill, spoke to a high-school class, talking to them about the importance of the Arapaho language:

Wonoo3ee' niiyou nuhu' heetoono', heetoh'uune'etiino'.
There are many words for where we are, for where we live.
NiitohP . . . heneenentou'u'u hi'iihi'. . . . ni'iiP ni'ii3eihiinou'u.
Where . . . there are words for . . . [the places] have names.
Hii[t] wooniihi' niiciihehe' cebinoo'oo' 3ebhoowuniihiihi'.
Here closer[?] the stream that flows past here, on downstream.
Wohei 3ebkox3iihi' hi'in ni'ii3eihiinoo'.
Well over there on the other side of the hill, that big stream [Big Wind River] flowing that way, it has a name.
Hii3e' hee3ebxookuuni coo'oowuse'.
Over there after it [flows] through the reservoir [Big Wind River becomes Bighorn River after flowing through Boysen Reservoir].
HeeneiP kox3i', hooxono'oo, cee'eyeino'oowu', xonouu'oo', koonootoohoene', boo'oowu', sosoni'.
Big Wind River area, Riverton, Fort Washakie, Thermopolis, Arapaho Ranch, Hudson, Shoshoni.
Heetne'P heetniinihiitowunee.
You will use/say all those names.
Hiit howoo nono'ei, konouutosei', heenei'isiihi'.
And here also, Arapahoe, Ethete, and so forth.

(ELAR 15sppt2)

Again, place names are valuable symbolic capital, and they also symbolize the value of the Arapaho language—though note in this case the elder is also speaking to the students in Arapaho, urging them to use the names. Fluent speakers also commonly share information about place names with each other, just as they do with personal names (see ELAR 18a).

Beyond general patterns of usage, I would like to look more closely at the fate of the type-2 place names that occupied so much of our attention in the first part of this chapter. Today, the Arapaho women's quillwork society is defunct. Beadwork is still done, but knowledge of the meaning of motifs is either gone or only being recovered via a reading of Kroeber's or Anderson's work. Traditional painting occupies the same position. Much of the loss of knowledge of these traditions seemed to have happened quite early—among the first two generations or so to move onto the Wind River Reservation, at the same time as the traditional age-graded societies were becoming defunct. Knowledge of traditional narratives continued longer—fluent elders today maintain a knowledge of quite a bit of this tradition, though certainly there has been a good deal of loss here as well, especially in the interpretive traditions that surround the narratives themselves (see Cowell, C'Hair, and Moss 2014:28–33; Toelken and Scott 1981). In general, knowledge of the symbolic system that undergirded type-2 place names in Colorado in the nineteenth century is much reduced. More importantly, the *practice* of that knowledge largely ceased in many contexts as early as the 1910s and 1920s, and even in the case of traditional narratives, their regular telling greatly diminished after the 1940s and 1950s among most families—though certainly in the Offerings Lodge, sweat ceremonies, medicinal interventions, and similar settings some of this knowledge continues to be practiced. Nomadic movement has of course also ceased, though Arapahos continue to move about the large reservation quite extensively for seasonal purposes such as hunting and gathering edible and medicinal plants. So in this context, what then has been the fate of place names among the Northern Arapaho at Wind River, especially type-2 names that are so closely linked to the lost practices oriented to MTH power?

A survey I did prior to 2010 showed that place names of types 1 and 3 continued to be very common. Place names of type 2 were quite rare, in contrast. There were just six names based on resemblance to human parts or products, and only two old ones inherited from pre-reservation times seem possibly symbolic ("black tipi" = Black Hills; "hammer/club" = Bighorn Mountains). Names based on resemblance to animal parts were even rarer, with just three, and all were old inherited ones ("broken/single horn" = Devil's Tower; "bear's tipi" = Bear Butte, S.Dak. [also now sometimes used for the Black Hills as a whole]; "buffalo bull's backfat" = area of Tyler, Wyo.). Note that among the type-2 names listed, all are for areas off the current reservation. Virtually no new type-2 names had been created for reservation locales encountered since the 1878 arrival at Wind River, and none on the reservation itself were obviously linkable to narrative, myth, or ritual. This was a striking discontinuity with earlier practice. It seemed that since the reservation era, the Arapaho had virtually ceased to use place names of the type that would be associated with traditional sacro-symbolism, despite the continuance of certain aspects of that practice.[11] The loss of this naming pattern, while the other two have remained intact, reinforces the sense that the pattern was fundamentally connected to either symbolic thought or nomadic existence and that Arapaho ethnogeographic perspective has undergone fundamental changes over the last 150 years. Such a finding corresponds to other situations where "the culture previously embedded in the landscape is no longer being passed down from generation to generation" (Schreyer 2006:231). Discontinuities in place-naming practices have been noted for other Native American groups (see Hanks and Winter 1986:275 on Inuit; Kelley and Francis 1994:97 on Navajo). In this case, it appears that upon the Arapahos' removal from Colorado, the older ethnogeographic perspective embedded in the former landscape simply never became embedded in the new landscape after 1878, at least with all its components.

More recently, however, I have discovered that some "analogical resemblance" names do occur on the Wind River Reservation. These include a mountainside location; a mix of north-facing forest slopes and south-facing slopes covered with sagebrush and grass, which from a certain distant angle resembles an eagle, with wings semioutstretched as if to take off in flight; and a cluster of rocks on a flat ridgetop, which resembles a turtle. The two locations are called *nii'eihii* 'eagle' and *be'enoo* 'turtle'. Even more interesting is a location whose name has fallen out of use: along the south bank of the Little Wind River west of Arapahoe is an area of rocks that was known as "buffalo bellies" because they resembled the stomachs of a buffalo. In the late 1800s and early 1900s, ghost dances were held below these rocks. One key goal of the ghost dance was to bring about the return of the buffalo, and this location was chosen in particular because of the appearance of the rocks. Thus the sacro-symbolic mode of thinking found in Rocky Mountain National Park did continue in practice for some time on the Wind River Reservation. Interestingly, the continuation was in conjunction with a new, nontraditional ceremony, of the type that Loretta Fowler (2010) notes as occurring in the 1890s and early 1900s in Oklahoma and Wyoming (see chapter 1)—the Ghost Dance, Crow Dance, and peyote ceremony. As she notes, these were often done by younger men seeking to escape the ceremonial authority of elders and find alternative pathways to power. This is a striking early example of the way in which older Arapho ideologies about MTH power were shared across generations, yet the shared ideology was embedded in new forms of practice that resisted elder authority. An ideology is of course not an external force acting on individuals, whereby continuity of ideology "imposes" continuity of practice. Rather, ideologies must be continually regenerated by individuals in practice, and quite often the impetus for this regeneration is as part of a *change* in practice.

While the name "buffalo bellies" has fallen out of use, the "turtle" and the "eagle" continue in use, now primarily in Arapaho English. These names raise a number of interesting points. First, given that I worked on the reservation for over ten years before hearing these names, there is certainly a continued reticence to talk about such names and places. Second, the Eagle and the Turtle are central ceremonial figures in Arapaho, so the tendency to look at the landscape through the lens of symbolic culture remains intact at least to a degree. Third, however, note that in this case the names are not animal parts or products but species names—in this sense, the names depart from those of type 2 documented in Colorado. Fourth, at least some elders contest the legitimacy of these names as true "place names" and/or the practice of using such types of names. More specifically, they argue that there is no "story" connected to the places, by which they mean both a story regarding the origin of the name in some event or moment of power and a story or explanation that would clarify the deeper symbolic significance and power of the places and names today. Ron, a son of Paul Moss (whose story of Buffalo Wheel was examined earlier in this chapter), was one notable elder who took this view. For some of these elders, the names denote "just" resemblances, which lack any connection to power in the landscape and thus are "just" names.[12] At least for many older individuals, the continuing effort to practice type-2 place naming and homelanding is not connected to a practice of reciprocity with the land based on tenured holding and MTH power. Note that reciprocity itself, from the view of the dissenters, is mediated not just by place or place names but by shared narrative and memory about both places and their names.[13]

There are also, I learned only recently, four "sacred" mountains on the periphery of the reservation (whose location Arapahos prefer not to share). The parallel to the situation around Estes Park, Colorado, reported by one consultant above, is obvious. Four is the sacred number for the Arapaho and central to traditional ceremonial processes. Thus it is not at all surprising that Arapahos would impose this kind of ceremonial order on the landscape. But again, some of the same elders who question the names of "eagle" and "turtle" question the importance of the four sacred mountains for the same reasons. They are "just" mountains, they argue, at the edges of the reservation, with no story connected to them. Of course there are others who take these mountains much more seriously, and the efforts at maintaining or reinstituting type-2 place names can be seen in the context of other Northern Arapaho efforts to reinvigorate older artistic motifs (sometimes associated with place names).[14] Most importantly, the essence of the argument is not over place names per se but over the underlying practices of visioning and reciprocal relationships with power—underlying ideologies of language and ethnogeography in other words—that generate place names. For elders such as Ron, continuity of naming practice masks a discontinuity of ideology, which then delegimates the practice.

On the other hand, there are several sites on or near the reservation that many Arapaho people agree are "powerful" (*nono'o3oo'*). These include old burial areas (less so for modern cemeteries) and certain hilly areas without human occupation (Whites Hills between Mill Creek and Arapahoe, Red Hills west of Ethete), as well as some areas used for vision questing, certain lakes and springs, and areas with high concentrations of medicinal plants. I have collected numerous narratives about the first two types of areas (Cowell and Moss 2006; Cowell 2014), but none about the remaining three. The power of the first two types of areas is incarnated in the form of ghosts (and ghost stories) rather than in spirits who might provide help and access to MTH power, so the areas are not really comparable to those in Colorado. In fact, the very lesson of many of the ghost stories is about modern Arapaho people's inability to correctly read the landscape and thus act with the proper respect and reciprocity toward it. One narrative, told by John (who is highly devoted to AC), discusses the area of the reservation's modern Beaver Creek housing development, which he says was placed on top of an older battleground and burial ground. John has been extremely interested in getting his views "on the record," so speak, in Arapaho, and has often requested that I come and record stories and narratives from him, in an explicitly documentational fashion. In this case, I was the only audience for this story, though John clearly wanted it shared with the broader community. As he tells the story, his grandfather, Beaver Dodge, is relating the true story of the area to him, along with a warning about the kinds of *improper* relationships with ancestors that can occur when graves are disturbed out of ignorance (I provide the English translation only):

> *That's when we rode over there (to the Beaver Creek housing area). Then he showed me the graves. There were a pretty good number of them. Then we, we didn't stay too long. We rode downstream this ways again. "Okay, my grandson," he said. "There will be houses here. Sometime," he said, "there will be a lot of them. But they won't know about* (hetneihoowoe'iyootiin) *the graves here," he said. "They will not know about* (hetneihoowoe'inowuu) *it. These old men know it* (hei'inou'u), *and these old women, that they were buried here, that they were killed here. These old men, these soldiers attacked them* [referring to attack on Chief Black Bear's Band, 1870]. *They killed them. And* [after the massacre] *then they rode here, some. Some Arapahos rode here. Then they buried them, after they have dug graves for them there. . . . And all the old men that were here, they killed them all, where they are buried. And then they tied up their pants/leggings, they cut them up. They made them into something like a rope. . . . You cannot tell about this," he said to me, "wherever these, where they are laying, and these young people, and newborns. Little children are buried here too. Don't bother* (ciibeh'iicoo'outii) *them. Well they will build houses here. Up here then holes will be dug, where [the graves] are at. They will come bother* (heetniicihwoncoo'u3ei'i3i') *them. They will be seen/visible, these (deceased) old men and old women.* [The narrator elsewhere goes into more detail about little children in particular seeing visions of the dead men and women at the Beaver Creek housing units.] *They will be looking for help. They can't do that. They can't play with that area where they are buried," he said. "Yes," I said to him, "but why are they not bothered* (tihciicou'u[heihi3i'])*?" "They are not bothered* (hiihoowucou'uheihiinoono)*,"* [he replied]. *"They were the ones who had these medicines. They shoot people them with them* [refers to common Arapaho belief that illness is caused by being shot by a ghost]. *You don't feel good because of this/it makes you sick," they said.* (Cowell 2014: "Graves and Ghosts")

In this narrative, John enacts, through the very structure of the narrative, the type of knowledge transfer that is closely associated with AC: he does not tell the story himself but presents himself as the recipient of the story from an older, more knowledgeable ancestor (note the many uses of verbs with the root *he'i-*

'know'). The story includes a detailed description of the way the individuals were buried, which indexes the knowledge as location and time specific to this site. In contrast, John presents this type of knowledge transmission as broken for the tribal officials who have developed the Beaver Creek housing (note the many uses of verbs with the root *cou'u-* 'to bother, molest'). As a result, rather than being in a position to receive help and MTH power from ancestors, the modern Arapaho now receive unwelcome visits—and illness—from those deceased ancestors, who ironically ask the *modern* Arapahos for help. I would argue that this request for help from the old people represents a symbolic call by John for a reinvestment by modern Arapahos in a traditionalist, AC relationship with the land—help the old people, help the land! This would reactivate the relationships of reciprocity that might allow the (good) medicines of the old people again to be available, and it would also reactivate more general relationships of reciprocity with the land, leading to renewed access to MTH power. Crucially, proper knowledge is intimately tied to respect and not "bothering" the old people.

Ghost stories and burial stories are thus an especially favored modern type of place (and place-name) narrative. They often play with notions of MTH power and its location in ways similar to Bill's story of "The Two Sons" in chapter 2, highlighting the ironies of a relatively disempowered position for modern Arapahos—though his story focused on the spatial domains of power and disempowerment, while John's focuses on temporal domains. Also of note is the fact that the places that are the foci of these stories do not have symbolic place names so far as I have been able to determine, being named descriptively as *nonookoteyoo'* 'white hills' and so forth. The other types of places often still associated with power—lakes and springs, fasting sites, sources of medicinal and ceremonial plants—are more comparable to the sites of power discussed earlier in this chapter. But they also lack symbolic place names. In other words, the names used for modern areas of power do not function symbolically to evoke power, even though a broader ideology of power in the landscape seems to remain active, if sometimes only in the inverted form of ghostly places.

In summary, there is apparently more continuity with the past than initially appeared to me in 2010 in terms of the ethnogeographic tendency to find powerful places in the landscape—but that tendency has been largely severed from symbolic (type-2) place-naming practice. Conversely, where place-naming practice itself seeks to at least marginally reinscribe continuity with the symbolic type of name, some elders challenge this continuity based on what is effectively a claim of discontinuity of ethnogeographic relationships with the land—at least of the sort those names would evoke. In both cases, symbolic names are severed from landscape power. In addition, with the loss of—or lack of—stories about such controversial places, the place names and related stories no longer form the basis of the knowledge exchanges that are a key factor in reciprocal relationships in Arapaho society. In more theoretical terms, we could say that the elders who are critical of these practices see a discontinuity between ideology and practice of the sort described in the introduction—in this case, where ideology has shifted, but where some degree of practice continues.

PLACE NAMING, POWER, AND MODERN ARAPAHO SOCIETY

With regard to the type-2 place-name naysayers, three competing theoretical claims could be put forward, which address not just place-name and MTH power but the very nature of Arapaho society, and which allow us to understand the views of different COPs. First, recalling Basso's description of the temporal sequencing of the Apache relationships to the landscape, one could argue that these Arapaho elders are suggesting that the Arapaho have simply not been present, not dwelled long enough at Wind River for the landscape connection to become deep enough to attain levels of sacredness. They are still simply exploring, describing, and settling in. Alternately, and more pessimistically, they could be suggesting that the power is not just not *yet* there but that it is no longer there at all: there is no power to be had through the land. I do not think, however, that this is what most elder Arapahos are claiming, though this is a position that many Assimilationists take, and it is a position that is taken overtly by many Evangelical Christians. The land is a place to live and a source of resources and revenue, but named places do not offer direct access to either MTH or social power and prestige.

Alternately, the elders could be seen as arguing that a certain mode of seeing and naming the landscape is no longer possible in Arapaho culture or that it at least has not been followed by the particular namers and users of the names of these new features. The power is still there, but the Arapaho cannot access it. This is a discourse used by some speakers about the Arapaho language in general: they argue that the language will never be gone—it will always be present in the sounds of the wind, the leaves, the water, and the birds and animals—but speakers will no longer be able to access and understand that language (and the associated power) once it is no longer spoken. More specfically for place names, studies of the Apache (Basso 1990, 1996), Navajo (Kelley and Francis 1994:40–42), Tolowa (Collins 1998b:134–48), and Kiowa (Meadows 2008:248–50) all underline that places, people (including ancestors), and stories must be intimately connected through time in order to legitimate and validate—empower—homelands. As Kelley and Francis claim in talking about the Navajo, "Place names are a vehicle for conveying knowlege from one person to another" (1994:49). But the knowledge must be conveyed through stories about place, not just the names themselves. If place names no longer (or do not yet) have stories, then in a sense they are not vehicles of knowledge, or at least their vehicularity is quite limited. We could say that they have little power to create reciprocal social relationships among users—in contrast to the power that Basso finds for Apache place names used in "speaking with names" (1990:138–73). Type-2, "analogical resemblance" place names have the least amount of literal "information" within the name itself of any type of Arapaho place name. Thus they especially require stories to perform their function. Without stories, their vehicularity as a true "place name" can be denied. The people who take this position seem to be prominent members of AC for the most part, as opposed to members of Pan-Indian or Politico-Tribal COPs (who seem less concerned about the lack of a story for these names). In fact, Pan-Indian and especially Politico-Tribal affiliates are often interested in stories about all types of place names because those stories are a way of cementing the shared histories and experiences that are a key basis for cohesion among these COPs. But the stories are not seen as maintaining or activating MTH power in the landscape in the way that AC affiliates seem to understand them, and they are thus optional benefits rather than necessary components of the name.

A very different objection is that such places—and/or such type-2 place names—*do* have power, and that it *can* still potentially be accessed. But without stories as a guide to the nature of that power and therefore to the precautions and respect necessary, this type of place naming could be seen as potentially dangerous—not powerless, but too powerful. What the Arapahos would lack in this case would be the length of experience with a place necessary to *control* its power. Those who resist the use of such symbolic place names are also among the older individuals on the reservation who are most cautious about power generally and ceremonial power in particular. These individuals (including Ron) often state that MTH power can be very dangerous and that because (especially younger) people today are "crazy" and lack caution and respect—both toward elders and toward power—they should not have access to certain traditional forms of power and should not "mess with" it. This attitude is reflected in Paul Moss's claims in his stories that the elders of earlier generations *nihnohkce3ei'oo3i' hiwoxu'uuwunoo* 'left with their medicines' (Cowell and Moss 2005a:61; ELAR 12b). In other words, because they saw the younger generations becoming "crazy," they were afraid these people would hurt themselves if given access to various forms of power. Thus they did not pass on their knowledge when they died. Similarly, ceremonial leaders at Wind River earlier resisted attempts to revive quillwork because this sacred art could be dangerous without proper knowledge of how to carry it out (Anderson 2013:22–23, 88–89). Type-2 place naming raises the same issues as reviving quillwork or "messing with" other rituals: such rituals are always accompanied by knowledge—that is, stories—that both explains the ritual and also provides the crucial restrictions on it that allow one to avoid danger to self or others. The argument that there is no story to places such as the "turtle" or the "eagle" must be understood in this light: symbolic place naming involves power and danger, and without knowledge of a controlling narrative, one is simply "messing with" the land. It is quite literally a practice that Arapahos today lack the knowledge to do safely. Power is not gone from the land—at least not entirely—but it has become too dangerous to maintain a reciprocal relationship with it, some elders argue. This is a position taken by a number of members of AC. Note that this is a highly restrictive view of AC and its membership and, in fact, a terminal view of AC. The claim is that the ethnogeography of MTH power in the landscape has not been, will not be, and cannot be passed down from the current AC elders and speakers of the language to the next generation—and thus the AC ethnogeographic perspective will terminate with the passing of these elders. While this position certainly solidifies the social capital and prestige of such elders while they remain alive, it has little appeal to younger Arapahos for obvious reasons, other than a small subset who may be privileged to learn from these elders and receive their imprimatur.

Most generally, we must understand the process of homelanding as a necessarily ongoing cultural activity—as the process of obtaining tenure of a landscape. As Ingold (1987) argues, tenure is fundamentally a social process, and in the same way, place names on the landscape are elements of a social process. Disputes over the legitimacy of place names and the stories—or lack thereof—connected to them are thus social contestations. Is Arapaho society fundamentally "out of order" not just with respect to place naming or ritual but with respect to everything, including the land? Has it gone too far off the track of continuity that it should have maintained with the past? Has this produced an inability to access MTH power or control it correctly? This is the argument of many elder AC-affiliated individuals. Or, on the other hand, is the society more continuous with the past than some more conservative elders might claim? In this case, do younger members of the society—in particular younger individuals who affiliate with AC and are interested in type-2 place names—have the right to seek prestige and social capital through ritual (and linguistic) practices that certain elders might seek to deny them—or that certain even-younger members of the society might seek to deny to the middle generation, based on the authority of the elders? In the worst of cases, since MTH power is understood within AC as the motivating force of all reciprocal relationships, both vertically with the sacred and horizontally with other Arapahos, what is now to be the basis of social relations and social authority in Arapaho society in the absence of MTH power? This is in fact a key question posed by many current Arapaho-speaking elders, though of course they do not pose it in quite these terms. Most commonly, they talk about the lack of "respect" in the society nowadays from younger people, both for other people and for ceremonial objects and processes, combined with these younger people's loss of knowledge about who their relations (relatives) are. They are asking questions about the very ordering bases of Arapaho society. The disputes about type-2 place names, while initially seeming fairly arcane, actually get at the very heart of this question, both within AC COP and among other COPs.

THE IRONIC RESPONSE

Among the Northern Arapaho, as among virtually all people, one of the best ways to resolve a dispute is through humor. A type of place naming that was perhaps uncommon among the Northern Arapaho in the nineteenth century (it is not documented among the Rocky Mountain National Park names) is joking and ironic place names. Some nineteenth-century examples do exist: Fort Fetterman was known as *ciiko'ootoowu'* 'stingy house' due to problems with BIA Indian agents and/or post traders. This has become a widespread practice—in both native languages and in English—among Native American tribes in the twentieth and twenty-first centuries (see M. Nevins 2008). Among Arapaho-language examples is Dubois, Wyoming, which is named *niisonoh'oho'*.

This word translates as 'two boys', roughly matching the pronunciation of the name Dubois in English. Such naming corresponds to the subversive bilingual "translation pairs" reported by Samuels (2001) for the San Carlos Apache. A crosslinguistic pun from the Crow Reservation involves the name of Hardin, Montana, a town famous for drinking establishments, which is known as *biinohooo* in Arapaho, a word that means 'digging stick' or 'crowbar', punning on the words "Crow bar/saloon" in English. Not a pun, but certainly intended as a comic name, is *hohookeeno'oowu'* 'crazy house', the old name for the Wyoming Life Resource Center (originally known as the Wyoming Home of the Feeble-Minded and Epileptic) just east of Lander. There are also ongoing comic reinterpretations of certain names, similar to the practice of folk etymology. The town of Hudson, Wyoming, was named *boo'oowu'* 'there is red water' due to its location on the Little Popo Agie River, of the same name. However, during the 1930s through 1950s, in particular, it was a hotbed of bars and prostitution, and thus many people today account for its name as a reference to all the red wine that once flowed there, though most people seem aware of the original nature of the name. And in the most extreme examples of this practice of capitalizing on the ambiguity of place names, some English names are reported to be corruptions of original Arapaho (see Samuels 2001:279 for the same practice among the Western Apache). For example, the town of Hannah, Wyoming, is based on the Arapaho *heenoo*, meaning 'customarily, necessarily', according to one speaker because the town is near the place where Arapahos would customarily travel from Wyoming into North Park, Colorado (via a pass known as *tecenoo* 'the door' in Arapaho).

Another comic or at least whimsical naming practice is to name—or rename—towns based on sports mascots. In Gros Ventre, Missoula and Bozeman have become known as Grizzly Town and Bobcat Town, in reference to the mascots of the University of Montana and Montana State University (Cowell, Taylor, and Brockie 2016), and in the same way, the Arapaho often call Laramie, Wyoming (formerly *niitokooxeeetiini'* 'where we get tipi poles'), *touhoono'oowu'* 'cowboy house/town' in reference to the mascot of the University of Wyoming.

Other locations on the Wind River Reservation have acquired English place names, but names known and used almost entirely within the local Arapaho community. One new elder housing area on a hill was christened "Bengay Heights," while another new suburban-like housing area, notable for the many paint colors used on the different houses, was christened "Easter Egg Village." Other places include "Home on the Range" (known for its good views), "Jizz

Lake" (a trysting spot), and the "Jungle" (a drinking spot along the Little Wind River). Not quite place names, but similar in their joking spirit, are the use of "LA" (as in Los Angeles) to describe the area officially known as Lower Arapahoe (a settlement area on the east side of the reservation) and the moniker "Ethiopians" to describe people from the Ethete settlement area.

Once one begins thinking about these names, one is struck by the fact that many involve "analogical resemblance" and association and, even more specifically, human or animal parts and products (Easter eggs, Bengay, college mascots, etc.). They are, in a sense, the new type-2 place names of the Arapaho. One important difference from the names recorded for the Rocky Mountain National Park area is that the resemblances are not just visual but also in some cases linguistic, either in the sense of pure sound (as in Dubois/'two boys' and Ethiopians), or in the multiple meanings that can be assigned to a word from two different cultural eras and contexts (as in Hudson/'there is red water'/'there is red wine' and LA). Yet the search for multiple meanings on the basis of sound alone—indeed for power (or humor!) hidden in language—is a characteristic Arapaho practice, as discussed in more detail in chapter 5 on folk etymologies. Broadly speaking, the names attest to a continued search for connections, in the visual, the aural, and the cultural realms more generally, even if the connections produce more humor than power.

Another important point to make is that whether in Arapaho or English, these names are largely confined to the Arapaho community. As such, they function in the same way as similar White Mountain Apache place names, to "constitute the reservation as an interpretive community" (M. Nevins 2008:191), though the Arapaho names do not draw on contemporary media discourse for the most part in the same way as the Apache ones. A key part of Arapaho identity is knowledge and use of the local network of English place names, similar to other Native American communities (see Meadows 2008:217–18 on Kiowa). M. Eleanor Nevins's work on the Apache is especially interesting in that it builds off the earlier work of Basso, which is much more focused on traditional naming practices. Like the Arapaho situation, the Apache one seems to offer marked discontinuities in practice and/or ideology around place naming at first. Yet Nevins argues that there is a common language ideology at work in both Apache- and English-language place names on the reservation, which involves "indexical contrasts between the Apache and English languages" (2008:192). She also argues for continuity in patterns of usage of the names, as well as in judgments about appropriate place names (2008:192, 196–99, 204–6).

Much of the more specific detail that Nevins reports for the Apache also applies to the contemporary Northern Arapaho. She argues that the English-language humorous Apache names serve to "highlight and comment on the difference between the isolated single-family residential patterns mandated by government housing developments vs. the extended family multiple dwellings characteristic of more longstanding settlements" (2008:193). The same types of housing occur at Wind River, and the humorous Arapaho names such as Bengay Heights and Easter Egg Village have been applied to the same prefab, government-designed housing areas that are the special targets of Apache humorous names. Nevins also argues that the decontextualization and recontextualization processes that produce the humorous place names are part of "strategic acts of community definition in political engagement with the dominant society" (2008:193) and, more specifically, "strategic engagement with the problem of domination by the surrounding society" (2008:195; see also Samuels 2001 on the Western Apache). Names such as Two Boys and Crowbar serve the same functions, as does Crazy House: English-language forms and euphemisms are reduced to their essential element, and towns are renamed according to their essential function. In the process, the humor indexes an Arapaho ability to penetrate external discourses and naming practices—to see through to the "truth"—while maintaining local coherence socially and linguistically, in order to resist the pressures of the outside discourses and the societies that generate them. These place names are thus vehicles whereby multiple Northern Arapaho COPs—AC, Pan-Indian, and Politico-Tribal in particular—maintain a degree of coherence in relation to external White society, both with other Arapahos and with the larger Native American community. Moreover, because the names in question involve humor rather than MTH power, they allow even Arapahos affiliated with the Evangelical Christian COP to maintain solidarity with others in the tribe (remember that this COP tends to be heavily oriented around small, kinship-based, Arapaho-only churches, so elements of Arapaho identity that avoid connections to traditional MTH power and ceremonialism can remain appealing). This situation can be contrasted with that described for Tolowa by James Collins, where the focus of efforts to create Pan-Tolowa identities is centered on documentation of old place names, "old words," and their associated stories (1998b:10, 134–35, 140–41, 180, 195). While such work is also going on among the Arapaho, it is clearly of a much more contested nature, and this allows us to see that the dynamics of place naming are certainly not the same across Native America.

PLACE NAMES IN CONTEMPORARY USAGE

Before concluding this chapter, I want to examine further the usage of place names in discourse, particularly in Arapaho-language discourse, as opposed to their role as a *topic* of discourse. We have already noted above that use of Arapaho place names has been on decline, even when speakers are otherwise speaking Arapaho, and that many recent places (buildings, senior centers, and the like) do not have formal Arapaho place names, with speakers switching to English for these names. However, the situation is far more complex than this.

A fact to note that is of central importance in relation to homelanding is that there seems to be a preference for deictic forms in lieu of actual place names among Arapaho speakers when referring to local sites—similar to what we will also see in chapter 4, where relationship and kinship terms are preferred over personal names among close associates. Thus instead of naming the two main towns of Ethete and Arapahoe as destinations, people often say they will *hihcini-ihkoohu-* 'drive upstream' to go to Ethete and *hoowuniihkoohu-* 'drive downstream' to go to Arapahoe. Depending on where one is on the reservation, of course, other local sites may be upstream, downstream, or "over the hill" (*kox3i'*), another commonly used directional for discussing places. In the case of kinship terms as opposed to personal names, use of the former (deictic) terms—"your mother," "my father"—indexes the family connection and the importance of kinship structures. In the case of place names, the preference for deictic forms seems to usually index local knowledge, both of the geography itself and of the pragmatic status of the knowledge for speaker and addressee. This could be compared to usage in English, where one might say to a good friend, "I'm going across the street," with the assumption that the friend understands that across the street is the location of the speaker's girlfriend's house. In the following, old friends and relatives John and Roger are telling me about a hunting trip they went on together and talking about a favorite spot along the Little Wind River. In the excerpt, *cih-* indicates 'to speaker', *neh-/eh-/uh-* indicates 'away from speaker', *ce'-* indicates 'back', *ceb-* indicates 'along/past', *3eb-* indicates 'there', *niih-/iih-* indicates 'along a stream', *oowu-* indicates 'down', *eec-* indicates 'to one's home', *no'-* indicates 'arrive at a location', and *ihci-* indicates 'up' (*koohu-* is 'drive'):

Yeheihoo, he'ce'iistoonooni? Noonoko' heet-**eh**-'**eec**-koohunoo.
*Gee, I wonder what I can do now? I might as well go **back home there**.*
Heet-**eh-ce'-ceb**-koohuni' hiit.

*We will drive **back along that ways** now.*
Hiit, **3eb-iih**-koohu'.
*Now here, we drove **along** the river **that ways**.*
Ne'nih'iiyoo3-**no'**-koohu' ho'oowuu'.
*Then we **arrived** safely at the house.*

. . .

Noh kokoh'u3ecoonoo, neibeex-**uh-'ihci-niih**-koohube.
*And I was thinking, we should drive **up along** the stream **that ways** [again].*
Beebeet **cih-ce'-oowu-niih**-koohu'.
*And we were just driving **back down along** the stream **this way**.*

(ELAR 56b)

The entire passage is about the home of the speaker, located in Arapahoe, and the Little Wind River, yet the speaker never mentions the locations by proper name. Not only does the extremely rich set of deictic and directional forms index shared knowledge, but it also serves to micro-specify the events and locations, in ways that place names alone could not. The deixis also establishes the hunting spot as the point of view for the entire passage, though I myself had never been there, thus reinforcing the import of the *-ni'/-'* exclusive first-person plural inflections: this story is "about Roger and me and *our* favorite place; it is *not* about *you*, the listener." Put another way, local place names are crucial for homelanding on the intertribal level, but not needing to actually *use* them may be nearly as crucial on the intratribal level. In fact, even when knowledge is *not* shared, we can find the same preference for deixis. Later in the same conversation, John questions Roger:

JOHN: Heetniice'iinoo'einee, that next day.
        You guys were going hunting again, that next day.
ROGER: Nihi'koohuni' **kox3i'**.
        *We drove **over the hill**.*
JOHN: Koohuut heih-'**oowu-niih**-koohube?
        *Was it here that you drove **down along** the stream?*
ROGER: Ne'-**noo'oe**-koohuni'.
        *Then we drove **around** [along the river].*
JOHN: Yeah . . . hini' nihii **xonouu'oo'** heetou'u', on this side, or . . . ?
        *Yeah . . . that uhh where **Thermopolis** is at, on this side, or . . . ?*

ROGER: Hee.
Yes.

(ELAR 56b)

Only as a last resort does John actually use a place name in this discussion, to clarify the situation.

There is certainly no general restriction on the use of place names among Arapaho people, however, and they are commonly used. Whether people are speaking Arapaho or English, the default is now to use an English-language place name. This is similar to the situation we will find for Arapaho personal names, but the distinction is not nearly so pronounced as with personal names, which are quite rarely used. Arapaho-language place names are used relatively commonly when people are speaking Arapaho (though almost never when they are not). This is actually variable by place name, however. As an example, in an automated search of eighty different Arapaho-language videos, I found the following results, arranged in order of ratio of English to Arapaho:

TABLE 2 Arapaho-Language versus English-Language Occurrence of Certain Place Names

LOCATION	NUMBER OF ENGLISH TOKENS	NUMBER OF ARAPAHO TOKENS
Casper/bei'i'einiicie	7	3
Arapahoe/hinono'ei'	7	4
Lander/howoh'oowuu'	12	10
Saint Stephens/heninouhu'	12	21
Denver/niineniiniicie	5	10
Riverton/hooxono'o	4	17

While three names occur more often in English, three occur more often in Arapaho. Many of the videos were specifically made to document the Arapaho language (others were of ongoing discourse and events), so one would expect speakers to be more likely to use Arapaho than English place names in these cases; I would say the counts overestimate the relative occurrence of Arapaho-language forms in neutral everyday conversation, based on general subjective observation. Certainly when an Arapaho-specific linguistic, historical, or cultural topic is under discussion, the likelihood is much higher that the

Arapaho-language name will be used, similar to what we will see for personal names. As marked forms, Arapaho-language place names index Arapaho-ness and affiliation to Arapaho identity. Even in these types of settings, however, English-language place names are clearly often used, as the tallies from the videos show. As far as why the ratios vary as they do for individual names, a full response would require looking at many more place names and examining individual contexts of usage, as well as distinguishing actual uses of the names in discourse from instances of talking about the names. Arapahoe/*hinono'ei'* is problematic in that many speakers use the form *hoowuniihiihi'* 'downstream' to express the same idea, so the count could be deceptive. Another problem is that *hooxono'o* can refer to 'overseas' generally as well as Riverton specifically. Otherwise, roughly speaking, Lander and Casper are places where not many Arapaho people live, compared to Saint Stephens and Riverton. Few live in Denver either, but when people go there, it is often for very Arapaho-specific reasons (language and culture conferences, powwows, etc.). So places more closely associated with Arapaho-ness would appear to be more likely to be named in Arapaho, which is hardly surprising.

To reinforce the earlier point about the preference for deictic and directional forms over place names in daily discourse, I will note that a search of the same exact videos just mentioned revealed 113 tokens of *-oowu-niih-* 'down along [the stream]' and thirteen tokens of *-ihci-niih-* 'up along [the stream]'. While the number of tokens of 'up along the stream' is comparable to the occurrence of the various common place names in the table above, the difference between 'up' and 'down' is striking. In theory, one would expect to be going upstream and downstream about the same number of times. But in fact, there is no place commonly referred to as "upstream" in the way that Arapahoe is referred to as "downstream." This suggests that the imbalance is due at least in part to the fact that people are referring to Arapahoe a lot, and referring to it as "downstream" in particular, much more than by its formal name of *hinono'ei'*, since the imbalance in tokens between the latter and the former is so great. As another example, the directional root *koxut-* and its allomorphs, meaning 'over the hill, to the other side', occur thirty-one times in the same corpus—more than all but one of the place names examined above. These tokens are certainly not all place references, but the number of tokens gives an idea of the prominence of these types of roots in everyday Arapaho discourse and of their role at least in part as indices of local knowledge and identity.

We have seen earlier that English-language joking place names ("Bengay Heights") also index a certain kind of Arapahoness and local identity. In many hours of recorded conversation, however, and much additional listening, I have virtually never found examples of people speaking Arapaho but using an English-language joking place name, even though they commonly use English-language place names such as Ethete or Arapahoe or Lander when speaking Arapaho. Older Arapaho speakers have in fact been reluctant to share such English-language joking place names with me or identify their exact locales, whereas they are quite happy to talk about Arapaho-language joking place names (*niisonoh'oho'*/Dubois). This is not because the places are "secret" or "sacred" but rather that, for older speakers, the joking English names seem to index a non-AC affiliation and to be not worthy of serious attention. In part, this has to do with the documentation aspect of fieldwork: certainly many individuals index and perform a (sometimes exaggerated) AC identity for me when working explicitly on "documentation." But after over fifteen years of my observation on the reservation, it is clear that the avoidance of these names is a general feature of the discourse of older speakers, though they certainly use the names at times, almost always when speaking English.

CONCLUSION: IRONY OR CONCEALMENT—OR CRISIS?

We can see at least two attempts at continuity of past and present in Arapaho place-naming practices—each with embedded discontinuities with the past as well. First, there has been an effort by some speakers to continue to find symbolic power in the landscape and to index this power through place names. Others contest this, however, arguing that without narratives, such place names are no longer acceptable as legitimate or meaningful—or safe.[15] In other words, there is a continuity of name type but a discontinuity in the ideology that would allow for these names to convey a proper reciprocal relationship with the land. The lack of very many place names of this type points to a general sense that these names may in fact be either hollow or dangerous gestures, which cannot be applied successfully in the absence of their ethnogeographic undergirding. These attempts at place naming and name usage can be associated most closely with the AC COP, though the Pan-Indian COP is also involved in these efforts, while the AC COP is by far the most prominent in resisting these attempts as well as making them.

Second, there has been an effort to continue the spirit of type-2 names, through a search for analogical resemblance (of a comic nature) in English. The names are part of a system of cultural commentary and ironic resistance that serves to reinforce the cohesiveness of Arapaho people as well as Indian people, while underlining their differences from other groups—notably Whites. They are most closely associated with the Pan-Indian and Politico-Tribal COPs. In the former case, they can be seen as consonant with similar practices among other tribes—not just the Western Apache but also the Gros Ventre and groups as far afield as the Maliseet (Perley 2011:14). This is likely an evolving Pan-Indian style of place naming, found on other reservations as well. In this latter case, the style can be seen more as a way of cultivating insider practices of lived experience and shared community that provide cultural reinforcement to the political nature of neotribalism, but without relying on more intensive and more traditionalist practices such as the Sun Dance, the Native American Church, or the Arapaho language. Perley (2011) describes a similar process among the Maliseet, where "indigeneity" is becoming the new preferred category of identity, and where a focus on shared lived experience is being used to enhance the otherwise limited legal and political nature of the term *indigenous*.

For both of these COPs, the new English names perform a fundamental function of homelanding, and it is a function that appeals to many in the AC COP as well (though there are definitely some elder Arapaho speakers who have little interest in these non-Arapaho-language names, and a few who even see them as part of the breakdown in respect among younger people). In this sense, despite the surface form of the names being in English, and the particular set of resemblances being chosen from a very different discursive frame than the one of the nineteenth century, one can actually see more continuity between these names and the past than in the case of the attempted Arapaho-language type-2 names. This is attested by the growing number of these humorous names. Thus I would agree with Nevins's analysis of the same type of names in Apache. She argues for continuity there, and the same is true for the Arapaho.

However, on an even deeper level, there is still a key discontinuity: the analogical/symbolic-resemblance type of name, which in the nineteenth century was tied to the invocation of MTH power, is now tied to acts of internal community maintenance and external resistance. Put another way, a landscape of power has been replaced by a landscape attuned much more to irony. Horizontal or lateral reciprocity *on* the land and within Arapaho (or the larger Native American) society remains strong, as does the desire for distinctiveness in relation to other (notably White) peoples on this same land, but a deeper vertical reciprocity with the landscape itself as a source of power is fundamentally altered, at least as viewed through the lens of place names.

I do not wish to claim that some Arapaho people either cannot or do not maintain a relationship to traditional MTH power, or that this relationship is no longer mediated through the land, since some Arapahos still do go on vision quests or gather medicinal plants, and many hunt. Some Arapaho people themselves do in fact claim that relationships to MTH power are either greatly attenuated or no longer possible. But many others would maintain that this claim is false. What is true is that Arapaho place names—in Arapaho or English—largely no longer function to index this relationship with power. According to some Arapahos, this is because there is nothing for this type of place name to do, so to speak—the power is not accessible. For others, the power is there and available, but place names do not index it and do not function within a larger multimodal system of ethnogeography. Perhaps this is in part because Arapaho people do not believe that English itself is powerful enough as a language to be used for this purpose, while Arapaho is now known by too few people to be very functionally useful for place naming. The third possibility is that such names are concealed, not only from outside researchers such as myself, but from those not part of AC as well. In any case, it appears that contemporary Arapahos, in the realm of place naming, have adopted an attitude of silence toward power in the landscape: they do not give it overt symbolic names. Given how many years it took before I became aware of the few examples of names of this type, and the tradition of reticence around matters of MTH power and ritual, this is not a surprising conclusion. But whereas in the nineteenth century that silence focused on the concealment of the explanation of names, in the current era it focuses even on the names themselves and the very possibility of naming.

James F. Weiner, speaking of the place names of the Foi of Papua New Guinea (and inspired by Heidegger), says that "names . . . expose things in their being, that is, in terms of their true relation to our life condition" (1991:32). If this is so, then a strategy of silence, in the face of the enormous pressures of Euro-American society on the Arapahos, is quite consistent with the strategy of irony that has been adopted with regard to the new place names that are "on the map" and thus on record. Weiner underlines "the role that naming plays in constituting this world as an intersubjective, social one" (1991:32). In other words, place names are used in, sustain, and are sustained by relationships. When the subjects with whom one interacts change drastically over time, as they have for the Arapaho since the 1850s in Colorado and Wyoming, then place names and their usage change as well in order to reconstitute these new intersubjectivities. In the case of the Northern Arapaho, these include relationships with Euro-Americans and their society and also, perhaps—for many younger people at least—reconfigured relationships with elders and with the concepts of elder knowledge and elder reciprocity. Internally to Arapaho society, the rise of relative silence with regard to the landscape as a powerscape suggests that the vertical transmission of knowledge and power via place names and their stories, from MTH sources of power through elders to younger members of the society, may be confronting moments of trouble or even crisis. Place names go away or go silent when the relationship contexts within which they are used go away—or need to go silent.

Looking at place names in relation to those outside of Arapaho society, the picture is different. Symbolic names were part of an earlier homelanding strategy, in which the Arapaho laid claim to tenure of the landscape in relation to other tribes. In a certain sense the names advertised the Arapahos' power to do this (at least to themselves, and perhaps to others) using an appeal to ideologies of landscape and power *shared* with other tribes. In contrast, ideologies of landscape and power are fundamentally different between the Arapaho and the Euro-Americans who surround them. Strategies of both silence and concealment on the one hand, and irony on the other, can serve in response to this situation. Both strategies recognize—and seek to maintain—the distance and *incommensurability* between the two groups, as well as the solidarity of the Arapaho with each other and, potentially, with other Native Americans as well.

4

PERSONAL NAMES AND NAMING

OF ALL THE NAMING PRACTICES among the Northern Arapaho, the process of giving and receiving personal names is the most salient for many members of the community. Personal names in nineteenth- and earlier twentieth-century culture were intimately tied to well-being and accomplishment and, at their most profound level, to personal access to power (see J. Moore 1984 on very similar ideas among the Cheyenne). Today, receiving a personal name in Arapaho—and the question of what name is received, its history and meaning, and who gave it—are still key community topics. In this chapter, I will begin by describing the many components involved in and surrounding Arapaho-language personal names and then consider some of the changes that have occurred over the last few decades. Hilger (1952:58–67) provides an extensive account for the period prior to 1940 (see also Anderson 2001a:128–32). Here I concentrate on the practice as it occurs in the lives of current Arapahos and their near ancestors, mostly during the twentieth and early twenty-first centuries, though many of the practices and ideologies match those described by Hilger and Anderson.

THE NAMES THEMSELVES: LINGUISTIC STRUCTURE AND CONTENT

The grammar of Arapaho personal names is quite interesting in that an older grammatical system of the language, which has otherwise largely disappeared in modern speech, has been retained in personal names. In order to make this more understandable, we need to first look at the history of Arapaho morphology and syntax.

In contemporary Arapaho independent clauses, there are two different sets of inflections used, one for affirmative statements and another for nonaffirmatives. The nonaffirmative set derives directly from Proto-Algonquian independent clause inflections. However, the affirmative set derives from Proto-Algonquian inflections that were originally used for what Algonquian specialists call the *conjunct order changed participle*. That particular label and the details of the usage of those forms do need not detain us here—suffice it to say that the forms were often used in relative clauses. Thus, originally Arapaho would have had a grammatical structure something like the following (third person "s/he" has no inflectional prefix) in independent and relative clauses:

1a. he-niibei he-ihoowu-niibei
you are singing *you are not singing*
1b. 0-niibei 0-hoowu-niibei
s/he is singing *s/he not singing*
1c. he-noohow-oo he-ihoowu-noohow-oo
you are looking at him/her *you are not looking at him/her*
1d. neniibei-t
the one who is singing

As the language changed, however, the Proto-Algonquian changed participles (the form in 1d) began to be used in independent affirmative statements. These forms use inflectional suffixes rather than prefixes, and they also lengthen the initial vowel of the verb stem (when it is short) or insert /en/ or /on/ (when it is long, as in 1d: *n-en-iibei*).

This has led to modern Arapaho forms:

2. neniibei-t   0-hoowu-niibei
S/he is singing *S/he is not singing*

Personal names, however, have retained the form of the original, Proto-Algonquian-style grammar. A common example is:

3. hisei be'eih
woman red = 'Red Woman'

In the spoken everyday language, where a name is not involved, this would be *bee'eihit hisei*, with initial change (*e* > *ee*) and a suffixed inflection marker (*-t*), as in examples 1d and 2. The form of 'red' in the personal name above looks exactly like in the Arapaho negative sentence *hoow-be'eih* 's/he is not red', however. So personal names have retained the old-style grammar for affirmative clauses, which otherwise exists in contemporary Arapaho only in nonaffirmative clauses. There are a few personal names that look like modern affirmative verb forms, but speakers typically interpret these as headless relative clauses (i.e., the old-style usage of the conjunct participle forms) of the form 'the one who . . .' as in 1d: 'the one who is singing'.[1] Thus Arapaho personal names have not only their own grammar, but an archaic grammar.

Arapaho names are all in principle descriptive and translatable. There are no forms that serve only as names and have no other meaning to speakers, in the sense of English "Andy" or "Kathy." Not all Arapaho personal names are verbs—some are nouns, either simple or modified:

4. *biixonoo*   'Plume'
5. *nouuh-usei*   'Kit fox-woman'

Verbs can also occur modified: *teiitoon-niibei* 'quiet-sing', 'Singing Quiet'. Nouns and active verbs can also occur together: *hono'cebisee* 'sky walk', 'Walks in the Sky'. Other names can be participles or even bare roots. Bare roots can only be used in names, not elsewhere in the language. The nominal suffixes *-(i/u/e)sei* 'woman' and *-(i/u)nen* 'man' are commonly used, with the first being much more common than the second. In fact, gender-neutral forms of names appear to be most commonly considered as default masculine forms, and the *-sei* suffix is then added to create feminine forms. There is also a shortened form of "woman" that occurs simply as *-s* and that occurs only in personal names: *niibei-s* 'Singing Woman'. Based on an examination of several hundred Arapaho personal names, the semantic contents are highly reflective of salient symbolic elements of Arapaho culture. The four sacred Arapaho colors are red, white, black, and yellow, and these are the most common colors in personal names. The most common birds and animals are the eagle, hawk, crow, bear, and buffalo, which are also important in Arapaho ceremony, subsistence, and traditional narrative. To the extent that body parts are mentioned, the face and eyes are the most common. Few or no insects or plants occur as parts of actual names, although consultants did not rule out the possibility.[2]

There are a number of detailed rules regarding the syntax of personal names, in terms of noun and verb order, depending on the types of nouns and verbs in question. Those are described in Cowell and Moss (2003). The most important one, as seen above, is that the order of nouns and verbs in Arapaho personal names is opposite that of normal syntax used in discourse (note that English-language adjectives are verbs in Arapaho)—instead of saying *hini' bee'eihit hisei* 'that red woman', one says for the personal name *hisei be'eih*, literally 'woman red.' Interesting, this same pattern of reversal occurs in some Lakota names as well (Powers 1986:32). The most important point for this discussion is that the word order and overall form of personal names is much more tightly constrained than is the case for the spoken language generally (which has free word order). This should not be surprising as we have already seen similar tight constraints on the various forms that place names can take. More generally, the grammatical system of personal names is clearly highly conservative. In fact, the only other place in the language where the older style of affirmative grammar has been retained is in traditional myths. In such texts, the narrative past-tense prefix *he'ih-* 'it is said to have happened' is used, and when this prefix occurs, the verbs look like those in personal names:

6. he'ih-niibei he'ih-cii-niibei
   S/he (is said to have) sang   *S/he (is said to have) not sang*

These forms can be compared to examples 1b and 2 above. Note also the more archaic negative form *cii-* rather than more modern *ihoowu-* here. The grammatical conservatism of personal names (and the traditional narratives) is all the more striking in that Arapaho has otherwise undergone extensive changes not only in morphology and syntax in comparison to its Proto-Algonquian roots (as already seen in this chapter) but also in its phonology. Overall, the speakers of the language seem to have been highly willing to innovate, as much as for any other Algonquian language, yet in the realm of personal names, that innovation has been resisted. (We should note, however, that the phonology [sound system] of the personal names matches that of the everyday language—the conservatism has been in structure [morphology] rather than pronunciation.) It is also important to note that the structure is not frozen, existing only in past names handed down to the present. If fluent speakers are asked to invent a new name today that otherwise is not documented for the community, they productively use the older grammatical system of personal naming to do so. This actually fits with the observation on pronunciation: it is not the names themselves, in either structure or sound, that have necessarily been handed down over time in a fixed, frozen form (i.e., the "Andy" and "Kathy" English-language model), but rather the systematic structure of personal naming itself, as an active practice that indexes names and distinguishes them from other components of the language, in the same way that *he'ih-* indexes a traditional narrative. This is another example of second-order iconism and the iconography of syntax (and morphology) that was discussed in chapter 3 (J. Weiner 1991:85, 87). As Powers says about Lakota, "Sacrality is frequently achieved through patterning of common words" (1986:127), rather than a turn to archaic words. This is true for both personal and place names in Arapaho.

THE LANGUAGE IDEOLOGY OF NAMES

The obvious question to ask is why there is a conservatism with regard to personal names and why it is this particular type of structural conservatism, rather than a "frozen" type of conservatism as seen in English. The answer lies in the ideology that surrounds personal names in Arapaho. The basic belief is that individual names carry power associated with them: power to heal, power to change one's behavior or personality, power to bring long life, power to transfer elements of the personality or spirit of a previous owner to a new one. The names have typically been imbued with this power by being attached to certain respected, powerful, long-lived, and successful individuals. This is a broader ideology found on the Great Plains and elsewhere. Blackfoot scholar Betty Bastien writes of "the significance of names in relation to our connections with our ancestors and the support they provide in our daily living" (2004:122; see J. Moore 1984 on Cheyenne). She tells of a relative who said to her, "I would call my name and remember who I am. Somehow I would find the courage and strength to overcome my challenges" (Bastien 2004:122). Arapaho personal names are similarly forms of prayer (see Lombard 2011 on Blackfoot as well).

Among the Arapaho, one old man who was himself a noted giver of names, Gary, told me that when he was young he was weak and sickly. In response, his parents went to an old man named *beh'eihehi'* 'Old Man' and asked if that man would give his name to their son, in the hopes that the son would live to old age as the current possessor had. The old man agreed, and Gary eventually lived well into his nineties. Note that in this case, it is not the semantic content of the name ("old man") that was most important. Rather, it was the fact that the name had been possessed by someone who lived to old age. Other names with no semantic relationship to age can convey exactly the same blessing on a new owner. Nevertheless, Gary reported that his parents were especially interested in this name due to the added benefit of the semantic force of the name. But had its possessor not been old himself, the name would not have been sought.

The stories associated with names also contribute to their gendering. There are no names in Arapaho that are specifically gendered male or female in the sense of English "Bill" or "Jane," other than gender-neutral forms to which the "man" or "woman" suffix is added. Women can have names such as *biikoonehe'* 'Kills at Night', which an outsider might expect would be given only to a male warrior. But once a name has been held by a woman or man within a family, it typically becomes associated with male or female gender at least within the extended family circle, and often much more broadly within the tribe. Thus a name like "kills at night" can become effectively gendered as female, though if the name goes out of use for several decades and the original holders are forgotten, it could then be used for a man.

It should be noted that although currently there are no names formally restricted by band or clan structures, Arapaho names are often passed down specifically within family groups, although apparently never without skipping at least one generation.[3] Name givers also tend to respect family naming "territory" and not give names to individuals in one family if they are traditional within another family. Thus many young people's names match those of a grandparent or great-grandparent. In fact, older individuals can voluntarily give away their names to favored relatives or those in need without even being asked. Conversely, younger people can ask older relatives for their name. If this is done following proper protocol, the request cannot be refused.[4] In such a situation, the older person can choose a new name for themselves unilaterally and announce it to the community. This is the only instance in which a person can name him- or herself.

In other cases, names could come directly from natural sources and inspiration and be imbued with power from those sources. Bill, who named a number of people over the years, stated that a traditional name giver would "walk around . . . looking for a name. . . . Somebody might say something to him . . . even animals talked to them. It was powerful [in] those days. Those old fellows had, had that power. [They would] thank the spirits [for the name]" (Wiles 2002:3).[5] This remark clearly situates names as similar to divine blessings obtained by fasting and vision quests and other ritualized suffering, coming from similar sources and having similar power. Indeed, the name is conceptualized as an independent agent by Bill (see Lombard 2011:48 for a similar idea in Blackfoot): "This name I got for this grandson here, I kinda had a rough time finding that name. [By having that name], in that way your grandson's gonna live—[he's] gonna live to see many things change. Gonna live to be an old man. That's how that name's gonna take care of him all the way" (Wiles 2002:3). Similarly, he also added, "As he goes along . . . that name [will] be with him, carry him through" (Wiles 2002:5). The name giver will often in fact address the name itself as part of the name-giving ceremony. Moss describes another name giver as follows: "He's pointing at his grandson . . . 'watch him that way, wherever he goes. Be with him' [he says to the name and powers associated with the name] . . . Gonna give him that name. 'And I want you to be with him as he goes on. Watch him. Be his shield'" (Wiles 2002:4).[6]

In other cases, if a person's life is going badly, they may seek a new name simply in hopes that the change will do them good. Even if they do not acquire a new name with associated power (though, of course, ideally they hope to do so), they have at least rid themselves of a name associated with failure to prosper: names can thus have negative as well as positive power.

These attitudes at least partially explain the linguistic conservatism with regard to personal names. If a name is powerful, then power can come to be associated with the specific form of the name qua name and thus tend to impede changes to the individual name. In part, this is related to the sound of the name: its actual (correct!) pronunciation is the key to its power to act in the world. This is part of a more general Arapaho and Plains Indian (and beyond) language ideology that privileges the power of sound itself, especially linguistic sound, to effect changes in the world (Anderson 2001a:272; Bastien 2004:122–23; Sullivan 2000:12–13). It is not just sound but iconic linguistic form and structure that is also involved, however. As we have seen, there are quite specific rules regarding the construction of Arapaho names. These rules must be understood as a form of linguistic compartmentalization as well as iconization, which indexes the names as such and isolates them from the rest of the grammar of the language. More importantly, the linguistic compartmentalization is both the expression and index of power, as well as the constructor and maintainer of that power, just as in the case of place names. If one can talk about "respect" for language and language form itself, then the grammar of personal names in Arapaho is a form of respect that speakers pay to personal names themselves (and of course to the possessors of those names), and most generally to MTH power. The iconic syntax of both personal and place names is also a domain where the notion of the sacredness of the language can be understood as directly linked to linguistic form.

The same process of compartmentalization occurs with meanings as well as forms of names, though in a slightly different manner. When a name is given, the name giver tells the individual (if he or she is old enough to appreciate it) or the parents the story behind the name: what inspired it, who formerly possessed it, why it is appropriate for the new owner, and so forth. Thus personal names, like place names, are actually bipartite, consisting of the formal name with its content and structure, and an associated interpretive and historical tradition (see Mithun 1984:46 on Mohawk; P. Moore 2007:288–89 on Kaska and Dene Tha; Lombard 2011:44 on Blackfoot).[7] And like place names, personal names whose associated story is lost or unknown are seen by most elders as partially or even entirely lacking in power and efficacy. In a certain sense they are "just" names, in the way that some elders say that "eagle" or "turtle" are "just" place names. However, unless there is a perception that the personal name is completely illegitimate (i.e., not given or received in the proper manner at all—see more below), there is still a belief that some power is potentially associated with the name, and thus it is deserving of respect. For this reason, elders refuse to give firm opinions on names for which there is not an available associated story or some general community knowledge. This is particularly the case with certain names that have lost their transparency as glossable forms, occasionally due to language change and time or, more commonly, due to garbling by nonnative speakers. When asked, "What does my name mean?" the answer in these cases will be "I can't say." For more traditionally oriented Northern Arapahos, it is considered taboo to speculate on the meaning of powerful objects and practices of the culture without firm knowledge. In other words, personal names are compartmentalized interpretively as well as semantically and structurally.

THE NAME-GIVING CEREMONY

This general ideology of power embedded in linguistic structure and content helps explain many of the broader social practices around naming. There is a great deal of variation in the formality or informality of name giving. At its simplest, a family (with a new baby, for example) or a young person (who was not named as a child because the parents did not take this step) can ask a respected elder (usually a member of the immediate or extended family) to provide a name. The elder thinks for a few days about an appropriate name and then announces it to the individual and his or her family, normally at a ceremonial meal cooked for him by the family, where he also receives some gift. They then will typically inform others in the community on a more or less informal basis. Probably most name giving at Wind River today occurs in this fairly informal way.

It is considered a great honor to be asked to name someone. Formerly, noted warriors were often asked to do this. Normally the person asked is perceived as having good knowledge of the Arapaho language and of Arapaho culture, as being a thoughtful and serious person, and as having a good knowledge of his or her own extended family and its history and personal names. Both men and women give names regularly. Additionally, if someone is known to have given other names that are admired in the community (either for their content or for the success that they have brought to the named person), that individual may be especially sought out, so that certain elders have become especially noted as givers of names. One such elder showed me a long list of names (written out in English translation since he could not write Arapaho, but actually read back to me in Arapaho), which he had recorded so as to be ready when additional requests came.

Somewhat younger individuals can be extremely touched and moved when first asked to give a name, as in the following conversation:

LINDA:	"Never, never thought I'd see the day when I was going to be asked, to be asked to name my grandchildren," [he said].
ALICE:	Uhh-huh.
LINDA:	That one was his great-grandson [name].
JANE:	Yeah.
ALICE:	Yeah.
LINDA:	Almost brought tears to his eyes. He said, "I never thought anybody would ever ask me."
JANE:	Uhm-hmm.
LINDA:	"It means a lot to me."
ALICE:	Yeah.
LINDA:	"It means a lot to me. I'm gonna name them."

(ELAR 63f)

Being asked to give a name is thus often perceived as a change in one's status, at least within one's extended family, and potentially within the larger community—a step on the way to elderhood. Since personal names are obviously extremely important, being trusted with the task is clearly honorable. As we have seen, the power of a name is associated with the richness of the narrative that accompanies it. But in at least an indirect sense, it is associated with the power of the person who gives the name as well. In certain cases—when young adults ask an elder for the elder's own name, and the giver is also the owner—this is very obvious. But even in cases where the elder gives some other name—the older, wiser, more admired, and more powerful the elder, the more power and prestige is associated with a name. Thus if a person happens to mention to someone his or her Arapaho name, the very first question asked is almost always, "Who gave you that name?" Just as the name *itself* has an associated story, the *event* of the *bestowing* of the name also has an associated story, as is classically the case in ritual gift exchanges. In my own case, for example, it is important to explain that my name is *Co'ouu3ii'eihii* 'High Eagle'; that the name is associated with a white cowboy and actor named Tim McCoy, who was a friend of the Arapahos many decades ago and who also had the name (thus I am marked symbolically as a "friend of the Arapahos"); and finally that the name was given to me by Joe, a noted name giver, who bestowed it on me impromptu at a public feast not otherwise intended as a time for naming, in recognition of my help providing documentation and curriculum in the language.

In a more formal type of naming, which is truly ceremonial, an elder is asked well ahead of time to think of a name. He or she, as well as extended family and friends, is invited to a feast put on by the immediate family of the one to receive the name. There is usually an effort at the feast to provide the traditional Arapaho foods (stew, fry bread, corn, chokecherry gravy). Once everyone is finished eating, a prominent member of the immediate family will make a short speech to all present about the circumstances and importance of the event. Then, the elder is formally asked (usually by this same person) to provide the name, in what amounts to a prayer, or prayerful request, to the elder. Gifts are then given to the elder (again, usually including traditional symbolic gifts such as blankets, linens, tobacco, and cash). The elder will then often give a talk to those assembled, formerly in Arapaho but now usually done in both Arapaho and English due to language loss, covering general moral rules of Arapaho culture, as well as the specifics of why naming is important. At the end of this speech (see Cowell, C'Hair, and Moss 2014 for a very formal example), the Arapaho name is formally announced to those gathered, along with a translation of the name, a description of the deeper meaning of the name, and the origins of the name (especially if it was formerly held by someone else). The elder may talk directly to the person being named in some detail if that person is older and can understand. If it is a baby that is being named, the elder normally talks about the baby to the others present but still addresses some specific comments both to the child and especially to the parents of the child about the name and its significance. The elder sometimes presents the child by name to all in attendance, one by one. Typically everyone is asked to say the name together once the child has been presented. The elder may also go outside and walk around the home, pronouncing the name in the four directions, or walk around the inside of a community hall. The elder also pronounces a prayer for the long and happy life of the newly named person. Once this is done, the elder is thanked, and the gathering returns to relaxed conversation and celebration.[8]

At its most formal, name giving is part of larger public ceremonies, with the name giving as an adjunct to these ceremonies. The elder chooses the name that will be given to the child, goes through the name-giving ritual much as described above, and then announces the new name to all those present at the name giving and, symbolically, to all those in the tribe. He or she then, in the most formal of events, goes outside and announces the new name to the four directions, symbolic of the traditional Four Old Men. Such public, ceremonial name giving of this sort seems to be done only by a narrow set of highly respected elders who have the confidence to speak and pray in public in Arapaho (and English). While in some Native American groups, knowledge of an individual's personal name is highly restricted (as is, obviously, the use of the name), among the Arapaho there is prestige associated with having one's name widely known—and even more importantly, with having the stories associated with the name and naming event widely known. The power of the name is enhanced through collective knowledge and understanding, just as prayers at ceremonies are considered more efficacious if large numbers of people join in collectively (in spirit, not actually orally). For this reason, the most elaborate and formal (and costly) namings happened in the past at large public events such as the Sun Dance, and they still occasionally occur in this way.

It is worth reflecting on the fact that Arapaho names are widely known, given that for many American Indian societies, especially in the past, there were taboos surrounding knowledge or use of personal names (D. French and K. French 1996). In those cases, the power of the name—and the social networks that it created and maintained through transmission and usage—was limited to immediate family, one's clan, a religious/ceremonial entity, or some other restricted group. In contrast, the Arapaho largely lacked such clan-restricted networks of power in the past, favoring instead models of vertical and horizontal integration through the Offerings Lodge and age-graded societies open to all men of the appropriate age. The fact that these very ceremonies were often the occasion for the announcing of a new name emphasizes the truly "tribal" importance of individual names, to be understood as markers of tribal social integration, and this is still largely the case today. In contrast, Arapaho has a rich set of vocative terms tied to kinship relations, and it is these forms—the preferred form of address when applicable, at least in the past—that serve to maintain and solidify more localized family and clan connections. Personal naming is thus a key point of juncture for MTH power, as well as social prestige, power, and respect.

NAME USAGE

Just as there is no taboo on the public use of personal names, there is no taboo on the names of the deceased as occurs in some tribes (D. French and K. French 1996). Obviously from what has been said above, the opposite is true: the names of the deceased live on and are reused, not only to help the living, but as an honor to those now gone, in a form of reciprocal relationship with ancestors. On the other hand, Arapaho personal names in the past were certainly used less often than personal names in English. As noted, Arapaho has an extensive set of vocative forms. Outside the family, there are also widely used vocative forms for 'friend' (*noto'u* [f], *be* [m]), and the vocatives for 'grandmother' (*neiwoo*) and 'grandfather' (*nebesiiwoo*) are widely used as honorifics, bestowed on individuals as varied as elders who help young people at ceremonies and classroom teachers at school, especially in Arapaho-language classes. In talking about relatives, people also tend to say "your older brother" or "her younger sister" without mentioning a name unless necessary for clarification, especially in Arapaho. In fact, in opposition to most claims about person reference, it appears from an ongoing study by one of my graduate students that in Arapaho discourse a kinship term (rather than a personal name) is the more common and least marked way of initiating reference to someone (Irina Wagner, discussion with author, 2016), a feature that has been reported for other strongly kin-based societies (Alford 1988:120). This practice is less about avoiding personal names than about showing honor and respect and especially about indexing kin relationships, which are a key organizing principle of Arapaho society. For this reason, both in the past and in the present Arapaho names are more often used for third-person reference than for direct address, a distinction noted for other societies that value kinship-oriented or other similar types of names that index social networks and solidarity (Sillander 2010:103, 111–13; Fiskesjö 2010:157; P. Moore 2007:287). Otherwise, personal names were commonly used in the past. Today, especially at large ceremonial gatherings, speakers often make a point of letting everyone know their Arapaho name.

Members of AC are especially likely to use Arapaho personal names, both in everyday conversation as well as on more formal occasions, even when they are speaking English. They are most likely to use them in the context of interactions such as master-apprentice work, where the language overall is particularly salient, and where large amounts of Arapaho are used. Usage of Arapaho-language personal names in discourse is in fact a key indexical marker of AC membership. In a few cases, individuals who were seen as extremely AC-affiliated were in recent times addressed and talked about using primarily their Arapaho name: these included Francis Brown (real name) (*wo'oot* '???') and Edward Willow (real name) (*noo'oeneecee* 'all-around chief'). This was done even by non-Arapaho speakers, and by Arapaho speakers even when speaking English. Other individuals are addressed by their Arapaho name as a sign of respect, especially in Arapaho-oriented contexts. At Wind River Tribal College, several elders were invited to talk to a class of students about language and culture, and the following typical exchange took place:

WILLIAM: So you know right now a lot of our students you know, they have to read, you know really read what they write and what they want to say [in Arapaho], but you know to me, the greatest thing is they're making an effort, to help, you know, preserve or revitalize our language. And so you know the next person that's gonna say something is gonna be uhh. . . .
MARY: Noh Nookonohwoot . . .
And Dances All Night . . .
WILLIAM: Sosoni'. Wohei . . .
[this half] Shoshone. Okay . . .

MARY: Nookonohwoot, while Helen, while Noo3een and uhm Heneecee Niiseiht are in here, can you uhh answer the question that was . . . that I asked you earlier?
Dances All Night, while Helen, while ??? [Helen's Arapaho Name] and uhm Lone Bull are in here, can you [now addressing the elders] uhh answer the question that was . . . that I asked earlier?

(ELAR 36c)

As the speakers' initial use of English followed by a switch to the Arapaho name shows, however, it is actually more common among both nonnative and native speakers to speak in Arapaho but use a person's English name. In the same discussion just cited, one can also find the following, where Mary (a nonnative speaker) mentions something she was told about a particular custom. Helen and Lone Bull (George), both native speakers, present an alternative explanation, and then Helen concludes:

HELEN: Nee'ee3e'inowoo.
That's what I know about that subject.
GEORGE: Yeah.
HELEN: Henee' heesinihiin Mary?
Who told you that, Mary?

(ELAR 36e)

The same two speakers are involved in initiating another response, along with William (a nonnative speaker):

WILLIAM: Ciibehnih'oo3ouyeiti!
Don't speak English [when you answer]!
GEORGE: Hei'towuuninee, Helen.
You tell her about it, Helen.
HELEN: Hotou3e'in?
What do you know about it?

(ELAR 36e)

In both cases, English names are used by native speakers, within a matrix of speech that is otherwise entirely in Arapaho. These examples illustrate two important points. First, as with place names, the unmarked behavior is to use

English personal names, with use of Arapaho personal names being a marked behavior, engaged in more often by AC students and learners than by elders themselves, as in these examples. The markedness of the names is further indicated by the fact that in many cases when people use an Arapaho personal name, they then use the person's English name immediately afterward, suggesting they suspect the Arapaho personal name may not be widely known or used (a pattern also commonly seen with place names), as in the following example from a native speaker, Helen:

Hi'in tihteebe, hiit tihniisi3einoo, ne'nih'ii'niiP niiteheiwou'u:
When I first started working here, that was when I helped them out.
George, nuhu' Ceneeteenii'ehisei, Roberta, yeah.
George [and] Bluebird Woman, Roberta, yeah.

(ELAR 28g)

Nevertheless, whether talking to or about someone, an effort is made by students to use Arapaho names to show AC affiliation. Secondly, when using a name to directly address someone, the use of the Arapaho name is indexical of elder respect: as seen four examples previously, Mary uses Arapaho names toward her older brother and two elders, while the elders use English names toward the student and even each other.

It is quite rare for older speakers to use a younger person's Arapaho name, especially outside of grandparent-grandchild contexts, but this does occur in some master-apprentice pairs. The consistent use of the Arapaho name by the elder seems to be a recognition by that person of the hard work and progress of the learner. In the following conversation, one teacher, who presented at a conference with one of the apprentices, is telling another teacher about the event:

DAVE: Niiteiniini heenetini'.
        We spoke one after the other.
        Neneeninoo, nookhoosei niibei, nih'eenetini'.
        Me and Singing Sage, we spoke.
        Niini'inihiini'.
        We said good things.
        Koe'sP koe'sohowuunei'ee3i', tihbee3tiiP, bee3tooni'.
        They applauded for us, when we finished.
HENRY: Yeah.

DAVE: Yeah. Ni'P ni'i3ecoonoo.
Yeah, I was happy.
Howoo, howoo nuhu' hono' niibei, howoo hentoot.
Also, also this Singing Sky was there.
'oh hih'oowkohtowuuni, hih'oowkohtobei, wo'ei3 teiitoonokut.
But she didn't, didn't do/say anything, she just sat there quietly.
Beebeet neniP neneeninoo noh nookhoosei niibei nih'eenetini'.
Just me and Singing Sage spoke.
Neeseh'e [personal name in English] nohco'oot.
My older brother [p.n.] took part [too].
HENRY: Uhm-hmm.
DAVE: Ceceecesibeit nuhu' [personal name in English] beenhehe'.
This [p.n.], he made some angry-type comments, a little bit.

(ELAR 22e)

The last two individuals mentioned (whose names are omitted for the sake of anonymity) are native Arapaho speakers, yet their English personal names are used. Clearly the speaker knows the Arapaho name of his older brother, and the name of the other individual is well known in the community as well, so unfamiliarity is not an issue. Yet the teacher chooses to name only the two master-apprentice students in Arapaho (one of whom is present in the room listening) while using the English names of two prominent Arapaho speakers. His usage here recognizes and legitimates the efforts of the apprentices as exemplary younger members of AC.

I should note that nicknames are not uncommon among the Arapaho. These were formerly in Arapaho, but now they are mostly in English. They tend to be humorous and teasing.[9] They most commonly refer to a physical characteristic or to some memorable, funny past event or remark with which a person has become associated. Thus when one baby was born years ago, an older woman said, "Why, he's as white as a snowball!" and that individual is commonly and affectionately called Snowball (in English) to this day. Such names can come from virtually any source.

It is also possible to joke with or about a person's actual Arapaho name, though this is a fairly restricted practice. It is normally done by the individuals themselves, by close friends only, or by elders toward younger people. When it is directed at elders, only those who are known to be especially jovial and accepting of this kind of behavior are targeted, and even then only by other elders who are very close acquaintances or lifelong best friends, as joking about a person's name can potentially be highly insulting to them and diminish the value of the name. The following occurred when two older men were sharing stories with me and each other, and then the daughter of one of the men and the niece of the other came in and interrupted. Seeing that this was an Arapaho-salient moment, she urged them to share their Arapaho names with me:

D/N: Daddy, Uncle, tell them your Indian names. . . .
CHARLIE: We introduced ourselves. I already told him. Red Shirt and . . .
JOHN: Be'biixuut.
 Red Shirt [is my name].
CHARLIE: Nii'eihii Kokteeneih. Spotted Bird.
 Spotted Bird [is my name]. Spotted Bird.
JOHN: [We are] Bird and Shirt.
 Nehe', niinih'ohut nehe'.
 This one, he flies around all over this one.
D/N: Shirt and pants . . .
JOHN: Wotooho, neihooweix.
 Pants, I don't wear them [just a shirt].
CHARLIE: I got no pants on, that's what he said. No diaper. (laughter)

(ELAR 69a)

Here John mocks both himself and Charlie by joking about the personal names. This is a display of solidarity between these two lifelong friends, for the sake of both Charlie's daughter and me, most likely, in a way typical of joking relationships (see Basso 1979; C. Goddard 1992:109; Spielmann 1998:108–24). Milder forms of teasing can occur between somewhat less intimate individuals, as when the tribal college secretary (Helen) teased the janitor (George) one day when I asked him his Arapaho name:

ANDY: Hotousihi' hinono'einiihi'?
 What is your Arapaho name?
GEO: Neecee niiseih.
 Lone Chief.
HELEN: Neecee niiseih.
 Lone Chief.
ANDY: Niiseih.
 Single/alone.

HELEN:	Yeah, neecee niiseih.
	Yeah, Lone Chief.
ANDY:	Lone chief.
HELEN:	Uhm. Neniisneniit.
	Yep. He's all alone/lonely. (laughter from George)
GEORGE:	Neniisneniinoo.
	I'm all alone/lonely.
HELEN:	Yeah, neniisneniit.
	Yeah, he's all alone/lonely.

(ELAR 28g)

It is interesting to note that Arapaho speakers do not seem to play with official English names in the same kind of way. In other words, Arapaho names can be a site of solidarity-oriented joking, whereas English-language names, which are associated more with bureaucratic citizenship, are much less so—a distinction also noted for other small-scale egalitarian societies, who seek to establish boundaries between internal tribal solidarity and an external bureaucratic world (Sillander 2010:117; Rajah 2010:140, 144; Kun-hui 2010:217).

To give another example of this kind of practice that avoids potentially exposing someone else to ridicule, my own Arapaho name as noted above is *Co'ouu3ii'eihii* 'High Eagle'. However, the name was once mispronounced by one nonfluent speaker as *coo'u3eihii*, which means 'sexual molester' among other things. Since that time, the older men in the family into which I have been adopted have consistently called me by the latter name, always with great glee. They have not been shy about sharing this anecdote with others in the community. However, for many years no one outside the family, or even younger members of the family, ever called me by this name or teased me about it, which fits well with the general patterns and restrictions of personal-name joking in Arapaho. Since I came to know a broader set of people in the community well, a number of older men and (less commonly) older women outside my adopted family have occasionally teased me: one said, "What's your name, *cooxuceneihii*?" The last word means 'meadowlark'. Other than the rough resemblance in sound, the joke plays on the fact that meadowlarks are supposedly always talking—and in particular, always talking dirty—plus the fact that nonfluent speakers of Arapaho, when they make mistakes, are typically described as "talking dirty" as well, on the theory that every mispronunciation ends up being accidentally off color or worse. (In my experience, this is true, alas.) Others pretend to misunderstand (even when the name is told to them by other fluent speakers) and come up with comic twists such as "high buzzard" or "high turkey" or "high meadowlark." Given how little joking I have seen with other people's formal Arapaho names (though it is very common with nicknames), I suspect that my outsider status contributes to the fun in these particular examples. At the same time, it indexes a form of insiderness, especially since the speakers are well aware that I understand their Arapaho jokes. Milder joking on personal names occurs between native speakers and younger learners within the community as well and is a key form of cross-generational inclusiveness. On one occasion, a number of fluent speakers were at the tribal college, waiting for a meeting on master-apprentice procedures to begin. They were chatting, when one advanced learner (William) entered. He was addressed using his Arapaho personal name, showing respect and acknowledgment of his language efforts. The speaker then mentioned his name again to the group, inviting a potential joking response, which did occur:

JOE: Wohei, nonookonohwoot.
Hello there, Dances All Night.
WILLIAM: Wohei.
Hello.
JOE: Nonookonohwoot, nenee'eesih'it.
Dances All Night, that's his name.
RON: Neneeninoo, nonookoneiP, nonookonebiihineenoo.
Me, I'm "Gambles All Night."
(laughter)
JOE: NonookP nonookonebiihineen.
You're "Gambles All Night."

(ELAR 108a)

The joke was all the funnier because the second speaker was someone who was widely known for being seen in the casino gambling at all hours of the night, and his self-deprecation was greatly appreciated. But the joking also signaled that the advanced learner was enough of an insider to AC both to understand the joke and to put up with the play with his name in good spirits. The self-deprecation served indirectly to appreciate the younger learner, elevating his status and inclusion in the group.

The other common setting for personal-name joking is among sisters-in-law and brothers-in-law. On one particular occasion, as I was trying to work with some older women on a "don't drink and drive" lesson in Arapaho, the women, who were in-law relatives of a particular man with whom I often work closely, decided to pretend that this particular man had been out drinking and then gotten stopped by the sheriff for driving drunk. They then made up an entire narrative of how that situation would have played out. One of the moments that brought the house down was when they played off both this person's nickname (Johnny Cash) and his Arapaho name (*3oo3ouuteiseet* 'Ridge Walker') and said that when the sheriff got hold of him, he made him "walk the line" (a line from a popular Johnny Cash song, "I Walk the Line")—that is, take a sobriety test by walking the road line in the middle of the pavement. The women expected (correctly) that I would report back on the session to my consultant and share their teasing with him.

As one final comment about usage, I should note that if a person does not have an Arapaho name, he or she can be (and is) called by the joking/insulting name *Woo3tineet* 'Shit Ass'. Those who arrive in the community and stay long enough to be more than just casual passers through, but who have not been present long enough to get themselves a name (such as me at one point in my fieldwork), must go through a period of having this name applied to them (including face-to-face). The name signals a lack of full legitimacy as a member of Arapaho society; all researchers who maintain a long-term presence in the community do eventually receive Arapaho personal names.

There are again restrictions on the usage of this teasing name. It was only older men who had already gotten to know me at least minimally who used this term toward me, a younger man, and the ones who used it the most were the ones most closely associated with me—and eventually the ones who actually named me 'High Eagle', illustrating a general lesson of Arapaho life: closeness and involvement in a specific family network bring both much respect and support and much teasing, as two sides of the same coin. Most interestingly, the teasing name signals a liminal status in Arapaho society: true outsiders receive no name, while potential insiders are the ones who are called *Woo3tineet*—while insulting, the name is a signal that one now *should* have a name and has earned that right. Other situations where the name is used can be among older men themselves—if, for example, a grandfather gives his name away to a grandson, his close friends will jump on the opportunity to apply this epithet until he announces a new name for himself. It can also be used from grandparents to grandchildren in a teasing way (while also suggesting that the young person should hurry up and ask for a real name). This is normally within gender lines.

I have seen this occur once between a grandfather and granddaughter, but some older women raised disapproving eyebrows at this usage.

Joking with names is reported to have occurred in the past much as in the present, and under roughly the same conditions, so there is a good deal of continuity in both practice and ideology here. Of course now only a few people have both the personal relationships and the command of Arapaho to engage in this behavior successfully, so it has the added function of indexing one's linguistic capital. The practice is interesting because it shows that the ideology of personal names as forms of prayer and as vehicles of power is not in force at all times. Rather, it seems to be in force especially whenever someone is ill or suffering misfortune—one does not joke about a person's name in this situation, as this is when the name's power component is most needed. It also seems to be in force when potential transfers of power are at stake in a relationship: in other words, in relation to those older than oneself or to whom respect is due, or in any ceremonial context. When no such potential transfers are at stake—outside ceremonies, with equals, or with those younger than oneself—then joking with names is allowable, provided that the two parties have a close relationship. Such joking in fact indexes that relationship, and secondarily creates a sense of good feeling among all present, since it indirectly indexes the quality of solidarity generally, in a way similar to what Basso (1979) describes for mock insults between good friends among the Western Apache. More commonly, however, joking occurs with nicknames since these carry no power, and thus there is little threat to either the name or its bearer in joking in this way.

Outside of the joking context, the function of Arapaho personal names in everyday discourse has changed markedly over time. Due to language shift, they have gone from being an unmarked form of personal address and person reference to being a quite marked form. The names have acquired several new indexical functions in discourse. These include AC membership for the user; respect directed to the addressee or referent; indexing of a relationship with the older addressee or referent who is close enough for the user to know the person's Arapaho name; linguistic capital via display of the ability to pronounce the name correctly; and establishment of the AC COP as the relevant interaction framework generally, and Arapaho-language saliency more particularly as relevant within that broader framework.

As the preceding examples also show, fluent speakers of Arapaho typically use English names, even when speaking Arapaho, while it is nonfluent speakers (who use primarily English) who often switch to Arapaho for personal names.

Nonfluent speakers' usage of personal names reflects the increasing "nominalization" of endangered languages that was discussed in the introduction: a few salient nouns and especially names may be the only words regularly used by some younger people. On the other hand, the elders' lack of usage of Arapaho names seems all the more curious since personal names are one of the most salient areas of the Arapaho language today, in terms of the amount of interest in them, desire for them, and discussion of them. The names are indeed heavily *discussed* and used in this context, and people make great efforts to report on others' names, as will be clear in the following section. However, native speakers very rarely actually *use* the names in simple personal address or person reference, even when speaking Arapaho (the master-apprentice pair above being a notable exception), outside of highly Arapaho-salient and formal contexts. The key point here is that Arapaho-language personal names and the narratives surrounding them—even more than the language generally—have become much more a form of elder *knowledge* and much less a vehicle for social work, especially outside the AC COP.

The elder-knowledge component is in some ways consistent with past practice, but language loss has heightened this component of personal names further. The decline in utility as a vehicle for social work is much more discontinuous with past practice. There is also a feedback loop at work here: rarity of actual usage serves to make the knowledge ever harder to come by and thus more valuable, while anything considered high-value knowledge has a tendency not to be deployed very often, especially in everyday contexts, and not to be used casually. Therefore for members of AC, the ideology of personal names has undergone several radical shifts. In this context, the insistence on *using* the names in daily discourse, especially by native speakers, must be understood as a practice of resistance to reideologizing personal names as a form of knowledge.

TALKING ABOUT NAMES

Based on the preceding discussion, it should not be surprising that talking about names is a common Arapaho activity, especially among older people.[10] Since the symbolic capital of a name is linked to its history, previous possessors, the person who gave it, and the manner and time in which it was given, in traditional AC it is important to share this information widely and accurately with family and acquaintances. In a sense, names could be compared to gift objects in traditional gift exchanges, as understood in anthropology generally through gift theory (Godbout 1998; Godelier 1999; A. Weiner 1992). It is not the literal semantic content of the name that matters any more than it is the "market" value of gifts that matters. Rather, highly valued symbolic gifts (such as in the Melanesian Kula Ring described by Malinowski) have specific individual histories attached to them, including a history of who has owned the object in the past. And when such objects are given, they create a ritual relationship between giver and receiver and are imbued with the personality and reputation of the giver as well as the receiver. Just as medieval charters recorded important gift ceremonies, Arapaho discourse and oral tradition preserves the memory of the giving of names and of the names' symbolic capital more generally. A name undiscussed, unrecounted, or misunderstood risks losing both symbolic capital and power—that is, it risks losing its story.

One example involves two older men, who had the following exchange:

LARRY: Yeah. Axe Brown. They were known as Old Hawks. Pete Brown and Boniface . . .

JAMES: Ho'noox.
Axe.

LARRY: Ho'noox, Axe Brown, [and there was his brother] Vincent Brown. Oh Andrew Brown, and the last one Vincent Brown. Five boys. They used to call them Old Hawks. But I don't know where they got this Lone Bear [as the current family last name]. But I do know this Pete Brown, the oldest, his name, his Indian name was Lone Bear. Then these boys was ahh. . . .

JAMES: Records burned [maybe].

LARRY: Yeah.

JAMES: Be'enoo Beh'ei.
Old Man Turtle.

LARRY: Be'enoo Beh'ei was Axe Brown . . . [no, I mean] Vincent Brown. Ho'noox [was Axe Brown]. Uhhh, boh'ooohoox, Mountain Lion, nehe' Boniface [*boh'ooo'* = 'badger', speaker momentarily mistranslates it as 'mountain lion'].

JAMES: huh!

LARRY: Ceece'eseihi3i'. Badger. . . .
They were all different. Badger. . . .

(ELAR 59f)

Neither of the speakers is closely related to the family in question, so this is purely a case of two older men (both in their eighties at the time, good friends, but unrelated) sharing cultural capital. The conversation also shows that even quite long ago in the twentieth century, people were commonly known by their English names, so that knowing someone's Arapaho name became a form of cultural capital once the name was not the most commonly used one. It was also fairly common for an individual to become known by the English translation of their Arapaho name, as with Axe Brown. In addition, personal names of family patriarchs ("Lone Bear") often became assigned as a family name. Like kinship relations, Arapaho personal and family name histories can become quite confusing over time without continual repetition and checking.

Later in the same conversation, the same two men continued:

LARRY: Cebii'ouh. That was Francis Brown's brother. Half-brother. Uhh, Dick Brown's Brother. They used to call him Charley. The Mexicans used to call him *chivato* ['kid, young goat']. That's [a] Mexican name. When you say that, *chivato*, old lady didn't know how to say it, Jenny Brown. Couldn't say, couldn't say Charley, or *chivato*. So she, he, she just called him Cebii'ouh.

JAMES: Ohhh.

LARRY: And that's where this name started. Old lady died, and that [other] old lady, Morris Whiteplume's old lady was Wosookuteih. Crooked Teeth. [She] kind of picked him up. Cebii'ouh. Took him to Ethete.

JAMES: That was Wosookuteih ['Crooked/Bad Teeth'].

LARRY: Yeah.

JAMES: Married to Tyler?

LARRY: No, she was married to Morris Whiteplume.

JAMES: Ohhh.

LARRY: But anyway, that's where CebeiP, Cebii'ouh was raised, by that old lady Wosookuteih.

JAMES: Ohhh.

(ELAR 60c)

Part of the humor of this anecdote is that *cebii'ouh* means 'little one just born'. Note the concern with providing the proper Arapaho personal name for people when they are mentioned, and in the context of language loss, making sure that the proper meaning is noted. And note finally the preference in this case for referring to the person by using that name, even when the rest of the conversation is in English. This kind of historical knowledge of personal names is a key form of social capital in the community since it is related to the ability to bestow names. When cultural capital is at stake, the name is in Arapaho even when the conversation is in English, whereas earlier we saw that in everyday conversation, one's personal name is typically in English even when the rest of the conversation is in Arapaho.

Women are equally able to bestow personal names and are equally interested in this topic. The following was a conversation recorded while a group of Arapaho-speaking women were cooking. Linda is telling the other women, Jane and Alice, about how her grandson was given his name by a relative who remembered the child's great-grandfather (only "grandfather" is used by most Arapahos):

LINDA: I think he named him after [our grandfather] [p.n. in English].
Now if I can remember that name. Elk, I think it was elk.

JANE: Yeah, after so many generations, we have fallbacks [to the names of people in previous generations].

LINDA: Yeah.

JANE: From way back.

...

LINDA: "Yeheihoo, henee3neenee'eenee3ookut hibesiiwoho'."
"Gee, he really has eyes just like his grandfather" [the name-giver said].
Wox Nookeih.
White Bear [was his grandfather] [wox = 'bear'; hiwoxuu = 'elk'].
'ii, what was his name?
Oh golly, what [exactly] was his name?
Do you remember my grandfather's name? NookuuP, white something. White Elk I think it was.

JANE: Uhm.

LINDA: He named him. "Nih'eenei3ookut nebesiibeh'inoo," he said.
He named him. "That's what kind of eyes our grandfather had," he said.
Yeah, nonoocoo'. Hiwoxuu Nookeih, yeah, that's what his name was.
Yeah, it is white. White Elk, yeah, that's what his name was.

ALICE: Ohhh yeah!

LINDA: Hiwoxuu Nookeih.
White Elk.

ALICE: Yeah.

LINDA: Neihnee'eesih'oobe, yeah.
That's what we must have named him, yeah.

(ELAR 63f)

Later in the conversation, the same two women are speaking, but now it is Jane who takes the lead, as she is contemplating giving a name:

JANE: Uhh niibeetP uhh nehe' [personal name in English], hoono' hoowP, I've been trying to think of the name.
Uhh, I want to, uhh this [p.n.], I have not yet, I've been trying to think of the name.
'oh nih'iibeetbiino' [p.n. in English]'s name. 'oh neihoowoe'in he'iitP
And I wanted to give him [p.n.]'s name. But I don't know what it was,
You know I mean, hee'inowoo, but uhh, niibeetP uhh bebiise'inowoo.
You know I mean, I know it, but uhh, I want to, uhh, know it properly.

LINDA: Yeah.

JANE: Noko3 Be'eih. Nooko3 Be'eih. Ne'nii'P uhh, nee'eesih'it, [personal name in English].
Red ??. Red ??. That's what, uhh, that's what [p.n.] is named.

LINDA: You know they used to call that morning star nookoox [morning star].

JANE: Uhh-huh.

LINDA: "Nookoox" nih'ii3oo3i', probably 'cause it was like a cross.
"Morning Star/Cross" they called it, probably 'cause it was like a cross.

JANE: Yeah.

LINDA: Maybe that's what it was.

JANE: Yeah, Nookoox Be'eih.
Red Morning Star/Red Cross.
. . .
I can't remember now. But I'm still trying to find out for sure.

(ELAR 63f)

Although the conversation continues for a good while after this point, with Linda sharing cultural information about the morning star, Jane remains unsure about the exact Arapaho form and meaning of the name that interests her. While she is interested in Linda's information, she is not willing to accept it as "sure" information about the particular name in question. Without such information, she cannot formally give the name to anyone.

Personal names are a key area of community documentation interest among the Northern Arapaho as well. Ron, one of the two cochairmen of the Northern Arapaho Language and Culture Commission, collected a great deal of language information, including hundreds of Arapaho personal names, with correct spelling and translation and the identity of the owner. He said that this is the topic about which he was contacted most often by members of the community.

CONTESTATION AND NAME GIVING AT THE TURN OF THE TWENTY-FIRST CENTURY: THE POWER OF ELDERS

The practices and beliefs described above are not without their internal inconsistencies, as with any set of social practices. The language ideology of "name power," at its most extreme, suggests that names are independent agents, with power literally embedded in their linguistic form (though they require oral performance of the name's historic narrative and meaning in order to maintain that power).[11] Conversely, the understanding of names as symbolic objects that carry symbolic capital places the emphasis less on the name itself than on who gave a name, how it was given, and to whom it was given—that is to say, on the process of transfer, on the "gift" ceremony and the relationship between giver and receiver, and on the capital accrued to both in the giving process. It is the human agents in the process that are central, from this perspective. In part, this is simply a distinction between overt Arapaho descriptions of the ideology (which focus on "name power") and my description of the social processes surrounding naming, which Arapahos understand well and enact regularly but do not necessarily conceptualize in the same way as the names themselves.

In theory, if names are powerful independent agents, they should be able to be conveyed to anyone in the tribe and carry their power with them. The fact that, instead, boundaries of the extended family are typically respected in the circulation of names suggests that the power of names must be understood in part in terms of networks of kinship and extended-family reciprocity. Personal names and the processes surrounding them are constituents actively used by people for the maintenance of those social networks, and they draw their power and prestige in part from the standing of those human agents. On the other hand, people within these relationships care as much as they do about personal names in particular because of the power understood to be embedded in the names themselves, as independent sources of power. It is the exchange of highly salient social capital that always brings issues of proper relationships most to the fore. In any case, the Arapaho view of personal naming corresponds closely in many ways to what David Maybury-Lewis (1984:8) says for central Brazilian peoples:

> Names and the principles of their transmission among Central Brazilian peoples form an integral part of their theories concerning the ideal social order. The Central Brazilians are constantly struggling to prevent this ideal order from being contaminated and undermined.

It is the transmission process, as much as the names themselves, that deserves the closest scrutiny, and in fact it is in this domain that struggles over Arapaho social order are most evident.

Whether one is focused on names themselves or on their transmission, it is clear that name giving is closely tied to the MTH and social power of older men and women. This includes the social power to determine membership and positioning of younger individuals within extended units of friends and relations. The agreement to give a name, as well as the exact name given, can be an important symbol of an individual's place within networks of reciprocity. Indeed, one can occasionally hear younger people who have recently acquired a name complain that they have been given an excessively common or uninteresting name by an elder. The explicit reason for the complaint is that the elder seems not to have thought carefully enough about the name. Underlying this complaint is a sense of being disrespected or undervalued by the elder, who has not thought enough of *the person* generally. MTH power is also involved, as with other ceremonial roles where the elder is the one who acts as "gatekeeper" or guardian of access to that power. A common or uninteresting name may also be a less powerful name. In both social and MTH cases, names and name giving are part of a hierarchical system of vertical exchanges that works to reinforce the standing of elders.

In the context of language loss, that standing has actually greatly increased in some regards, since there are far fewer individuals who can be trusted to give proper Arapaho names, and the knowledge of the native speakers is more and more valued. Indeed, one can now hear complaints that certain elders are asking for what is considered exorbitant payment in exchange for giving names (hundreds of dollars). Other elders criticize this practice, saying that one should simply accept whatever the individual or family can afford and that one should not be in the name-giving practice for profit. Of course, if the names are truly as powerful as many people believe, then the former elders would argue (though certainly not in my specific terms here) that the economic capital to the giver should reflect the symbolic capital of the name.

In general, the personal naming practices and ideologies described above continue in force most strongly within the AC COP, with many adherents among the Pan-Indian COP as well. Within AC especially, personal-name giving is an arena where the relative social power and prestige of the remaining Arapaho-speaking elders has increased markedly over the last decades, as a result of the continuity of ideology and practice, along with parallel language loss. For obvious reasons, the ideology of the independent power and agency of personal names appeals less to many of these individuals than the ideology whereby the proper giving of the name, by the proper person, is central to activating the power of the name.

RECENT CHANGES

PHONOLOGICAL RIGIDIFICATION

As more and more people lack knowledge of Arapaho, there are growing numbers of cases in which people become confused about their names and forget or mispronounce them. Indeed, a new genre of Arapaho anecdotal narrative is the "garbled name" story. Many of these simply remark on the failure to get the name correct, but some recount amusing results. The following remarks began by recounting a name giving and then followed up with the garbling:

LINDA: "Nehe' heiniisih'oonin," nih'iit.
"This is what we have named him," he said.
Nii'eihii 3i'ok, I think, Sitting Eagle.
Sitting Eagle, I think, Sitting Eagle.
JANE: Oh yeah, yeah.
LINDA: Nii'eihii 3i'ok.
Sitting Eagle.

>Uhh, we asked him, uhh, what's your Indian name?
>"Hey that buck," nih'iit.
>*"Hey that buck," he said.*
>*(laughter)*
>You know, when they're just learning to talk, kookon niinihiit,
>*You know, when they're just learning to talk, a person says just anything,*
>whatever it sounded like [in English].
>
>(ELAR 63b)

Of course, more mature individuals do try to verify the correct Arapaho version of their names. But in the context of language shift, Arapaho linguistic conservatism with regard to personal names is now producing a number of interesting changes. Now that many nonspeakers do not actually understand the internal semantics and grammar of their own names, there is a tendency for names to become garbled in pronunciation in Arapaho as well as in English. Thus a name like *Hisei Be'eih* 'Red Woman' can come to be pronounced as *Sebeih*.[12] In other words, in the absence of Arapaho-language competence, the *linguistic* conservatism fails to function effectively, and rapid change can occur in the name. (I should note in passing that Arapaho personal names are often shortened in everyday usage by native speakers, in the same way that "Andrew" is shortened to "Andy" in English, but when this is done in Arapaho, the name remains meaningful.[13]) On the other hand, the generalized *ideological* conservatism surrounding personal names remains in full force for at least some people. As a result, whatever form a name may have come to have over (recent) time can become truly "frozen" in place—at least for the current owner in the present. In other words, a nonspeaker of the language whose name has come to be pronounced *Sebeih* will often strongly resist efforts by others aware of the actual name to correct the pronunciation, responding, "That's the way it was told to me." Even fluent speakers now largely accede to this attitude, out of an extension of an older attitude that one should not speculate on names. Ron, the language and culture commissioner who made a habit of collecting as many personal names as possible, mentioned to me several times that so-and-so's name did not seem to make sense and that there was "something missing there" in the pronunciation, but he recorded the name as reported to him by the speaker and did not attempt to correct him or her.

In summary, the *linguistic results* of Arapaho ideological conservatism with regard to personal names have changed even as the underlying sociocultural ideology has remained in force: when full language knowledge was shared by all, the result of this ideology was *morphosyntactic* conservatism; now that this knowledge is being lost, the result is *phonological* conservatism, even when that conservatism involves radical loss of morphosyntactic (and semantic) information. This is a case of discontinuity between ideology and practice of the type discussed in the introduction, and it is seen with place names as well and is similar to the unexpected results that arose when the cultural metaphor of center and periphery was extended to White towns, as seen in chapter 3. As a result, instead of a productive indexical *structure* for personal names being maintained, *individual frozen forms* may end up being maintained, thus converting the naming system into a collection of nontransparent forms—ironically much like Anglo-American names. Thus we see a very interesting case where language shift causes a shift in the linguistic manner in which a language ideology is expressed, even while the ideology itself remains intact. And this ideology itself—in the form of fluent speakers' refusal to correct problematic names—is now ironically contributing to more and more potential linguistic change in the names. Moreover, further misuse, misinterpretation, or mispronunciation may violate the original power and sanctity of the form, diminishing or destroying its effectiveness. The process very strongly resembles the one described more generally for Kaska by Barbra Meek (2010): in an effort to maintain respect for elders, Kaska speakers are avoiding speaking Kaska because, in the context of language shift, Kaska is now seen as the prerogative of those elders. Thus the conservative cultural ideology of respect actually exacerbates cultural change in the form of loss of the language, one of the key elements of the traditional culture.

IDEOLOGICAL SHIFT AND "HOLLYWOOD" NAMES

For other members of contemporary Arapaho society, however, the ideology of personal names is undergoing major changes. In particular, many younger people, especially from less traditional families (i.e., more Pan-Indian and Politico-Tribal affiliated), lack a name and seek out elders to give them one, often when they are in their teens or twenties. But they sometimes now reject names that elders suggest to them, especially if they do not like the meaning of the name (as noted above, names such as "Crooked Teeth" are fairly common in Arapaho). Gary, who was often called on to give names, kept a list of around 150 traditional names, divided by gender. He complained to me, however, that the young people often did not want the names that he tried to give them but instead wanted "fancy" names, including names that originated in English and then had to be translated into Arapaho as new creations. Another fluent speaker complained that "the young people today want Hollywood names, like Singing Star Woman and names like that." This complaint explicitly about "Hollywood names" is something I have heard echoed by several older Arapaho speakers.

Shifts in name preference have been reported for others, such as the Palokhi Karen (Rajah 2010). In that case, while older personal names are often based on events, newer ones may often be based on euphony or on direct references to exemplary qualities. These types of shifts can often be linked to changing norms of gender, age, and tribal identities. A similar situation can be detected for the Northern Arapaho. It appears that the young people in question simply no longer think of personal names in terms of MTH power. The name itself does not necessarily need to originate with an elder, nor does it have to have any traditional linguistic or sociocultural capital associated with it. It does not need a history or a story. Rather, the name serves as an index of both Arapaho and Native American identity, in the context of the Politico-Tribal and Pan-Indian COPs, as well as for those in AC who are less tightly bound to traditional ideologies. It needs to be in Arapaho to meet the first criterion of Arapaho identity, and its specific semantic content needs to relate to the most positive images of evolving Native America that are available to young people on reservations. Otherwise, many young people in this subset have no knowledge of Arapaho and often little interest in the language overall, as they are not affiliated with the AC COP. In some cases, the name may be literally the only word they know in the language, although there is a great deal of variability in this regard. Moreover, these young people and their friends may never actually use the name, except perhaps in very rare formal circumstances. The name is effectively a reified possession rather than a vehicle for interaction. In some cases, people ask, "Do you have an Arapaho name?" and, if the person says yes, that can be the end of the exchange (although more normally "What is it?" and "Who gave it to you?" would be follow-up questions).

The elders' invocation of Hollywood stereotypes is interesting in that it suggests that elements of younger Native Americans' own models of identity are borrowed in part from largely non-Indian American media. In other words, the name used to establish Indian identity, as opposed to Euro-American identity, is ironically a product at least in part of Euro-American communities of practice. But the main force of their criticism seems to be more about a perceived "inauthenticity" of such names, with "authenticity" understood as providing links to MTH power. Bill noted that the power of a name is efficacious only if the name is given in the traditional ceremonial manner: his grandmother suggested his name to a group of elders, one of whom said *beeseyeinoo* 'I approve/endorse it'. The same word is used for endorsing a treaty. The grandmother felt that she could not give the name herself in an efficacious manner, but once the older men gave it, she said to them, "And I really thank you. I thank you for what you done for [my] grandson here. Pass that name on to him, so that name can be with him" (Wiles 2002:6). Bill himself then added, "And just the way I heard them old fellows talk, just the way that old fellow prayed, it's still with that name. It's still with that name" (Wiles 2002:8). Clearly without this ceremonial procedure, the power cannot "be with" the name, and the name as a source of power cannot "be with" the individual. And clearly the ideology of the power of names is linked within Arapaho culture to the power position of the elders who operationalize that power. Here we can see a clear link forged between the concept of names as independent power agents and the somewhat different conception of names as symbolic elements manipulated through the agency of elders and drawing their power in part from them—in particular, through proper means of transmission, as well as proper deployment in discourse and ceremony.

This same ideology likely controlled the use and oral tradition around place names in the nineteenth century and, as we have seen, leads some elders to question the efficacy and legitimacy of symbolic-resemblance place names today since these names lack the stories—and the elders with the authority to tell those stories—to be properly operationalized. One of these elders, speaking of personal names this time, said to me that if one does not have a "real" Arapaho name, then there is "nothing to look forward to" and "nothing to live up to." The "real" personal name is conceptualized as a model for one's life course (based on the model provided by the life of the previous holder of the name), as well as a vehicle that "potentiates" a person (Bodenhorn 2006:150). In this case, the full power of the name is only incipient and dependent on being actualized through a proper life trajectory. That trajectory is of course one that would be highly conservative in many ways, reenacting the life pathway of the earlier elder from the past who first possessed the name—in other words, following the prototypes of the AC COP. From this point of view, not only does the power of personal names come *from* an elder giver, but it is only fully attainable if the recipient seeks to *become* such an elder in the future and follows the models that the elder has set. The MTH power of the name and the power of elders in the community are completely inseparable in this conceptualization. Furthermore, this view of the role of the personal name sets up a lifelong relationship of reciprocity between the name holder and the elder/ancestor who previously held the name: as the name holder honors the path and model of the name, he or she receives increasing power from the name and the ancestor but also gives the name itself increasing power in actualizing its potential and, more symbolically, renders more and more power to the ancestor. As seen in the previous chapter, place names, especially symbolic-resemblance names, are a key nexus of power and reciprocity with the land. Personal names, particularly "real" ones, are a key nexus of power and reciprocity with the past and ancestors. And both types of names are mediated by the power of elders, who give them, use them, and tell their stories, thus guarding their efficacy as power nexuses. Conversely, just as AC elders rejected certain types of place names, they reject certain types of personal names, and for exactly the same reasons—the names do not engage with the proper ideology of knowledge and MTH power, and the names are not given within the proper form of reciprocal respect relationship.

We can also think back to the tribally specific nature of homelanding discussed in the previous chapter, which links to the power needed to dwell in the landscape, as opposed to Pan-Indian or at least Pan-Plains models of place naming, which do not. In the same way, the "Hollywood" epithet used by elders concerning some personal names can be understood as a version of "non-Arapaho," in that the names resonate with Pan-Indian or even White models of identity and belonging, rather than with AC models. For elders, the names are seen as being *in* the Arapaho language but not *of* AC value systems, in terms of the deeper historical and ideological positions and social relationships that are embedded in and around them. Bill said (already cited once in the introduction), "A lot of times they just, they just want a name, you know (laughs). 'Can you give me [an] Indian name?' you know, like that (laughs). I said, 'wait a minute . . . there's more to it . . . But you kids here, you probably don't know that. You just want an Indian name'" (Wiles 2002:8). While the word *Indian* can often stand in for *Arapaho* in Arapaho English, in this case, the idea of an "Indian name" is clearly devalued. Ignorance and an "Indian name" are contrasted with traditional AC values and a true Arapaho name.

In sum, the elders see the desires of the younger people as threatening their role as name givers, as well as their role as holders, transmitters, and managers of cultural knowledge generally and knowledge of Arapaho names and their history more specifically. We could say that young people's desire for charismatic "Hollywood" names reflects a decline in both the language ideology of "name power" and elders' association with this power, and also a decline in the young people's willingness to engage in patterns of reciprocity that tend to privilege elders and their manipulation of symbolic capital.

Note that, ironically, younger people who pursue these "Hollywood" names tend to be strongly interested in transparency of meaning since it is the literal semantic content of the name that is centrally important. Thus whereas in the case of younger affiliates of the AC COP, we saw continuity of language ideology leading to phonological rigidity at the expense of semantic transparency, in the case of the Pan-Indian and Politico-Tribal COPs, there is a change in language ideology, with names being associated with identity rather than MTH power, and this leads to concern with semantic clarity (though not necessarily phonological accuracy—indeed, such names are often reported only in their English gloss, not the Arapaho version).

As with place naming, the personal naming concerns of many young people are now oriented horizontally or laterally toward their peers, within a broader Pan-Indian setting where affiliation with "Indian" identity as indexed via an Indian name is a central concern. They are also oriented laterally toward Euro-Americans, from whom they seek to differentiate themselves. Orientation toward the elders is for many of them much less strong. There is a shared cultural resource—personal naming in Arapaho—that is quite salient within the community. But the ideology that drives the practice, at least in these cases of "Hollywood" names, seems clearly not to be shared with the elders among non-AC COP affiliates. The gulf between the ideologies seems so broad that it points to entirely different models of social relations, power, authority, agency, and distribution of resources—clearly completely different communities of practice. Yet *within* each COP, the logic of the ideologies and practices around personal naming is quite understandable and sensible.

ELDERS TALK BACK; YOUTH RESPOND

Not all young people share the desire for "Hollywood" names, however. Others, more AC oriented, value traditional Arapaho names and see access to both social and MTH power as crucially linked to traditional tribalism and names with a deep and powerful tribal connection. Indeed, some of these younger people actually complain when an elder gives them a name that seems too common or too "Hollywoodish," as noted above. What is occurring today among younger Arapahos is a complex negotiation of identity in relation to elders, family and clan, tribal identity, Pan-Indian identity, the relevance and force of history in their lives, and the location and nature of power and agency in their existence. Every one of these issues can be expressed in the process of obtaining, keeping, changing, pronouncing, and glossing one's personal name within Arapaho society. Thus it is not surprising that naming ceremonies remain important traditional ceremonial activities in Arapaho society and that Ron's list of personal names and their meanings was—among his many similar efforts with place names, old vocabulary items, stories, and prayers—his "best seller" and most requested item.

At the same time, there is a clear recognition of the contested nature of the naming ceremony. I attended an official naming ceremony in May 2006. It was held in the gym of Wyoming Indian High School as an adjunct event to a powwow going on there, and it was conducted by a widely respected, Arapaho-speaking man, Burton Hutchinson (real name; see Wiles 2011:138–41). Immediately after he offered a prayer in Arapaho, Hutchinson spoke in English about the importance of such ceremonies. He noted that the ceremony was being done on this particular day in connection with an event (the powwow) especially popular with younger people in order to encourage more young families to hold the naming ceremony. Hutchinson then made a similar series of remarks (again in English) as he began the ceremony. He spent a good deal of time talking about how the ceremony would be done and the significance of the different parts—clearly feeling that his audience needed such information. He stressed the importance of the ceremony within Arapaho culture and made a particular point of noting that he had received official authorization to conduct such ceremonies—in this case from Ben Friday Sr. (real name), who passed away in the 1990s. This remark was targeted to audience members who might be tempted to simply "take" a name in a nonceremonial way and suggested the inefficacy of such a procedure. Indeed, in talking to me, one of Ben Friday Sr.'s daughters said on a different occasion that children often "take" things today without proper authorization, "taking" contrasting clearly with "giving" and "receiving." Hutchinson's remark also targeted older individuals who might be tempted to conduct a version of the official ceremony but without full authorization to do so—again, the implied claim was that names received in such a way would not be efficacious. He went on to stress that a properly given Arapaho-language name was symbolic of the larger value of Arapaho language in religious and ceremonial contexts. Appropriately, given these claims, he went on to conduct the actual naming ceremony entirely in Arapaho, and he received several gifts from parents and relatives once it was concluded.[14]

The use of Arapaho, while efficacious ceremonially, also served performatively to underline another necessity of proper naming ceremonies—an Arapaho speaker. A series of metalevel claims was embedded in the ceremony, about the power of names, the power of the Arapaho language, the power of ceremonies, and the power of proper transmission of ceremonial authority—all implicitly linked to the privileged status of elders within Arapaho society, and all implicitly recognizing the unstable and contested nature of this language ideology within contemporary Arapaho society.

LANGUAGE REVITALIZATION AND NAME REVITALIZATION

Over the last few years, there have been ongoing language revitalization efforts on both sides of the Wind River Reservation, in the communities of Ethete and Arapahoe (see Wiles 2011:102–5, 154–57). Each community has had an Arapaho-language immersion preschool. The two schools have taken fairly different approaches to teaching, however. In the Ethete school, all the teachers are fluent speakers. In the Arapahoe school and community, older fluent speakers have been paired up with younger adults in a master-apprentice approach, and the younger adults have been either assistant or primary teachers in the classrooms, backed up by the elders. There are also differences in the usage of Arapaho names. In the Ethete school, children are called by their English names, not their Arapaho names.

In the Arapahoe school, however, the apprentices (especially the most dedicated pair) consistently call each other by their Arapaho names—even when they are otherwise speaking in English. Moreover, the children in the school are often called by their Arapaho names as well. The teachers (elders and younger people in conjunction) actually assign provisional Arapaho names to some children who lack them. These behaviors in Arapahoe show an interesting mix of tradition and innovation. Obviously, using Arapaho personal names is a strong statement about Arapaho identity and its linguistic expression. Nowhere on the reservation are Arapaho personal names used more than at this school. On the other hand, giving children Arapaho names as the teachers do, in a nonofficial and informal way, is a new behavior that works outside the traditional ceremonial and extended-kin networks for naming. More fundamentally, there does not seem to be a worry that potentially ill-considered or inappropriate names could harm the children (a key part of the "power of names" language ideology). Of course the elders supplying the names are quite knowledgeable and generally careful about such possibilities. They do not assign Arapaho names on the first day they meet the children, for example, but wait to see what the children are like as individuals. Nevertheless, there is no true ceremonial thought process leading up to the names, and the behavior is seen as cavalier by some in the larger community. The teachers themselves respond by lamenting that some of the children's parents have not bothered to procure real Arapaho names for them and suggest they are making up for this lack. I have seen a similar process occur in Arapaho-language classrooms at Wind River Tribal College: there is a strong usage of Arapaho personal names and willingness to provisionally assign Arapaho names to at least some of those associated with the class who lack such names. Once again, we see a case where an effort at continuity of practice actually involves a shift or even discontinuity in the ideology of personal naming.

A somewhat similar trend involves reclaiming traditional family names, at least in their English translation. As mentioned earlier, when families arrived on the reservation in 1878, the personal name of the leader of the extended family in its English gloss (Lone Bear, Ridge Bear, Runs Behind, etc.) was often used as the family name for that group. More often, however, these glosses were further anglicized, so that the names above became "Brown," "Ridgely," and "Behan," respectively. Other strategies were followed as well, such as arbitrarily giving famous Anglo surnames to families (Vanderbilt, Shakespeare, etc.). Anglo first names were also largely randomly assigned. Refusing to use these personal and/or family names within the local Arapaho community was one key element of sociocultural resistance. Thus George Caldwell (real name), one of the last traditional Arapaho chiefs, was known to all by the name of Yellow Calf (see Wiles 2011:31–33).

More recently, members of the preceding families and others have begun changing their last names back to Lone Bear, Ridge Bear, and so forth. These changes have also generated increased storytelling (mostly in English) about the original holders of these names and their origins. Thus in this context of resistance to earlier colonial naming practices, not only names but the stories connected to them—and the relationship pathways along which these stories circulate—are being revitalized. At the same time, the names are now in English and are applied to entire families, rather than indicating a special relationship between one former bearer and one current bearer. Thus the new names continue to have an element of Euro-American-style family patriarchy associated with them, even as they resist the patriarchal relationship between Euro-American and Arapaho society that is represented by names such as Brown or Vanderbilt (see Anderson 2001a:200–223).

To me, the most interesting thing suggested by these situations is that efforts at language revitalization are always in an ambivalent relationship to language ideologies. "Traditionalists" tend to want to respect the deeper cultural and ideological framework that surrounds the language (key aspects of the "linguistic ecology," one might say [Mühlhäusler 1996]) as part of their efforts at language revitalization. Yet this very framework and ecology have led to and/or are reflective of language shift and loss. True revitalization almost by definition involves a larger ideological reframing of the language itself, its relationship to the COP, and the broader linguistic ecosystem within which it functions. In some cases, this can mean that practices are continued but that the symbolic meaning of those practices actually differs radically from in previous time periods. The respective decisions of the two immersion schools can be seen as more traditionalist (Ethete) and more innovative (Arapahoe, as well as the tribal college) in many different ways (elders only, avoiding assigning Arapaho names in Ethete vs. elder-apprentice teams, assigning Arapaho names in Arapahoe), and the two schools could be seen as two different COPs within the larger AC COP. Ironically, the "traditionalist" choice includes using English personal names, while the "innovative" choice involves using Arapaho ones.

The apparent meaning of a language practice can obviously be highly deceptive if one does not appreciate the language ideologies and ecologies that produce this usage. The respective choices in usage of personal names at the two schools reflect larger choices in maintaining or reframing ideologies within a COP. The more innovative choices by the Arapahoe school can be understood as a partial breaking up—by elders themselves—of the traditional networks of vertical reciprocity, kinship relations, and authority over MTH power that have favored elders in Arapaho society in the past, but all in the service of preserving the Arapaho language and AC more generally. This makes sense because even though elders are strongly associated with the Arapaho language, they are also now associated (by at least some younger people) with the sociocultural frameworks and ideologies connected to language shift and loss—a point made implicitly by the student discussed in chapter 1 who was resistant to elder restrictions on the "Northern Arapaho Experience." Thus elders recognize the potential resistance they face to stricter interpretations of AC—which, as we saw in chapter 3, can be both exclusionary and even terminal versions of AC in the long run. Choices in personal-name giving and taking and personal-name usage reflect the varying range of reactions on the part of younger people to the traditional status of elders: some have no interest in Arapaho names; some seek identity-oriented names, with little commitment to a relationship with the name giver; some seek traditional tribal names, often from a fluent older relative; and some seek full-fledged naming ceremonies run by "authorized" namers. As with conflicts over place names, these choices are reflective of deeper struggles over the relative agency of the young and the elders in Arapaho society, as well as over the very sources of agency and power in Arapaho life. When Arapaho speaker and Sun Dance ceremonialist John told me in October 2010 that not giving Indian names to everyone is "a big downfall for us" as a tribe, he was recognizing that personal names, their usage, and the process of their transmission are central to the social order of AC and that the Arapaho Tribe as a whole could not be identified with AC, as much as he wished it were the case.

As with place names, personal names are as much about intersubjective experience and relationships as they are about naming people or places. As sociocultural and linguistic ecologies shift, new relationships evolve, old ones disappear, and others shift their function and meaning. Personal names inevitably are transformed as well in this process, in both usage and ideology. For both personal and place names, we have seen a purist version of AC that argues for tight restrictions on the legitimacy of the names and the processes by which they are given and used. These restrictions offer a strong view of MTH power, which can be attractive to a subset of individuals; on the other hand, they risk not only separating AC from other COPs at Wind River but even splitting AC itself.

Conversely, we have seen ways in which multiple COPs can coalesce around cultural resources such that these can become at least partially shared across the COPs; in the case of place names, this involved the use of ironic, humorous, and punning type-2 place names (in Arapaho but especially in English), which showed continuity of *ideology*—at least to a certain extent—with more traditional names of this type. In the case of personal names, however, we find that it is the names themselves, in Arapaho, that become a shared *practice* across multiple COPs, even though the ideologies behind the names are variable or opposed. Although this seems puzzling at first, the answer to why the two choices are made is the same: there is a general questioning of the traditional, Arapaho-specific concept of MTH power across the COPs at Wind River. The ideology of the new type-2 place names actually breaks with the issue of MTH power, while maintaining cohesion with the broader search for cross modal correspondences in image, sound, or concept. It provides coherence within most of Arapaho society and provides resistance to Euro-American society. In the case of personal names, the traditional ideology is highly problematic for certain COPs, but the more generalized practice provides a valuable symbolic resource that can maintain continuity with the Arapaho past and thus legitimize the practice of the various COPs while also producing coherence of practice among them, as well as resistance to Euro-American society. In addition, whereas it is hard for a nonspeaker to know dozens or hundreds of Arapaho place names, it is relatively easy for him or her to remember one Arapaho personal name—one's own. Thus many Arapaho individuals are manipulating cultural resources in ways that seek out social coherence across multiple competing COPs, erect boundaries between Indian and Euro-American identities, and maintain continuity with some elements of the Arapaho past that can legitimate current practices and/or ideologies.

5

FOLK ETYMOLOGY AND LANGUAGE PURISM

INTRODUCTION: THE IMPORTANCE OF FOLK ETYMOLOGY

There is a river in southeastern Colorado, whose Arapaho name is not recorded, which the Kiowa call Xō-vāu or 'Rock River' (Meadows 2008:287). French trappers, arriving more recently, knew it as the Purgatoire (Purgatory) River. Later, Anglophone settlers decided that the name must surely be the Picketwire River, based on an adaptation of the French pronunciation to English sounds and meanings. This is a classic case of folk etymology—popular explanations for the origin and original meanings of words. It has taken years of effort by linguists, lexicographers, historians, and geographers to try to get the name corrected back to Purgatoire, but the local people of southeastern Colorado still insist today in many cases on using the term *Picketwire* when referring to the river. And why shouldn't they? After all, it is their river, running past their ranches and farms, not the river of linguists and lexicographers.

The study of folk etymology is not a very active area of contemporary linguistic anthropology. Perhaps this is because the very definition of folk etymology points to error and falsehood: explanations are called "folk etymologies" because they are wrong, from a technical linguistic perspective. If they were correct, they would simply be "etymologies," with a stamp of linguistic approval. Indeed, much work on folk etymologies—especially in the realm of place-name studies—involves attempts to correct these etymologies, which constitute a different type of purgatory for linguists and historians frustrated by blissful popular ignorance of matters multilingual.

Instead of mere ignorance, however, we should recognize that the use of "Picketwire" is an ideological gesture by the local people of southeastern Colorado, which works on several levels. First, it illustrates a continuing refusal to return to the Kiowa name of the river or to any other potential Native American name. It thereby erases a certain portion of the land's history. Second, it also erases the Spanish and/or French history of the same land. Instead, the pronunciation is an act of homelanding, not so different from the strategies we saw in chapter 3, which makes the land the property of a specific group of Anglophone settlers. It is also a gesture that shows disdain for or at least disinterest in a certain other group of Anglophones (professor types, for example, and other potential name correctors, busybodies, and do-gooders), many of whom live in places like Boulder and Denver, and whose political and economic interests often appear antithetical to those of the rural Colorado ranchers. And of course the use of the pronunciation helps identify "locals" or "insiders" and build solidarity within that community. In an important sense, "Picketwire" is not an error but is the truth of the name of this river for these Coloradoans.

Even more profoundly, the use of the term implicitly makes a claim about the nature of language itself. Language is analyzable, or it should be: it is not just sounds but deep meanings. And language is descriptive and motivated, not a series of arbitrary letters or sounds applied to places, people, things, actions, and the world. "Picketwire" does not just sound like Purgatoire—it describes the long fences of posts and barbwire running across the Colorado ranch lands, much like the river itself runs across the landscape. It advertises the ownership of the land by these rural Coloradoans and the very lifestyle through which they maintain that ownership.

The more we think about this name, the more we come to appreciate folk etymology as a powerfully creative linguistic act, deeply embedded in social, cultural, linguistic, political, and economic ideologies. It is not just a way of naming the world but a theory of how the world should be—or should have been—named. In more technical terms, it can be considered a key feature of certain communities of practice and a key indicator of language ideologies, both in the contents of the specific etymology and in the urge to pursue such etymologies generally. Were we to have the opportunity to pursue research in the Picketwire basin, we would almost certainly find that the deployment of the name in discourse is closely linked to acts of stance taking, social affiliation, and the indexing of identity.

ARAPAHO PRACTICE AND IDEOLOGIES

With a renewed appreciation of folk etymology, we can now return to the specifically Arapaho forms of this practice. Arapaho speakers, like those of any language, have a partial knowledge of the linguistically valid etymologies of the words of their language, a partial knowledge of the relationships between words. Virtually all native Arapaho speakers know that the word *woxhoox* 'horse' was formerly pronounced as *hiwoxuu-hoox*, and this latter pronunciation makes the derivation of the word from 'elk-dog' clear. But the complexity of language change through time means that while some etymologies are relatively transparent, others are obscure, controversial, or completely unknown—even to linguists and lexicographers and all the more so to the average speaker. One example from contemporary Arapaho is the name for 'sneezing medicine': *3owoxu'uno*. This word used to be pronounced *hi3owoxu'uno* and is derived from *hi3ib-i-* 'to sneeze' and *-oxu'uno* 'grasses, roots'. The underlying form is *hi3iwoxu'uno*. The shift to *hi3owoxu'uno* seems to be based on a reanalysis of *hi3ib-* as *hi3eb-*; /e/ then changes to /o/ due to vowel harmony with a following /o/ (/i/ does not), and /b/ changes to /w/ preceding an /o/. A common shift in modern Arapaho is loss of initial, unaccented /hi-/ in nouns, leading finally to *3owoxu'uno*. Meanwhile, the verb 'to sneeze' remains intact as *hi3ibi-*. While older speakers recognize the relationship between the verb *hi3ibi-* and the noun *3ow-(oxu'uno)* 'sneezing medicine', younger speakers often do not, and one proposal from a speaker was that the medicine word is related to words with the root *3owoy-* 'to pieces, crumble' because sneezing medicine breaks up the mucus in the nose.

The preceding examples illustrate several features of Arapaho folk etymologies and of common language ideologies more generally (see Mithun 1984:51–52 for remarks on Mohawk folk etymologizing; Powers 1986:5–6 on Lakota; and I. Goddard 1984:97–99 for a more general discussion). First, there is a strong commitment to the maintenance of and/or belief in the transparency of linguistic forms. As we will see in chapter 6, Arapaho speakers have largely resisted borrowing from English or other Native American languages, at least until recently, in favor of lexical extensions and redescriptions. This neologism strategy has the result of maintaining lexical transparency in the language and can be seen as complementary to the practice of folk etymology since the latter rests on the assumption of lexical transparency. Second, the commitment to such transparency means that there is actually an oral tradition among speakers of passing down etymologies for words that might otherwise risk losing transparency. The reason most speakers know that *woxhoox* comes from *hiwoxuuhoox* is that speakers actively share this information with each other, and it has often been pointed out to me as well, spontaneously. This kind of oral tradition exists not just for the sake of idle curiosity or showing off of arcane knowledge but rather as part of the deeper commitment to lexical transparency. Third, the assumption of transparency leads to active attempts to explain partially obscure forms (such as "sneezing medicine") by appealing to principles of linguistic analysis that are not that different from professional linguistic practice. In particular, the speaker above sought out morpheme-level correspondences (*3ow-/3owoy-*), which would also be motivated by real-world knowledge and practice. And finally, the assumption is always that all elements of the Arapaho lexicon are in fact Arapaho in origin (a corollary of the first point) so that the principles in the third point can in fact be applied successfully. Since this assumption is in fact largely true, most Arapaho folk etymology, unlike that seen in the Picketwire example, concerns analysis of the Arapaho language itself rather than of borrowings from other languages. For the same reason, little Arapaho folk etymology involves changing the pronunciation of existing words to make them fit native speech patterns in the way that Purgatoire was changed to Picketwire.

The "sneezing medicine" example is actually not typical of Arapaho folk etymologies in some ways, however. It arose as part of my own language-learning efforts and focuses on a word that is not particularly salient in contemporary Arapaho life. Most folk etymologies that are recounted within the community focus on highly salient lexical items, often associated with ceremony, myth, history, or Indian–Euro-American relations. These explanations are part of a larger oral tradition of such etymologies: they are widely known and discussed rather than being made up on the spur of the moment as the "sneezing medicine" one likely was (though certainly new ones are made up on a regular basis). The result is that for many important words, the folk-etymological oral tradition is as much a part of the meaning of the word as are the word's direct denotations, and these traditions are thus "true" in a sociocultural sense, even if they are perhaps "false" in a narrow technical linguistic sense.[1] The etymologies are also a central area of philosophical speculation and sometimes contestation within Arapaho life. Unlike the Picketwire example, where folk etymology appears to have been largely a gradual and unconscious process, the Arapaho version of this practice often involves overt discussion and debate and a conscious engagement with linguistic meanings. A number of highly salient words have competing folk etymologies, and the different explanations offered for words are embedded in larger differences in perspective and ideology within the community. Extensive knowledge of these etymologies, and especially the ability to convince others to accept one's own etymology, is a key component of linguistic and cultural capital in the community. Furthermore, folk etymology is used not only to analyze the internal content of words but also to explain the reasons why words were extended to new meanings. For example, the word *nih'oo3oo* means 'Trickster' and 'spider' but was extended to mean 'White Man' during the nineteenth century or earlier. This is an uncontroversial bit of linguistic history, known by all Arapahos. But the question of exactly why this word was chosen to apply to the White Man is a continuing question among Arapaho speakers, and there are multiple, institutionalized folk explanations offered to explain this conundrum—each with its own unique perspective on Arapaho–Euro-American relations.

In this chapter we will see that the practice of folk etymology among the Arapaho is all about power. On the one hand, it is a search for correspondences in language. These are understood to reveal the basic connectivity of the world, as expressed through linguistic similarity. The word for 'meat' and 'flesh' is *hoseino'*, and the reason this is the word, according to Arapahos, is because the Sun Dance or Offerings Lodge is the *hoseihoowu'*, where one gives away or sacrifices things (*hosein-* 'to sacrifice' [TI], unrelated to *hoseino'*), including one's own flesh (at least in older times when piercing was practiced or when one's fingers were given away via ceremonial amputation). The discovery and awareness of such linguistic similarity—lexical or morphemic parallelism, we might say—gives access to knowledge and understanding that is itself a form of MTH power (*no'otehiit*) embedded in both language and the MTH world that language indexes. Since this is the case, it is not surprising that many of the institutionalized folk etymologies occur in the domains of Arapaho life where *no'otehiit* is of most concern, such as the Offerings Lodge. Ritual MTH power and linguistic MTH power are intricately related in that they both are often based in correspondences of sound, image, or thought. It is sound more generally, not just linguistic sound, that can connect to power, and sound is just one field for symbolic and analogical thought (see Anderson 2001a:272, 276–77; 2013).

At the same time, the deployment of folk etymologies in discourse and society—both inside and outside of ceremony—is a form of performance closely linked to social influence and status. Debates over which etymology is the correct one likewise must be understood at least in part as contests for social influence and competing ideological positions. In summary, folk etymology is a central part of Arapaho oral tradition and linguistic practice, and it plays in social life a key role that is difficult for anyone from Euro-American societies to appreciate.

THE CASE OF THE TRICKSTER AND THE WHITE MAN

Among the most commonly etymologized words is that for Whites, with the Arapaho word being *nih'oo3oo* (see Anderson 2001a:279–81). This word originally referred to 'spider' as well as to the Trickster (a similarity also found in Cheyenne and Gros Ventre). At the same time, the word *Hihcebe' Nih'oo3oo* 'Above Trickster' was used for the Creator and was transferred to the Christian God in the late nineteenth century. Like the Cheyenne and the Gros Ventre (and the Lakota), the Arapaho transferred their word for Trickster to the White Man. When and exactly how this occurred would be interesting to know, but at this point, such a question is largely idle speculation. More interesting are the various accounts given by the Arapaho themselves about the reasons for the assignment of *nih'oo3oo* to Whites (see Powers 1986:154–59 for a discussion of similar ideas about Iktomi/spider/Trickster among the Lakota).

One common explanation given is that Whites built fences across the prairies, thus reminding the Indians of spiders weaving a web. Historically, this is highly unlikely to be the real origin of the transfer of the name, since contact with Whites, and transfer of the word *nih'oo3oo*, occurred far before any fences were built on the Great Plains. But the folk etymology indexes an underlying distinction that is pervasive in Arapaho discourse—the idea that Whites seek to take possession of land as private property and exclude traditional users, who lack a notion of private ownership of land. Even today, older Arapaho women complain about having been fenced out of especially good chokecherry patches in the recent past. Thus the etymology serves both to index and to reinforce certain salient identity distinctions between Arapahos and Whites that continue to circulate among the Arapaho.

Another very common explanation is that Whites are like the Trickster—always going too far, getting into trouble, prying into everything, seeking after powers that they should leave alone, and otherwise abusing Arapaho notions of proper individual and social ethics. This folk etymology is part of a much larger set of stereotypes elaborated around Whites. For example, the Trickster is often qualified as *hohookee* 'a crazy person'. Within the semantics of Arapaho, the word "crazy" refers not to mental states or disturbance but to antisocial behavior or, more specifically, to someone who seems to disregard the proper norms of social behavior and be unbounded by a sense of self-restraint. The Trickster is the prototype of such "craziness" in traditional Arapaho thought, and not surprisingly, the term *crazy* in this sense is now applied pervasively to the behavior of Whites. Indeed, "that crazy White guy" is a phrase one hears virtually every day, usually used in a semijoking manner. Many Arapahos would slyly point out that the phrase seems redundant. More to the point, this particular folk etymology indexes a key distinction between Whites and Arapahos in traditional Arapaho thought, but one that is fairly different in import from the stereotypes evoked by the "web of fences" etymology. While the first is primarily economic in orientation and concerns limitations on subsistence lifestyle, the second is primarily social and focuses on White-Arapaho personal interaction styles as well as stereotypes of what used to be called *ethnopsychology*.

It is very important to note that these etymologies are not mutually exclusive: the same person can invoke different ones on different occasions, deploying the one most appropriate for the context in question. To the extent that two or more Arapahos suggest alternative etymologies in the same moment, this is less a debate on which is "correct" in an academic sense than it is a debate about which is more applicable as a diagnosis of the problem with White people that one may be experiencing at the particular moment. Thus these folk etymologies must be understood as social diagnoses and social theories. The notion that both etymologies can be "true" at the same time is widely accepted—especially with regard to Whites, since the types of problems with them are endless!

Another common explanation focuses on the fact that Whites are hairier than Arapahos. The explanation relies on an underlying association with certain types of spiders and, in particular, on the analogy to *biis-nih'oo3oo* 'tarantula' (lit. 'hairy spider'). The suggestion is that Whites seemed especially hairy and were thus compared to tarantulas, so finally the general term for spider was extended to Whites. Thus Arapahos will say jokingly, "You're a spider!" or "You're a hairy spider," in English.

At the same time, the word *biis-nih'oo3oo* itself has been extended in Arapaho to mean 'monkey' (lit. 'hairy White man' in this case). Thus the folk etymology that evokes hairiness serves to indirectly index both the comparison of Whites to monkeys and that of Whites to scary spiders. It is the monkey comparison that is most salient today—a standing joke among the Arapaho is to talk about a White person as *biisnih'oo3oo*. This can be done whether the person is hairy or not, but if one happens to have a beard or even a mustache, one is almost assured to be greeted by this term, often in a purely joking way (I myself often still get this greeting from certain older men with whom I am on good terms).

This latter etymology evokes a further layer of meaning in that the term *biisnih'oo3oo* is itself a more polite, mixed-company term for monkey, with the slangier, joking term being *3o3okouhu'* 'it plays (sexually) with itself'. Thus the evocation of *biisnih'oo3oo* often carries with it the other, absent term *3o3okouhu'* and associated issues of both sexuality and institutional gender relationships (brother-sister respect versus in-law joking). In summary, a folk etymology centered on hairiness almost inevitably evokes the term *biisnih'oo3oo*, which then can evoke both the ludicrous image of a monkey (and excrementality, since monkeys like to throw their feces) and potentially aberrant sexuality/gender behavior—including the fact that Whites stereotypically are seen as enacting more transgressive and "looser" norms of gender behaviors. Of course the full panoply of associations is not activated in all contexts where such a folk etymology is used, but one can see the range of potential associations available just in this particular etymology, not to mention the other two competing etymologies for the same word.

ETYMOLOGIES IN THE CREATION STORY AND ORIGINS

While the word *nih'oo3oo* is largely one big joke, etymologically speaking, other folk etymologies are or were taken and used very seriously and are closely tied to ceremony. One excellent example is in a creation account recorded by George Dorsey and published in 1903 in his study of the Sun Dance. This is the most detailed Arapaho creation account available. Though it is in English, Dorsey includes a number of Arapaho words—in particular, words associated with folk etymologies—so these etymologies must have been pointed out explicitly during the documentation process, attesting to their importance for the consultant.

The turtle is the hero of Arapaho creation accounts, since it succeeds in bringing up mud from the bottom of the waters to allow the creation of dry land to proceed. Thus the turtle is the focus of intense symbolic associations. Some of these are visual: "His whole body shall represent the creation or earth with all things; that is to say, the markings on the back of Turtle shall represent a path, its four legs typifying the four Old Men or Watchmen . . . by its shield are represented mountain ranges and rivers" (Dorsey 1903:200). But tied in with this visual symbolism are linguistic connections: "Its legs or feet shall be somewhat red" (Dorsey 1903:200). The word for turtle is *be'enoo*, while the Arapaho root for red is *be'-*. The two are not connected etymologically, as the word *be'enoo* can be traced back to a Proto-Algonquian form **mexkenaahkwa* (Aubin 1975, entry #1285), but red is the most sacred color for many ceremonial purposes, so it makes sense to seek a connection between this color and this animal.

In addition, the turtle itself is reported as saying, "My name will mean, to cleanse the sick, to comfort the bereaved, and to paint" (Dorsey 1903:200). The word for 'paint oneself red ceremonially' is *be'i'ei-* (AI), while if one paints someone else, the word *be'enei'i-* (AI) can be used, producing an even closer resemblance to *be'enoo* 'turtle'. Dorsey then adds, "The Arapaho term for turtle is, to paint—blood-egg, or blood stain" (1903:200). The Arapaho word for 'blood egg' would be *be'i-noon*, closely resembling *be'enoo*. And the word for 'blood' is *be'*, plural *be'iwo*, closely resembling both 'red' and the initial syllable of 'turtle'.

The further implications of "blood egg" are not clear, but one of the central components of Arapaho cosmology recounts how the sun and the moon came into conflict over their wives (at their camp along the Turtle River, by the way), and eventually the sun's wife jumped onto the moon, leaving her menses on its face, still visible today. So the notion of bloodstains in relation to the turtle could have a number of connections with Arapaho myth. The account then goes on to tell of the other animals central to the creation and of their place in the Sun Dance ceremony. Then *Nih'oo3oo* arrives: "The people knew him and called him Nih'ãⁿçaⁿ, Bitter-Man, from the fact that he reached the gathering toward the last part of the creation, carrying a cane, such as a leader uses" (Dorsey 1903:203). The root for bitter is *nih'ou*, while the word for cane is *hookoto*.

Later, the account provides an explanation for the four sacred Arapaho colors and again links them etymologically to the concepts of 'red' and 'blood' epitomized in the turtle: black paint (*wo'toobe'*) linked to 'dark blood' (*wo'teen-be'*); yellow paint (*nihoonoobe'*) linked to 'growing blood' (*niii'oon-be'*); and red paint (*hinow*) linked to 'man's blood/veins' (*hinen hini'iwo*) (Dorsey 1903:204).

Obviously, the connections proposed in this passage are not dependent on any inordinate amount of resemblance with the base word in question. A single key syllable is enough to allow the connections to be made in some cases. But as stretched as some of the connections are (none are etymologically "correct" from the standpoint of historical linguistics), the passages are examples of both etymological and aural thought at their most serious. The understanding of the world put forth in this passage relies on weaving together by means of sound, key semantic components of Arapaho myth, ceremony, and ideology into a more coherent whole, centered on such key morphemes as *be'-* 'red'. From this perspective, a deep understanding of the world lies hidden but recoverable in the resonant sounds of the language and especially in their resemblance.

ANALOGICAL THOUGHT IN AC

Such an attitude fits well with Arapaho "fetishistic" attitudes toward the material world, as reported by Alfred Kroeber ([1902–7] 1983:418–54). Kroeber gives many examples where analogical thought links certain material objects to desired human powers and outcomes: If labor is difficult, the woman must grasp a smooth, slippery shell ([1902–7] 1983:453). If one wants a horse to run fast, one must attach pronghorn antelope hooves to it as amulets. If one wants to scare away ghosts, one must put a walnut around a child's neck on a string, because the base of the nut looks like a skull, and in this case, like will repel like ([1902–7] 1983:437–38). All these "fetishistic" examples rely on searching out analogies between materials and qualities of the natural world and human needs, or on what is sometimes called a *hermeneutics of correspondence*.[2] Analogy is the key in all these cases to obtaining power or "medicine," which is understood to lie embedded and hidden in the extrahuman world. Likewise, Arapaho folk-etymological thought, as presented by Dorsey, should really be thought of as *aural analogical thought*. This approach seeks analogies of sound that will offer access to power and medicine—not just conceptually or metaphorically, but literally—in the natural-world connections that the aural thought processes reveal. As such, the Arapaho creation accounts can be compared to such classics of aural mythic thought as the Hawaiian creation chant, the *Kumulipo*:

> Born is the Umaumalei eel living in the sea
> Guarded by the 'Ulei tree living on land. (203–4)
> Born is the Paku'iku'i fish living in the sea
> Guarded by the Kukui tree living on land. (207–8)

> Born is the Laumilo eel living in the sea
> Guarded by the Milo tree living on land. (213–4)
>
> (Beckwith 1951)

The turn to aural resemblance and a folk-etymological perspective in order to classify the world is thus certainly not unique to the Arapaho (see Evans 2010:22 on Australia), but it is part of what have classically been seen as fetishistic (or shamanic) attitudes (see Thompson 1997), though in fact they occur to a degree in Western philosophy as well. Pierre Bourdieu, for example, discusses the rhetoric of Heidegger and of philosophy more generally. His central point is that words are borrowed from "ordinary language" but are transfigured by appeals to etymology, aural resemblance, or "the systematic accentuation of morphological relations" in order to create a "special language," which works to distinguish philosophy from ordinary language as a special discourse. More particularly, "association by alliteration or by assonance" comes to function in lieu of other forms of reasoning in order to "bring to light a hidden relation between the signifieds or, more probably, to bring it into existence solely by virtue of the play on forms" (Bourdieu 1991:140–41). Arapaho folk-etymological thought works in exactly the same way and can be seen as a key rhetorical strategy for implementing "philosophical" thought more generally among the Northern Arapaho.

The account from Dorsey shows that Arapahos have been thinking carefully about the nature of *Nih'oo3oo*, among other topics, for quite some time using folk etymology and that this type of thought has a deep place in Arapaho culture. Such a process relies on a fundamental belief that resemblance is real, whether that resemblance is material or aural. Not only is it real, but it is powerful in the sense of the Arapaho words *beeteenoo'* 'it is holy/sacred' and *nono'o3oo'* 'it is powerful, frightful'. It also rests on a belief that revelation and power lie in spoken language and sound more than in pure inventive or speculative thought. Creatively *listening* reveals the most powerful connections.

Not surprisingly, Kroeber's field notes from 1899 and 1900 are peppered with folk etymologies: someone who is the leader or most important member of a group is *heneeteihit* 'important, influential', thus the buffalo bull (*heneecee*) is the head of the buffalo (notebook 10, p. 41); if someone has died, one says *nih-nece-'* 'he died', but the word for water is *nec*. This shows the connection between the two, for without water there is no life (notebook 6, p. 74); the cottonwood tree (*hohoot*) is so called because it is *hoohooteihit* 'not durable; awkward, clumsy' (notebook 12, pp. 4–9); the meadowlark (*cooxuceneihii*) is so named because he imitates the Comanche (*coox*) (notebook 2, p. 59); and, once again, *Nih'oo3oo* appears, this time explained as due to the fact that the spider has a slender body at the middle (based on the root *nih'oo-* 'tight'), according to Cleaver Warden (real name) (notebook 13, p. 1; this seems to be based on the practice of White women in particular wearing tight-waisted clothes); but alternately, he is so named because he is hairy and also good at making nets (*noyoot* 'net, trap' but also used for 'spiderweb'), according to Phillip Rabbit (real name) (notebook 6, p. 46). In this last case, it is a shared secondary term (*noyoot*) that links the White Man and the spider, as much as a direct resemblance within the word *Nih'oo3oo* itself, reinforcing the finding that the process of etymological thought can be quite complex and multilayered.

Ceremonial or serious philosophical folk etymologizing still goes on today. Jeffrey D. Anderson's 2001 ethnography of the Northern Arapaho contains many examples, though he does not clearly distinguish between true etymologies and folk etymologies (almost all of what he reports is folk etymology).[3] One particular problem in dealing with Arapaho field notes for anyone who is not extremely familiar with the language is the question of how to recognize folk etymologies as such. The Doris Duke Oral History Collection at the University of Oklahoma has a rich set of Arapaho notes, which contains many folk etymologies. It appears the collector did not actually know Arapaho, however, and reported many of these etymologies as technical linguistic fact. I fear that future users will take the notes at face value, leading to a good deal of potential linguistic confusion. Among the contributors to those notes, Jim Warden (real name) in particular stands out as someone who etymologized quite freely. He came up with etymologies that I have otherwise never encountered and ones that are in some cases far removed from the original words—often more so than is normally tolerated by other Arapaho speakers in actual interactive settings, in my experience. Elicitation sessions done by non-Arapahos who do not know the language likely encourage this kind of freedom on the part of speakers, and it can produce highly interesting and creative results, even perhaps bravura performances, but the results can also be highly idiosyncratic and not necessarily representative of the more institutionalized Arapaho oral tradition in this genre.

In any event, common examples from the present Northern Arapaho oral tradition include:

One's body (*beteneyooo*) is sacred (*beeteenoo'* 'it is sacred').
The buffalo bull (*heneecee*) is so called because it is the chief (*neecee*) of
  the buffalo.

A dance (*betooot*) is holy because it means "he is acting holy" (*beeto'oot*).
The crow (*houu*) is the messenger to the Creator (*houu*).[4]
The Sun Dance/Offerings Lodge (*hoseihoowu'*) is so called because in the old days one sacrificed one's meat or flesh (*hoseino'*).

As these examples make clear, folk etymologizing remains heavily centered on moral and ceremonial issues and thus shows a great deal of continuity with past practice. It is certainly not restricted to this domain, however. One amusing example involves the word *wookec* 'cow'. Officially, linguists claim that this is a rare example of an Arapaho borrowing, from Spanish *vaca*. But the Arapaho story goes as follows (paraphrased):

> One day the Arapahos were out by the Oregon Trail, watching the wagons go by. There was this one White Man who had a team of oxen. You know oxen can be pretty slow to get moving. So this man had a whip and he was whipping those oxen, and he kept saying "gee, walk, gee, walk, gee, walk." And so the Arapahos decided the name for those animals must be *wookecii* 'cows'. And that's where that word comes from.

This example illustrates that not only are folk etymologies part of the oral tradition, but a number of them have stories connected with the etymology, and those too are part of the oral tradition. And once again, we come back to White people, this time in a story that contrasts the easygoing, relaxed, bemused Arapahos watching the no doubt hot, dusty, sweaty White Man futilely straining away with his animals, trying to get somewhere as quickly as possible, always in a hurry, always angry and frustrated. The etymology, as well as its story, indirectly evokes a reference frame that is once again a theory and diagnosis of White people, and the joke cannot really be appreciated without an awareness of this common cultural reference frame (which the retelling of the etymology obviously serves to reinforce).

ETYMOLOGY, ETHNICITY, AND IDENTITY

Ethnic groups are one of the most common foci of etymologies. For example, there was previously an Arapahoan group, the Beesoowuunenno', who joined with the Arapaho proper in the nineteenth century. There are various competing etymologies for this word, which I list in order of relative frequency in the community. Pitch accent marks are included to indicate the slight differences in pronunciation:

Big lodge people < béex-óowú-unén-no' = big-lodge-man-PL
Wood lodge people < bex-óowú-unén-no' = wood-lodge-man-PL
Great Lakes people < béex-óowú-unén-no' = big-water-man-PL
Big-bellied people < béex-óoowú-unén-no' = big-belly-man-PL
All-the-lodges people < bey-óowú-unén-no' = all-lodge-man-PL

In fact, none of the proposed etymologies fit the real word from a strict linguistic standpoint. However, most of the etymologies involve attempts to associate the Beesoowuunenno' with more eastern locations or lifestyles, in connection with a modern Arapaho awareness that they are an Algonquian people who likely came from somewhere to the north and east of their current location. A general belief is that the Beesoowuunenno' were the original holders of the Sacred Pipe (which itself was part of the creation of the world) and that all Pipe Keepers until recently were part of that group. This is reflected in the etymology 'all-the-lodges people' because the Arapaho name for the overall religious system is *beyoowuu* 'all the lodges'. The deeper claim behind this etymology is that the Beesoowuunenno' are the source not only of the Sacred Pipe but of all the Arapaho religious traditions. This etymology was reported by an individual whose family has Beesoowuunenno' blood, according to the family oral tradition. It was reported in the context of a story about the origin of another sacred object, where the speaker said that the story he had told about the object's origins was itself a Beesoowuunenno' story passed down in his extended family. After the story, he clarified to me:

JOE: The ones that, that try to figure this out, you know, they have many theories, okay. Beesoowuunenno' they say ahh, the people of uhm the big waters. So we say the Great Lakes people, from the Great Lakes and what not. And then uhh, but the way that their uhh, their way is, is that all, alllll of these [ceremonial age-graded] lodges that, that, all the way from you know uhm, *ho3o'huuho'* [Star Society], *hice'eexoowu'* [Tomahawk Society], *he3owoowu'* [Dog Society], all the lodges like that, they each had a ceremony. And then when they put all of these lodges together, they called it *beesoowu'*, that's a BIG lodge. It was all the lodges combined. Today that's, that's, that's what the Sun Dance is supposed to be, supposed to represent, supposed to be. And then they, some still call it uhh *beyoowuu* [all the lodges], it means every, every, every lodge.

(ELAR 104s)

In contrast, the "Great Lakes people" etymology attempts to associate the Beesoowuunenno' with the supposed Algonquian homeland, as part of an effort to see them as the Mother Tribe of the Algonquian peoples generally (Mooney [1896] 1973:955 reports a contrasting claim that the Northern Arapaho are the Mother Tribe). Given the privileged relationship between the Arapaho and the Beesoowuunenno' described above, this would then mean that the Arapaho are the truest of Algonquian peoples, the inheritors of the traditions of the Mother Tribe. This is a claim reported by Paul Moss on several occasions in his historical narratives, such as in the story of "White Horse" (Cowell and Moss 2005a:165–209; I give only the English translation here and cite by the section numbers used in the text):

Red willow men, Great Lakes men; that [is the place] where we came from, that place where there are lakes. Algonquians; Arapaho; where our relatives are located; (26)

And this Arapaho, Arapaho, he was specially chosen. Around here the Arapahos, Arapahos, red willow [Northern Arapaho] people, he's the mother tribe of all, he's the mother tribe. (56)

Here's my uncle, Bill Shakespeare [Arapaho historian and anthropologist], that's how he found out about those things. The Arapahos were the mother tribe. He knew all that . . . around here . . . (57)

That's it. Arapahos, red willow people, that Great Lakes tribe, we migrated here, to here. Our relatives [still] live over there; they stay somewhere there, the ones there who are related to us somehow. (103)

In a discussion with another elder (with several nonfluent speakers also listening) Paul's son Ron brings up this etymology. The context is a discussion of the words for 'corn' and 'boat' and other cultural items related to the eastern woodlands. Ron then uses *nooxeihi'* 'maybe' as a polite and respectful way to suggest a topic addition:

RON: Nooxeihi' nuhu' "beesoowuunenno'," nehe'nih'ii3oo3i'.
Maybe these "beesoowuunenno'," they call them that.
Hinee cenih'iitiseeno'.
We came here from there.
"Beesoowu'," ni'iitou'u.
"Big water," they call it.
Big lake, big water. That's the Great Lakes.

JAMES: Neih'oowoe'in, hii3oobein.
I didn't know that, you're right.

RON: Yeah. thiiP, tih'iiP, cihP, huut hee3eecihnouuto'oneino' nuhu' nih'oo3oo.
They forced us out of there, to here, the Whites.
"'oh nuhu' beesoowuunenno'," nih'iit, "niinonih'inihii3i' nono'einiihi'."
"And these beesoowuunenno'," [my dad] said, "they have forgotten how to say it [correctly] in Arapaho."
Big house people.
Big house people [is what they think it means].
Nih'oo3ou'u, nih'oo3ouniihi', 'oh nih'iisinihiitooni' "beesoowuunen, beesoowuunen."
The White [researchers], in English, well they would say it [as if that's what it meant].
Neisonoo, "hoowuuni."
My father [said], "no, [that's wrong]."
"Beesoowuunenno', hinee beesoowu', nee'ee3oo', big water.
"Beesoowuunenno,' that big water, that's where [the word] is from, big water.
Great Lakes people, nenee3i'."
They were the Great Lakes people."
Nenee'. Nih'iixooxouuwooyei'onoot.
That's it. He straightened them out on that.

JAMES: Big belly.

RON: Ahh, neisonoo, neeP, "big water people,"
Ah, my father [said], "big water people,"

JAMES:	Oh yeah. Yeah, right.
RON:	"Beesoowu'" nih'iit, yeah. "Beesoowu'."
	"Big water," he said, yeah. "Big water."
JAMES:	Right, Great Lakes.
RON:	Yeah. Great Lakes people, beesoowu'.
	Yeah, Great Lakes people, big water.
JAMES:	Yeah.
RON:	Yeah, Cenihnee'eetiseeno'. Yeah.
	Yeah, that's where we came here from. Yeah.
JAMES:	Yeah. Well, I, I never understood it that way.
RON:	Yeah.

(ELAR 18a)

This sample of the conversation shows that the folk etymology is invoked by Ron in the context of a larger discussion of origins, with the Beesoowuunenno' being the key bridging ethnic group who link the Arapaho back to the Great Lakes and a broader Algonquian origin, both historically and—most crucially— etymologically. James at one points tries to invoke an alternative etymology, but Ron is very insistent on his father's proposal, which serves to suggest that the Arapaho could or should still be in the original Great Lakes area, if not for the Whites, thus denying their seemingly peripheral status (in terms of geography) among the Algonquian peoples. Note that he speaks almost entirely in Arapaho, which serves to underline his language knowledge and the legitimacy of his etymology, and he also attributes the etymology to a wiser elder of the preceding generation. In contrast, though James is fluent in Arapaho, he responds entirely in English (though he was using Arapaho in the preceding discussion of corn and boats). In this context, his English usage likely can be understood as an indication of his unwillingness to challenge the etymology. Indeed, he clearly concedes the point at the end of the discussion. He then returns to using a mix of Arapaho and English in the following segment of the conversation, which continues the discussion of early Arapaho migrations.

All these different etymologies are to some extent mutually reinforcing, reflecting a general Arapaho consensus about the special nature of this Arapahoan group in their history. But among the claims, some emphasize individual family positions more strongly,[5] others take a general tribal position,[6] and some make more sweeping claims about the status of the Arapaho than others. But they are all theories of Arapaho history and the origins of Arapaho religious practice, embedded in speculation and debates about etymology.

In passing, it is interesting to note that when people are overtly challenged with regard to a folk etymology's legitimacy, a common response is something like, "Well, the language has changed over time." In other words, sound changes have obscured original correspondences. A less common and somewhat different response is, "Well, that was probably a Beesoowuunenno' word." To put it differently, the lack of exact correspondence between two words is attributed to the fact that one of them may have come from the language of the Beesoowuunenno' originally, thus leading to dialect differences. Both responses show that the Arapaho language is not conceived of as a complete, self-contained whole, wherein all connections are to be found between concepts. Rather, it is itself part of a potential larger whole, with "power" connections to other languages or tribes. This viewpoint is clearly revealed in a discussion between two elders on their way back from Montana and a visit to the Gros Ventre tribe (who speak a language closely related to Arapaho). They were discussing what they had learned from visiting the Gros Ventres, and what the Gros Ventres had learned from the Arapahos. They were also discussing how they had a hard time understanding the Gros Ventre language:

JOE: Toonheeneetoh'uni, huut neneenino'.
Wherever [the two tribes may have been], here we are [now].
LESTER: Yeah.
JOE: HeeneetohP toh'uuni nenee3i'. . . .
Wherever they [may have been] . . .
LESTER: Uhm.
JOE: Wohei ne'P heeneihii3iihi'. . . .
Well then, from those places/times/experiences . . .
LESTER: 'oh ne'iini ce'eeneixoxonetiino'.
Then we will fill out [our knowledge] again.
JOE: Yeah.
LESTER: ToonheeP toonheesiini, 'oh nuhu' he3ebiicxooyeiniihi', toonhei'cih'iine'etiino'. . . .
However things go, after some time of separation from them, once we have lived up to some point/time . . .
'oh nuhu', nuhu' nuhu' heeneine'etii3i', 'oh heenoo heetce'eseiti3i'.
Then this, the way they live, they will eventually, necessarily speak differently.
Honouuneenee'eesoo' nooxeihi' nenee'.
That is just naturally how this is, maybe.

>   Nuhu', cihcei'soo' nuhu', tohuuce'eseitiitooni', 'oh hinee
>   hosei3iihi'. . .
>   *This, it's become different now, because people speak differently, but back
>   in the past . . .*
> JOE: Hee, hini'iitiino, nuhu' beebeet 'oh tohP, nuhu' hee3oxoneeno'.
>   *Yes, those things [are different], but just this one thing [stays the same],
>   the color of our skin.*
>
>   (ELAR 51b)

The discussion then continues, concerning the use of language in ceremonies, with this being the place where the language is most intact and most powerful, but even here, there is a feeling that something may be missing. In response, Joe suggests:

> JOE: Wohei, wohei niiyou nuh'uuno, hiteenetiitooninoo, nee'eeteecise'.
>   *Well, well here is, their language, this is where it fits into the puzzle.*
>
>   (ELAR 51b)

In other words, gaps in Arapaho understanding and even "missing" words from the language can be resolved by contact with the Gros Ventres. Similar attitudes are revealed in the widespread interest of Arapaho speakers in other Indian languages, particularly Algonquian ones. It is common for them to note that another language has words "like ours." There is also a widespread story that some lost Arapaho group went off to the north into Canada and may still speak Arapaho. In many versions of the story, a priest from Wind River actually heard speakers of this language at some event in Canada several decades ago and reported back to the Arapaho that he had understood the language of the Canadian group—but their exact identity has never been clarified. At first, non-Indians may be tempted to treat these kinds of remarks and this linguistic interest as simply linguistic curiosity. But if we take the words of the conversation above seriously, then we recognize that much more is at stake in the search for linguistic correspondences and lost connections to languages and ethnic groups. New nexuses, and new access to understanding and power, are waiting in the aural realm.

This finding helps explain better the special Arapaho interest in the etymology of ethnic names. Not surprising, given the close linguistic connection, the name of the Gros Ventre tribe is also a focus of etymology. They are called *hitóuunénno'* in Arapaho, usually understood as 'begging men' (*hitouu-nen-no'* beg-man-PL). But one family tradition—from a family associated with the Gros Ventres through marriage—suggests that the actual name is *hítounénno'* 'men who take something out of the water' (*hit-ou-nen-no'* get/take-out of water-man-PL). The reference is to a part of the creation story in which someone is called on to remove earth from the water. This version was told by a teacher at the Arapahoe Immersion School, Dave, talking to me in the classroom as he simultaneously helped young students with their work (those side remarks to the students have been edited out). The occasion of the telling was the fact that the teacher's grandson is part Gros Ventre. After the teacher talked about the grandson and his Indian name, he then added after an interruption:

DAVE: Ni'ii3oo3i' "hitouunenno'" ni'ii3oo3i'. 'oh hoowunee'eesoo.
They call them "beggar people" they call them. But that's not how it is.
Bebiisiihi' 'oh "hitounenno'," nee'P nee'eesih'i3i'.
Properly, "bringing it out of the water people" they are called.
Hitounenno', hitouyei3i'.
Bringing-it-out people, they bring things out [of the water].
Hini'iit hentou'u' nec,
At that time when water was everywhere,
teexokut. Niinou'oot.
he was sitting [on a raft]. He was floating around.
Notiihoo[3i'] nuhu' notiihP 'oh notiihooni3i cese'ehiiho nuhu' biito'owu'.
The animals were [diving down] looking for the earth.
"Nihcihbixou'oo3i'," nii3i'.
"They floated back up to the surface," they say.
Neetih'ebi3i'.
They were drowned.
Neetih'ebi3i'.
They were drowned.
Noh ne'nii'hitounoot.
And that is when [the Gros Ventre man] scooped [earth] out of the water.
Nenee3i' hitounenno'.
They are the Gros Ventres/scoopers.
HoowuuP hoowuu[ni] beggars hitouunenno'.
The Gros Ventres are not beggars.

ANDY: Oh, okay.

DAVE: Hitounenno'.
Gros Ventres/scoopers.

ANDY: Oh okay, hohou.
Oh okay, thank you.

DAVE: Yeah, yeah, "hitouno'."
Yeah, yeah, "he scooped it out of the water."

(ELAR 40a, 40b)

This example illustrates that the folk-etymologized word often comes with a complex narrative attached to explain the etymology and that it is often embedded in even more complex mythological or other types of narratives (as with Beesoowuunenno'). In this sense, folk etymologies in the oral tradition resemble etiological narratives, such as those about how the skunk got its stripes or how the bear got its short tail: complex moral and social ideology is attached to a single, salient word or natural phenomenon. This example also again shows the speaker using almost entirely Arapaho and insisting on the point until the listener clearly accedes to the claim, at which a final "yeah" seals the discussion—the successful etymologist always gets the last word.

Note finally that here as with the previous examples the etymologist invokes a competing etymology in order to resist it, even though that competing etymology has not been raised by the other person in the conversation. These examples illustrate "oppositional" folk etymologies, where someone argues against commonly held community etymologies and understandings. This type of etymology is especially fraught with problems of speaker authority and potential loss of face. The use of *nooxeihi'* 'maybe' by Ron in initiating his proposal to James reveals his awareness of this issue, as does his appeal to the knowledge of a previous generation. I once heard someone argue that the name of Denver and the South Platte River, *niinéniiniicíe*, refers to Moose River (< *hinénihii* 'moose (PL)'), whereas the more normal understanding is Tallow River (< *niinén-ii* 'tallow (PL)'). On facing doubt, he then added, "At least that's what my dad said." Oppositional etymologies are normally offered only by the most respected and knowledgeable individuals. Given the potential loss of face, one might ask why they would be proposed. One reason is the high-stakes work in both directions: convincing others of the validity of an oppositional etymology brings significant cultural capital to the etymologist, and the name of the etymologist is often attached to the etymology ("A. explained that . . .") when it is repeated later. More importantly, in both cases the etymology serves to enhance the power and prestige associated with the word being etymologized. The Beesoowuunenno' are not just "wood lodge" or "big lodge" people, but people of the Great Lakes and thus the Mother Tribe, who have bestowed that legacy to the Arapaho (including the speaker). The Gros Ventres are not "beggars" but the heroes responsible for the creation of land—and this includes the grandson of the speaker. These oppositional etymologies greatly "empower" their target word or ethnonym, those associated with this identity, and the etymologist. Mocking, disempowering etymologies do occur, but they are relatively less common and usually are taken less seriously. An example is the claim that Chief Washakie of the (traditional enemy) Shoshone tribe was so named because he was always asking the White people for whiskey but could not pronounce the word correctly. Likewise the Shoshone (*sosoni'ii* in Arapaho) are "swelled up" (*niisoneihi3i'*) from being falsely flattered by their White allies.

In contrast, one can also invoke "community" etymologies, in which there is complete consensus and one is simply drawing on that consensus for increased rhetorical or ideological effect. The ceremonial leader Richard made the following remarks to his people in English at a special Arapaho powwow in Boulder, Colorado, in 2002, as he opened the event (XXX indicates indecipherable segments, as the speaker was using a microphone with poor acoustics):

RICHARD: And one, one of the things uhh we need to try to get back is our language.
XXX create the XXX as we go.
XXX I want to say, XXX big part of our people,
they're, they're uhh, occupied with some bad things.
XXX drugs and alcohol XXX gonna go away.
XXX one of our XXX
Uhh, uhh, my, my uncle used to always tell me,
Just uhh, respect your body, it is ahh sacred.
This, this uhh heart, they call it beteneyooo [body], it's uhh, it means uhh
that this body is sacred [beeteenoo'].
And then this uhh, uhh this heart is uhh betee [heart].
It means that's holy [beeteenoo'].
And your backbone, they call it hesiicoot,
And that's, that's the same word that they use for our Sacred Pipe [hiicooo].

> So you're, you're uhh, try, try to respect yourself.
> Try to, try to be XXX, that's what he said, you know.
> Respect yourself.
> Work, work together and love one another.

In invoking three different folk etymologies, he provides a linguistic basis for seeing the body as a holy and sacred site, to be protected from the contamination of drugs and alcohol. Another elder, Ron, suggested to me at a different time that the body (*beteneyooo*) is really a "holy lodge." He drew on the connection not only to being sacred (*beeteenoo'*), but also to 'putting up a ceremonial lodge' (*yoohu-*). These etymologies all further empower the body itself and its different parts and offer a powerful behavioral rationale. And as Richard himself explicitly recognized in the speech, these kinds of etymologies are only available within the Arapaho language: the sound correspondences do not transfer to English. Thus the realm of folk etymology is a key area where language loss means a true loss of knowledge, belief, and social cohesion—Arapaho Vernacular English just will not do. Richard also implies here—and others have stated this to me explicitly—that one need not consciously know or be aware of an etymology. Rather, simply by one's knowing and speaking the language, the power that resides in the aural connections is automatically activated and acts upon the speaker and the community to empower and regulate their behavior. This is not a claim that is made for all folk etymologies: the oppositional ones, for example, seem to require overt explanation. But for uncontroversial etymologies, the overt mention is intended not to create a linkage of power through aurality but rather to point out the existing linkage, while both demonstrating the knowledge and cultural capital of the etymologist and encouraging the listeners to seek other such connections on their own.

FOLK ETYMOLOGY AND "BEING ARAPAHO"

There are also "speculative" etymologies, where there is no general community understanding—this would be the case for attempts at etymologizing on a word that has not been previously considered. And finally, there are cases of multiple etymologies existing in a kind of complementary distribution, most or all of them considered possible or acceptable. As one might imagine, the name Arapaho itself (*hinono'ei*) receives a great deal of etymologizing attention, and it is an example of a complex of multiple etymologies (see also Anderson

2001a:243–44). The word has no clear technical linguistic analysis. Some common competing suggestions include:

> 'wandering people' (*hiinon-* 'wander, roam'; *o'owuu-* 'land'; *neito'ei-* 'my relative')
> 'blue sky people' or 'sky people' or 'cloud people' (*hiinono'et* 'cloud'; *(h)ono'* 'sky')
> 'wrong rooters' (*non-* 'mistakenly, in error'; *o'-* 'break through a surface')
> 'red' or 'red willow' people, because they always use red paint (*hinow*), reinforced by the fact that Southern Arapahos call Northern Arapahos *bo'ooceinenno'* 'red willow men'

The first suggestion clearly evokes the prototypical Arapaho lifestyle of the eighteenth and nineteenth centuries. The second evokes a common Arapaho naming usage of the present time—the gym/community hall at Ethete is known as "Blue Sky Hall," for example, and the tribal higher education office is "Sky People Higher Education." The third suggestion refers to the story of the "Porcupine and the Woman Who Fell from the Sky" (see Cowell, C'Hair, and Moss 2014). This story is a quasi-creation narrative, featuring a porcupine (thus evoking sacred quillwork) who also turns out to be a star, the act of digging for wild turnips (thus evoking women's food gathering and the most important wild root plant on the Great Plains), and the origins of the culture hero Found-in-the-Grass, as well as versions of the story of the sun versus the moon and their jealous wives (referred to earlier in this chapter in the discussion of the "blood egg" and women's menses). The terms 'sky' and 'cloud' people evoke this and related narratives as well. The fourth etymology draws both on an existing ethnonym used by the Southern Arapaho and on a connection to the most sacred of all ceremonial paint colors for the Arapaho, red (see Dorsey's creation account, discussed earlier in this chapter). All the etymologies tie the Arapahos directly or indirectly to key mythological—or better, cosmological—narratives of the Plains Indians.

The exact etymology one proposes will often depend on the context and goals of the interaction. In the following, the two older men already cited above in relation to the Beesoowuunenno' are again talking. The first of them invokes a common etymology for the word 'Indian', and the second then invokes a second one to reinforce the general claims being made, in an act of affiliation:

JAMES: Well [the old-time Arapahos] done a lot of traveling and moving around.

RON: Yeah.
JAMES: When they had hunting problems and uh, uh, pressure and war problems you know, they moved on. I think the Arapaho word is, is . . . moving people, 3owo3neniteeno'.
is . . . moving people, Indians, Indians. [lit. 'upright people']
Hinono'ei.
Arapaho [were 'upright people'].
RON: Uhm-hmm. Nihii, nehe' nihii, Jim Warden [real name], keihcee'inonoo?
Uhh, this uhh, Jim Warden, did you know him?
JAMES: heeyou?
What?
RON: Jim Warden.
JAMES: Hoowuuni.
No.
RON: Yeah. Noowunen.
Yeah. Southern Arapaho.
NiiP niisP heeyowuuni biiceiniisiis nihno'useet.
Every June he would come here.
Nih'iiniinii3P niiniibeihetiit.
He took part in the singing.
JAMES: Yeah.
RON: Hoseihoowu'.
At the Sun Dance.
JAMES: Warden?
RON: Jim Warden, yeah.

. . .

"Nuh'uuno hinono'eino', hiinono'wuuhunenno' ne'nih'iisih'i3i'," nih'iit.
"These Arapahos, wandering people, that's what they were called," he said.
JAMES: Uhh-huh.
RON: "Roaming Tribe," nih'iit.
"Roaming Tribe," he said.
JAMES: Uhh-huh.
RON: They used to travel all over.
Nuh'uuno "hinono'eino'," nih'iibi'tou'kuutii3i'. "Hinono'eino'" niibi'ii3oo3i' nuhu'.

> *This "Arapahos," they just shortened the word. "Arapahos" they just call them this now.*

JAMES: Hee hee.
> *Yes, yes.*

RON: 'oh hiiP "hiinono'wuuhunenno' nuhu', ne'niisih'i3i'," nih'iit, "roaming tribe."
> *But this "roaming people, that's what they were called," he said, "roaming tribe."*

JAMES: Hee, hee.
> *Yes, yes.*

(ELAR 18a)

Ron manages to show his own social capital and knowledge, while also reinforcing James's point, and James enthusiastically accepts this affiliation. Ron told me on a different occasion in October 2002, however, that the name *hinono'ei* came from the fact that the Arapahos used a lot of sacred red paint (*hinow*). This was in the context of discussing traditional narratives and ceremonies, where red paint was a very salient topic. A different context produced a different etymology from the same speaker.

As another example of this, on one occasion while taking a break outside the Arapahoe Immersion School, I was told by one of the teachers the mythological story of Bluebird. Bluebird is trampled to death by a herd of buffalo, leaving behind a giant cloud of dust in the sky. The dust is a signal to Bluebird's relatives, however, and they send a magpie to look for him. The magpie finds a speck of his blood left over and is able to re-create him from this. The teacher concluded the story by adding that this proved that the old-time Arapahos knew about DNA. He then added to me:

> There's a lot of stories like that, which uhh . . . I just heard 'em, I didn't really think nothing about 'em. Later on I come back to think about 'em. Oh yeah, you know, like that, that kind of stories. Hinono'eiP hinono'eino' [Arapahos], they're, they're one of a kind people. Their, their name, nuhu' [this name], it come from the sky, from the clouds.
>
> Hiinoono'eti' you know, hinono'eino', you know, that's cloud people, sky people.
>
> *It is cloudy you know, Arapahos, you know, that's cloud people, sky people.*
>
> (ELAR 48c)

This etymology serves to link the Arapaho back the story of Bluebird, via the blue imagery as well as that of the sky, dust, and clouds. More importantly, it symbolizes the power and knowledge of the Arapaho, as encapsulated in the story and the teacher's interpretation of it. Yet this same teacher, Dave, when talking at a later date about problems at the same immersion school, said that the problems there were ultimately due to the fact that things always went wrong for the Arapaho. He noted that the name *hinono'ei*, and thus *hinono'ei-tiit* 'Arapaho language', comes from the fact that the tribe made some kind of mistake in the past (*non-o'-*), and thus things always have to go wrong for the Arapaho.

One might be tempted to engage in an "aha!" or "gotcha" moment and claim that the speakers were contradicting themselves in these examples. But in fact there is no reason that more than one set of sound correspondences cannot be found in an Arapaho word. Folk etymologies can be equally and multiply true, because the *sound* resemblance is true in both cases. Folk etymologies can thus be considered resources for affiliation, reflection, contestation, or other social purposes, rather than single, absolute truths to which one must be committed in the sense that a linguist would be. This is true of many linguistic ideologies as well as practices—they can be deployed situationally to index certain identities or perform social work, as needed by a speaker, and a speaker need not maintain consistency over time in the use of ideologies or practices, or feel limited to a single one (see Briggs 1998:240). An appreciation of the emergent quality of identities—and COPs—allows one to see these varying moments as exemplary of creativity and agency rather than contradiction.

ETYMOLOGIES AND AUTHORITY

The folk-etymologizing process involves not just standard techniques of linguistic comparison and standard foci of etymologizing interest but also social expectations regarding the conduct of the process. Only fluent elders engage in this process today, and in the past, even when all Arapahos were fluent in the language, contemporary accounts suggest that only older respected individuals would propose folk etymologies, at least in public settings—although anyone can *report* an etymology proposed by someone else. In fact, one folk etymology captures this very idea. When talking about the four directions and their symbolism, people say that the north (*neneb-iihi'*) is associated with the fourth stage of life—the elders—because the white snow represents their white hair. They then add that the north is so called because the knowledge of the elders is sacred and dangerous (*neenebee'*). The folk etymology captures why one should be cautious about engaging in folk etymologizing! Folk etymologies thus not only are a part of the oral literature tradition of the tribe but have a status as knowledge, similar to medicinal or ritual knowledge, and are linked to authority. Further evidence for this is the fact that when people offer a folk etymology, they will quite often cite the name of the person who shared the information with them. They thereby underline the knowledge status of the item and enhance their own social capital through demonstrating their knowledge connection to a prestigious elder of a previous generation. For all these reasons, the practice of folk etymologizing is almost entirely restricted to the AC COP. Even secondary reporting of folk etymologies is largely restricted to AC, since the folk etymologies are almost entirely oral knowledge at this point, and one must participate in AC to hear them. Two exceptions are the terms for "Arapaho" and "White Person": at least some of the proposed etymologies for these are known more broadly at Wind River. These make sense: while most folk etymologies are oriented around questions of MTH power and vertical connections to the sacred, these two terms obviously connect closely to the laterally oriented identity concerns and boundary maintenance that are important to Pan-Indian and Politico-Tribal COPs, while also allowing points of commonality between those two COPs and AC.

Not surprisingly, few people are willing to overtly contest folk etymologies, especially today. Indeed, overt disagreement is rare in any circumstance—much more commonly, an alternative suggestion is offered, and people are free to choose which to accept. Most actual contestation comes in private: one elder may offer an etymology at a public gathering, but often days later another elder who was present will assure a subset of the audience (including me) that "the word really means . . ."—or more mildly, "the way I was told, the word means . . ." Thus folk etymologies constitute a running topic for discussion and reflection in the AC community. Convincing others to accept one's proposed etymology is a way of creating affiliations within families and other social circles. Accepting someone else's etymology and then sharing it—especially with due credit to the source—is a way for younger individuals to engage in affiliation and association with an admired elder, as well as showing their own knowledge of the language. Certain etymologies—such as the one for Gros Ventre mentioned above, as well as the one for the Beesoowuunenno' as 'Big/Great

Lakes People'—clearly run in specific AC-oriented families and are more restricted than widespread examples such as the body being holy. This is not just an accident of social adjacency but a conscious strategy of social cohesion, which matches some of what Anderson (2001a) finds regarding the family-based orientation of many aspects of Arapaho practice. Thus nonfluent individuals do continue to share folk etymologies today, using English to explain the Arapaho words. This mode of thought—or at least respect for this mode of thought—shows strong continuity with the past within AC.

FROM POWER TO IRONY

Due to lack of fluency in Arapaho, fewer and fewer people are in a position to create new etymologies. And though the belief in the power and revelatory wisdom of folk etymologies continues, Arapaho is considered the only language (along with related Native American languages) worthy of etymologizing on: I have never heard anyone propose a serious folk etymology concerning English. Arapaho is viewed as a language containing power, whereas English is not. Arapaho holds hidden aural correspondences that provide keys to a deeper understanding of the interrelationships in the world between various domains. English is a language that for the Arapaho lacks this depth (cf. Gómez de García, Axelrod, and Lachler 2009).

This is not to say that Arapaho people do not pick up on sound correspondences in English. However, much as is the case with modern Arapaho-English place names, they tend to ironize on these resemblances, through jokes and puns, rather than seeing them as nexuses of power. For example, in August 2004 during a field trip to Rocky Mountain National Park, I was told that if you touch a thistle, you will get horny (sexually). This idea fetishistically connected the quality of the thistle plant to an English slang term, but in a completely nonserious way. The Arapaho word for thistle (*tooxu'oo'* 'it is sharp') and the word for 'horny, sexually desirous' (*hiiwo3eihi-*) do not resemble each other, nor does the latter Arapaho word for "sexually desirous" make any reference to prickliness.

Arapaho people also of course make innumerable puns and jokes with the Arapaho language, many of them based on sound correspondences, and some of these take on a folk-etymological character. For example, people explain that the devil (*hoocoo*) is so named because he fries people in hell (the word for a 'fried thing' or a 'steak' is *hocoo*). Irony is not something limited to any one language—it works everywhere. Folk etymology, however, works only in Arapaho, and within that language, primarily in semantic domains associated with MTH power, or with boundary maintenance between groups with greater or lesser claims to MTH power—the domains of creation, ritual, ceremony, ethnic group origins, and personal identity. As we have seen often in this study, MTH power is a key component of social power as well. Folk etymologies are forms of knowledge and creative performance whose circulation establishes networks of ideological, kinship-based, or other types of affiliation or contestation, as well as bringing social capital and prestige. Jokes and puns, on the other hand, bring admiration and friendship but not deep social respect or affiliation in the way that serious folk etymologies do.

In concluding this chapter, it is important to note that Arapaho speakers themselves do not recognize a category of "folk etymology." They simply seek to pass on to each other and their descendants an understanding of the full meanings and connections of words in their language. Many of these are linguistically "true" meanings and connections, in the technical sense. Others are not and thus are "folk etymologies" for linguistic anthropologists. But as we noted earlier in this chapter, the meanings associated with words as part of folk-etymological oral traditions are equally "true," functionally speaking, whether for the Arapaho or the inhabitants of the Picketwire River valley. One might ask if it is not patronizing to apply a linguist's extrinsic distinctions to Arapaho speakers and their language. On the contrary, my goal in this chapter has been to underline the linguistic and intellectual creativity of Arapaho speakers. In highlighting their interest in going beyond the most solid and obvious linguistic connections, in order to speculatively explore the aural realm of their language and their world to the fullest, we can truly appreciate the nature of this creativity. Most importantly, this chapter helps to show from an additional angle Arapaho speakers' interest in bridging conceptual gaps to connect separate domains of thought, by the process of analogy. While in the case of place names, that analogical bridging occurred primarily in the visual realm, here it occurs in the aural realm. In both cases, it is oral tradition that cements the bridge to MTH power, while simultaneously constituting the key mechanism of reciprocity in social relations, via the transfer of story knowledge. And in both cases, we see that a shift to English (the Arapaho English version of American Indian Vernacular English, in particular) is tied to a reluctance to "name" power through language or to find power in English language and names. William, an educational leader, in a presentation in June 2012, stressed that students must "study the [Arapaho] language," and then they would "see connections . . . see how things relate in the language." He said that "if you really want to learn, you try to understand all the relations of things," and cited elder Howard Antelope (real name), who said, "When you learn [Arapaho], you will start to see . . . all the relations in life." Antelope also said, "When you speak that language, it brings everything together, and you understand why you do the things you do." Only with a full understanding of Arapaho language ideologies about folk etymology can one understand the full depth of these comments. These words also allow us to see that folk etymologies—and naming more generally as understood broadly in this book—can function much like traditional narratives. Writing of the Yukon, Julie Cruikshank says that stories "unify interrupted memories" (1998:46) and "incorporate unfamiliar events into larger stories" (1998:47). In the same way, creative folk etymologies can unify disconnected parts of language, culture, and thought and incorporate unfamiliar words or events into larger cultural complexes of thought and metaphor. The same occurs with neologisms, as we will see in chapter 6, and of course place names are a quintessential example of this process. Indeed, this entire book is about the unique "paradigms" and "institutional arrangements" (Cruikshank 1998:52) through which Arapaho indigenous knowledge(s) and identity(ies) are encoded.

In the English context, however, analogy is now turned increasingly toward an ironic confrontation with Euro-American society and the standard English language and away from seeking nexuses of power. As with chapter 3, the claim here is not that MTH power is not sought or found by Arapaho people but that it is not "named" or connected to through English by AC members. Even the ironic usage of folk etymology, due to its dependence on knowledge of Arapaho, is largely used only by AC members—unlike the case of place names, where ironic English-language names are available to Pan-Indian and Politico-Tribal COP members for usage. As a result of this, folk etymology is a relatively uncontested ground in terms of competing ideologies from competing COPs. It shows strong continuity with past ideologies and practices. However, if the Arapaho language is completely lost, it will be reduced to a fossilized process at best. At the moment, few of the institutionalized examples seem to be widely used by nonspeaker members of AC, even though in principle they can be memorized, and a small subset of them currently are.

An important point to consider for shifting and endangered language communities is that where a practice (and associated ideology) is unchanged and unchallenged, this will very likely be because the practice is too hard to carry over into the new language and faces extinction as a productive process if language shift proceeds completely. In the case of place names and especially personal names, the contestation around these practices is a sign of continuing vitality, or at least attempts to maintain vitality—it is not a sign of "crisis."

It remains to be seen how irony-directed, Arapaho-English-based folk etymology will develop and continue as a productive process—in the absence of the motivating impetus of MTH power quests—as a means of creating greater identity-based solidarity across multiple Arapaho COPs, as Arapaho English place names can do. Certainly the investigation of folk etymology has allowed me to realize much more fully what it means for Arapaho people—especially speakers—to say that Arapaho is "our" language in a way that English can never be. It also makes clearer why the language itself is considered "sacred" by AC affiliates. And it has allowed me to see a way in which one kind of Arapaho knowledge and oral tradition can likely never be translated into English or any other language very successfully—at least not without very major shifts in the ideologies of Arapaho as an MTH power language and English as a prosaic, utilitarian language.

All of these realizations lead one to recognize the cruel irony that this domain, which provides such a powerful argument for the preservation of a living knowledge and use of the Arapaho language, is also a domain that for this very reason makes it difficult for the larger Arapaho society to capitalize on this language resource for the purpose of broader social reproduction and continuity. When a process is extremely closely tied to one language, this turns out to be a double-edged sword in terms of broader efforts at social reproduction and continuity. In the case of place names, a general ideology of seeking resemblances can be maintained even as the language (practice) shifts. In the case of personal names, the practice in the Arapaho language is somewhat maintainable since it does not require advanced knowledge of the language, and the ideology around the practice can be shifted as well. But in the case of folk etymology, the ideology and linguistic practice are so closely bound to each other that it seems highly unlikely one could be maintained without the other. This tight binding means that folk etymology is less manipulable as a generalized cultural resource across multiple COPs.

In the introduction we discussed what is often seen as the "problem" of discontinuities between ideology and practice, either across time or across the metaphorical space that separates different COPs. But in reality, the opening up of such discontinuities can be part of a creative process of adaptation—evidence of a living process of contestation, as mentioned above. The *lack* of discontinuity *may* be a negative sign, and the lack of *possibility* of discontinuity can certainly mean that a cultural resource—like a highly specialized biological species intimately bound to one narrow environment—is restricted in its potential for creative appropriation and redefinition. This idea should not be pushed too absolutely, however—as we have seen, there is a long tradition of folk etymologizing on ethnic groups in relation to their claims to power, which can and is being partially adapted toward lateral affiliation and boundary-maintenance purposes in the realm of identity.

Nevertheless, this characteristic of tight ideology-practice (and therefore ideology-language) binding is likely a general rule in the area of language maintenance and revitalization, though it requires much more investigation. Domains where language-specific practices are most obvious may be the best ones to appeal to for language *maintenance* (where the language continues to be spoken fluently). But where this is no longer the case for the vast majority of the community, as in language *revitalization*, these very same, highly appealing practices may be among the hardest to operationalize among younger learners because of the high-level knowledge required of the language. More importantly, they are likely not the best sites around which to attempt to build broader social consensus on local identity among multiple COPs, since they are so unavailable to most of the community, at least as a living practice. On the other hand, I have found in teaching workshops that presenting these folk etymologies draws extremely favorable response from participants and leads to high levels of initial motivation. The interest of the learners must be understood as conceptual and symbolic, however: they grasp the *idea* of folk etymology and find both the concept and specific examples highly appealing, but they are not yet in a position to productively propose, detect, or appreciate folk etymologies in their own practice of the language.

6

NEOLOGISMS AND THE POLITICS OF LANGUAGE MAINTENANCE

HISTORICAL NEOLOGISMS: MOVING ON TO THE GREAT PLAINS

Like speakers of any living language, Arapaho people have created new words as they have confronted new objects and new concepts.[1] This process has been going on for hundreds of years—indeed, for as long as Arapaho has been a linguistic and cultural entity. The process intensified when the Arapaho moved onto the Great Plains several centuries ago. Faced with a plethora of new plants and animals, they relied in part on a common stock of Proto-Algonquian (PA) forms, which they extended to new objects, with the old semantic value often being lost. Thus the PA cognate for 'moose' (*mooswa*) has been shifted in Arapaho (*bii*) to mean 'buffalo cow', the cognate for '(tree) squirrel' (*anyikwa*) has been shifted (*honi'*) to mean 'ground squirrel', and the cognate for 'caribou' (*atehkwa*) has been shifted (*hote'*) to mean 'bighorn sheep'. Similarly, the cognate for 'poplar tree' (*asaatiwa*) has been shifted (*hohoot*) to mean 'cottonwood tree' (as well as 'tree' generally), and the cognate for 'rock' (*aʔsenya*) has been shifted (*hohe'*) to mean 'mountain'. In a related development, several general PA words have been shifted and applied to a more specific object in the natural world, which is inevitably the central and prototypical member of its type in traditional Arapaho culture. The word for 'berries' (*miinali*) has come to be used specifically for 'chokecherry' (*biino*), and the word for 'male ungulate' (*ayaapeewa*) now means specifically 'buffalo bull' (*heneecee*).

In many other cases, as the Arapahos encountered new animals and plants, they were simply described, in some cases as modified nouns, in others as verbs. Thus the black-footed ferret is *coo3oniiseihon* 'prairie dog weasel', the pocket gopher is *nouuciitoo3eit* 'it blows (dirt) out (of the ground)', the lark bunting is *nook3e'enii'eihii* 'white-winged bird', and the narrow-leaf cottonwood of the Rocky Mountains is *sesiin(h)ohoot* 'bitter tree/cottonwood'.

A closer analysis of the new descriptions in Arapaho as well as the semantic shifts and extensions suggests some interesting findings. Below is a list of Arapaho names for animal fauna, divided by both structure and origin of the name (here, an asterisk indicates an animal not in the range of Central Algonquian groups):

1. Descriptions (including compounded modifications):
   *mountain goat = 'it has a hairy chin'
   *grizzly bear = 'it has white arms/shoulders'
   bobcat = 'short-faced mountain lion'
   lynx = 'pointed-eared mountain lion'
   wolverine = 'weasel bear'
   *pocket gopher = 'it blows (dirt) out (of the ground)'
   chipmunk/striped ground squirrel = 'striped squirrel'
   red fox = 'big swift fox'
   *prairie dog = 'enemy/Comanche squirrel'
   wood rat = 'big mouse'
   *jackrabbit = 'it has black(-tipped) ears'
   white-tailed deer = 'it has a dog tail'
   *opossum = 'it has a naked tail'
   raccoon = 'striped-tail one'
   *black-footed ferret = 'prairie dog weasel'
   moose = 'normal one', 'it has flat horns'
   snowshoe hare = 'it makes flat tracks'
   *pika = 'rock(?) rodent'
2. Nondescriptions, but also not inherited from PA (i.e., likely borrowings):
   *pronghorn antelope (*nisice*, possibly cognate with Cheyenne *vo'kaa'e*)
   *badger (*woh'ooo*', cognate with Cheyenne *ma'háhko'e*)
   (*?)buffalo (*hii3einoon*, cognate with Cheyenne *esevone*)
   *coyote (*koo'oh, koo'ohwuu* [PL], possibly cognate with Cheyenne *o'kóhome*)
   wolf (*hooxei*)

*mule deer (*bih'ih*, possibly based on a borrowed form meaning 'little moose', possibly connected with Navajo and Tewa [Shaul 2014:152])

tree squirrel (*no'ou[h]*)

3. Semantically shifted terms:

(*?)buffalo bull < male ungulate

(*?)buffalo cow < moose

*bighorn sheep < caribou

*swift ("kit") fox < red (and gray?) fox

*marmot < woodchuck

*ground squirrel < tree squirrel

animal < bison

cottontail < snowshoe hare

4. Retained PA terms:

(black) bear, skunk, otter, weasel, beaver, muskrat, elk, porcupine, mouse, mink(?)

The division above is interesting for a number of reasons. First, it is obvious that animals that the Arapaho would not have encountered in a putative earlier homeland to the northeast or north of their nineteenth-century location (the asterisked terms)[2] would have needed to acquire names. The Arapaho seem to have used three different strategies roughly equally: shifting existing terms in the language to new meanings once the older animal referred to was rare or absent from Arapaho life (the "caribou > bighorn sheep" strategy); borrowing words from some other language (the "pronghorn antelope" strategy); and describing animals (the "pocket gopher" strategy).

Where there was continuity in knowledge of animals, there was also a fair amount of continuity in the names—in other words, PA terms have remained in continuous usage, with the same meaning (list #4). However, it is interesting to note how many more northerly or easterly animals, which one would expect to have remained at least a minor part of Arapaho ethnozoological experience over the years, ended up getting renamed via description or borrowing (i.e., the nonasterisked terms in lists #1 and #2). These include white-tailed deer, raccoon, and bobcat (easterly animals); lynx, moose, snowshoe hare, and wolverine (northerly animals); and red fox and tree squirrel (occurring in both zones). None of these are prototypically Great Plains animals, but all at least range along plains riparian zones and/or occur in the Rocky Mountains. It is as if a new lifestyle in a new location demanded new names for animals, even those that had already been known and named in the older, more northerly and/or easterly locations.[3] Certainly Arapaho has undergone very major phonological and morphological changes compared to the Central Algonquian languages, and many of these may be indirectly associated with major sociocultural changes and/or contact with new language groups as the Arapaho shifted their occupation area over time. With such a history, it should not be surprising that major changes in the lexicon also occurred.

Two facts are notable with regard to the borrowings, however. First, they are largely associated with new Great Plains fauna, not new Rocky Mountain fauna (mule deer being the only likely exception). Borrowing seems to have occurred primarily in relation to the zone with which the Arapaho would have had the least familiarity, while it was largely avoided in relation to a zone more similar in flora and fauna to earlier homelands. In other words, the borrowing has the appearance of a kind of last-resort strategy, occurring at the far margins of linguistic and cultural experience (at the time of the borrowing). This finding bears a certain resemblance, at least by analogy, to the patterns of homelanding seen in chapter 3: the existence of tribally specific and transparently analyzable place names (as opposed to loan translations or borrowings) is a key aspect of claiming a core area as a homeland. Second, if one looks at the partial or full cognates between Cheyenne and Arapaho in the borrowings, it is clear that these forms have changed greatly from the common source (likely a shared borrowing by both languages). Some of the cognates could date to the early post-PA era, as they show the same Arapaho/Cheyenne sound correspondences as true PA cognates in the two languages. Thus few of the borrowings look recent ("coyote" being an exception).

This is not the place to explore the early history of Arapaho linguistic acculturation in great detail. The key point is that the majority of the new animal names that the Arapahos needed in the past were not borrowed, and the same is true in other domains as well, such as plant or bird names. Rather, the existing Algonquian stock of their language was used. As such, the Arapaho are an example of an ideology of language purity—the avoidance of "foreign," non-transparent words.

SOUND CORRESPONDENCES, ANALOGICAL THINKING, AND THE IDEOLOGY OF NEOLOGISMS

A very different process for creating new words—but one that will be familiar by now—involves extensions of names based on analogical appearance or behavior. This is the same mode of thought that accounts for type-2 place names (symbolic or analogical resemblance names), which we saw in chapter 3. Thus the word for pronghorn antelope (*nisice*) has been extended to (or from?) the water strider insect, and the word for buffalo bull (*heneecee*) has been extended to (or from?) the water beetle insect, based on similarities of general behavior. Meanwhile, the word for turtle (*be'enoo*) has been extended to 'fog' based on the Arapaho belief that the turtle controls moisture of a foggy or drizzly sort (as opposed to snow or thunderstorms), and the word for whirlwind or tornado (*neyooxet*) is also used for the caterpillar, based on the resemblance of the spinning of the cocoon to the whirling of wind. Symbolic resemblances across domains are the motivation for the naming practice here, as with place names, and the visual domain is the method of linkage. It is important to recognize that these resemblances are not "mere" overlapping names: in at least some cases (turtle, whirlwind), they are true indicators of nexuses of power. For example, an older Arapaho belief is that if one is plagued by foggy and drizzly weather for four days, one can draw a picture of a turtle on the ground in the dirt, then beat it with a stick, and this will drive away the bad weather. Water beetles and caterpillars both occur as design motifs as well (Kroeber [1902–7] 1983:139).

Related to this are modified onomatopoetic forms. Pure onomatopoeia plays a relatively small role in Arapaho, but the combination of this approach with what we could call "retranslation" is an interesting feature of Arapaho. One example is 'raven': *woxuuxoneihii*. This word can be glossed as 'one who makes the sound *woxuuxon*', with the form in italics being an onomatopoetic imitation of the bird's call, and -*(e)ihii* being a noun suffix indicating an agent. But the form also glosses as 'eater of bad things' (*wox-uuxonee-ihii* = bad-eat thing-agent). The natural call of the bird was apparently first noted (first gloss), and then that call was retranslated into Arapaho (second gloss). The word for 'chickadee' functions in a similar way: the call of the bird is described in Arapaho as *biiceyeihii*. This can then be glossed as 'one who makes the sound *biiceyei*' but has been retranslated as 'one who brings summer' (*biicen-yei-ihii* = summer-making-agent). Similarly the word for 'killdeer' (*ti'iihii*) is based on the call of the bird but can be glossed as 'the one who makes the sound *ti*". The word for 'snipe' is *ceecee'iheihii* 'triller, ululator'. This is not an onomatopoetic form strictly speaking, but the name is based on the resemblance between the courtship flight call of the bird and women's trilling or ululating, as widely practiced in Plains Indian music and ceremonies. All these names are much more interesting than simple onomatopoeia because they recall the mode of analysis seen in the previous chapter with folk etymology: a search for meaningful sound correspondences that can be explained in terms of the Arapaho language.

While the meadowlark (*cooxuceneihii*) is not named based on sound resemblances, its call is retranslated into Arapaho, and it is generally believed to speak Arapaho (cf. Powers 1986:28 for the same idea among the Lakota, that the meadowlark speaks Lakota). It is often described today as "talking dirty." Suggested glosses in early sources include *hinenitee ceitokusee* 'person, crawl toward me!' (Kroeber [1902–7] 1983:317–18) and 'go, cook!', which would be something like *neecis(ee), bii3ihi!* (Hilger 1952:42). A common modern retranslation is *wooxubouhut* 's/he stinks', as if the bird is insulting someone, with the name of the insultee added prior to the verb. Kroeber (field notes:MS 2560a, NB5:78) also says that the bird was believed to be calling one away to death and that children were therefore told not to imitate it. On the other hand, if a child has difficulty speaking, it can be fed a meadowlark, and this will "loosen its tongue." The crow (*houu*) is often understood as a messenger to the Creator (*houu*), and it too is understood as talking Arapaho when it calls. Suggested glosses are 'grandma, bread!' (*neiwoo, co'ocoo*) and 'come here!' (*neheicoo*) (Hilger 1952:41). The call of the screech owl (*bee3ei*) is associated with ghosts and death but—as far as I have found—is not retranslated into Arapaho. Note that the crow and meadowlark are considered to use everyday Arapaho, in nonwondrous ways—this is very different from birds or animals who communicate with humans in vision quests or traditional narratives.

The most important thing to recognize with all these examples from bird calls is that Arapaho speakers look for aural correspondences between nature and their own language, and they seek to find meaning in those correspondences in a way exactly parallel to the folk etymology process described in chapter 5. The names that are then applied to these birds can be understood once again as indicating nexuses between domains that are associated with knowledge and power. The analogical animal names (turtle/fog) participate in the same process, though by means of visual or metaphorical associations rather than aural ones. As the oral wisdom around these names and bird calls suggests—especially the crow and meadowlark—the nexuses are serious and truly powerful, potentially even life threatening or linked to the Creator. Overall, the Arapaho practice of analogical thinking and the ideologies associated with it can be linked to more specific *language* ideologies and practices, including both folk etymology and the symbolic thinking involved in place names. These can then be linked to even more specific practices and ideologies in the creation of new common names for birds and animals. Most generally, the practices can be linked to a general Arapaho belief that language, song, and nature are connected. I have been told on multiple occasions about songs being created in such circumstances as someone hearing the wind whistle through a slightly open door, which swung open and closed a few inches with each gust of wind, or someone else riding in a car and hearing the sound of the tires hitting cracks on the road as the wind simultaneously whistled through a partly open window. In these cases, it is not simply that the sound inspires the melody for a song but rather that the melody is actually *given* to the composer by the sounds and by the wind, and the composer has only to listen closely to "catch" the song. At a language conference in 2008, Joe, a native speaker who is a strong proponent of language preservation, addressed the largely Arapaho audience and said that the Arapaho language would never be fully "lost," despite worries about language endangerment. Rather, he said that his grandfather had told him it would always be present in the calls of the birds, such as the meadowlark, in the sound of the wind in the trees, in the rushing waters. The language would never die, his grandfather had told him. But the people might someday no longer be able to *understand and access* the language—this was his fear.

We can also start to understand the deeper reasons why Arapaho speakers over time have been devotees of language purism and have been relatively resistant to borrowing, using this process for less than one-third of new plains animal names, for example, and even less in other domains such as birds and plants, where virtually every name is either of PA origin or a new description. In chapter 5, we saw that a key Arapaho language ideology is that of transparency, which simultaneously arises from and licenses the process of folk etymology. We can see in this chapter that transparency is a broader phenomenon, however, which exists not just in language concepts and sounds but across all symbolic domains, from the aural to the visual to the tactile. Given the importance and complexity of this system of analogical thought, it is not at all surprising that speakers would seek to keep it intact and extend it coherently where possible. Borrowing "meaningless" words from other languages would be a severe threat to this system, unless those words could be reinterpreted and retranslated in relation to existing Arapaho language—somewhat in the way that has been done with onomatopoetic bird calls, or with the word *wookecii* 'cows' as seen in chapter 5. While some of this retranslation has been done, for the most part speakers have strongly preferred new descriptions or extensions (sometimes with modification) of existing lexical items, over borrowing from other languages. Knowledge and power depend on this, within the broader ideologies of AC—both the MTH power found in the correspondences, and the social power involved in conveying and explaining those correspondences through the oral tradition.

TWENTIETH-CENTURY PRACTICE: LEXICAL AND TAXONOMIC EXTENSIONS

All the features of traditional Arapaho practices of linguistic innovation, as seen in the adaptation to the Great Plains and then the Rocky Mountains, carried over into modern Arapaho linguistic adaptation to Euro-American culture during the period from first contact in the early nineteenth century (or earlier, at least indirectly) through the period in which Arapaho remained the primary language of all Wind River (through the 1940s and 1950s) or at least of important parts of the Wind River community (into the 1960s and 1970s). An obvious example of semantic extension—and then shift—is items of clothing. Initially, new European clothing likely had a special modifier attached to the original extended noun, but today, such modifiers do not occur or else now occur with the old, traditional item of clothing, which is relatively less used. Thus *wo'oh* originally meant 'moccasin', was extended to mean 'shoe', and now occurs with both uses, though the term *niscehinono'oh* 'buckskin/antelope-hide shoe' is now often used to refer specifically to moccasins, while the base term now prototypically refers to 'shoe' rather than 'moccasin'. Further extensions of the base term include *touhoono'oh* 'cowboy boot' (lit. 'cowboy shoe') and *heyo'oono'oh* 'work boot' (lit. 'tall shoe'). Leggings (*wotoo*) are now prototypically pants, women's dresses and men's traditional shirts (*biixuut*) are now blouses for women and buttoning collared shirts for men, and interlacing fasteners (*hoxkuhuut*) are now buckles and zippers.

The preceding examples show that even when new items are integrated into a language's existing semantic system, the prototype associated with a word can shift from the older, more traditional item (moccasin) to a newer, originally imported item (shoes). It is difficult to simply integrate new items "cleanly" into an existing system. More radically, shifts can occur in an entire classificatory system. One good example in Arapaho is the names for indigenous as opposed to introduced plants.

The traditional plant taxonomy has five levels. Level 1 is the term *plant* itself: *bisiii'oot* (*bis-iii'oo-t* = appear-grow-PARTICIPLE = 'growing thing'). Level 2 indicates general growth forms:

NOUN	NOUN-FINAL	VERB MEDIAL CLASSIFIER	MEANING
hohoot	*-ohoot*		tree
coo'oo'oe'	*-(h)iis*	*-oo'-*	bush, shrub (medial = 'wood')
woxu'	*-oxu'*	*-es-*	grass, forb, root plant
cee'ese'einoo'		*-e'ei-*	flower ('head')
biibinoot	*-ib*	*-ibin-*	fruit, berry

The final category of fruit or berry is ambiguous in that it refers not to a growth form but to a specific product of a plant. However, berries were so central to Arapaho life that plants that produced edible berries were almost always identified by this characteristic: it was essentially a "growth form." Note in this connection that plants whose berries were not a major food resource (red osier dogwood) tended to not be named in terms of berries. See additional comments regarding level 5.

Level 3 consists of generic names within the level-2 categories. These generic names all have multiple subtypes/species in the genus. Types of trees include *see3* 'pine' and *hohoot* 'cottonwood'. Types of shrubs include *nookhoose'* 'sage'. Types of flowers include *wohoono'* 'mint' and *woniihiiho'* 'beans'. Types of berries include *yeino'* 'rose'.

Level 4 involves species-level names. Some of these are compounds involving level-3 generic terms plus a modifier, while others are compounds involving level-2 terms plus a modifier—in both cases, effectively binomial terms. Others are compounds using other features of a plant (stem, bark, etc.). A few are uncompounded monomial terms. Thus: *siisiiyei-biis* 'snake bush' (greasewood); *hox-wuus* 'rotten/pitted bush' (box elder); *hiteeh-ib* 'heart berry' (strawberry); *bees-ib* 'big berry' (plum); *ne'-ib* '?-berry' (golden-flowered currant); *to'-see3* 'short pine' (common juniper); *nooku-see3* 'white pine' (lodgepole pine); *hiwoxuu-yeino'* 'elk rose' (mountain prickly currant); *wox-wohoono'* 'bear mint' (elk mint); *ceeneeteen-e'einoo'* 'blue head' (mountain blue bells); *kouhuy-e'einoo'* 'sticky head' (gumweed); *ni'ibootou-nookhoose'* 'sweet smelling sage' (mountain sweet sage); *bo'-oocei-biis* 'red stem bush' (red osier dogwood, "red willow"); *bee'-exooti'* 'red bark' (mountain birch); and *woo'teen-exooti'* 'black bark' (eastern redbud).

Level 5 involves individual parts of a plant. For some very important plants there are different names for different parts of the plant itself. In all cases, the different parts of the plants are employed for very different uses—most commonly the berries are eaten, but the bark of shrubs are used medicinally. For example, the name *yeino'* is used for wild roses, but this refers specifically to the rose hips. The bush is referred to as *yein-iis* 'rose hip bush'. The flowers are referred to as *be'-e'ei-* 'red head'. The name for mountain bluebell flowers is *ceeneeteen-e'einoo'* 'blue head', while the root is referred to as *he3owoon-oxu'* or *hi3owoon-oxu'*, usually glossed 'good root' (used medicinally and ceremonially). Chokecherries are called *biino*, but the bush is called *hoowoo'* or *hoowoo'uu-biis*.

In sum, Arapaho shows four general growth categories of plants: trees, shrubs, grasses and other inconspicuously flowering forbs, and flowering forbs. A fifth category, important berry-bearing plants, cuts across the other categories. There are four well-developed layers to this taxonomy, with a fifth occurring for certain highly important plants.

The Arapaho have partially maintained this system in their naming of new types of fruits and vegetables, relying on level-2 and level-3 base terms to form binomial expressions like those in level 4:

biis-ib = hairy-berry = 'peach'
ce'-woniihiiho' = spherical-peas = 'English peas'

More interesting is the speakers' adaptation of the name *cee'ee'*, originally the wild Indian potato, now also used for domestic potatoes. Faced with a variety of large fruits and vegetables, the Arapaho have adapted this form as a new classificatory item, parallel to those in level 2. It is now widely used in forming level-4 binomial names, involving both root vegetables and large fruits that are not included in the berry category.

bee'i-ce'ee' = red-potato = 'apple; radish'
niihooni-ce'ee' = yellow/orange-potato = 'orange'
nonooku-ce'ee' = white-potato = 'turnip'
niisci-ce'ee' = sweet-potato = 'sweet potato'
seesiini-ce'ee' = sour-potato = 'lemon'
3onouuyi-ce'ee' = oblong/pointed-potato = 'pear'
ceeneeteeni-ce'ee' = green-potato = 'avocado'

Like the "berry" classifier, the "potato" one obviously crosscuts growth forms—potatoes themselves of course are roots, as are turnips, radishes, and sweet potatoes, but all the other items above grow on trees. In general, the naming of newly encountered fruits and vegetables has relied less and less on references to growth form. We find that items actually grown by the Arapahos in early farming times do respect the growth-form criterion for the most part—sweet potatoes, turnips, and radishes are in fact varieties of large root plants similar to the Indian potato. But more recent names for items that grow only "at the store" almost universally do not pay attention to growth form. The potato category in general, like the berry category, tends to focus attention on the physical characteristics of the edible berry or root, and both of these categories have expanded rapidly. Other examples of names for new foods that describe what they look like in the store include *hiiniinsiinoo'* 'it is horn shaped' (banana), *niiscibouhut* 'it smells sweet' (cantaloupe), *see'kooti'* 'it has flat leaves' (cabbage), and *hi'iisoono'* 'maggots' (rice). Thus there has been an overall shift in the Arapaho plant-naming taxonomy, from a largely growth-form-based system to a largely appearance-based descriptive system that ignores growth form. As with the earlier move on to the plains, the regular trip to the supermarket has left its mark on the lexicon, but the more profound shift from hunting and gathering to purchasing at the store has left a deeper mark on the overall ethnobotanical classification system embedded in the language. When one has largely ceased gathering, then the identifying growth form of plants becomes less and less relevant, and appearance on the shelf becomes the central concern. Thus even when borrowing is resisted, semantic acculturation is almost never as simple as a mere extension of lexical items or taxonomic categories. Just as the center-periphery cultural metaphor has been partially "colonized" via its extension to towns and White society, and clothing terms have acquired new, Euro-American prototypes, the plant taxonomic system has been similarly colonized, in ways that subtly remove Arapaho language and people from the land, even in the context of lexical continuity (i.e., continued use of the Arapaho language).

REDESCRIPTION AND HUMOR

The tendency to rely almost entirely on redescriptions or extensions and modifications of existing words remained intact through the twentieth century. Even earlier borrowing was comparatively rare but did occur, as some of the animal examples above attest (for example, *wookec* 'cow' directly or indirectly from Spanish *vaca*). The one area where this resistance was less pronounced is in names for other tribes. Data from the late nineteenth century in Oklahoma (Albert Gatschet's field notes) attests to several borrowings of new tribal names: *sonoci'* for Cherokee, *cik'soo* for Chickasaw, *cikowu'* for Kickapoo, and *yeebenak* for Delaware (from *wabenaki*). Arapaho names for the Osage (*wosoot-*, *wosoos-*), Shoshone (*sosoni'-*), Omaha (*howohoo-*), and Bannock (*beneht-*) have no analyzable meaning in Arapaho and are clearly borrowed. Many other Arapaho names for tribes are loan translations, widely shared across the plains (Pawnee are 'wolf men', Kiowa are 'river men', Oto are 'sock men'). This is a curious exception to general practice in the language. It is a version of the same situation seen in chapter 3 with place names, where there was a regional plains place-naming tradition, in which names of major rivers and other features were loan-translated into many different languages with the same meaning. Both the loan translation and borrowed tribal names in Arapaho are widespread in other tribal languages as well (see the "synonymy" sections at the end of each tribal entry in G. Goddard 1996). Thus Arapaho participation in a regional linguistic area—likely enhanced by the use of Plains Sign Language—explains this particular feature of the language. More fundamentally, one does not linguistically "homeland" or "make one's own" another tribe and its tribal name in the same way one does with local place names, personal names, or etymologies and metaphors in one's own language. The strategy of borrowings and loan translations used with other Native American ethnic group names actually indexes a specific type of political and linguistic relationship with those groups. More generally, as with place names and fauna names, we see once again that borrowing and loan translation strategies are not uniformly or randomly distributed throughout the language and lexicon: both are specific to certain domains and have certain ideological bases. Different neologism strategies index different relationships to the land and its human and animal inhabitants, and to material culture.

In the twentieth century, *ciiis* 'cheese' and *ceebini* 'Germany' are clearly borrowings, but the list ends quickly after that. The language ideology that resists borrowing is part of a larger purist ideology. It is expressed most powerfully in the idea that no "outside" elements should occur in the most symbolically salient aspects of Arapaho life. In the Sun Dance, only traditional materials are allowed to be used for construction, dress, and so forth—paints are supposed to be only natural earth paints. In contrast, for the Pan-Indian powwow, material innovation is common, especially for the showier dances, where one often sees bundles of feathers with a DVD attached in the middle to produce a shimmering glow. There is also a strong prohibition on the use of English—even of single English words—in formal Arapaho genres such as prayer, speeches, or traditional narrative, even as everyday speech is peppered with code-switching from English to Arapaho and code-mixing (where English words, with English pronunciation, are embedded in Arapaho prefixes and suffixes). For this reason, it has been imperative for Arapaho speakers to invent new words based on the Arapaho language in order to discuss evolving modern topics.

Note in passing that Arapaho language purity in many ways does *not* look like the kinds of purity reported for Pueblo peoples (Debenport 2015; Kroskrity 1998). Arapaho speakers are not particularly concerned with distinguishing themselves from speakers of other Native American languages in the way that occurs in the dense network of Pueblo settlements, with many closely related languages and dialects. They also are little bothered by code-switching and code-mixing outside of ceremonial and formal contexts. In addition, they have shown very little concern with keeping the language "secret" (again with the exception of specifically ceremonial language) and indeed have actively participated in producing grammars, dictionaries, and anthologies and in putting the language on the web and on Facebook, as well as teaching and sharing it with anyone interested, including local Euro-Americans. Rather, Arapaho purism traditionally focused on maintaining a *transparent* language for the purposes of access to MTH power, with that language used in ceremonial and formal thought and action. When the Arapaho were monolingual, the same transparent language was used in everyday situations. With bilingualism, it has been seen as widely acceptable to code-switch and engage in "impurity" on an everyday basis, as long as the transparent and pure language remained known and available for formal ceremonialism; Arapaho language was never the basis for Arapaho identity in the way of Arizona Tewa, for example, among the Hopi (Kroskrity 1998, 2000a). For these reasons, everyday Arapaho language has been generally conceived of as open to everyone—it is only certain ceremonies that are closed off to outsiders.

This ideology as it relates to borrowing seems to have actually become more pronounced recently in several COPs, and it is especially strong in the context of language revitalization efforts today. The hardening of the attitude toward borrowing—especially from English—in a revitalization context parallels that reported for at least one other Algonquian language, Sauk in Oklahoma (Sammons 2009), and seems characteristic of Native American revitalization contexts generally at present. The implications of the ideology have changed in this recent context, however: in addition to a desire to maintain linguistic transparency, the ideology now expresses a general political desire to resist the influence of English and Euro-American culture and to ground Arapaho/Native American identity (cf. B. French 2010:34–37 on Mayan neologisms). Put another way, Arapaho practice in this domain is continuous with the past, as is the associated ideology, but a newer ideology has been calqued onto the older one. Now language purity expresses both a desire for continued connections to MTH power and a desire for boundary maintenance in relation to Arapaho and particularly Native American as opposed to Euro-American identity. One way in which this boundary maintenance is accomplished in speech is what I would call *framed borrowing*. This involves a speaker using an English word but, rather than simply using it, framing the word by saying "as the White people say ..." before using the word. This is an important strategy especially in more formal contexts, where there is normally a desire to avoid switching to English. Thus in a daily prayer in an immersion school for the students in the classroom, a native speaker, Dave, said:

Nuhu' hesowobeihiit, heetciinoono'useenoo' nuhu' ni'iitou'u nih'oo3ou'u swine flu, he'ii3P he'ii3P he'ii3ou'u.
This disease, it will not come here, this Swine Flu the Whites call it, whatever it is, whatever it is.
Heetihciino'useenoo' huutiino.
Let it not arrive here.

(ELAR 39b)

This strategy of overtly framing such uses as "what the White people say" rather than "what we say" is a way of demarcating words as non-Arapaho (or non-Arapaho-English) and of framing language gaps as in some sense due to cultural differences with Whites or negative White influences newly arrived in the area.

All these ideologies can be seen at work—and being actively reinforced—in a 2015 conversation among several speakers at Arapahoe School. They had gathered previously to participate in a project to record Arapaho words for a new mobile application. In the process of coming up with the words that would go on the app, they had come across a few words in English for which they did not have terms. Now at the follow-up meeting, they were sitting around the table chatting (and code-switching) as they waited for the technical team to arrive. One speaker initiated the discussion in English, noting that they had gotten stuck on the word "rooster." The conversation then moves to other missing words, at which point one speaker uses the topic to focus on differences between Euro-American and Arapaho culture:

JOE: We still didn't, we still haven't really settled in on this one yet. We never agreed on it. This undertaker.

. . .

JOE: Yeah, because traditionally we didn't bury each, ourselves.
ALLEN: Yeah, hii3oobein.
Yeah, you're right.

The first speaker then recounts previous suggestions for such a word:

JOE: I remember uhh, I asked different ones, uhm . . . Who is it now, uhh, hin'iit uhh, uhm, Redman, what's her name, that one that runs that program up there?
DAVE: [personal name in English]

. . .

JOE: Well, they said, "I think you know I think my mother might have . . . I think I heard my mother say 'niinkoohuu3ei'it.'"
I think I heard my mother say, "He drives people around."
I said, "Well, that could be a taxi driver."
(laughter)
And [personal name in English], he said, "niiciineyei'it."
And [p.n.], he said, "He puts things down [into the ground]."
Everybody said, "No, that's a farmer."
(laughter)
Yeah, I never did come up, come under with that. I never did find out about a mortician.
ALLEN: wootii I think that you know it's just uhm, hiihoote', you know, that covers everything, you know.
I guess I think that you know it's just, he is dead, you know, that covers everything.

. . .

"Toothetciineneih?"

	"*Where will s/he be buried?*" [they ask].
	That's about all they say.
DAVE:	Yeah that's all they say.
ALLEN:	"Toothetciineneih?"
	"*Where will s/he be buried?*"
JOE:	Yeah, where they're gonna go plant 'em.
DAVE:	Where they're gonna plant 'em.
ALLEN:	Hohoo3P
DAVE:	???
JOE:	Wooce', a bunch of little guys growing up.
	You know, a bunch of little guys growing up [out of the ground].
	(boisterous laughter)
ALLEN:	You know there's a lot of, there's a lot of humor in this Arapaho boy!
	(ELAR 133b)

Clearly all the suggestions involve descriptive terms. In addition, there is a clear commitment to arriving at a precise description that will avoid vagueness or overlap with other words. The concluding joke is based on the fact that burial is literally 'putting someone into the ground' (*ciinen-*), which is closely related to planting crops/putting seeds into the ground (*ciineyei-*). Thus the speaker produces an image of the Arapahos farming/raising new people by "planting" the old ones who have passed away. The Arapaho lack of a word is related on this occasion to the prototypically Euro-American practice of farming, which is rendered vaguely strange and absurd by the logical extension of the practice from seeds to people, and by the further extension back to the idea of an undertaker, already explicitly mentioned as culturally foreign. The word gap is turned into an index of cultural difference, as well as of the strangeness of the practice associated with that gap. It is almost as if the Arapaho speakers want to refuse to have a word for this concept in order to maintain the indexical gap. The result is a humorous look at Euro-American-style farming, undertaking, and burying, as well as an explicit appreciation of the potential richness and humor of Arapaho.

From this example, it is not hard to imagine that if a name for 'undertaker' were eventually arrived at (none ever was in this discussion), it would be a humorous term that would make fun of Euro-American culture. In fact, many Arapaho neologisms do exactly that. In some cases, they mock the new object in question through a description that associates it with a humorous (or often, sexual or scatological) conceptual frame; in other cases, the descriptions are also puns, often of a crosslinguistic nature. Examples of the first category include *tontinoc* 'donut' (lit. 'asshole bread'); *hi'iisoono'* 'rice' (lit. 'maggots'); *cee3ibino* 'kidney beans' (lit. 'fart berries'); *biisnih'oo3oo* 'ape' (lit. 'hairy White man'); *biihiino'oowu'* 'outhouse' (lit. 'defecating house'); *3o3okouhu'* 'monkey' (lit. 'he plays with himself [sexually]'); and *bo'os* 'gearshift lever' (lit. 'head of the penis'). The forms for donut, kidney beans, outhouse, and gearshift are slang terms that have more polite equivalents, while the other words are standard forms. Virtually all examples of crosslinguistic puns are slang terms: *houubenoheino'oowu'* 'crowbar' (lit. 'Crow Indian saloon/bar') is one common pun (the more standard word is *biinohooo*, which also means 'digging stick'). A standardized nonslang example is the Arapaho verb for 'pawn'. It plays on the similarity of "pawned" to "pond" (especially for a nonnative speaker of English). The verb used is *hinowoun-* 'put it under water' (i.e., 'pond it'). An Arapaho English example is one of the stomachs of a cow, traditionally called *biiswoo*, now called "Bible" in English, because the many food-absorbing flanges of the stomach lining are said to resemble the pages of the Bible. As with all slang, the boundaries between formalized usage and puns invented in the moment are not always clear. In June 2004, Henry recounted two brief anecdotes to his wife and me, one of which illustrates one of the words above:

Nihnii3oxoeyei3i', [personal name in English] and neiteh'eihoho',
  nihnii3oxoeyei3i'.
They were fixing fence, [p.n.] and my friends, they were fixing fence.
Wohei ne'P, "heetonounoot nuhu'."
Well then, "I'm going to use this," [p.n. said].
"Wohei cih'iteninee hinee houunen benoheino'oowu', cih'iteninee," nih'ii3oot,
  hih'iinii3niisi3eiwo'o.
"Wohei get that Crow Bar for me, get it for me," he said to the one who was working with him.
Noh hoowoe'in hini', hi'in hihnii3niisi3eiwo'o.
And [the other one] didn't understand, that thing he was working with.
Hoowoe'in nih'iisinihiit.
He didn't know what he was saying.
"Get that crowbar," ne'ii3oot nih'oo3ouniihi'.
"Get that crowbar," then he told him in English.
Houunen benoheino'oowu'—commercial word.
Crow bar/saloon—a commercial word.[4]

That guy didn't know—hoowoe'in, hini' hihnii3P nii3oxoeP nii3oxoeyei3i',
hinee hihnii3nii3oxoeyoowunoo.

He didn't know, that one they were working with.

Hoowoe'in nih'iisinihii3oot nuhu', nih'iisinihiit: nehe'nih'iisinihii3eit.

He didn't understand what [p.n.] was saying to him, what [p.n.] said; that's what [p.n.] said to him.

Hinen ci', he'ne'he'iiteihi3i he'ihno'usee nehe' [personal name in English], hito'oowuu'.

A man too, then someone arrived at [p.n.]'s house.

Wohei ne'wottonoot, teebe heetwottoneet nehe' [p.n.].

Well then he was going to light a fire for him, this [p.n.] is just now going to light a fire.

Noh ne'P he'ihceenok.

And then [the visitor] sat down.

Wohei heehehk, "heetneyeiwottoneenoo," he'ih'ii3ee hinee hihno'useeneet.

Well [the host] said, "I'm going to try and light a fire," he said to the one who had arrived.

"Beebeehiiho', heetnoo3ou'u.

"Barkers [i.e., barking dogs], I am going to fetch some.

Heetne'wottoneenoo nuhu'."

Then I will light this fire."

Noh ne'P he'ih'ei'towuun[ee], "cih, nei'okun," hihno'useeneet.

And then he told [his visitor], "Gee, you're just sitting there like a lump on a log," [he said to] the one who had arrived.

Wohei huut cihneenoniisei'it.

Well [the visitor] was just sitting there looking dumbfounded.

"Yeah heeyou, tohuu3eih nuhu' beebeehiiho'" [pronounced slowly and quizzically]?

"Yeah, what kind of thing are these barkers?"

(laughter)

The actual Arapaho word for 'bark (from a tree)' is *hinooox*. This anecdote suggests that many of these new joking lexical items may have arisen out of crosslinguistic punning moments such as the ones told here, with some now rising to the level of institutionalized puns (as have both of these) and thus slang, and others to the level of standard terms for the items in question. They can thus be appreciated as both the result of and the tools for the maintenance of certain kinds of interpersonal relationships. The anecdote also suggests that these terms can now be key resources for indexing full membership in AC and full linguistic competence. Since both puns are well known among core native-speaker members of AC, the individuals who failed to get the references are being singled out by Henry for covert criticism. His repeated use of "he didn't know" at the end of the first anecdote (reported in a somewhat incredulous tone) underlines this point. And of course, secondarily, since the anecdotes were told in the context of a session with me, an outside linguist, they index Henry's own competence and full membership in AC.

Also interesting is his use of the term "commercial word," which he used on other occasions as well. Arapaho is a serious language, full of power, while English is a "mere" instrumental language, used for commerce and related activities, he implies. These puns and this slang, even though in Arapaho, are really part of an English and Euro-American COP in terms of their standing as lexical items, he suggests—though the broader punning *practice* here is full-fledged AC. This remark shows a common ambivalence about such slang among AC members: on the one hand, it celebrates Arapaho linguistic ability and creativity, but on the other, it tends to "corrupt" and "degrade" the language and even import English semantics into it. Common examples include expressions like *be3o'uuten-* 'take it hard', based on the English expression 'to take it hard' when one hears bad news, and *koxo'uuten-* 'take it slow', based on the English expression 'to take it slow' when relaxing or recovering from illness. The Arapaho verb *hiten-* (*-uten* noninitially, with vowel harmony) does not have the metaphorical sense that English 'take' does, so the expressions sound humorous and bizarre in Arapaho, as if picking something up slowly off the ground, for example. Some Arapahos find this hilarious in some contexts, while others claim that such usages are ruining the language. These usages are strictly avoided in formal contexts such as prayers or ceremonies, in the same way that English is avoided. In other words, Arapaho shows an ideology not just of language or lexical purity in these contexts, but also of *semantic* purity.

Rather than being used to police COP boundaries, however, these slang neologisms can also be used to engage new learners. In fact, the speaker just cited used the exact same forms (in company with his good friend, also a native speaker) in an informal master-apprentice session that I observed and filmed. The session consisted of a series of humorous Arapaho literal translations of English words, such as "don't fall in love" translated as *ciibeh3eiicensii bixoo3etiit*, literally 'don't fall into love', as if love is a hole in the ground or a container.

The apprentice had to figure out what the Arapaho meant and, in doing so and having the humor explained to her, was learning the different semantic nuances of Arapaho forms, while also engaging in a practice that rendered English practices (and vocabulary) strange, foreign, and bizarre. The two native speakers then added related terms, such as *3eneiicenisi'* 's/he has fallen into it' to build off the verb form. Eventually, Henry brings up the story he had told me several years earlier, this time recounting it to the apprentice, Paula:

HENRY: Howoo that crow bar. They were, they were, nihnii3P nii3oxoeyei'i3i'.
Another [joke] is that crowbar. They were, they were, they were fixing fence.
"Woow ceitinee hinee houunen benoheino'oowu'," [p.n.] said, that guy.
"Now bring that crowbar here," [p.n.] said, that guy.
"Cih! Heeyou nenee'?" he said, "what is it?" that guy.
"Gee, what is that?" he said. "What is it?" that [other] guy [said].

PAULA: Huh.

HENRY: "Yeh, crowbar, get that crowbar," nih'ii3oot.
"Gee, a crowbar, get that crowbar," he said to him.
You know Crow.

PAULA: Yeah.

HENRY: And a bar. You know Crow, Crow bar.

ANDY: Houunenno' benoheino'oowu'.
Crow bar.

DAVE: Benoheino'oowu'.
Bar.

PAULA: Yeah.

ANDY: Hardin, Montana, nee'eesih'iitou'u.
Hardin, Montana, that's what they call it.

PAULA: Nee'eesih'iitou'u.
They call it that.

DAVE: Hardin, Montana, houunen, ne'niitP ne'niitiine'etiiwoohu3i'.
Hardin, Montana, Crow People, that's where they reside.

. . .

PAULA: Hardin.

DAVE: A lot of benoheino'oowuu, wonoo3ei'i.
A lot of bars, lots of them.

PAULA: Uhh-huh.
HENRY: Yeah.[5]

(ELAR 56a)

Since knowledge of these puns is important for membership in AC, the two native speakers are providing the information necessary for the apprentice to be integrated into the community, while also simultaneously engaging in joking behavior with her (rather than simply explaining the joke), and also providing her with the means to engage in the same joking behavior with other speakers in the future. Even if she lacks the linguistic ability to repeat the full account, she can use the slang term for crowbar in an effective fashion to maintain affiliation with AC and engage in the linguistic joking that is central to AC relationships. Thus these neologisms and slang terms are a preferred mode of language-acquisition-related interaction across generations.

Another common conversational genre in AC these days is the "word search" discussion, where a speaker does not know a word, or where perhaps a word does not even exist. These discussions often end in humor, as in the following case where three women—all native speakers—are cooking a meal:

ALICE: How do you say potato salad?
JANE: That's what I was telling XXX. cee'ei'i. I don't know how to say salad.
That's what I was telling ???. Potatoes. I don't know how to say [potato] salad.
Cee'ei'i.
Potatoes.
ALICE: Salad. . . .
JANE: Salad, yeah. [pause] Cee'eito salad.
(laughter)

(ELAR 64b)

In this case, the joke ends the discussion, and no Arapaho word is ever arrived at. Faced with an awareness of language shift and her own loss of competence in the language, the speaker uses humor to dissolve the potentially distressful or embarrassing moment, while also showing linguistic creativity of a sort widely admired in AC. Here the "contamination" from English is even more pronounced than in the cases in the previous anecdote, and one might be tempted to focus on the discontinuity in semantics. But the speech practice itself—the performance—shows strong continuity with Arapaho joking and punning practices generally and joking naming practices in particular. The speaker enacts her ability in these practices and thus her strong membership in AC. As with ironic place names, the joking behavior here turns out to have much stronger continuity with past *practice* than the surface semantics would suggest.

A second example, from the same conversation, illustrates that the performance here is not simply a onetime innovation but a widely practiced strategy:

ALICE: [Personal name, in English], how do you say pickles?
LINDA: 'iiheihoo . . .
Golly gee . . .
ALICE: I just say yeinou'u.
I just say yeinou'u.
JANE: That's tomatoes.
ALICE: Tomatoes, yeinou'u, yeah.
JANE: Yeah yeinou'u is tomatoes.
Tomatoes, yeinou'u.
LINDA: I don't know.
JANE: I don't even know either.
Pickles . . .
[Pause]
PAULA: That sounds like Alfred. Said siisiiduck, 'innit?
JANE: Siisiiduck [smiling, laughing slightly].
PAULA: Yeah.
KATE: Siisiiduck! Crazy! Siisiiduck [laughing].

(ELAR 64b)

The joke here is that *siisiiko'* means 'duck'. Apparently someone could not remember how to say this word, and so the crosslinguistic joke form *siisiiduck* was offered by Alfred. In this case, the speaker does not create a form herself to resolve the pickles question but instead reports a similar resolution to a similar question done by someone else. The speaker who does this, Paula, is not a native speaker of Arapaho, though she is a helper in the immersion school and thus in a master-apprentice role. Although her linguistic ability may be limited, she is able to successfully enact this key AC-language *practice*, if indirectly. She thus humorously resolves the situation, as with the preceding example, while also indexing her membership in AC via her performance of this joking routine. In other words, she does what the two men were teaching another apprentice to do in the example above involving the crowbar. Two other women respond approvingly, repeating the formation, with the second one (Kate, also a second-language learner) adding "Crazy!" which in this context indicates approval of a successful humorous attempt. Thus these five women—three native speakers and two younger learners—come together to complete this joking routine successfully and affiliate as mutually supportive members of AC.

Note in this case that as with place names (and somewhat with folk etymologies), a particular type of ironic humor targeted toward English and Euro-American culture is the practice that allows the generations to come together most successfully. The actual COP "in play" here, as well as the emergent identities, is ambiguous, however. In part the moments of joking between elders and learners seen in this chapter (and see also the conclusion) serve as forms of lateral boundary maintenance in relation to identities, similarly to ironic place names. They all make salient the topic of English as opposed to Arapaho language, and thus they also make salient issues of Euro-American, Pan-Indian, and Arapaho identity (including both AC and Politico-Tribal). In the cases here, however, the humor could also be analyzed as serving a narrower AC-affiliation role. In particular, it helps bridge gaps in linguistic knowledge that might potentially disrupt a unitary AC community. Most profoundly, the humorous language practices help maintain the social relations that are potentially the source of both social and MTH power within AC. While such power is not directly at issue in this moment of interaction, the language and humor help maintain the pathways along which such power can flow on other occasions. Crucially, the older speakers have to recognize the continuity of deeper AC practice that is occurring and engage with this by being accommodating to surface-level discontinuities in Arapaho-language ability, as the three women are here. (In contrast, the first examples with "crowbar" and "bark" show cases where humor is used to exclude potential younger learners of the language, producing a much narrower version of AC.)

The fact that the joking examples among the women occurred in the kitchen of an immersion school, while they were cooking traditional foods in order to feed an older woman who was going to come and tell stories, reinforces the idea that this was a highly AC-relevant setting. Yet clearly we must recognize that clear-cut distinctions—even at the level of prototypes—among different COPS are not always possible, though they have their heuristic uses in this study. Moreover speakers themselves often play with and manipulate these ambiguities, as we saw in chapter 2. Even more importantly, a clear-cut distinction between vertical relationships oriented toward access to MTH power and laterally oriented relationships concerned with ethnic-identity orientation cannot be sustained. Joking about White people and English and strange Euro-American practices is a widely used resource among the Northern Arapaho, and it can be multifunctional not just from time to time and place to place but even at a single moment. Claims to differential MTH power obviously also strengthen the legitimacy and appeal of Politico-Tribalism and Pan-Indianism, while underlining ethnic differences obviously further strengthens AC. Thus these particular topics of joking strongly lend themselves to creating solidarity across multiple COPs, as well as accomplishing the multifunctionalism emergent in specific contexts. Certainly in some cases, the jokes are specifically about differentials in MTH and other forms of power between Arapahos and Euro-Americans (see chapter 2), which suggests a strong AC focus—or perhaps an attempt to erase distinctions within Northern Arapaho society and draw affiliates of other COPs into the AC COP.

In the conclusion to chapter 3, I argued that irony seemed to have replaced power in certain place-naming practices, and I raised the same possibility in the end of chapter 5. This led to the suggestion (reinforced in chapter 4) that there are major discontinuities between fluent elders and younger people and that linguistic "power pathways" in AC may have partially closed down, or at least are perceived as having done so by many elders. This may well be the case for younger people committed to Pan-Indian or Politico-Tribal (or Assimilationist) COPs. However in the examples here we can see that at least for the AC COP, irony and humor when deployed properly have the potential to serve as a "deferred pathway" to social and MTH power for both elders and younger persons. While this has likely always been the case in AC to some extent, this pathway is perhaps becoming increasingly important as loss of language ability among younger AC members makes direct pathways mediated via fluent language usage increasingly problematic. The fact that much of the humor here is about the English language and Euro-Americans should not lead us to assume automatically that the social function of this humor is merely lateral identity work in relation to that other language and society. Certainly that is part of the work, but the relationship work across generations is even more important in many cases. The specific topics of the English language and Euro-Americans are, in a way, just a particularly safe topic around which to engage in humorous relationship building.

Despite all the jokes about not having or finding words, of course new words are eventually arrived at sometimes. The discussion mentioned above at Arapahoe School, which began with the problem of the rooster, continued as follows:

ALLEN: Yeah, there's a lot of words that we're losing.
JOE: Yeah.
DAVE: Yeah, that's. . . .
JOE: 'oh we've been making some [up].
But, we've been making some up.
DAVE: Have to, we have to make new words too.
JOE: Yeah, we make words, you know. When we in Denver, we got computer and we got uhm Facebook and all that, terms . . .
DAVE: Yeah. Got cell phone too 'innit?
DARRELL: Yeah.
JOE: Descriptive terms.
DAVE: What did you guys settle on for cell phone, what have you got for that?
ALLEN: Yeah.
DARRELL: Yeah, woteikuutonehe.'
Yeah, small phone.
JOE: It's something about kind of a small, a diminutive of a phone.
DARRELL: Yeah, woteikuu3oonehe'.
Yeah, small phone.
JOE: Yeah, woteikuu3oonehe'.
Yeah, small phone.
DAVE: Woteikuu3oonehe'.
Small phone.
ALLEN: You know, tih'ini, tih'eenetini' howoo, hi3oowo', hii3oobein.
You know, when, when we spoke too, remember [we came up with words], you're right.
JOE: Yeah, yeah.
. . .
JOE: Yeah. And so rooster, yesterday I said I'm gonna call it, what did I say, "niinohkuseicetouuhut."
Yeah. And so rooster, yesterday I said I'm gonna call it, what did I say, "it hollers early in the morning."
ALLEN: Uhm-hmm.

JOE:	It hollers early in the morning, yeah.
ALLEN:	Yeah. That sounds, that sounds all right.
JOE:	Yeah, that's descriptive, yeah. That's what they do.
ALLEN:	Yeah.
DAVE:	Pretty accurate, yeah.
JOE:	Yeah, pretty accurate, yeah. Niinohkuseicetouuhut.
	It hollers early in the morning.
DAVE:	Niinohkuseicetouuhut.
	It hollers early in the morning.

(ELAR 133b)

The speakers further reinforce the ideology of descriptiveness and transparency, both in their comments on the annual Cheyenne-Arapaho language conference in Denver, where each year there is a discussion of new terms, and in their evaluation and approval of the new term proposed here. Facebook, by the way, is *ceeyobeet* 'gossiping, saying whatever comes to mind', while Twitter is *heces-ceeyobeet* 'little gossiping'. The discussion also allows for sharing of the proposed terms with other users (*ceeyobeet* is now in active use among some speakers), and as the terms for Facebook and Twitter show, the tradition of humorous commentary on Euro-American technologies and practices continues.

NEOLOGISMS AND THE FORMAL EDUCATION SETTING

Informal creation of new words seems to have slowed significantly sometime in the 1960s or 1970s, as English increasingly came to replace Arapaho as the predominant everyday language for more and more people. At this point, direct insertion of English words, with standard Arapaho English pronunciation, began to replace the formation of new description words. This occurs in two forms—usage of full English expressions or insertions of English words into Arapaho grammatical patterns. There is a standard grammar of foreign word insertion in Arapaho: nouns add *-hii* plus an affix (*garage-hii-ne'* 'at/in the garage', with locative suffix), and verbs add *-hii* for intransitives, *-hiih-* for transitives, and *-hiihee-* for middle voice (*Heet-won-dialysis-hiihee-noo* 'I am going to go get a dialysis treatment'). The second insertion pattern is the one preferred by fully fluent speakers: they state that the ability to use the proper

Arapaho affixes with the English shows that a person really knows how to speak Arapaho.

As evidence for the timing of the shift away from new-word creation to English borrowing/replacement, we can note that there are widely known words for television, movie, record player, typewriter, and other examples of mid-twentieth-century technology (even photocopier), but until recent formal, institutionalized word-formation processes were established, there were no widely known or used forms for cassette player, computer, videotape, or other technological innovations introduced in the 1980s or later. It appears likely that the word-formation process did not so much simply stop as lose the power to produce full lexicalizations within the speech community: the decreasing use of the language often apparently led to a failure of uptake of proposed new terms since they did not have enough opportunity to be widely heard and spread through the community. Individuals can be found who can offer Arapaho terms for these more recent technologies, and they claim that the terms have been in use for many years, but on checking it is difficult or impossible to find others in the community who know them. Small groups such as close friends or a single family seem to have shared a term, while other such clusters had equally narrowly known equivalent terms. It should be noted that even for older, more standardized terms, there is variation, such as for 'banana' (*hiiniinsiinoo'* 'it is horn-shaped', *niihooyoo'* 'it is yellow') and 'elephant' (*honookowuubeet* 'it has a bent nose', *see'eteet* 'it has flat ears'). However, in these latter cases, speakers all seem to know both forms and will even alternate between one and the other as the mood strikes them, whereas in the former cases, knowledge of alternate or competing forms is absent.

A new and quite different wave of neologism formation began to occur in the 1980s and 1990s, largely under the impetus of the Northern Arapaho Language and Culture Commission (NALCC), which was formed in the early 1980s and was highly active through the mid- to late 1990s. In this context, committee-based neologisms began to become common. In some cases, the entire committee (which originally consisted of six members) would meet and create new words. In other cases—the more common procedure recently—a single member of the committee has been consulted and asked to suggest a word when the need has arisen in a given school. Out of this process came words such as *koonoh'e'inoo* 'computer' ('it knows everything'), *bei'ci3eini hi3konoo3oo* 'magnet' ('metal inhaling/sucking-up thing'), *hoseinouniixoneihii* 'carnivore' ('meat eater'), and *neniteeno' kookoh'ouheihi3i'* 'anthropology' ('people are examined').

Many of these new word formations were driven specifically by the creation of bilingual school curriculum, which flourished during this period, particularly in the Ethete area, where NALCC cochair Ron was highly active. Note also that quite a number of the terms are actually loan translations from either English or the original Latin and Greek meanings of the words (carnivore and anthropology, also 'nocturnal'—*niinoo'ei3i' biih'iyou'u*, lit. 'they hunt at night').

This stage of word formation was highly bureaucratized, with paid employment on the NALCC and in the schools for teachers and administrators. This was a time when knowledge of how to read and write the language was a major source of cultural and economic capital. A process was developed for certifying teachers and other Arapaho-language employees, run by the NALCC. Curriculum development often had to respond to state standards and expectations that made little local sense for AC and were a major challenge to the NALCC and curriculum developers. Ron told me that he was told in one case that he had to develop a book with sentences concerning forty animals, forty parts of the body, forty place names, and so forth. He did so in a bravura performance, incorporating complex linguistic forms, a great deal of local knowledge, and characteristically Arapaho humor with distinctive Arapaho English translations (see Cowell 2002b). For 'elbow' he came up with the Arapaho "If you don't wash that elbow, it's going to look like a prune," and for the verbs section, "He smokes so much he looks like a walking stovepipe." In an oblique reference to the requirements for the animals that he had to include, the Arapaho sentence about giraffes was "That's the first time he ever saw a giraffe around here." Ron was justifiably proud of this effort and felt that perhaps no one else on the reservation could have come up with all the necessary names and forms.

Unfortunately, as might be imagined, the curriculum produced from these efforts tended to be at too high of a linguistic level—a level beyond that attainable by students in the Arapaho-language classroom or usable by teachers in those classrooms. Thus, while many of the new words appear in curricular materials (or in a revision of the 1983 Salzmann dictionary produced in 1998 with the help of anthropologist Jeffrey D. Anderson), they were never really learned by students. They were also never extensively used by Arapaho classroom teachers themselves—many of whom likely did not know exactly what terms like 'arthropod' meant in the first place, in English. Indeed, the word-formation process often involved someone with college-level or above learning—sometimes, though not always, non-Arapaho—explaining to the Arapaho language commissioners exactly what 'carnivore' or 'anthropology' meant, and then the consultant(s) translating that meaning into Arapaho. Thus the process of neologism formation was heavily driven by academic English in all its components. Little of the underlying semantic structure of Arapaho was employed in the formation of these words, and an Arapaho-internal redescription model was replaced by a loan translation model that was fundamentally discontinuous with the processes described earlier in this chapter and could possibly be considered an "inauthentic" process of neologizing, in the sense discussed by Leanne Hinton and Jocelyn Ahlers (1999) for California languages. Certainly the loan translation model indexed a specific type of relationship with Euro-American society that was active in the neologism process.

Official committee-style meetings designed to create new words became steadily less frequent after the mid-1990s, as did the production of new bilingual curriculum with its neologism-driving component, in large part because the most active coordinators of the effort (i.e., grant seekers) as well as participating elders either passed away, retired, or moved into other positions. At the same time, the number of speakers of the language continued to decline, and the existing school language-teaching strategies proved unsuccessful in producing new speakers. Due to the declining number of speakers and lack of adequate distribution and publication methods, few of the 1980s/1990s neologisms actively entered the vocabulary of general speakers: the overall tendency of the last forty years to simply insert the English terms has remained consistent outside of school settings. Thus there has been a growing division between the language of elderly speakers and the lexicon being used in schools, and even a rejection of school-derived neologisms—a phenomenon widely reported for other language revitalization efforts (Hinton and Ahlers 1999; Wong 1999; Neely 2012:104–6). This division between school-based language learning and community usage is also a product of two other important issues. First, especially due to the demands of largely Anglo-American-derived curricular expectations, topics of school-based learning are often quite dissimilar from the everyday concerns of native speakers, as shown by the 'giraffe' example. Students tend to learn words—especially isolated nouns—for things like 'penguin', but they do not know basic forms necessary for everyday communication and social interaction. Therefore they cannot actually talk about penguins or put the word to use in any communicative context, and if they did, fluent elders would not know the word anyway. The learning of "exotic" nouns in itself would not be a problem were intergenerational communication in Arapaho occurring; indeed, it would be a good thing, as it would be part of an overall survival and evolution of the language. But the second key issue is that the students virtually never acquire enough Arapaho to effectively use the nouns and other new words they are learning at school and integrate them into a meaningful conversation with fluent elders. Thus the world of "school Arapaho" often remains functionally isolated from the world of "everyday elder Arapaho," with the few fluent school teachers being insufficient to bridge the gap between the two domains.

More recently, this gap has begun to be at least partially bridged. Since roughly 2007, new models for at least semiofficial neologism creation have developed. To a significant extent, these are the result of the local Arapahos themselves taking charge of language-education programs on the reservations, replacing previous outside contractors or consultants. Rather than being driven by the needs of K–12 language classes, funded through Title VII, as was the case with the efforts in the 1980s and 1990s, the most recent efforts are driven largely by the needs of immersion preschools. The K–12 model, because it was grant funded, tended to involve official channels and designated paid workers, who were eager for these jobs and certainly did not welcome "free" contributions from others that might challenge the need for their position. The new model involves ad hoc meetings of groups of elders at broader language and culture conferences. Attendance at the conferences is much more open to the community than were the NALCC official meetings or curriculum-development efforts. Among the larger group of elders already present at the conferences, a smaller group will typically hold an ad hoc meeting in order to suggest new words, often at the encouragement of some particular teacher or occasionally collaborating linguist. The small ad hoc meetings are open to anyone interested in sitting around a table to listen and contribute, including nonspeakers, who might suggest needed words or interpretive glosses to be translated into Arapaho—indeed such people are commonly present. These meetings still primarily respond to the needs of students and teachers in Arapaho language-education programs, but they are notable in that they are not narrowly curriculum driven. Rather, they are a general response to pervasive new everyday technologies that teachers and especially students want to be able to discuss. At the first such meeting that I attended in 2008, most of the words created were for items like iPod, DVD, software, and the like, as well as terms related to casinos. More recent meetings at Cheyenne-Arapaho language conferences in Denver in 2012 and 2014 focused on terminology for describing football, basketball, track and field, and other popular AC sports. The results are now also being posted on a website hosted by the University of Colorado.

A second model used for creating the most recent wave of neologisms has occurred in the immersion preschools themselves, which have operated in Ethete for many years, and more recently since 2008 at Arapahoe, with some activity coming from regular elementary-school Arapaho classes as well, especially Arapahoe Elementary School. Again, the production of neologisms has been largely curriculum driven and school based. Initial elements of it were driven by Dr. Neyooxet Greymorning, who helped found and administer the Ethete school for a number of years. However, whereas the previous wave of neologisms tended to be a top-down process, in which curriculum was often centrally produced and then simply given to the teachers (with major limitations in success), the more recent process has been increasingly teacher and even student driven. At its most basic, it comes from students asking, "How do you say *astronaut* in Arapaho?" Equally common are teachers translating simple children's books into Arapaho, to read in the classroom, and asking how to say "rocket," for example. Also common is the need to teach basic content such as colors, shapes, and so forth in an immersion setting, thus producing a need for words such as rectangle, triangle, ellipse, and so forth.

The mechanism for the creation of these neologisms remains in one sense similar to that of the previous wave—consultation with elders—but the process is less formalized, and a given teacher often consults with whichever elder he or she may know best or feel most comfortable with, or with whichever one happens to be working at the particular school. Immersion schools also employ multiple elders, thus offering the opportunity for informal consultation over lunch. Thus both the words created and the creation process are markedly more bottom-up than top-down. One result of this localism, however, is that the two immersion preschools on the opposite side of the reservation have become competing centers of neologism formation: for example, the word used for triangle in Ethete is *neneesoonee'* 'it is made of three parts', while in Arapahoe the word *neneesouuyoo'* 'it has three points' is used. And the new words still remain largely confined to the school settings and population, though a few words such as *ceeyobeet* 'Facebook' have spread beyond these settings, and even to Oklahoma, as the teachers and language commissioners talk to each other and then to friends and relatives, and as the different revitalization programs work with each other.

The current overall process is more promising than that of the 1980s and 1990s because of its Arapaho student- and teacher-driven nature. The words are much more likely to be actually used in the classroom, and to be learned by teachers and students, since the demand comes out of actual usage situations (see Thieberger 2002). In many cases, the words are written down and posted in appropriate places in the school. The extension of these words beyond the communities of the schools themselves remains a very limited process, but the situation shows that even a small immersion program can give a degree of new impetus to a language in ways beyond simply the effort to produce new speakers.

In a related development, both immersion preschools also serve as de facto master-apprentice programs. In Ethete, language students from the Wind River Tribal College help the elder women in the classroom, while at Arapahoe, younger learners are paired with fluent elders in teams of two in each classroom. In some cases, particularly at Arapahoe, these relationships extend outside the classroom, with the younger individuals adopted as language protégés of the elders, so that they drive around together, eat meals at each other's house, or go to the casino together. One form of this relationship is extensive text messaging (in Arapaho) between some of the twenty- and thirty-something students and sixty-something teachers. This process has led to the development of new words for things such as "use up all the minutes on a prepaid cell phone" (*beetookoh-* 'use up a liquid, by means of an instrument' [TI]—an extension of the language for using up the gas in a car).

In summary, newer models involve: (1) semiformal meetings of elders and younger people, discussing suggested words at conferences; (2) neologisms created semiformally by groups of teachers at a school; (3) neologisms suggested by an external elder (often the two NALCC cochairmen) to one or more of the teachers at the school, responding to their queries—again a semiformal process, which recognizes forms of elder authority in that the paid chairmen of the NALCC are called; and (4) true single-person neologisms being created in one-on-one interaction. All these models involve degrees of counterhegemonic reaction to the highly formalized, bureaucratized, and Anglocentric calqued translations of the first wave of revitalization-era neologisms.

As much as these newer processes are from the ground up, it is still striking how central elder authority is to the process. These individuals are now seen as the only ones capable of creating new words in ways that maintain an Arapaho-centric and transparent perspective in the language (cf. Powers 1986:5 for the same views among the Lakota; M. Nevins 2013:218 and associated references on the Apache). Individual teachers for the most part seem very hesitant to create or suggest new forms on their own. The clear preference is for committee-based elder consultation, or for calls to culturally designated "experts"—the NALCC in particular. The one teacher who is notable for creating his own personal neologisms (including the cell phone minutes example above) teaches the language at Central Wyoming College, a high-prestige position, as well as at the University of Wyoming, which grants him a quite different position from the local K–12 teachers. I had the following conversation with a native-speaker worker at the tribal college, who often informally assists in language classes:

ANDY: They were looking for penguin the other day.
HELEN: Yeah, penguin, we gave, I spelled it out for, uhh [p.n.].
ANDY: What did you call it?
HELEN: Uhm, it was, what did Ron call it? I have it down.
ANDY: Oh.
HELEN: But he said it's in the mammal group.
ANDY: Oh. I would have said something like, wo'wuunii'eihii. Wo'wu-unii'eihii, like ice bird or something.
HELEN: No, it wasn't it.
ANDY: Oh, okay.
HELEN: But he gave us a name, a name, and I called [p.n.], because she kept asking me. And there was another one that they wanted to know. XXX. But these exotic animals . . . that they didn't have around here you know. They just had to more or less, you know, names for them like their environment. But that's what Ron said. It's in that mammal group, nih'iit [*he said*]. Yeah, [p.n.], they wanted to know.
(ELAR 71c)

We see here the reliance on a single expert—one of the cochairs of the NALCC in this case. There is apparently a great deal of reluctance on the part of either this teacher or the other teacher being discussed to come up with a name on their own. The name given by the NALCC head is considered "the" name, despite the fact that it was created by that person only earlier in the week, and it must now be respected almost like a personal name. An alternative suggestion is rejected out of hand. Yet the name is apparently so unfamiliar and nonintuitive that it must be written down and even then cannot be remembered. The teacher recognizes that the exotic animal is unknown and therefore difficult to name based on personal experience. She is aware that penguins are anomalous as birds since they do not fly, but she confusingly mixes this up with the idea that penguins are supposedly mammals (likely thinking about a platypus). Thus despite changes for the better in many cases, we see here a highly inorganic process for neologism creation, which looks to be very likely a failure. Of course most neologism suggestions in all languages are likely failures. But here we see some of the ways in which the continued reliance on elder respect produces a very problematic process.

In addition, students themselves seem to almost never create neologisms or suggest them in Arapaho—or even propose English glosses that could be translated into Arapaho to create new Arapaho words, though this does occasionally happen. And in situations of disagreement, the gloss proposed by elders seems to always win. I am not aware of any purely student-created words being used in opposition to elder-suggested forms. Thus in what has to be considered an ironic twist, the creation of "new" words in Arapaho is an area where *older* patterns of elder respect seem the most pronounced, even more so than in personal naming or place naming, where challenges to elder authority occur, as we have seen.

In reality, this can be fairly easily explained, and the explanation is similar to what we found for folk etymology. Both personal names and to a lesser extent place names are highly salient among many Arapahos and have important symbolic value. As a result, individuals who are otherwise only peripherally involved in language learning and preservation—people outside the AC COP—are often very interested in these topics. Such individuals are typically less deeply committed to the ideology of elder respect than others who are more centrally involved in the maintenance and revitalization process. Thus though they accept the symbolic value of the language, they are less willing to embrace attempts at embedding elder authority in language and process. In contrast, those most closely associated with the various schools and colleges—AC members—are more committed to the language as a whole, as opposed to just small symbolic components of it, and are also more committed to the key ideology of elder respect. Only these latter individuals are likely to be much concerned with neologism creation. It is much less salient and less closely linked to what we could call *symbolic traditionalism* than personal names or place names—although more closely tied to everyday processes of basic communication! Thus this process remains more traditionalist than others so far examined in this book, even though it engages with technological modernity most intensively.

Traditionalist does not mean consensus driven, however. It is interesting to compare what we have found so far in Arapaho schools with the situation described for the Western Apache by M. Eleanor Nevins. Clearly the integration of Arapaho language into education has the potential to be highly alienating in relation to traditional structures of language use, language learning, and elder authority. It is common to hear even today that "the language starts in the home." This phrase invokes the idea that the authority structures of schools are inappropriate for true learning of Arapaho language *and* AC practices. This is the fear that M. Eleanor Nevins (2008) describes for the Western Apache, and this is some of what appears to have happened in the 1980s and 1990s with the Arapaho—though even at this time, there were key ways in which elder teachers were able to integrate Arapaho cultural and performance traditions into the classroom effectively (see Cowell 2002b). Notably, even though Arapaho elders were intimately involved with the production of the curriculum at that time, the external bureaucratic processes that were central to its creation led to an inability to integrate it well into the classroom. There was also resistance by other Arapaho elders because of the lack of an elder-*consensus*-based (as opposed to just elder-based) process, and additionally, there was a great deal of distrust of some of the content of the curriculum produced. Thus complaints such as the following could—and still can—be heard from fluent speakers. This is an excerpt from a conversation in which an older man, Lester, is chatting with his wife, Linda, with me also present. His wife had been a certified teacher, whereas he had not attained this due to a lack of Arapaho literacy skills, but the main target of his critique is younger Arapahos who are nonfluent but teachers, and also me, as an outsider involved in the teaching process (I give only the English translation here):

> *Well what's more, this, when they recognize/certify [teachers], and now when these councilmen [sign off on it], it seems like they blame them [for not getting a job], and over there for I don't know how many years, we are always stuck. But I'm not. . . . They don't want to call me certified; and here is this woman, and here is this woman, where . . . also my older sister, it's like they [don't want to classify them as] certified. Also, somehow "are you certified, you?" [they always ask]. That one, that one, you are permitted [to teach], because you are white. Who certified you? . . . I guess I'm watching it, I guess this is not how we [should] live, I guess then things are all just entangled. I guess they can't . . . the Arapahos are going apart [from each other]. It is different [now] how . . . no longer . . . those ones say these things, they mention things [i.e., they pronounce the word, use it]. But only . . . they are really only words; they are not followed [i.e., the true meaning of the word is not understood or lived out]. . . . I guess that's how the White Man lives; we're headed that way. It's like this, because people don't respect each other, or because*

they don't listen to each other. The young people are the ones who give the commands/are in charge all around. And the elders are not listened to. (ELAR 44b)

This passage is a quite complete example of the critique of the education system heard from many AC individuals. Whites are too dominant, along with younger Arapahos who are allied with the Whites and think and act like them. Fluent elders are excluded through bureaucratic processes such as certification, which requires reading and writing ability. Most fundamentally, "respect" relationships do not exist—in other words, social relations based on reciprocity and elder authority do not exist. As a result, not only do many elders lack social power in this system, but MTH power is also vacated from the system, they claim. Because of this, the language itself is detached from flows of MTH power— and any serious meaning, according to some elders. People say words, but they are "just" words, in the same sense that elders argue that some place and personal names are "just" names—nominalized elements no longer embedded in proper systems of social relations. Without the language practices that mediate social relations and power transfers, the system crumbles. This is the system that especially in the past generated a series of neologisms that are also "just" words, which have largely not entered into the language as vehicles of social action and power and likely never will—though as we saw, it was as much elders themselves as the middle-aged generation who were responsible for much of this work, and these elders worked with the best of intentions, even as they did seek to maintain their social capital and prestige.

What we find here is actually a four-way split within AC around the issue of the language, the schools, and reading and writing practices, with three components of the split involving elders themselves. Some elders are simply not interested in engaging with the schools, due to the kinds of suspicions Nevins finds among the Western Apache, but this is actually not especially common at Wind River. Other elders, such as the one just cited at length, are not interested in learning to read or write but are interested in engaging in the schools. They most commonly explain their resistance to literacy as a resistance to excessively "White" educational practices that betray more traditional Arapaho culture, and they thus share some viewpoints with the previous group of elders. The lack of literacy excludes this second group of individuals from the classroom, however, other than as "resource persons." A third group of elders have learned to read and write and have relatively well-paying and prestigious positions in the schools, which they tend to protect by arguing against allowing nonliterate speakers to teach. Then there is a fourth group, of younger second-language learners or semispeakers, who often occupy teaching positions now and who are literate. The second and third groups of older individuals tend to resent these younger people occupying school positions, although the younger people often have much more extensive teacher training. Conversely, while some of these younger people show strong elder respect and reliance on them for neologisms, others are less pliant in this regard, and they of course resent the possibility of being forced out of their position by those elders, so this fourth group is split between those with more or less close alignments with elders. Thus teaching the language in the schools is a key point of contestation within AC (no other COP is much interested in the contested specifics of language teaching), and the differing approaches to neologisms are indirectly an expression of this tension, with group one ignorant of or ignoring them, group two critical of them due to their inorganic nature, group three promoting them but insisting on their restricted right to produce them, and group four split between trying to promote and use the forms on their own, and relying on the elders (in groups two and three) to provide them all.

As much as one can understand the criticism of the educational system as exclusionary of elder knowledge and the processes of respect relationships, we have seen in this chapter that too much respect for elder authority seems to inhibit the process of forming "real" words as well, since it is primarily young learners who want to actually use these words. There are signs that some elders and some students, working together, are moving toward a middle ground that may be more successful in meeting the needs of both groups, although it may be too late to save the language for the moment as a vehicle of communication. It is not just in informal moments of humor where this is occurring but also in school settings, on a site-by-site basis, where teachers and students are able to escape the tightest clutches of both the educational bureaucracy and extreme elder dominance. The immersion preschools are the exemplary location where this is happening. As noted in the previous chapter, apparent "discontinuity" can often be evidence of positive developments. The fact that the Ethete and Arapahoe preschools have different—but more importantly, actively used—words for "triangle" points to local processes of neologism creation that have "gotten on with business," so to speak, rather than being paralyzed by efforts to work with larger bureaucracies to create a pan-reservation term.

CONCLUSION

As we have seen in all the preceding chapters, the AC COP shows internal tension between those who advocate a narrower and more traditionalist view of AC, with strong elder control, and those with a much broader view, including greatly increased agency for younger speaker-learners and even nonspeakers of the language. This is a common situation in many language maintenance situations. What is less often recognized is that this is not simply an age gap between older, better speakers and younger, less fluent speakers (a point made strongly in Briggs 1998:243). Rather, some older and younger people both remain strongly committed to the idea of MTH power in language, and thus to ideologies of language transparency and "rationality," and thus to elder/expert control of neologisms in order to insure this. Elder-youth collaboration is therefore not just about fostering relationships in the moment, as new words are created, but also about maintaining the linguistic bases for all future relationships: the rationality and transparency of the language are what mediate productive relationships and effective flow of knowledge and power so that the language is not "just words." This rationality and transparency can only be achieved with continued strong elder/fluent speaker input. Some young people are very interested in more traditionalist relationships—including the prestige that comes from gaining wisdom and language ability through such relationships. Conversely, some elders are much more willing to compromise and consider new models of relationship, such as teacher-helper pairings, which grant greater agency in language usage and even neologism formation to younger people. This is similar to the differential degrees of traditionalism and innovation among the different immersion schools with regard to personal names. There is always a delicate calculus between the desire to have a more traditionalist relationship across generations and the possibility that this desire can effectively lead to no relationship at all.

Clearly, elders must be committed to relationships with younger people—and the linguistic practices of relationships—in order for new language to be created and flourish; they cannot just be committed to the language.[6] In this and other chapters, we have seen that humor is a crucial domain for the maintenance of these relationships. This is hardly surprising as a general statement. But we can see that there are deeper theoretical implications involved. First, although there is certainly such a thing as "sacred humor" in Arapaho, virtually all the humor we have seen in this book is a nonserious type that disengages with questions of MTH power—whether in place names, personal names, or folk etymologies and neologisms. This disengagement lowers the stakes, so to speak, in terms of MTH power. With the stakes lowered, it then makes it easier for elders in particular to accept a broader view of AC and even to integrate Pan-Indian or Politico-Tribal COP members, since the main points of contention both within AC and among the other COPs ultimately involve the issue of MTH power and its transmission in relationships.

We can now see the deepest implications of crosslinguistic punning in Arapaho as well—what the Dubois/*niisonoh'oho'/*'two boys' place name is really about, or what "*cee'eito* salad" really means. Since such punning plays with and violates notions of linguistic purity, it explicitly keys or indexes forms of communication and relationships that lie outside the domains of language purity, which are also the domains of MTH power. Thus not just joking and humor generally but crosslinguistic, "contaminating" joking and humor in particular can be understood as crucial practices for depressurizing relationship building and language learning, as well as providing spaces for the creation of solidarity across multiple COPs. Humor in general makes it possible for less fluent speakers to more easily engage in the actual linguistic practices that make relationships, since without MTH power directly at stake, the implications of language mistakes are greatly lessened. Crosslinguistic humor in this regard is preferable to Arapaho-only humor, since at least one-half of the basis of the humor (i.e., English) is available to the learners as well as the teachers.

The older speakers must of course recognize appropriate efforts at practice—and relationship building—and not focus only on Arapaho grammatical fluency for this to happen. I now begin to understand much more fully what Richard Littlebear, president of Chief Dull Knife Tribal College, meant when he said to me at a meeting, "You've got to be able to have fun with the language." A marvelous example (though it has nothing narrowly to do with neologisms or crosslinguistic puns) occurred as I was with three fluent speakers who were watching students put up a tipi. A daughter of the oldest speaker came over, and he said to her, "hesiho'. They're your uncles" *'[These other two men are] your uncles. They're your uncles'*. The daughter misunderstood the first word, not realizing the second sentence was a translation of the first, and said, "Hesneeno'?" *'[You said] "they're hungry"?'*. Rather than correcting her, the older speaker said, "Yeah," and the daughter then replied with "yeheihoo" *'gee whiz'*, which, though technically incorrect in that it is a male form (*'iiheihoo* is the female form that she should have used), was pragmatically spot on, as it expressed surprise and sympathy about the supposed hunger of her uncles. One of the uncles chuckled at her pragmatically correct response in the circumstances, and then the oldest speaker promptly engaged in some uncle-nephew teasing, saying: "Heesneet [points at one nephew] noh ceniini, ceniinoseino'" [pointing at the other nephew] *'He is hungry and he doesn't, doesn't have any meat'*. This produced loud laughter from all present. The youngest nephew then responded to the uncle "neneenin" *'you're the one [who's hungry, or who's got no meat]!'* (a typical response to a tease). The daughter then again responded perfectly from a pragmatic perspective, saying, "tebinou" *'poor thing!'* followed by the laughter marker "'iiih," which again elicited loud general laughter. Only at this point did she then greet the uncles with "tous" (the correct female form for 'hello'), at which point the eldest speaker then repeated, "hesiho' nenee3i'" *'they are your uncles'* (ELAR 28a).

Many things are striking about this moment. First, the elders do not correct the younger person's communication attempt (which would effectively shut it down). Rather, they open a space for it to continue, recognizing that the speaker knows Arapaho well enough to have heard a form wrongly, but in relation to another proper Arapaho form. This could be read as its own form of resistance to language "purity" or narrow correctness. The daughter is successfully able to jump into the space provided, albeit again without the exactly required form. Again, the elders accommodate, and the oldest speaker creatively *uses* the daughter's error in understanding (*hesnee-* 'to be hungry') as the basis for performing the teasing that the original phrase (*hesiho'* 'your uncles') implicitly evoked, since uncle-nephew is a prominent teasing relationship (and uncle-niece can be as well). The younger nephew jumps in with a counter, which allows the daughter to then produce the pragmatically expected and perfectly appropriate "poor thing" line. At this point, the appropriate relative greeting now occurs (the daughter reaches out her hand to shake hands with the uncles as she says *tous* 'hello'), and the oldest speaker circles back to the original point in Arapaho, that these two men are her uncles, with whom she should therefore expect to have a certain teasing relationship—the exact teasing relationship that the men have just demonstrated for her, and in which she has already successfully participated herself. Thus we have witnessed an extremely adroit and creative emergent performance by the three elders, and an impressive collaborative response from the daughter, all based on a willingness to let language *effort*, combined with a good awareness of AC pragmatics, overcome a lack of language correctness—and all leading to an enhancement of cross-generational relationships.

As in the conclusion of the previous chapter, we once again encounter a great irony, however. The desire to learn Arapaho among younger speakers is often closely tied to ceremonialism and MTH power, to the power in personal names and place names and the rest of the language. Yet in humorous moments disengaged from this question of power, one sees the most coherence within AC, as well as across COPs within Arapaho society. It is in these moments that one often sees the strongest sense of intergenerational relationship and the most use of Arapaho language by learner-speakers. Ironically, one of the key overt reasons for preserving the language (MTH-power orientation) is also one of the principle sources of contestation, relationship difficulty, and narrow exclusivity that often inhibit this preservation. Again, this point should not be pressed to extremes—there are several multigenerational groups of sweat lodge practitioners who are effectively using this occasion to maintain some use of Arapaho and even increase knowledge, for example. But more often than we recognize, the ideologies that enhance the prestige or power of the language can be the ideologies that also get in the way of the compromises and adaptations needed to maintain the practice of the language when sociocultural and linguistic ideologies shift. This discontinuity between ideology and practice in the language maintenance/revitalization setting has taken me many years to fully appreciate.

CONCLUSION

COMMUNITIES OF PRACTICE

A Linguistic Summary

In chapter 1 of this book, I began with an analysis of socioeconomic and sociocultural changes at Wind River over the last 150 years, examined the differing COPs that have developed out of those changes, and noted especially the ways the changes have impacted people in terms of gender, age, and ideologies of knowledge. The next five chapters of the book focused on five specific linguistic domains and the ways that those have changed over roughly the same time period. I want to return now to the COPs, as well as the questions of age—and also gender—in light of the details about the different linguistic domains.

I want to first clarify once again that I understand COPs to be somewhat similar to what are often termed *identities* in the literature of ethnolinguistics and anthropology—that is to say, high-level or predominant identities. A given individual can participate in multiple COPs, and these COPs are to a degree abstract prototypes, in the same way that identities are. My use of the term COP is roughly parallel to what James Collins calls *undertakings*; he notes, speaking of the Tolowa, that "each undertaking makes a slightly or substantially different claim about identity, about Indianness as a relation to the past and hope about the future" (1998b:163). The prototypes and their sociocultural efficacy are maintained as individual social actors move in and out of these identities, occupying and using them for the purpose of social work, then moving on.[1] Many of the specific individuals described in Wiles (2011) illustrate this pattern. Thus these COPs are groups of people "doing things"—that is, pursuing shared goals—at various times and places, not mutually exclusive groupings of individuals who "are" Politico-Tribalists or Pan-Indianists.[2] The COPs can be thought of in some ways as analogous to companies, political parties, or religious denominations—none of which completely define an individual in most cases.[3] The COPs are of course themselves internally complex sites of action and contestation, where individuals may occupy and enact various smaller-scale identities, positions, and stances, as we have seen throughout the book. Nevertheless, there are many individuals who predominantly participate in one or two of these COPs, and it is fair to say that Northern Arapaho people see certain individuals who are very heavily affiliated with one COP or a component of it as "being" Sun Dance people or Peyote people or Sweat people or Powwow people, or as "being" a "real" Arapaho person or not. Also, one can often say that an individual Arapaho person is definitely *not* a participant in one or more COPs. Thus when I say "these individuals" in the following, there is an ambiguity between individuals occupying this COP at a specific point in space and time, and individuals affiliated with this COP as an identity. This is part of the larger ambiguity that necessarily characterizes any attempt to talk about what Shaylih Muehlmann (2014:578) terms *social aggregates* in the context of postmodern linguistic anthropology—there is a tension between groups as empirical objects and groups as analytical categories.

The Assimilationist COP is the group with which I have had the least contact and discussed the least in this book, as my primary interest has been the fate of Arapaho-specific language practices and ideologies. Assimilationists largely reject the notion of MTH power as located in nature, ancestors, or the traditional Arapaho Creator. They also largely reject the AC form of interpersonal relationships that would mediate such power. They see personal power and prestige in much the same way as many in the surrounding Euro-American society—in terms of stable jobs and ideally prestigious careers and social positions, and command of adequate resources to afford nice homes, cars, and other material items, which themselves symbolize status and prestige. Interpersonal relationships are mediated by the pursuit of this form of prestige and power. AC practices and ideologies are not seen as an effective means for either group or individual agency. Older individuals in this group may have extensive knowledge of Arapaho language and culture but rarely practice it. Younger individuals may have an Arapaho name because a parent or grandparent thought it was important but often may not be sure what the name is, how to pronounce it correctly, or what it means specifically. Their knowledge of Arapaho place names is limited to English-language local names, the latter simply by virtue of local residence. These individuals lack any real interest in the Arapaho language and thus in neologisms. They may know one or more folk etymologies related to the word *Arapaho* (*hinono'ei*) itself by virtue of local residence, but rarely more than this. Similarly their knowledge of cultural metaphor is largely limited to knowledge of the path/journey metaphor, again by virtue of local residence and exposure. These individuals largely reject age- or gender-mediated forms of knowledge or respect relationships in the Arapaho-specific sense. They often have a positive view of Arapaho as a "heritage" but little or no practice of the AC features described in chapter 1.

The Evangelical Christian COP is the next least familiar to me in my own research. These individuals, like Assimilationists, reject AC-based forms of MTH power and the relationships that mediate them. They see MTH power as crucial to their lives but as located in Christianity, largely of a type consonant with local Euro-American Evangelical or Pentecostal Christianity. However, they often have a more positive view of Arapaho identity than the Assimilationists. In part, this is because they distinguish themselves from local Whites, in that they remain reservation- and kin-based in both residence and church affiliation (cf. Samuels 2004:7–8 on the Western Apache equivalent; as well as Nevins 2010). In addition, because of this local residence, and because of the mixed religious affiliations within virtually any extended kin group, they maintain fairly close ties to others more engaged in Pan-Indian, Politico-Tribal, and AC COPs. For this reason, they may sometimes be more interested in Arapaho personal names, though for lateral-type identity purposes rather than for purposes related to MTH power: they use these to distinguish themselves from Whites and affiliate themselves with Arapahos. Since the focus is lateral, they may be tempted more toward "Hollywood names" than traditional ones. They may likewise be more interested in local place names but again for lateral identity reasons rather than any connection to MTH power—and thus especially oriented toward local Arapaho-English place names. They are normally not strongly interested in Arapaho language, folk etymologies, neologisms, or cultural metaphors, though the last category (especially path/journey) is sometimes syncretically incorporated into Christian religious discourse, and some joking folk etymologies appeal for the same reasons as joking place names. Their use of and interest in Arapaho is overwhelmingly oriented to highly salient symbolic uses detached from MTH power (cf. Samuels 2006 for the Western Apache) and oriented to the indexing of Arapaho identity. The primary reason that

Arapaho language per se does not appeal is that the denominations they belong to have associated Arapaho ceremonialism—and the people most engaged in that ceremonialism and who use Arapaho language especially in that context—with "going to hell." Thus the Arapaho language is iconic of "paganism" or "heathenism" for the strongest Evangelical Christians.[4] Age, gender, and interpersonal relationships are mediated primarily by Christian models.

Those engaged with the Pan-Indian COP often overlap heavily in practice with Politico-Tribal and AC COPs. These individuals are often committed to ideas of MTH power that look similar to those of AC, and they are likewise committed to interpersonal relationships (like those of the AC sort) that would mediate this power. They likewise tend to be committed at least somewhat to gender and especially age-based distinctions in the possession and transfer of knowledge, similarly to AC. This is in part because "Pan-Indian" itself is not neutrally "pan" Indian but in the Northern Arapaho case most closely associated with related tribes such as the Cheyenne, Crow, Gros Ventre, and especially Lakota, who have shared a great deal of related practices and ideologies over centuries. Thus Pan-Indian practice is often quite consonant generally with long-term Arapaho practice. Conversely, many Pan-Indian practices such as specific powwow dances and the Peyote Lodge have been integrated into Northern Arapaho society (and even AC) in Arapaho-specific ways, including use of the Arapaho language. Peyote songs are often sung in Arapaho, and there are Arapaho-language origin stories for the various powwow dances such as Grass Dance and Jingle Dance.

The primary difference between Pan-Indian and AC COPs lies in the former's decreased commitment to Arapaho-specific modes of MTH power, interpersonal relationships that mediate that power, and ceremonialism. From a negative perspective, loss of tribal languages, as well as rampant intertribal marriage, has made such distinctions less and less relevant for younger people. From a positive perspective, for these people, an identity as "Indian" offers an appealing form of group agency and avenues to individual agency that can be maintained even as one moves from reservation to reservation—in other words, expertise in the Peyote Ceremony transfers from reservation to reservation and brings prestige everywhere, whereas expertise in the Arapaho-specific Sun Dance does not. Arapaho language thus represents less practical utility than it once did—it is not absolutely required in order to access MTH power or to carry on the interpersonal relationships that mediate this power. Neither of these are considered tribe- or language-specific within Pan-Indianism.

Nevertheless, there is within Pan-Indianism at Wind River a remaining strong commitment on the part of some to the notion that Native American languages (all of them, not just one's own tribal language) do provide privileged access to MTH power, as well as Pan-Indian knowledge, in a way that English does not. Middle-aged individuals have told me that the many younger kids want to learn Arapaho (or Gros Ventre or Cheyenne as well) not so that they can use it every day but so they can "gain wisdom" and "understand what it means to be an Indian" (my paraphrases). Of course for anyone from a specific reservation, one's tribal language is the most obvious and convenient Indian language for this purpose. Thus knowledge of the language as a communicative device among peers is not a main goal for Pan-Indian individuals, but knowledge of the highly salient realms of naming discussed in this book is indeed a goal for many of them. Personal names, place names, and the wisdom and perspectives contained in folk etymologies and cultural metaphors are key areas of interest, as is understanding what both older words and neologisms actually mean, in terms of their analyzability and glossability. Much of this knowledge involves understanding of a specific Arapaho name or word. The knowledge *about* the word, however—the story associated with it—is conveyed in English: it is only the name that connects to MTH power and needs to be known in Arapaho. And since the focus is on traditional wisdom, there is little interest in neologisms for the sake of continuing to speak the language daily and also comparatively little interest in creative extension of cultural metaphors to new domains.

For others among the Pan-Indian COP at Wind River, issues of MTH power seem less important than issues of lateral identity formation. For these individuals, Arapaho personal names and place names, or other knowledge of the language, function in a highly symbolic way, focused on high-saliency items that serve as "non-referential resource[s]" for laterally oriented identity purposes (Debenport 2015:50–52). In this sense, these individuals are similar to the Arapaho Evangelical Christians: they seek to define themselves as not White and also to affiliate with others—though in this case, not just with other Arapahos but with other Native Americans. Their Arapaho personal names are thus, functionally speaking, "Indian" names, which happen to be in Arapaho since the individuals are Arapaho. These are the individuals who are likely to seek "Hollywood names." For these individuals, type-2 humorous place names, humorous folk etymologies, and humorous neologisms—all of which normally involve elements of crosslinguistic puns that can be referenced to a shared knowledge of English or even expressed directly in English—are valuable tools for affiliation, which show local variants of Pan-Indian practices. Of course these individuals also tend to maintain strong ties to Politico-Tribal and AC COPs, so Arapaho-language forms specifically remain valuable in this regard. As one student at the tribal college said in June 2009, the language is what "distinguishes us from the rest of the world." But in general, these individuals show low interest in learning the Arapaho language—though the student in question was a notable exception—and their focus tends to be on the most high-saliency Arapaho-language items only, used for indexical purposes—especially personal names and place names.

Affiliates of the Politico-Tribal COP engage in many of the same language behaviors and practices as the second group of Pan-Indian COP members, as the two are quite similar. They seem weakly oriented toward issues of MTH power and mediating relationships, but they are often strongly oriented toward issues of lateral identity, in relation to Whites and other Native Americans. For this reason, Politico-Tribal use of and attitudes toward the various language domains are quite similar to that seen for the second Pan-Indian group, though affiliation is primarily with other Arapahos rather than Pan-Indian in orientation. The primary distinctions between these two groups are in the area of political and economic versus cultural bases for understanding group and individual agency. Politico-Tribal affiliates tend to be more strongly Arapaho specific, because this is the tribe with which they are politically affiliated and on whose reservation they live. They see Native American sovereignty, government-to-government relationships, trust lands, and political identity as enrolled tribal members as the best bet for future group and individual agency, and they are also strongly focused on shared lived experience at Wind River.[5] This leads to strong tendencies to be interested in the symbolic components of Arapaho, for the purpose of indexing identity, but little interest in the MTH-power components of the language.[6] Because this COP is less interested in the cultural/behavioral components of either Arapaho or Pan-Indian identity, its affiliates also are often less committed to age- or gender-graded distinctions in knowledge, relationships, or social roles of the sort common in AC and still commonly supported to a lesser degree among the Pan-Indian COP.[7] Members of this group often make overt statements about the very high importance of the Arapaho language but show little inclination to learn it themselves in depth or to provide tribal resources to support the language. Certain councilpersons have been notorious in this regard for "using" Arapaho-speaking elders for internal or external political purposes and talking often about the importance of the language, but refusing to actually appropriate money for tribal-language purposes.[8]

I should note in passing that the discourse of *indigeneity* is a potential new identity position and COP within Wind River and Native America, but it is not yet strongly established at Wind River. The term itself, as currently used globally, contains elements of Politico-Tribalism (there is after all an official UN declaration), of Pan-Indianism (since the political force of the term is to unite disparate peoples), and of AC (since it appeals to local specificity in language and other practices). What direction the term itself will take in various places around the globe, and how it might be inflected specifically within the context of Wind River, remains to be seen. It is at least possible to imagine that the term could be the basis of a broader alliance across multiple COPs inside and outside Wind River. What would the linguistic practices and ideologies of indigeneity look like among the Northern Arapaho? It is worth pointing out that all the practices discussed in this book—origins of personal and place names, of words and metaphors, and so forth—involve the maintenance or creation of what Debenport (speaking of Pueblo communities) calls "inherently local systems of knowledge" (2015:76). Many conversations cited in this book are specifically oriented toward sharing such local knowledge. As such, this knowledge is one part of a shared experience across the Wind River Reservation, which could eventually feed into a stronger sense of indigeneity that would combine many elements of the Politico-Tribal and Pan-Indian COPs with AC.

The AC COP, as we have seen, is strongly oriented toward the idea of MTH power in an Arapaho-specific sense and toward the human relationships that mediate this power. The views of place naming, personal naming, folk etymology, neologisms, and cultural metaphors are all oriented toward seeking out and maintaining MTH power through language—the Arapaho language specifically. As elders in this COP often say, "The Creator only speaks Arapaho." Not only do members of this COP value the various "naming" practices highly, but they value the everyday use of the language in the same way. I once mentioned to Ron, a cochair of the Northern Arapaho Language and Culture Commission, that someone was trying to use a cultural metaphor (concerning eagles and eagles' wings) in an interesting way on a poster. His reply was that unless the person could explain what the phrase meant "in Arapaho," it had no meaning and should not be used. In other words, not just the words and names but the stories and knowledge behind them had to be in Arapaho (contrast this with the Pan-Indian practice described above). And of course, such stories must be conveyed *to* someone, so it is really relationships overall that must be in Arapaho, from this viewpoint. This corresponds with research by one of my students, who wrote a senior honors thesis examining the reasons why students and teachers were engaged in Arapaho learning (Preciado 2010). The high-school students with whom she worked predominantly said that they wanted to learn Arapaho (again paraphrasing) "to talk to my grandparents." These students are AC affiliates, and they were clearly interested in more than just symbolic and identity-oriented uses of Arapaho. In contrast, several high-school teachers talked about the importance of Arapaho for the purposes of sovereignty and other symbolic uses.

Having spent most of this book teasing apart the different COPs, I would like to conclude by tearing down this edifice a little bit, however. As noted, many individuals move between multiple communities of practice and identities. Very few Northern Arapahos are wholehearted Assimilationists—virtually all maintain attachments to and orientations toward other COPs, and more and more Arapaho people are increasingly viewing their world in explicitly counterhegemonic terms. Conversely, however, very few, especially among the young, are wholehearted practitioners of AC. Life is complicated, and attitudes are ambivalent.[9] As one moves between different spaces and times, one moves between different COPs. More importantly, COPs overlap, and as seen in chapter 1, multiple COPs may be "in practice" at a given moment. More specifically, certain practices are shared across multiple COPs—most notably joking about and making fun of Euro-Americans (present author definitely included!) and of the English language. As we saw especially in chapter 6, core practices of one COP may also be recruited to serve important functions within another COP, and in certain moments, unity across COPs can emerge around practices such as crosslinguistic and crosscultural joking. Ambiguity is a useful strategy in many situations because it can allow bridges and connections to form, or at least to be perceived (cf. Samuels 2004:3–15). The average Northern Arapaho person experiences a kaleidoscope of daily experience and intersubjective practice, partly oriented toward assimilationist pressures or opportunities, part Native American, part member of the Arapaho tribe with all the legal, economic, and political consequences that entails, part oriented toward Arapaho spiritualism and MTH power, also perhaps attending a Christian church, often using the resources of one of these domains to enhance agency or legitimacy in another domain where possible—all while being an individual whose identities and practices exceed the bounds of any of the COPs elaborated in this book.

Yet people do have predominant orientations and special affiliations, and I believe that it is crucial to recognize not just heuristic or analytic categories but real times, places, ideologies and practices, and COPs, in order to make sense of—and fully appreciate—the kaleidoscopic experience of daily reservation life and indigenous life more generally (Clifford 2007, 2013; Canessa 2005). Too often, we search desperately for continuity and a "culture" in Native American communities, and when we fail to find enough of this, we dismiss such communities as "corrupted" and riven by "factionalism," as David W. Samuels notes (2004:14). My approach in this study has sought to avoid this and, in so doing, to show people on and around a reservation responding to their social situation in creative, diverse, multiple, and contested ways, as they move among contexts and encounters in their daily lives, and as they move through history.

LANGUAGE, AGE, AND POWER

While it may seek greater continuity with the past than do other COPs, the AC COP can no more escape the sociocultural transformations at Wind River than any other, and elders in general cannot do so either, despite the fact that many of them affiliate with AC as it offers the strongest discourse in support of elder prestige, authority, and agency. As we have seen in this book, younger affiliates of the AC COP also now more commonly challenge elder respect relationships and elder control of knowledge in the context of language practices and ideologies. Newer type-2 place names such as the Turtle and the Eagle are names without stories, not so different perhaps from the "Hollywood" personal names, which also lack stories. As Ron suggested above, a lack of stories also means a lack of elder-mediated relationships in the creation or transfer of knowledge. As noted in chapter 1, elders lost a great deal of socioeconomic status over much of the twentieth century. In other words, they lost access to socioeconomic power, and kinship relationships with those elders no longer mediated socioeconomic power in the way they once did. For Assimilationists, this is the end of the story. For Evangelical Christians, elders also have no privileged access to Christian MTH power. For Politico-Tribal affiliates, elders also have no special access to legal or political power. For Pan-Indian affiliates, linguistic mediation is also now less important for access to MTH power, and avenues to non-MTH prestige also increasingly involve performative venues that do not rely on elder mediation for participation (one can participate intertribally in many Sun Dances now, for example—though not very easily in the Northern Arapaho one, which still requires having an Arapaho ceremonial grandfather).

In the face of all these losses, one might wonder how age-graded respect relationships survive at all. Indeed, a key point of Jeffrey D. Anderson's study of Wind River during the 1980s and 1990s was the decline in the age-graded components of Northern Arapaho society (Anderson 2001a:199–204, 223–29) and a "widening disjuncture between senior and junior generations" (202), which is fairly different from what Fowler (1982) reports about Wind River.[10] Anderson also makes very similar points to those made in chapter 1—new forms of religion and ceremony and new performative venues all tend to require less elder mediation of knowledge (2001a:205–7, 219). He also suggests that the efficacy of Arapaho-specific MTH power itself has been increasingly called into question, even since the early reservation era (2001a:203, 205). I think it is fair to say that Northern Arapaho elders themselves today strongly feel that elders have lost influence and status over the last fifty to sixty years. They face challenges in maintaining their own status and influence, in promulgating the ideology of elder respect, and in adapting creatively to the changing society so as to find new positions for and new ways of being "elders" as the models and duties of this role continue to change (indeed the term *elder* itself is likely a linguistic Pan-Indianism).

For a not-insignificant number of younger Northern Arapaho people, "respect for elders" is in fact a mere symbolic ideology—the words index membership in certain COPs, or perhaps in Arapaho society generally, but actual practice is difficult to discern. Specific identities internal to the Arapaho tribe—the kinds of identities that once required mediation through and acceptance by older members of the tribe, such as ceremonial positions—are now far less important than externally oriented claims to general Indianness or Arapahoness. In this context, access to linguistic, ceremonial, or esoteric knowledge is important, but primarily as an (often shallow) symbolic vehicle for lateral identity claims rather than for actual access to MTH power. Elders may have such knowledge, but there is no desire for the reciprocal relationship with the elder that would be necessary to mediate access to MTH power. Rather, the desire is simply for the knowledge itself, which will then be deployed laterally and symbolically, outside the relationship with the elder (a few words of Arapaho, for example, to index Arapaho identity). If the knowledge can be acquired without the complex reciprocities involved in traditional elder-younger relationships, all the better for many younger people. Thus the lateral pressure on identity claims converts the elder from a source of knowledge and advancement to, at worst, a potential obstacle to the acquisition of this knowledge and, at best, an irrelevancy if this knowledge is obtainable by other means.

On the other hand, as we also saw in chapter 1, more recent shifts in job availability at Wind River have allowed some older people to regain status as they are able to keep working. In addition, in a still economically fragile society, broad kinship links that extend both horizontally and vertically across generations can be an important mutual benefit, just as they were in pre-reservation times of pulsed resources, and elder respect goes hand in hand with elder responsibilities to those younger than them. The main point here, however, is to understand the relationship of *language* to elder respect. Prior to language loss, this connection certainly existed. Elder prestige was associated with the practice of all the language domains discussed in this book as elders tended to have the greatest historical and linguistic knowledge, and of course they were also the privileged performers of various genres of prayer, ritual, song, traditional narrative, and other genres.

Today, language loss has led to *greater* prestige for elders among other affiliates of AC since they are the only ones who can speak the language authoritatively. Young AC individuals now say, "I learned my Arapaho from X individual" in the way they would have formerly explained how they acquired other kinds of specialized knowledge. Even when one is reduced to learning the language through recordings, books, or websites, one can still cite the source of the knowledge. In addition, we have seen that Politico-Tribal and Pan-Indian COPs place great importance on the symbolic value of the Arapaho language, and while fluent elders remain alive, they benefit from the cultural capital that accrues to them for this reason. The new status of the language also then combines with the trend to more white-collar jobs, in the form of membership on the Northern Arapaho Language and Culture Commission (a paid position), work as a language consultant, and especially work as a classroom consultant/resource person or classroom teacher, in a melding of Politico-Tribal and AC COPs. Thus there are clear bases for understanding why *certain* elders—those with jobs or those who know Arapaho, and especially those with both attributes—would remain influential in Northern Arapaho society, among several different COPs, and how they are able to use the discourse of elder respect successfully with some younger people to maintain or enhance their own status in the community. More particularly in the context of the language, they continue to give personal names, supply information on place names and even provide new ones (for immersion schools, for example), creatively produce neologisms and folk etymologies whose authority and legitimacy is recognized, and use and extend cultural metaphors, in addition to producing prayers, narratives, and so forth. The ideology of MTH power and mediated transfer of knowledge is crucial to the standing of many elders, as is the Arapaho-language-specific nature of this power and transfer; thus this ideology continues to be strongly supported by elders, for obvious reasons, and embraced by many younger AC affiliates in particular.

Yet while the MTH-power "names" (broadly understood, including words for common objects) that are the focus of this book are also the continued focus of interest in the language among AC affiliates, the stories that go with the names, and which activate and maintain this power—along with the everyday processual use of the language more generally—are now extremely eroded and continuing to erode, though some younger (and older!) people are trying their hardest to reverse this trend. As we saw in chapter 3, place names do not exist independently of each other but function in broader systems, and the same is true of all types of "names." More abstractly, while the Arapaho MTH-power names and words still exist (and are even found in the appendices of certain books), the pathways for their efficacious transmission and productive usage effectively no longer exist in the Arapaho language, with very few exceptions, and it is this transmission and usage that maintains functioning *systems* of names in relation to each other—as opposed to isolated, documented names, which are the dead artifacts of such a system. This, I believe, is the deepest meaning of the complaints among older AC individuals that there is no more "respect" among the Arapaho—they are indexing a loss of Arapaho-language-mediated pathways for transfer of knowledge and power, for they recognize that power does not subsist in names, words, or metaphors, but must be legitimated and activated in systemic processes of exchange.[11]

I believe that this is not just a discourse of nostalgia but an accurate and powerful diagnosis of the issue of language shift among the Northern Arapaho. It corresponds closely to what M. Eleanor Nevins and Thomas Nevins (2012) describe for the Western Apache. They talk about stories themselves as objects that are not being transmitted well enough. They write that "what is at stake is not simply the transmission of stories, but a kind of reciprocity between generations," as stories become "objects" that are primarily "documented, displayed" (2012:130). The stories become removed from intergenerational circulation and relationship-building functions. In the Arapaho case, names and words continue to exist in increasingly nominalized forms, but they are largely removed from intergenerational circulation and usage—a fact especially seen in the lack of circulation of the stories about the names and words. "Language loss" really means relationship loss. This translates into "not listening" and a "lack of respect" (M. Nevins and T. Nevins 2012:137). For the Western Apache, M. Eleanor Nevins and Thomas Nevins suggest that what I am calling Politico-Tribal features (culture centers, schools, museums, bureaucracies) are replacing intergenerational reciprocity (i.e., what we would call AC) as the site of stories and other cultural resources, and that this leads to a reification and a blockage of circulation (2012:141–42).

We can now see that the "naming" processes seen in the introduction, which are so salient at Wind River (and elsewhere), work in two different directions. I argued that, traditionally, "naming" involved "using language to touch, connect with, and access the MTH power of the world" through language. Naming was thus a process. We also saw that language endangerment tends to increase the salience of such naming practices as well as MTH-power practices, at least in the Arapaho language (and almost certainly in other Northern Plains Native American languages). But socioeconomic and subsequent language shift causes this process of naming to rigidify and calcify, breaking connections to younger nonspeakers. Increasingly, these younger people can access the names only symbolically, as reified objects out of circulation in relation to intergenerational reciprocity. At this point, naming ceases to be a process and becomes a state of being for certain words and cultural resources. This is the kind of nominalization that overtakes endangered languages. And as gift theorists have shown, that which is out of circulation is what is or becomes most "sacred" (Godelier 1999; A. Weiner 1992; Godbout 1998). There is nothing wrong with this kind of sacredness: as the theorists all show, sacred objects outside the realm of exchange can become the anchor that impels the system of exchange that goes on around it, with that circulation mediating access to the sacred. In language loss, however, the sacred no longer has a set of circulating objects mediating access to it through exchange processes. Names become "just" names, and the "sacred" is a label not for a process of accessing MTH power and social reproduction but simply for cultural resources no longer in effective intergenerational circulation. This is very similar to the fears that Arapaho elders have for Arapaho ceremonial objects: the elders say the objects will lose ceremonial efficacy without Arapaho-language-mediated relationships with the people.

While AC elders continue to talk about naming and the sacredness of the language in the older sense, most younger Arapaho individuals think in terms of the newer senses and functions of these terms just described—including almost all Politico-Tribalists and even many Pan-Indian and AC affiliates. This is yet another discontinuity within Northern Arapaho society that escaped me for years. To the extent that Arapaho-specific linguistic forms do remain in active use, mediating relationships, the (typically Arapaho-English or bilingual) forms tend to be oriented toward ironic counterhegemonic identity statements in opposition to Euro-American culture, and the relationships they mediate are lateral identity (and nonidentity) relationships with peers. These forms and relationships now have much more "power" in most of Northern Arapaho society because they work across multiple COPs and therefore contribute to social cohesion and reproduction, in a way that Arapaho-language-specific forms and relationships often cannot.[12] To the extent that Arapaho-specific forms are in effective use, they are increasingly being recruited as "resources" for use within or across other COPs and being redefined in ways that distance them from their earlier MTH-power connections. This is effectively what elders mean when they talk about younger people not listening or not showing respect.

LANGUAGE AND GENDER

Turning now to gender, we find a quite different dynamic in relation to the AC COP and especially in relation to language. Virtually all the socioeconomic trends at Wind River over the last 150 years have tended to increasingly equalize the position of men and women and reduce the distinctiveness of male and female roles. We have already seen that this is the case in relation to increasing numbers of nonmanual-labor jobs, in relation to roles and ideologies of participation in at least some Christian denominations, in relation to politico-tribal roles and positions (female councilpersons for example), in relation to performative venues such as the military, and in relation to Pan-Indian as opposed to Arapaho-specific ceremonialism. This is not to say that gender-based role distinctions do not exist at Wind River but simply that there is an increasing equality of opportunity and participation in many domains. This is in fact not a radical transformation from the past in some ways. Women give personal names just as men do, and they have apparently always done so. They produce neologisms and folk etymologies, name places, and use and extend cultural metaphors. As in the past, they continue to tell narratives and say prayers. The changes that have occurred around gender at Wind River over the years largely do not show up in differences in linguistic practice or ideology. The loss of respect for elders seems to be more strongly felt by elder men than by elder women, and that feeling does seem to reflect a reality.[13] But the reality appears more in socioeconomic and political domains than in language.

The following long excerpt from a conversation between two men in their sixties captures many of the issues around gender, ceremonialism, performance, and status. Dave is a Vietnam War veteran who saw intense combat. He is discussing with Henry the importance of Arapaho medicine and Indian doctors and arguing that Arapahos should prefer Arapaho doctors over White doctors. The discussion then moves to the idea that too many people now want to be Arapaho doctors without going through the proper protocol, before moving to the topic of gender (I give the English translation only):

DAVE: *Today, today, they all want to be doctors.*
HENRY: *Yeah, they all want to be [doctors] today.*
DAVE: *And women are participating/becoming doctors too.*
HENRY: *Yeah.*
DAVE: *They doctor, they take part too. It wasn't like that a long time ago. Yeah, it wasn't like that.*
HENRY: *It wasn't like that. This man, that's who it was, this man . . .*
DAVE: *Yeah, doctoring was only given to the man. It was not given to the woman.*
HENRY: *It wasn't.*
DAVE: *It wasn't.*
HENRY: *The women never took part.*
DAVE: *Yeah, yeah.*

. . .

HENRY: *This [place] where they are selected for these employment positions, [in the past] women were not [taken]. The man was the one.*
DAVE: *Yeah, yeah.*
HENRY: *But women are being taken in/hired [now].*
DAVE: *Yeah.*

. . .

Also long ago . . . today these [women] [act/do things] in this White way. Today these women serve in the armed forces. They take part in combat/ go to war.
HENRY: *Yeah, yeah.*
DAVE: *Female soldiers are appearing.*

HENRY: *Yeah.*
DAVE: *Long ago there were no female soldiers. There weren't, yeah.*
HENRY: *Yeah, there weren't.*
DAVE: *This White Man has brought this [practice], and . . .*
... [Henry discusses a specific female relative who is serving overseas]
Whenever she comes back, how will you treat these women soldiers? They can't ??? them, you know.
HENRY: *Yeah.*
DAVE: *Right away for them, they have an honor dance for them [with] those uhh like this Warbonnet Dance, that type [of dance].*
HENRY: *Yeah, yeah.*
DAVE: *But today, the women are fundamentally not suited for [such a dance]. Like that word . . . [i.e., the dance is supposed to honor bravery in battle, but since the women actually do not engage in combat (at least officially), it is not appropriate to have a dance for them]*
HENRY: *Yeah.*
DAVE: *But "might as well" [do it, they say] you know. That is what [they do]. Anyway [they] will [just go ahead and do it].*
. . .
It's like they are put in there, but this is not good, you know, this White style.
HENRY: *Yeah.*
DAVE: *Yeah. These Whites are crazy. They just . . . They just don't respect anything, you know.*
HENRY: *Yeah.*
DAVE: *Yeah. They just want to always know everything, you know.*

(ELAR 23b)

In this conversation, Dave invokes the AC idea of gender-specific forms of knowledge and power within AC and the erosion of gender distinctions in this area (see Anderson 2001a:202, 206). Henry then moves to the Politico-Tribal area of economics, noting that women are now increasingly hired for all tribal positions (thus potentially threatening men's predominance as family wage earners). Dave then moves into a Pan-Indian area of performative prestige, noting that women now have equal access to military service (though in fact women did sometimes participate in traditional combat in pre-reservation days) and receive the same public recognition for their service as male veterans—invoking in particular an AC-specific honoring ceremony. He then makes the common move of criticizing these changes in Arapaho society and AC as due to White influence and ideologies of knowledge (curiosity to know everything and implicitly to make everything available to be known, without respecting restrictions related to elders), thus suggesting that the changes be rejected from AC (and implicitly, Pan-Indianism and Arapaho Politico-Tribalism as well). He concludes by invoking a competing ideology of knowledge that is strongly AC, though with Pan-Indian elements. The comment about White knowledge ideologies and lack of respect serves to link the breakdown of gender-specific avenues to prestige in Arapaho society with a breakdown of the proper compartmentalization and management of knowledge by elders—elder men in particular. Language itself, however, is never invoked.

There is one key exception to the nonlinguistic focus of gender tensions, however, and that involves a new language practice—teaching Arapaho. There have certainly been male teachers of Arapaho, and this was especially the case in the early days of language revitalization efforts in the 1970s and 1980s. However, especially since my work began around the year 2000 at Wind River, teaching has become increasingly dominated by women. This is somewhat the case in public schools, but especially the case in the tribal college and the immersion preschools. I should clarify that language administrators have often continued to be men, but the actual teachers in the classroom have been predominantly (though never entirely) women. One of the reasons for this is that women have also been more willing to acquire at least the rudiments of the Arapaho writing system, which has been a key qualification for classroom teaching. As we saw in chapter 6, some men explicitly complain about this requirement.

This exception has a somewhat less strong parallel in that more of the learners of Arapaho have also been women. This includes especially some of the more committed learners, who have reached the point where they are partially productive speakers. Again, this is not unilaterally true, and there are a few younger men who have also reached partial productivity, but the most dynamic second-language speakers who have worked in the immersion schools in cooperation with the native speakers have all been women.

This is a fact that has not escaped the notice of the teachers themselves, and they often comment on this gender distinction. One female teacher, Linda, who was conversing with her husband (after her retirement from a reservation public school, where she taught Arapaho language and culture classes, preceded by teaching in an immersion preschool), noted this fact even for young children in the classroom:

Nih'onobeeneetowoo; niiP niini'eeneti3i' tei'yoonoh'o'. 'oh . . .
I enjoyed it; the children speak well. But . . .
Beebeet niiP niitiini, niitiinihii, cenih'ini, nuhu' hiseihih'o' noh honoh'oho', noh . . .
Where, where uhh, as things developed, these girls and these boys, and . . .
Nuhu' huseihih'o' niiheeP nihii cesiseeneti3i', 'oh nuhu' honoh'oho' huu3e', nih'oonoo3itouhu3i', hih'oowceh'e3tiino'.
These girls talk, uhh start talking. But these boys over there, they told each other stories, they didn't listen.
Huseihih'o' neene'inonkuutii3i'; 'oh nuhu' honoh'oho',
The girls catch on to it real quick. But the boys,
"Heihoowuni'itoobe. Neenei'towuunetinee," nih'ii3ou'u.
"You aren't acting right. You're talking to each other," I said to them.

(ELAR 44b)

Of course it is well known that preschool boys often lag behind girls in both learning and socialization, so one should not make too much of these remarks (which concern the preschool immersion program). But it is interesting that this is the one detail that this teacher chose to raise in commenting about her teaching experience, and it echoes comments I have heard from teachers at the elementary and junior high-school levels as well: boys seem more resistant to learning Arapaho than girls. The fact that most of the teachers are women might partially explain this, but the gender issues extend all the way to the elders. The following conversation between two other immersion preschool teachers occurred when they were sitting in the preschool kitchen, conversing simply for the sake of language documentation. They made very similar remarks about the better progress of girls as opposed to boys with regard to the language, then discussed the problems around middle-aged men and why they won't learn or use Arapaho better (I give only the English translation here):

ANNIE: *They are shy.*
RHONDA: *They are shy.*
ANNIE: *They are shy.*
RHONDA: *It's like . . . they don't want to be laughed at.*

ANNIE: *Yeah, they don't want to be laughed at. They don't want to be ridiculed. That's what they think, anyway. But people don't do that.*
RHONDA: *Unh-unh, it's not like that.*
ANNIE: *When people say something wrong, no one says anything about it. They are just shown how to [say it] properly.*

. . .

They are told about it.
RHONDA: *Then they get angry.*
ANNIE: *Then they get all angry.*

. . .

I think the past hundred years we have gone very shame based because of the treatment that we had. *So these men are shy.*
RHONDA: But women can take anything.
ANNIE: *The women give it a try. They always try.*

. . .

And they just finish what they're doing/carry things through to completion.

(ELAR 124b; see 124b and 124c more generally)

In this segment, the two women make two very interesting claims. First, the men have been differentially and more severely victimized by the historical experience of the Arapaho over the last century and a half. The shame that they carry from this experience makes them more liable to feel shame in public in front of other Arapaho people. But second, the women argue that this shame is actually a projection by the men onto those around them, which in fact does not occur among the audience.

It is certainly true that people often laughed at each other in the past for language errors, and this certainly does still occur sometimes today, but in my experience the women are right: public use of Arapaho is largely viewed supportively, and mistakes are more often simply corrected (if remarked on at all) rather than mocked, at least with the exception of more formalized settings (see chapters 1 and 2). Despite this, the two women argue that men's historical experience of diminished agency leads to an especially intense hyperawareness of appearances of public competence. This ideology regarding perfect public performance and avoidance of any errors is itself most associated with ceremonial and ritual public uses of the language; it is a kind of dominant ideology that can be—but certainly is not always—extended to other domains (cf. Kroskrity 1998). But this ideology inhibits actual language usage and practice, even as it highlights the great power that perfectly performed Arapaho has in such ritual contexts.

The women, however, suggest that women more generally are less concerned with these kinds of public mistakes and less influenced by the ideology or performance target of public perfectionism. This is again, in my experience, a valid point—though the women are of course also actively producing and strengthening this ideological point in their comments themselves. There are certainly women who will criticize Arapaho-language usage of others in public or who are very concerned with public speaking (as seen in chapter 2), but this seems to be most common among men currently—particularly public criticisms. On the other hand, the women simply "get down to it," so to speak, and try to teach and use the language—along with some men as well, of course.

It is interesting to compare these comments with the finding in chapter 2 that teachers tend to take a more agentive perspective on their engagement with the Arapaho language, while the ceremonial leaders cited there and other nonteachers tended to take a less agentive view of the language, depicting it as having independent agency. Once we recognize that most ceremonial leaders (including those cited in chapter 2) are men,[14] while most teachers are women (though one of the teachers cited in chapter 2 was a man), this agency distinction begins to take on a potentially gendered quality. We can further combine this gendered meta-agentive discourse about agency with the fact that actual agency exercised around the Arapaho language in the classroom is predominantly female, on the part of both teachers and learners.

In other words, speaking Arapaho fluently is not gendered within Arapaho society. Engaging with the language ceremonially or in public discourse (speeches about the language) and treating it as highly sacred and having independent agency does seem to be gendered, however—as masculine. In contrast, engaging with the language in terms of transmission and thinking about it more in terms of everyday processual usage seems to be gendered as feminine. Certainly this is not an overwhelming or exclusive gendering, but it is intriguing nevertheless, especially because it appears to be a newly developed language ideology, associated with the newly developed practice of formally teaching the language, and it is being actively promoted by some women, as we have just seen.

This finding fits with an earlier observation that although MTH power and ceremonialism is the reason often given by prominent public speakers in

Arapaho as to why the language should be learned, and this is a reason often echoed by more advanced students, such as in the tribal college, this ideology and its associated practices (or lack thereof) at the level of interpersonal relationships actually can be seen as impeding language learning and transmission. In other words, a focus on MTH power and ceremonialism and associated language ideologies such as purism and public perfectionism inhibits actual agency in transmitting the language, and in addition, we see that meta-agentive discourse *around* MTH power and ceremonialism also involves reduced speaker agency in relation to the language. In contrast, not only can a focus on low-saliency everyday processual behaviors potentially aid the relationships necessary for usage, learning, and transmission, but meta-agentive discourse *around* low-saliency everyday processual behaviors (such as classroom teaching) also involves a greater degree of speaker agency.

Putting this all together, we find that low-saliency Arapaho-language usage and transmission are at least mildly gendered female, while high-saliency sacred Arapaho-language usage (but lack of transmission) is likewise at least mildly gendered as masculine. Tendencies for language maintenance and revitalization practices to become gendered have been noted elsewhere (Collins 1998b:68, 172–79; Dalby 2003:76–81; Meek 2014a and additional references therein), and this can become especially the case in bureaucratic contexts (Meek 2014b).

It appears that fractal recursivity is occurring here within AC. Male association with ceremonialism has at a minimum remained intact over time, or likely increased, while female association with high-visibility ceremonial roles has declined—even as they are heavily involved in the actual cooking, money raising, and support for the more prominent men. Meanwhile, within language preservation programs, the same distinction has played out: men are officially heads of programs or cochairs of the Northern Arapaho Language and Culture Commission, and they often speak publicly on behalf of the language at tribal general council meetings or Native American conferences. But women are the ones doing more of the work of teaching and transmitting the language. And just as key ceremonial objects such as the Sacred Pipe are seen to have independent agency (see chapter 2), so is the language, in more ceremonial contexts (see again chapter 2). Meanwhile women highlight their own agency in relation to the language, as teachers—and keep busy cooking! New practices, new opportunities, new ideologies—all in order to maintain the continuity of the language. Looked at the other way around, maintaining the language is itself ironically a new opportunity wherein new ideologies can develop.

SO MUCH MORE TO SAY . . .

In concluding with a new finding regarding gender and the new topic of classroom teaching, I underline how much more there is to say. Among the topics I would have liked to discuss that are *not* covered in this book are the past versions and modern fate of traditional genres of song and oral narrative (except as related to names and places); gender-based distinctions in speech; stylistic distinctions and formal registers; prayer and ritual oration; the linguistic details of respect and joking relationships, including avoidance of a number of vocabulary items or entire topics in respect relationships; institutionalized puns, jokes, and humor; a broader range of cultural metaphors; slang; special evidential forms; politeness; uses of silence; uses of literacy; conversational practices such as turn taking; Plains Sign Language and gesture; paralinguistic and kinesic practices; translation practices; Arapaho English; many additional details of maintenance and revitalization activities; and the list could go on. There are in fact additional studies completed or in progress (though many are not diachronic in approach) on many of these topics.[15] One of the major lessons of this book is that the story looks different according to the topic one chooses, which suggests that it is very difficult to take one topic and treat the findings from it as representative of the group or groups under study (see Clifford 1988:31, fifth point). I have argued, however, that a combined look at several key areas of "naming" among the Northern Arapaho can give us some privileged insights—including as to why the language shift has occurred and continues to occur. The various continuities and discontinuities of language ideology and practice that we have seen in this book are almost all understandable in terms of the AC concept of knowledge and power—both in relation to the natural and ancestral worlds and in relation to social power operating in relationships between Arapaho individuals within the everyday society—and competing concepts and sources of knowledge and power (and relationships) within other Arapaho COPs. The ethnography of language shift is an ethnography of competing conceptions of power, of the struggle for continuity of MTH power within Arapaho society by the AC COP, and of that COP's efforts to use language as a key basis for maintaining this continuity. As a political position used to accomplish social work effectively and ultimately to accomplish social reproduction, AC must constantly evolve in order to remain efficacious for both individuals and the larger group adhering to the COP—if it fails to do so, it will be abandoned.[16] Perhaps the single most salient aspect of the ongoing changes in the AC COP is the debate over the role that the Arapaho language can or should play within AC's repertoire of practices, and the way that the repertoire is being forced to adjust to the loss of the language as an everyday discursive tool.

Put simply, language shift began because the majority of people in Northern Arapaho society decided that English was fundamentally *necessary* to provide access to jobs, education, modernity, cultural reproduction, and Christianity—versions of "power"—while the Arapaho language began to be seen as an *optional, additional* avenue to power—MTH power—in the post–World War II era, when assimilationist pressures were most intense. Then, beginning in the 1960s and increasingly ever since, there has been a partial reorientation toward Arapaho-specific bases for social reproduction and coherence. This reorientation, however, has been primarily based in Politico-Tribalism (with a strong component of Pan-Indianism as well) since sociocultural and political changes in the United States have made this an increasingly viable option. As a result, the forms of Arapaho-specific power that are now most relevant at Wind River are political, legal, and bureaucratic in nature, with secondary bases in performance venues and shared historical ("indigenous") experience. Whereas AC was available as a counterhegemonic COP in relation to Assimilationism during the postwar years, now Pan-Indianism and Politico-Tribalism represent additional—and often more empowered—counterhegemonic alternatives.

Meanwhile, as we have seen at many points in this book, the Arapaho language and AC provide many symbolically salient and attractive cultural "resources" that could serve as unifying factors across multiple COPs. There is certainly no reason that vertically oriented MTH practices cannot reinforce laterally oriented identity formation and boundary maintenance, and there is no reason that the latter cannot be used as a means of supporting the viability of the former. Gregory E. Smoak (2006:3) presents an interesting case where these two tendencies were mutually reinforcing in his study of the Ghost Dance at the Fort Hall Reservation: "On one level, [the dances] represented a culturally consistent appeal to a supernatural power aimed at restoring the flow of that power toward native people. But on another they were a vehicle for the expression of meaningful social identities [in relation to Euro-Americans]." We have seen similar crossovers between COPs and functions at many points in this study—indeed, this is virtually always the case, and there are rarely any completely "pure" practices or COPs. In a long discussion recorded around 1990 that I was able to listen to on tape, Arapaho elders Ben Friday Sr. and Paul Moss (real names) discussed the Sun Dance in Arapaho. They focused on changes in practice over time among the Arapaho, which they felt threatened the efficacy of the ceremony and access to MTH power. They also spent a great deal of time comparing the Arapaho Sun Dance to that of the Shoshone, Crow, and Cree, and tracing the paths of influence between the groups. This was clearly an effort to use the Sun Dance as a form of ethnic identity marker between neighboring tribes. More deeply, issues of ceremonial efficacy were inseparable from issues of ethnic and ceremonial purity and contamination: contamination is a key threat to efficacy, and the originary and purer nature of the Arapaho Sun Dance (merely copied in fragmentary form by the other tribes, according to Moss and Friday) is key to its greater efficacy. Here ethnic boundary maintenance and MTH power issues mutually reinforce each other, as a more powerful Sun Dance enhances the value of Arapaho ethnic identity, while maintaining those ethnic boundaries insures the continued superiority of the ceremony.

In the current social situation at Wind River, however—particularly in the context of advanced language shift—as long as the symbolically salient cultural resources are deeply embedded in the MTH-power discourses and relationships of AC, not only are they problematic for intergenerational reciprocity within AC, but they often cannot be easily extended to the kinds of lateral identity practices that would make them most appealing across multiple COPs. The struggle *within* AC today is between those who take a more purist perspective on AC language, knowledge, and relationships, and those who see compromises in all these areas as necessary in order to allow Arapaho "names"—and eventually possibly Arapaho-language-mediated relationships—to again enter into productive transfer on new terms. This is a problem that confronts many Native American groups where MTH power remains a key component in society. Speaking of the Arizona Tewa, Paul V. Kroskrity writes, "It is possible to argue that the community cannot reproduce itself without considerable transformation aimed at inclusion of those now outside the inner discursive circle" (Kroskrity 2012a:177).[17]

Such transformations among the Northern Arapaho will likely require a major shift in the concept of the sacred, especially in relation to the language, in order to allow the "resource" of "the sacredness of the language" to be a truly motivating and unifying rather than inhibitory force in revitalization. This will likely require different forms of intergenerational relationships as well. It will perhaps also require a much greater emphasis on the domains of joking and teasing in relation to language acquisition and teaching, since these often escape the constraints of MTH power and the carefully monitored discourses that surround it. As we saw especially in chapter 6, joking and teasing is a domain with high multifunctionalism—in the sense that it can work not just across but within multiple COPs simultaneously, doing *both* the relationship work that provides the basis of MTH power transfers *and* the identity work so crucial to several COPs. In my own documentation work, I have moved more and more toward video of conversation, in part for this reason: it documents *relationships*, often of an informal nature, including much joking and teasing, rather than just documenting language (cf. M. Nevins and T. Nevins 2012). Fortunately, virtually all individuals with whom I work have been open to this approach. This also allows documentation of names, neologisms, words, and metaphors—and stories—in use, in noncalcified ways. To the extent that I have documented high-saliency items, approaches like the video of conversation attempt to add stories to words, to make them more reusable and recirculatable. I am certainly not suggesting that one avoid documenting high-saliency practices and items such as place names and traditional narratives. These are the targets that can motivate language learning and revitalization at its earlier stages. But I think that we must recognize that some of these items may be the last to be reactivated and reentered into circulation as productive systems if and when revitalization advances. Document—and teach—relationships, not just language![18] I end with one final example that illustrates many of the points of the overall conclusion. The video was recorded in the tribal college and involves a second-language learner and native speaker who often assisted at the college. The learner Mary mentions another native-speaker helper (not present), first by a nickname, then by what she believes his Arapaho name to be, but the native speaker Henry says he knows this same person by another Arapaho name:

MARY: That uhh, Tokoubeihii, [p.n. in English]
That uhh One Who Makes Shade, [p.n.] . . .
[p.n. in English], his uhh his name is uhh Heneecee Niiseiht.
[p.n.] his uhh, his name [in Arapaho] is uhh Lone Bull.
HENRY: Ceitoosoo, nee'eesih'it.
Rain Is Coming, that is his name.
MARY: Oh what's, hinee, what's his name?
Oh what's, that one, what's his name?
HENRY: Ceitoosoo.
Rain Is Coming.

After a sequence in which the learner makes sure she understands the new Arapaho name, the speaker then instructs her on how to address the person in Arapaho:

HENRY: "Hee, Ceitoosoo," hetii3oo.
"Yes/hello, Rain Is Coming," you must say to him. [hee is a form used by male speakers]

MARY: I'm going to tell him, "tous, Ceitoosoo."
I'm going to tell him, "Hello, Rain Is Coming." [the learner successfully realizes that as a female she must use tous rather than hee]

The younger learner then comments that the person in question has "all kinds of names." She then tries to say this in Arapaho, using *wonoo3ee3i* 'there are many of them [animate]' rather than *wonoo3ei'i* 'there are many of them [inanimate]', however. She knows the word for *name* but asks now to make it plural. This is supplied by the native speaker, who, however, offers the form *wonoo3ei'i* **heniisih'iitono** 'you have many names'. In other words, he gives her the appropriate form to use to speak *with* the other man, rather than just talk about him, even though she has not specifically asked for this. After a sequence in which this sentence and its exact meaning are clarified, the native speaker then begins offering additional interactional tools for her to use with many names, again without her explicitly asking for these:

Wo'ei3 XXX "niitobeenoo, nuhu' hinenno' ceece'esih'einoni," hetii3oo.
Or, ??? "I heard about it, these men gave you lots of different names," you must say to him.

What Henry is doing here is teaching Mary how to tease an elder about his personal names—a key Arapaho practice, as we saw in chapter 4, and one heavily oriented toward solidarity and reciprocal relationships. Henry then interrupted this exchange to make a side comment to me in English about someone else knowing many Arapaho names, but I did not understand who he was talking about and asked in Arapaho, "henee'eehek hinee?" *'who is that [whom you're talking about]?'*. The learner likely did not understand my question but, seeking to say something in Arapaho to stay engaged in the interchange, responded to me by saying "ciibehnih'oo3ouyeiti!" *'don't speak English!'* (a common command around the tribal college). Although literally this comment is somewhat off target, it does the social work of reinforcing my shift of the exchange from English back to Arapaho, and the native speaker seems to pick up on this, because he then repeats her command back to her with enthusiasm, "ciibehnih'oo3ouyeiti!" The learner then shows that she has picked up on the plan to tease the absent elder about his many names:

MARY: Ahh, heet[n]ei'towuunin, "wonoo3ei'i, uhh, heniisih'iitono."
Ahh, I will tell him [sic, s/b—wuun-o'], "you have, uhh, a lot of names."
HENRY: Yeah.
MARY: KoohiiP, koohi3oobei?
Is that, is that right? [sic; s/b—3oobee]
HENRY: Uhm-hmm.

The elder concludes the session by instructing her to say the full sentence *neniitobeenoo, wonoo3ei'i heniisih'iitono* 'I hear that you have a lot of names'. He then adds more complex and colorful ways of doing this same kind of teasing:

"Tohuubiineihi3i', wootii niiseti', tohuubiineinoo, 'oh neneenin, 'oh he'iitP, he'iitoxei'i," hetii3oo, you know.
"When these [people] are given [names], it seems like [someone] gave me one, but you, I don't know how many [they gave you]," you must say to him, you know.

(ELAR 37c)

Here we see a relationship being built between the learner and the elder, as he teaches and models for her how to also build another relationship with a second elder.[19] I noted her small errors in verb inflection just to point out that the elder easily accommodates for these. Rather than maintaining a purist stance toward the language and correcting her as she speaks, he patiently repeats correct models for her later, and she shows a commitment to fixing her errors. The learner is able to use a mix of English and Arapaho to successfully do the social work to maintain the conversation in collaboration with a cooperative elder, by taking advantage of linguistic resources creatively. Her interactive skills are in a sense in advance of her Arapaho-language skills, as continuity in the area of interaction skills can be maintained across language shift to some extent, especially in communities where Native American Vernacular English is strong.

Finally, note that while the learner wants to talk *about* the absent person, the (strongly AC) elder insistently pushes her to approach language lessons as learning to talk *to* people in Arapaho, and she picks up on this point. The relationships are being built around humor, around personal names, and most particularly, around the circulation of stories and discourse about personal names that reactivate their relevance for intergenerational reciprocity, in a way that could appeal to several different COPs (though the use of Arapaho clearly identifies this as an AC moment). This informal, humor-focused, potentially cross-COP moment is emblematic of what can occur with Arapaho. Though learning efforts focused around ceremonialism also continue, this type of moment represents perhaps the most viable future for the language within Northern Arapaho society.

NOTES

INTRODUCTION

1. In this book, all names are pseudonyms, with the exception of Andy (which refers to Andrew Cowell, the author of this book) and Paul Moss, whose narratives have been published (Cowell and Moss 2005a), or where "real name" is included after the name.
2. See Kroskrity and Field (2009:21), where they speak of "attempts to reproduce traditional cultural ideals and practices" (i.e., what I am calling *continuity*), but where they also note that such reproductions "will be necessarily recontextualized to changing historical circumstances as partial reproductions" and that "members will rationalize the perspective of their generation's linguistic adaptation in the form of language ideologies of varying degrees of explication."
3. I use this term roughly in the sense that Kroskrity and Field use the term *cultural resources* (Kroskrity and Field 2009:3). They refer to these as "allowing communities to remake themselves, to adapt to transformed social formations, and to recontextualize traditional practices to ever-changing socio-economic patterns." Resources are thus especially open to creative appropriation by various communities of practice (COPs) within a society. See Irvine and Gal (2000:38) on "the discursive or cultural resources to claim and thus attempt to create shifting 'communities,' identities, selves, and roles, at different levels of contrast, within a cultural field." See also J. Hill and K. Hill's use of the term *symbolic resources* (1986:1), which include linguistic "definitions, attitudes and techniques," and Samuels (2004:10) on *symbolic material*.
4. Cf. B. French (2010:6) and her discussion of "ongoing, competing projects" among the Highland Maya. See also M. Nevins (2013:116), where she categorizes arguments about language and discourse among the Western Apache as "an argument about where and with whom to attribute the agency to shape the present and the future."

5. Kroskrity insists on the need to relate "microanalysis" to "political economic macroprocesses" (2000a:1–2) and especially argues against "the autonomy of discrete levels of microanalysis" in favor of "the linkage of microcultural worlds of language and discourse to macrosocial forces" (2).
6. There are minor variations between citations in the book and those in ELAR, where I have made corrections to the earlier versions. Thank you to the many RAs and students who have worked with me over the years helping to compile this data, including Richard Sandoval, Allison Sanders, Irina Wagner, Jena Huang, Jenette Preciado, Katie Brown, Finn Thye, Hartwell Francis, and Hannah O'Brien. Hohou!
7. For discussions among Arapaho speakers on the value and importance of the language generally, see ELAR 15sp, 20c, 20n, 27a, 35a, 35b, 50a, 63b, 63e, 68c, 68d, 68e, and 79b.
8. The orthography used here is standard for Arapaho (see Cowell and Moss 2008). The apostrophe indicates a glottal stop, while the number 3 is used as a letter, representing the sound *th* as in *three* (IPA theta, θ).
9. See Griffin-Pierce (2000:128) and the term *greater-than-human* power. Anderson (2001a) uses *other-than-human* power in talking about the Northern Arapaho, but the "more" seems important here, thus my choice of MTH.
10. See also Harrod (1987:163), where he says that the aim of Plains Indian religions is "to acquire power and thus to establish a sense of identity and destiny within the group."
11. Anderson 2001a is an extensive study of traditional Arapaho ideologies of knowledge and the ways in which relationships mediated its flow. He pays close attention to both age-related (119–72) and gender-related (173–84) components of this process, which he terms *life movement*.
12. Bourdieu argues that "all symbolic domination presupposes, on the part of those who submit to it, a form of complicity.... It is inscribed, in a practical state, in dispositions which are impalpably inculcated ... by the linguistic market" (1991:50–51). In this book, I am less interested in potential symbolic "domination" imposed by English, for example, on Arapaho speakers, than on the way in which any society includes a market in which struggles for power are enacted. To engage in this market is already to be complicit in "domination" in a sense, but I do not wish to imply the kind of political domination practiced by nation-states and official languages, which is the immediate context for the quote from Bourdieu given here.
13. See also Powers (1986:9) on Lakota: "Much of the Lakota world ... is a linguistic universe and ... the process of naming people, objects and places gives them ontological status."

CHAPTER 1

1. See "Bad Dreamers," "The Arapaho Boy," "The Enemy Trail," "The Shade Trees," and "The Forks" in Cowell and Moss (2005a) for good examples of this relationship

structure in Arapaho narratives. Often a larger portion of the narrative is spent describing the ceremonial preparations for battle or hunting, led by elders, rather than on the battle or hunting itself, carried out by the younger men.

2. Note: in this book, all Arapaho cited within the text is in italics. Conversely, in block quotes, all original text is in standard font, and all translations are in italics.

3. See ELAR 14a, 14b, 15sp, 18a, 18c, 21b, 22b, 23b, 24a, 25a, 32a–c, 34e, 35a, 35b, 44b–d, 48c, 66a, 68b–d, 71d–e, 79a, 79c–d.

4. Wiles (2011:166–69) recounts an event that illustrates some of the components of what could be called *pulsed distributions*. She notes specifically that "once, gatherings like this, in which both men and women displayed traditional horsemanship skills, were common. Families in outlying locations would host one or more days of activities; they would butcher a beef and cook and feed everyone" (210). She documents a contemporary example of such an event and notes of the organizer that "he and his family, by sponsoring Indian games and races, hope to bring a more traditional Arapaho way to horse events" (210). This is an excellent example of an attempt to use a reinvigorated pulsed-resource event (there was a major giveaway of material items) and its associated social and ritual practices to maintain Arapaho-style relationships across individual and family lines. See also Wiles (2011:132–37) on hunting and meat distribution in current times.

5. Fowler (1982:232–39) offers a survey of the economics of Wind River through 1978.

6. The attitudes here are very similar to the ones Kulick reports for Gapun villagers: "Language is a collaborative activity primarily concerned with the elaboration and manipulation of social relationships." He argues that "the villagers' continual embedding of talk in social relations and contexts both reflects and influences their notions of what language is and what it is for" (1992:190).

7. The youngest fluent native speaker of whom I am currently aware was born in 1953.

8. There are important differences, however. Kulick reports that the Gapun villagers see "power" as largely located in schooling, Christian religion, books and literacy, and White people (1992:182–85). In contrast, many Arapaho people evince a great deal of ambivalence and even resistance toward these external power sources, and they counterpose an ideology of the power of the Arapaho language, orality, and traditional ceremonialism quite overtly. Unlike the Gapun (1992:188), many Arapaho still also see value and power in links to ancestors.

9. Thus the Northern Arapaho are a case of what Pye (1992:75) calls *defective bilingual acquisition*.

10. Fowler (1982) offers a very interesting study of political leadership and processes at Wind River through 1978. See especially pages 256–99, where she shows how leaders at the time of her study mediated between political (i.e., Politico-Tribal), "traditionalist" (i.e., AC), Christian religious, Pan-Indian, and assimilationist pressures, seeking to maintain coherence with past symbols of authority and more generally to maintain the continuity of Northern Arapaho society, through creative responses in practice and ideology.

11. Faudree and Hansen note that "understandings of the past are the result of semiotic processes in present micro-contexts of interaction" and that "trajectories of past events lead to formations of semiotic complexities . . . that structure and define particular pasts while influencing the present as well" (2014:227). Basically everything known about pre-reservation Arapaho language and linguistic practices is an "interested reconstruction," involving the interests of consultants and of the linguists and anthropologists working with them. Nevertheless a wide range of early sources—notably Mooney (1896) 1973; Kroeber (1902–7) 1983; Dorsey 1903; Dorsey and Kroeber (1903) 1997; Hilger 1952; and field notes of Kroeber and Gatschet (a good deal published in Cowell, C'Hair, and Moss 2014)—at least provide differing perspectives.
12. See, however, Debenport (2015:105–18), where she presents a very interesting analysis of the concept of *nostalgia*—specifically in the context of language and culture revitalization movements—as a sometimes useful, future-oriented strategy for building stronger communities and collectivities. See also Cruikshank (1998:xii) on the value of "optimistic stories about the past."
13. See also M. Nevins (2004:280) on the Western Apache, where she notes that "the view of language loss, then, within the Apache discourse of the family identifies that loss with a crisis in cooperative participation" and also that "language loss in Apache discourse is envisioned not only as the loss of the language itself, but more saliently as a weakening of the relationships from which it springs" (282).
14. Anderson (2001a:229) notes that "there is a growing sense that the [Northern Arapaho] 'tribe' is now a political entity."
15. Readers may wish to compare this list of COPs to a list of five "identity types" given in Dauenhauer and Dauenhauer (1998). Their #2 ("substantial") roughly corresponds to AC. Their #4 ("civic") corresponds fairly closely to my Politico-Tribal. Their #1 ("traditional") has elements of both AC and Pan-Indianism. Their #5 ("past") could be compared to my Assimilationist. Their #3 ("optional") is similar to my recognition that no one occupies the AC position at all times and places, and COPs correspond not only to different sets of practices but to different identity positions.
16. Margaret C. Field (2012:115) nicely states this same point, that knowledge and stories are not simply objects transferred but "forms of linguistic structure, or interactional strategies, through which identity is discursively produced" (and relationships are established and maintained, I would add).

CHAPTER 2

1. See Gómez de García, Axelrod, and Lachler (2009:100), where they note that "several of our current consultants have commented on the necessity of maintaining their ancestral language because their culture, their ceremonies, and their spiritual history and values can only be transmitted through the metaphors inherent in the language and through the cognitive imagery these metaphors invoke." For more

on the Hopi, see Glowacka and Sekaquaptewa (2009). Vest (2006:52) notes that Haudenosaunee metaphors are "direct links between the concrete and the spiritual realms." Sekaquaptewa and Washburn (2004:466) stress the importance of these metaphors for maintaining reciprocal relationships.

2. Vest (2006:53) terms these metaphorical practices "sympathetic ritual association" or "mimetic sympathy." Sekaquaptewa and Washburn (2004:466) stress even more forcefully the "active" quality of metaphors and their extension to multiple domains, as with Arapaho metaphors, folk etymologies, and neologisms.

3. Anderson (2001a:246–48) contains further discussion of the concepts of camp circle and periphery for the Arapaho.

4. I should note that there are other ways of expressing the idea of "assimilate" in Arapaho. *Woohonkoohu-* 'run together, into unison' and *woohonisee-* 'walk together, into unison' are common.

5. This image is pervasive in Arapaho quillwork. See Anderson (2013:31–33, 36–38, 41–42, 44, 48–49, 51, 53, 57, 59, 65, 78–79, 81).

6. Kelley and Francis (2005) discuss Navajo narratives and songs as actual verbal maps and travel guides; Laird (1976) documents similar and even richer connections of this sort for the Chemehuevi. Thompson (1997) examines the importance of the journey as a theme in narratives recounting the acquisition of shamanistic power among the Koyukon Athabaskans. Fienup-Riordan (1994) likewise discusses the journey theme and also the central importance of the metaphors of "clearing a path" and the opposite image, barriers to travel, in Yupik oral traditions. Ahlers (1997) looks explicitly at "life is a journey" as a cognitive metaphor in Hupa. Glowacka and Sekaquaptewa (2009) discuss this metaphor in Hopi ethical thought.

7. James Mooney ([1896] 1973:1000) notes that "the prairie idiom for directing or commanding [is] to 'give a road' or to 'make a road' for the one thus commanded. To disobey is to 'break the road' and to depart from the former custom is to 'make a new road.' The idea is expressed in the same way both in the various spoken languages and in the sign language."

8. McCarty and Watahomigie (1999:5) discuss the idea of the Navajo language as a "shield" for the people—another example of the language as independent and protective agent.

9. Cf. Palmer (2012:32–33) for very similar Kiowa metaphors, including "lay down your language," "going down the wrong road" (because the language was laid down), and "put your language aside."

10. See Meek (2009:165) and associated references there for more on the idea of "independent agency" in indigenous languages.

11. For the sake of completeness, we should also note other descriptions of language loss. These include the idea of "knowing" (*he'in-*) or "remembering" (*toyou'uuwuu-*, usually used to refer specifically to remembering moral lessons or teachings) versus "forgetting" (*nonih'i-*) the language; the notion of "presence" (*hentou'u-*) versus "absence" (*hiiyohou-*) of the language; and likely more surprising for speakers of English, the idea that the language has become buried in the ground and must be

dug back up and brought to the surface (*ce'biscitii-* 'dig an object up and into view again'). The last one is actually a common Arapaho idiom, also used when talking about someone who remembers an old song that is long forgotten: the person has "dug the song back up and brought it into the open" or "uncovered it."

12. Davidson (1999:30) notes the connection between language as "specialized knowledge" and the development of "loyalty to the primary consultant/counselor" in such situations, where extremely close connections are established between learner and teacher (which mimic those among ceremonial or medicinal apprentices, for example).

13. Following is a personal introduction delivered at a conference at Wind River Tribal College by a second-language learner:

> Wohei neito'eino', nii'i3ecoonoo tohno'useen.
> *Well my relatives, I am happy that you are here.* [sic: you SING, s/b PL]
> Neneeninoo hohoot niibei.
> *I am Singing Tree.*
> Neneeninoo hinono'ei.
> *I am Arapaho.*
> Neinoo noh neisonoo nei'eibehe', nebesiibehe', nihco'oneeneti3i', nuhu' hinono'eitiit.
> *My mother and my father, my grandmother, my grandfather, they always spoke this Arapaho language.*
> Beeteenoo'.
> *It is holy.*
> Niibeete'inowoo nuhu' neeneiseenetini'.
> *I want to know how we speak this [language].*
> Nuhu', niiitowoonoo heetihce'eenetini' hinono'eitiit.
> *This, I am asking that we again speak Arapaho.*
> Neniisi3ei'inoo co'ouutou3eino'oowuu'.
> *I work at the college.*
> Nenee' nuhu' niitneyei3ei'inoo.
> *That is where I go to school.*
> Noo'eino' neyei3einotii.
> *I drive the school bus/van.*
> Niitehei'inoo hinono'eitiit.
> *I help out the Arapaho language.*
> Hohou.
> *Thank you.*
>
> (ELAR 36c)

14. See Neely (2012:102–3 especially) for a description of similar changes in language acquisition strategies, elder/child interaction routines, and language ideologies among the Kiowa, as well as the resistance to this from some quarters of the community.

CHAPTER 3

1. See especially Cowell and Moss (2005a:251–53) for a further discussion of the symbolic meanings of the wheel and the notions of center and periphery in the narrative. See also the story "The Forks" for further discussion of the use of the wheel image symbolically (Cowell and Moss 2005a:313–33).
2. Moreover, as Bodenhorn and vom Bruck (2006:12) note, "Knowledge of the ritual significance of named places may be the sine qua non of political claims to, for example, voice, position, authority and/or land ownership." This is an especially important point in relation to the type-2 place names discussed later in this chapter.
3. A more fine-grained classification, along with more in-depth discussion of linguistic details, can be found in Cowell and Moss (2003).
4. Investigation of Gros Ventre place names (Cowell, Taylor, and Brockie 2016) reveals the same pattern in those names.
5. In discussing the Foi of Papua New Guinea, James F. Weiner (1991:43) gets at a similar idea when he writes that "places can be morally invigorated, as it were, by naming them after significant human events."
6. Arapaho traditional religion, very broadly, could be interpreted as an effort to overcome potential or actual separation between humans and MTH power, particularly through rituals that depended on symbolic mediation or sought symbolic inspiration. The rituals in question often focused on specific animal parts. Thus in addition to seeing the type-2 place names as symbolically marking points of power in the landscape, the very specific choice of animal-part semantic content for these "analogical resemblance" names—as opposed to other possible choices such as human parts and products—can be understood as evoking the mediatory nature of the relationship to both the landscape and the animals that live there (see Kroeber [1902–7] 1983:418–19, and especially 450–54 on animal parts).
7. See Kroeber ([1902–7] 1983:429ff and 433ff) for examples of painted items that represent dream sequences. In addition, although Kroeber does not report it, the item described on p. 109 (figure 2 of Plate XIX) seems quite possibly to recall the Arapaho story of how the coyote defeated the Trickster "white man." White man turned himself into an elk, buffalo, antelope, and deer, but he was unable to fool the coyote. On p. 134 is a description of an unequivocally narrative design on a bag.
8. Anderson (2013:17) describes these as "metonymic connections among levels of space and time" and talks of "a unique Arapaho way of seeing, voicing, and understanding motion, shape, and connections in language, art, and narrative" (72). Speaking specifically of "ornamentation," he says that "many core connections and patterns of language and culture were conveyed or reinforced through them" (95).
9. Cf. Levinson (1996:355): "Frequently one can see direct connections between classical questions of cosmology, aesthetics and art style, practical activities like hunting or herding, and the linguistic resources used to make spatial distinctions in different cultures."

10. More generally, Pearce and Louis (2008) discuss "indigenous depth of place" and give an illustration from Hawaii of the way in which many different linguistic, cultural, and performance resources are involved in creating this depth of place (see esp. 113–15).
11. This would lead one to speculate that the seeming continuity of rituals such as the Sun Dance masks an altered relationship between such rituals and the way they encode the landscape and cosmology, but that is a topic beyond the scope of this book.
12. See Cruikshank (1998:18), where she writes of a Yukon elder, "John Joe . . . explained his view that there is a causal link between understanding the [place] names, knowing the stories associated with the names, and living in the world as an adequate human being."
13. See similar ideas expressed concerning the Tolowa: the "legitimating and locating of subsistence activities, which was mediated through the social structure of extended kin and patrilineal wealth asymmetries, had other place-bound spiritual and ritual dimensions." The village headmen "owned songs, connected to sites and necessary to properly initiate the first hunting or fishing activities for a given season" (Collins 1998b:138). Thus knowledge controlled by elders mediated access to the power and utility of places (as well as their names).
14. See Wiles (2011:206–11) for one discussion of the reinvigoration of traditional design motifs on women's clothing, including both the turtle's and the bear's paws, which link to a place name in Rocky Mountain National Park.
15. It is worth noting that some Arapaho-speaking AC elders have made efforts to reconnect with the type-2 place names that occur in Rocky Mountain National Park. Because there are in fact stories associated with some of the place names in the park (recorded in Toll 1962), AC elders have shown noted interest in tours of the park where they can see the sites and at least read the associated stories (see Wiles 2011:220–24).

CHAPTER 4

1. For more details on the linguistic structure of Arapaho personal names and the subtypes of structures, see Cowell and Moss 2003.
2. P. Moore (1984) examines the semantic content of Cheyenne personal names and finds similar tendencies.
3. Bill gave away his name to his grandson, stating, "My great-great grandpa, Chief Bull Thunder of Oklahoma . . . that's the name I want my grandson to have and to carry on" (Wiles 2002:5).
4. One must go to the elder's home, remove one's shoes, knock on the door without saying anything or announcing oneself, and wait humbly at the door to be asked to enter the house. Once inside, the petitioner must stand over the seated elder, place both hands outstretched over the person's head without touching it, and

make the request. The same procedure is followed when requesting someone to be a ceremonial "grandfather" at the Sun Dance.

5. Betty Bastien (2004:122) reports that a relative told her that in times of difficulty, "I would call my name and remember who I am. Somehow I would find the courage and strength to overcome my challenges."

6. Similarly, Lester, a noted ceremonial healer, told me that "an Indian name is supposed to protect you."

7. An example: in August 2014 I was in Estes Park, Colorado, with several Northern Arapahos for a National Park Service event. One tribal councilman told the group that as he was driving up the road to Estes Park, he remembered that his grandfather Ben told him once that Ben's own grandmother's uncle named his niece *Siiyoniiniibei* 'Singing in the Rocks'. This occurred in the 1800s, when the uncle was traveling through the same canyon and heard singing. He followed the sound and discovered that it was wind in the cliffs. Inspired by this, he decided to give his niece this name. The councilman then concluded by saying that the name has been kept alive in the family ever since. Thus personal naming, family identity, family and tribal history, claims to the land and belonging, and personal authority and legitimacy were all wrapped up in a single personal name story, recalled by passing through this canyon again.

8. See Wiles (2011:88–93) on one such formal ceremony, Wiles (2011:138–41, 172) on name givers, and the entire book more generally for individual biographies and Arapaho personal names.

9. These names could also be used for social reprobation, however. Hilger (1952:48) relates the case of a brother and sister (in Arapaho definition) who lived with each other, thus violating the incest taboo. The man was called "Skunk" by the rest of the tribe.

10. See ELAR 18a, 21b, 26c, 28f, 28g, 41a, 48b, 60c, 60e, 63b, 63f, 69a, 69c, 69e, 79b, 79c, 80c, 80d.

11. As an example of the concept of the independent existence of a name, in the Arapaho language a name without an owner or a family with which it is associated (perhaps all members of the family have died out) is described as *heniiniiwo'oo'* 'wandering aimlessly without a home' (the same verb used to describe a widow without a family). Such a name can go to anyone in the tribe at this point.

12. Another example is the name *Nii'eihii Niitowuh'o* 'Bird Flying First', which has been condensed down to *Towuh'o*. *Niitow-* means 'first' and *uh'o[hu]* means 'fly', but *Towuh'o* means nothing, or could perhaps be interpreted as *Tow-uh'o* 'Flies Broken'—clearly not the intended meaning.

13. For example, the name *Nii'eihii Koyih'o* 'Eagle Flying Away' was commonly shortened to just *Koyih'o* 'Flying Away' for one man (see account in ELAR 18a), and *Nooko3onii'ehisei* 'Golden Eagle Woman' was commonly shortened to *Nooko3on* 'White Rump' [of a young Golden Eagle] for one woman (see account in ELAR 28g).

14. See Wiles (2011:170–73) on another highly formalized and public naming ceremony by a prominent family strongly affiliated with AC.

CHAPTER 5

1. See I. Goddard (1984:98–99) on this same distinction between the functionally "real" meanings found in institutionalized etymologies that are associated with the words they explain and merely "ad hoc explanations" that are invented on the spur of the moment.
2. Anderson (2001a:267) refers to this as "what Sapir called 'form-feeling,' the sense of connectedness and vitality carried in forms."
3. Anderson (2001a:41, 49–50, 103, 147, 162, 243–44, 261–62, 263–64, 280).
4. The word for crow (or raven) comes from Proto-Algonquian *kaakaakiwa* (Aubin 1975, entry #503). The word for the Creator likely comes from or is related to Proto-Algonquian *kaakiki* 'forever, eternal' (Aubin 1975, entry #507).
5. To cite another example, one younger woman once noted to me that her grandmother Cleone Thunder (real name) spoke or at least remembered Beesoowuutiit language. She said that *beesoowu'* meant 'Great Lakes' and that those ancestors were the more "traditional" branch of the family.
6. Ron reported in summer 1999 that his father said that the Beesoowuunenno' spoke the "real old, original Arapaho."

CHAPTER 6

1. See especially Brown (1999) for a survey of different strategies of lexical acculturation and differences from language to language.
2. Bison receive a partial asterisk because they were present in the northern woodlands (wood bison) but very clearly acquired a much more salient place in Arapaho life after the shift onto the Great Plains.
3. Of course some change simply happens as a result of linguistic drift—though drift can be accelerated in the context of major sociocultural changes. Today, there are a number of variant names for the same animal in Arapaho, which would be the source for potential shift to one of those names in the future, should the language survive. Thus 'moose' is both *hinenihi'* and *see'iini3eet* 'it has flat horns', and 'wolverine' is *(hi)seihiwox* and *tooxu'ookuteet* 'it has sharp teeth'.
4. See ELAR 18a.0995 for another example of this same word and joke by another speaker.
5. Several other examples of this sort of joking occur throughout ELAR 56a and 57f, with the same speakers.
6. See especially McCarty, Romero, and Zepeda (2006:39–40). In the most extreme cases, linguistic goals may not be achieved in interactions, yet the social work of building relationships can be achieved, and this may be the most important outcome for future language success. Meek (2010:49–50) makes this point for Kaska

language workshops she has observed, which are failures linguistically but not socially.

CONCLUSION

1. Compare this to similar ideas about ethnicity. Gregory E. Smoak, partially citing Fredrik Barth, writes that "interethnic boundaries are not impermeable walls but rather 'entail social processes of exclusion and incorporation whereby discrete categories are maintained despite changing participation and membership in the course of individual life histories'" (Smoak 2006:6, Barth 1969:9–10). Cf. Smoak 2006:5 on "identities" as well.
2. Readers may wish to compare this discussion to Perley (2011:156–73) for Maliseet. Perley draws similar distinctions between more linguistically oriented identities, similar to AC; more culturally oriented ones, similar to AC and Pan-Indianism; and more politically and experientially oriented ones, similar to Politico-Tribal. He links the different identities to different age cohorts quite explicitly. This age-related schema could be roughly applied to Northern Arapahos as well, at least on some kind of statistical-prevalence basis, but all the Northern Arapaho COPs cross age lines, and they are also not mutually exclusive identity positions. The largest difference between Perley's analysis and mine is the lack of Maliseet-oriented MTH-power issues, due to early Christianization and a more advanced move on the part of many Maliseet toward generalized "aboriginality." See also House (2002:12–13) for Navajo, where she discusses "assimilation" (12) and in contrast "traditional" practices, "pan-Indianism," indigeneity, the Native American Church, and "Navajo nationalism" (13) as counterdiscourses of Navajo identity that correspond fairly closely to my categories. See also Neely and Palmer (2009) and Neely (2012:95) on competing Kiowa ideologies concerning tradition, power, and authority.
3. See Ortner (2006:11–18), where she critiques traditional practice theory and suggests that we treat the concept of *culture* in overtly political and economic terms (see also Gal 1998:319–20). England (2003), in her discussion of the Maya movement in Mexico and Guatemala (which initially used its supposed cultural orientations as a disguise for political goals), and Friedman (2003), on the cultural politics of the Hawaiian language renaissance, are good explicit examples of the way culture and, in particular, language as culture can be understood as overtly political in indigenous "cultural revival" contexts.
4. The situation at Wind River contrasts with the Northern Cheyenne, where Christianity, Cheyenne language, and Cheyenne literacy are closely connected for many people. Likewise, both Southern Cheyenne and Southern Arapaho people have a long tradition of integrating indigenous-language hymns and prayers into Christian religion, including Evangelical varieties. Similar conditions occur among the Western Apache (Samuels 2006; M. Nevins 2010). At Wind River, the Bible has never been translated into Arapaho, the Summer Institute of Linguistics has never

been active, and Evangelical Christianity in the indigenous language has never really developed.

5. There has been a significant increase in interest in the Sand Creek Massacre over the last two decades, including formal runs commemorating the event (Wiles 2011:178–89). This focus on past historical experience as a bonding element among Arapahos—of all generations—could be seen as a response to perceived weakening of other forms of bonding, such as AC-style relationships. The interest in Sand Creek is most strong among Politico-Tribal and Pan-Indian COPs. See also Wiles (2011:212–15) for Northern Arapaho involvement in even broader affiliations based on shared history, such as Martin Luther King Day.

6. See B. French (2010:82–100) on urban Highland Maya people, for whom the Mayan language is now an evolving component of a "modern" Maya urban identity but no longer something that they individually speak.

7. Cf. Richland (2009:81) where he notes (citing Elizabeth Joh) that "the call for custom and tradition in tribal jurisprudence has more to do with articulating cultural identity different from dominant non-Indian society than really reflecting contemporary indigenous beliefs, values, and everyday social practice." If one removes "tribal jurisprudence," one could make similar claims about Politico-Tribalism.

8. Anderson (2001a:200, 207–10, 218, 223) makes a strong argument that Northern Arapaho society has been sectioned into a series of family interests and positions. This claim is not radically different from my claim about multiple COPs within Northern Arapaho society. I believe that the COP approach is more useful, however, in that it accounts for differences across family groups as well as generational differences within families. Anderson (2001a:227) notes the increase in "personal choice" in relation to religious, political, and other involvement, and he discusses (2001:328) "various and at times conflicting perspectives on knowledge, life movement and personal relations . . . [that] generate views about the future of the tribe." His presentation points to the society as chaotic and full of contradictions, whereas I see it as offering an increasing series of choices in an increasingly complex "debate" about how the coherence of the society itself will be maintained. Certainly individuals and groups oppose each other, but this does not mean that the society itself is riven with contradictions or disfunction. (See Muehlmann 2014:584 on the link between a COP-based approach and expectations of contestation as opposed to consensus.)

9. Collins (1998b) on the Tolowa is a nice parallel example of a similar analysis (see especially pp. 163–64), though he does not argue for separate COPs and thus maintains a somewhat more "single culture" view than I do, despite explicitly questioning whether there is any stable unity called "Tolowa" (1998b:7).

10. I have found great value in the writings of both Fowler and Anderson. Fowler's fieldwork was completed in 1978. She finds overall a strong element of continuity in Arapaho culture. Anderson's fieldwork was primarily completed in 1988–1994, with some later visits, and his most extensive book was published in 2001. In contrast to Fowler, he finds a great deal of intergenerational discontinuity—a point

that he made later as well (2009). I suggest the following resolution to the seeming disparity. In the 1970s, language shift was fairly low in visibility at Wind River. As a result, there was a strong rhetoric of continuity in the community, even though, below the radar, actual language practices and ideologies were undergoing radical shifts (Fowler was of course a historian as well, not focused on language). The late 1970s and early 1980s were a time of greatly increased awareness of language shift—linguist Zdenek Salzmann was brought in to produce an orthography, dictionary, collection of narratives, and curricular materials. Anderson arrived after this period and was also heavily involved with the language itself. He was exposed to a much more pronounced rhetoric of discontinuity within the community—a rhetoric that remains very strong to this day. Thus discontinuity was below the radar for Fowler, while continuity was below the radar for Anderson. Also, both Fowler and Anderson tended to view the Arapaho more as a single "culture." The more fine-grained approach offered by the concept of COPs allows one to recognize *both* discontinuity *and* continuity more clearly. In accord with Anderson's findings, I would suggest that Arapaho society at Wind River is experiencing increasing differentiation and contestation among various COPs and a substantial loss of the ideology of elder respect within some of those COPs. But in accord with Fowler's findings, I would suggest that the AC COP has shown surprising amounts of internal continuity and coherence, even as its overall position within the constellation of COPs at Wind River has been weakened.

11. See O'Neill (2012:62–63) for a description of the way "names" and vocabulary are being reconnected to accompanying stories—and generations are being reconnected—in a language-revitalization setting. See also Debenport's analysis of a Pueblo dictionary project, where indigenous participants in the project are interested in "regenerativity" for the language, not "memorialization" (2015:38–42). AC elders are also clearly interested in the regenerative power of names, not just in memorializing them as dead objects of documentation.

12. Compare M. Eleanor Nevin's (2013:216–17) words about entextualization: "The attributed object-like quality of entextualized discourse allows what people identify as 'the same' text to serve as a boundary object across contrasting regimes." While Nevins focuses more on misunderstanding or contestation, "boundary objects" (or "cultural resources") can also unify "regimes" or COPs—a point Nevins recognizes as well (see 2013:ch. 7).

13. See J. Hill (1998) for a similar finding about respect and gender among Mexicano speakers.

14. We have noted that female-gender-specific forms of knowledge, knowledge transmission, and ceremonialism within Arapaho society (quillwork and so forth) have declined significantly. Men's roles have declined in this area as well, but not as significantly as women's. (There are also some roles such as Pipe Keeper and Wheel Keeper that can be held by either a man or a woman.)

15. These include Cowell (2002a, 2014), Cowell and Moss (2005a, 2005b, 2006), and Cowell, C'Hair, and Moss (2014) on narrative; Cowell (2002b) on the uses of

literacy; Cowell (2007) on politeness; Sandoval (2016) on Plains Sign Language and gesture; Densmore (1936), Nettl (1951), Lah (1980), Anderson (2006), and Cowell, C'Hair, and Moss (2014) on song; Anderson (2001b) on translation; and Greymorning (2001, 2003) on the preschool immersion programs. The ELAR deposit provides excellent documentation of conversational practices; uses of silence, gesture, paralinguistic, and kinesic practices; and Arapaho English; and much future work in this area is to be expected.

16. See J. Hill and K. Hill (1986:1), where they speak of "the struggle of people of the Malinche to construct for themselves a useful identity and to organize their world in order to survive and prosper in it."

17. See also Collins's (1998b:197) remarks about the Tolowa, including the "conundrum of identity politics" and the problem of "how to recognize the differences that comprise humanness while building political solidarities."

18. See Debenport (2015:117), who, relying partly on the work of Vincent Crapanzano, critiques the tendency of language documentation programs to focus on "instrumentality" and saving "concrete object[s]" and "examples" of morphology, phonology, and so forth, in ways that are much more memorializing than regenerative. See also Cruikshank (1998:41–43) on narratives as "equipment for living" and as social activities rather than objects or data.

19. Cf. Debenport (2015), where she examines the ways both a dictionary project and curriculum for an indigenous language program insistently seek to model idealized relationships for the learners (and construct "future conversations" [2015:71]), rather than simply teaching them words and information.

REFERENCES

Abu-Lughod, Lila. 1991. "Writing against Culture." In *Recapturing Anthropology: Working in the Present*, edited by Richard G. Fox, 137–62. Sante Fe, N.Mex.: School of American Research Press.

Adley-Santa Maria, Bernadette. 1999. "Interrupting White Mountain Apache Language Shift: An Insider's View." *Practicing Anthropology* 21 (2): 16–19.

Afable, Patricia O., and Madison S. Beeler. 1996. "Place Names." In I. Goddard 1996, 185–99.

Ahlers, Jocelyn. 1997. "Cognitive Metaphor in Hupa." *American Indian Culture and Research Journal* 21 (3): 63–73.

Albers, Patricia, and Jeanne Kay. 1987. "Sharing the Land: A Study in American Indian Territoriality." In *A Cultural Geography of North American Indians*, edited by Thomas E. Ross and Tyrel G. Moore, 47–81. Boulder, Colo.: Westview Press.

Alford, Richard D. 1988. *Naming and Identity: A Cross-Cultural Study of Personal Naming Practices*. New Haven, Conn.: HRAF Press.

Anderson, Jeffrey D. 1998. "Ethnolinguistic Dimensions of Northern Arapaho Language Shift." *Anthropological Linguistics* 40 (1): 43–108.

———. 2001a. *The Four Hills of Life: Northern Arapaho Knowledge and Life Movement*. Lincoln: University of Nebraska Press.

———. 2001b. "Northern Arapaho Conversion of a Christian Text: The Our Father." *Ethnohistory* 48:689–712.

———. 2006. "The Poetics of Tropes and Dreams in Arapaho Ghost Dance Songs." In *New Perspectives on Native North America: Cultures, Histories, Representations*, edited by Sergei A. Kan and Pauline Turner Strong, 122–61. Lincoln: University of Nebraska Press.

———. 2009. "Contradictions across Space-Time and Language Ideologies in Northern Arapaho Language Shift." In Kroskrity and Field 2009, 48–76.

———. 2013. *Arapaho Women's Quillwork: Motion, Life, and Creativity*. Norman: University of Oklahoma Press.
Aubin, George F. 1975. *A Proto-Algonquian Dictionary*. National Museum of Man, Mercury Series, Canadian Ethnology Service, paper no. 29. Ottawa: National Museums of Canada.
Barth, Fredrik. 1969. *Ethnic Groups and Boundaries: The Social Organization of Culture Difference*. Boston: Little, Brown.
Basso, Keith. 1979. *Portraits of "The Whiteman": Linguistic Play and Cultural Symbols among the Western Apache*. Cambridge: Cambridge University Press.
———. 1990. *Western Apache Language and Culture: Essays in Linguistic Anthropology*. Tucson: University of Arizona Press.
———. 1996. *Wisdom Sits in Places: Language and Landscape among the Western Apache*. Albuquerque: University of New Mexico Press.
Bastien, Betty. 2004. *Blackfoot Ways of Knowing: The Worldview of the Siksikaitsitapi*. Calgary, AB: University of Calgary Press.
Bauman, Richard, and Charles L. Briggs. 1990. "Poetics and Performance as Critical Perspectives on Language and Social Life." *Annual Review of Anthropology* 19:59–88.
Beckwith, Martha. 1951. *The Kumulipo: A Hawaiian Creation Chant*. Honolulu: University of Hawaii Press.
Bender, Margaret. 2009. "Visibility, Authenticity, and Insiderness in Cherokee Language Ideologies." In Kroskrity and Field 2009, 123–47.
Bodenhorn, Barbara. 2006. "Calling into Being: Naming and Speaking Names on Alaska's North Slope." In vom Bruck and Bodenhorn 2006, 140–56.
Bodenhorn, Barbara, and Gabriele vom Bruck. 2006. "'Entangled in Histories': An Introduction to the Anthropology of Names and Naming." In vom Bruck and Bodenhorn 2006, 1–30.
Bonvillain, Nancy. 1989. "Noun Incorporation and Metaphor: Semantic Processes in Akwesasne Mohawk." *Anthropological Linguistics* 31:173–94.
Bourdieu, Pierre. 1977. *Outline of a Theory of Practice*. Translated by Richard Nice. Cambridge: Cambridge University Press.
———. 1991. *Language and Symbolic Power*. Edited by John B. Thompson. Translated by Gino Raymond and Matthew Adamson. Cambridge: Polity Press.
Briggs, Charles L. 1998. "'You're a Liar—You're Just like a Woman!': Constructing Dominant Ideologies of Language in Warao Men's Gossip." In Schieffelin, Woolard, and Kroskrity 1998, 229–55.
Bright, William. 1957. *The Karok Language*. University of California Publications in Linguistics, vol. 13. Berkeley: University of California Press.
Brown, Cecil H. 1999. *Lexical Acculturation in Native American Languages*. New York: Oxford University Press.
Buchholtz, Mary, and Kira Hall. 2010. "Locating Identity in Language." In *Language and Identities*, edited by Carmen Llamas and Dominic Watt, 18–28. Edinburgh: Edinburgh University Press.

Bunte, Pamela. 2009. "'You Keep Not Listening with Your Ears!' Language Ideologies, Language Socialization, and Paiute Identity." In Kroskrity and Field 2009, 172–89.

Canessa, Andrew. 2005. "Introduction: Making the Nation on the Margin." In *Natives Making Nation: Gender, Indigeneity, and the State in the Andes*, edited by Andrew Canessa, 3–31. Tucson: University of Arizona Press.

Clifford, James. 1988. *The Predicament of Culture: Twentieth-Century Ethnography, Literature, and Art*. Cambridge: Harvard University Press.

———. 2007. "Varieties of Indigenous Experience: Diasporas, Homelands, Sovereignties." In *Indigenous Experience Today*, edited by Marisol de la Cadena and Orin Starn, 197–224. New York: Berg.

———. 2013. *Returns: Becoming Indigenous in the Twenty-First Century*. Cambridge: Harvard University Press.

Collins, James. 1998a. "Our Ideologies and Theirs." In Schieffelin, Woolard, and Kroskrity 1998, 256–70.

———. 1998b. *Understanding Tolowa Histories: Western Hegemonies and Native American Responses*. New York: Routledge.

———. 2003. "Reclaiming Traditions, Remaking Community: Politics, Language and Place among the Tolowa of Northwest California." In *Language and Social Identity*, edited by Richard K. Blot, 225–41. Westport, Conn.: Praegar.

Cowell, Andrew. 2002a. "The Poetics of Arapaho Storytelling: From Salvage to Performance." *Oral Tradition* 17:19–52.

———. 2002b. "Bilingual Curriculum among the Northern Arapaho: Oral Tradition, Literacy, and Performance." *American Indian Quarterly* 26:2–43.

———. 2007. "Arapaho Imperatives: Indirectness, Politeness and Communal 'Face.'" *Journal of Linguistic Anthropology* 17 (1): 44–60.

———. 2014. *Stories of Charles Piper*. 2 vols. Boulder: University of Colorado, Center for the Study of Indigenous Languages.

Cowell, Andrew, William C'Hair, and Alonzo Moss Sr., eds. 2014. *Arapaho Stories, Songs, and Prayers: A Bilingual Anthology*. Norman: University of Oklahoma Press.

Cowell, Andrew, and Alonzo Moss Sr. 2003. "Arapaho Place Names in Colorado: Form and Function, Language and Culture." *Anthropological Linguistics* 45 (4): 349–89.

———. 2004a. "Arapaho Placenames in Colorado: Indigenous Mapping, White Remaking." *Names: A Journal of Onomastics* 52 (1):21–41.

———. 2004b. "The Linguistic Structure of Arapaho Personal Names." In *Papers of the 35th Algonquian Conference*, edited by H. C. Wolfart, 61–74. Winnipeg: University of Manitoba.

———, eds. and trans. 2005a. *Hinono'einoo3itoono: Arapaho Historical Traditions*. Told by Paul Moss. Winnipeg: University of Manitoba Press.

———. 2005b. "Three Stories." Told by Richard Moss. In *Algonquian Spirit: Contemporary Translations of the Algonquian Literatures of North America*, edited by Brian Swann, 472–94. Lincoln: University of Nebraska Press.

———, eds. 2006. *Modern Arapaho Narratives: Hinono'einoo3itoono*. Told by Richard "Dickie" Moss. Boulder, Colo.: Wyoming Council for the Humanities.

———. 2008. *The Arapaho Language*. Boulder: University Press of Colorado.
Cowell, Andrew, Allan Taylor, and Terry Brockie. 2016. "Gros Ventre Ethnogeography and Placenames: A Diachronic Perspective." *Anthropological Linguistics* 58 (2): 132–71.
Cruikshank, Julie. 1998. *The Social Life of Stories: Narrative and Knowledge in the Yukon Territory*. Lincoln: University of Nebraska Press.
Dalby, Andrew. 2003. *Language in Danger: The Loss of Linguistic Diversity and the Threat to our Future*. New York: Columbia University Press.
Dauenhauer, Nora Marks, and Richard Dauenhauer. 1998. "Technical, Emotional, and Ideological Issues in Reversing Language Shift: Examples from Southeast Alaska." In *Endangered Languages: Current Issues and Future Prospects*, edited by Lenore A. Grenoble and Lindsay J. Whaley, 57–98. Cambridge: Cambridge University Press.
Davidson, Jill. 1999. "Reflections on Linguistic Fieldwork in Two Native American Communities." *Practicing Anthropology* 21 (2): 28–33.
Debenport, Erin. 2015. *Fixing the Books: Secrecy, Literacy, and Perfectibility in Indigenous New Mexico*. Santa Fe, N.Mex.: School for Advanced Research Press.
Densmore, Frances. 1936. *Cheyenne and Arapaho Music*. Southwest Museum Papers no. 10. Los Angeles: Southwest Museum.
Dorsey, George. 1903. *The Arapaho Sun Dance: The Ceremony of the Offerings Lodge*. Field Columbian Museum 75, Anthropological Series, vol. 4. Chicago: Field Columbian Museum.
Dorsey, George A. and Alfred L. Kroeber. (1903) 1997. *Traditions of the Arapaho*. Lincoln: University of Nebraska Press.
Eckert, Penelope, and Sally McConnell-Ginet. 1992. "Think Practically and Look Locally: Language and Gender as Community-Based Practice." *Annual Review of Anthropology* 21:461–90.
Eggan, Fred. 1955. "The Cheyenne and Arapaho Kinship System." In *Social Anthropology of North American Tribes*, edited by Fred Eggan, 35–98. Chicago: University of Chicago Press.
ELAR (Endangered Languages Archive). *Arapaho Conversational Database*. Deposited by Andrew Cowell. Hans Rausing Endangered Language Project, Endangered Languages Documentation Programme. SOAS University of London. Publicly accessible at https://www.soas.ac.uk/elar/.
Enfield, N. J., Paul Kockelman, and Jack Sidnell, eds. 2014. *The Cambridge Handbook of Linguistic Anthropology*. Cambridge: Cambridge University Press.
England, Nora C. 2003. "Mayan Language Revival and Revitalization Politics: Linguistics and Linguistic Ideologies." *American Anthropologist* 105 (4): 733–43.
Errington, Joseph J. 1985. "On the Nature of the Sociolinguistic Sign: Describing the Javanese Speech Levels." In *Semiotic Mediation*, edited by Elizabeth Mertz and Richard J. Parmentier, 287–310. Orlando, Fla.: Academic Press.
———. 2003. "Getting Language Rights: The Rhetorics of Language Endangerment and Loss." *American Anthropologist* 105 (4): 123–32.
Evans, Nicholas. 2010. *Dying Words: Endangered Languages and What They Have to Tell Us*. Chichester, UK: Wiley-Blackwell.

Faudree, Paja, and Magnus Pharao Hansen. 2014. "Language, Society, and History: Towards a Unified Approach?" In Enfield, Kockelman, and Sidnell 2014, 227–49.

Field, Margaret C. 2009. "Changing Navajo Language Ideologies and Changing Language Use." In Kroskrity and Field 2009, 31–47.

———. 2012. "Kumiai Stories: Bridges between the Oral Tradition and Classroom Practice." In Kroskrity 2012b, 115–26.

Fienup-Riordan, Ann. 1994. "Clearing the Path: Metaphors to Live by in Yup'ik Oral Tradition." *American Indian Quarterly* 18 (1): 61–70.

Fiskesjö, Magnus. 2010. "The Autonomy of Naming: Kinship, Power, and Ethnonymy in the Wa Lands of the Southeast Asia-China Frontier." In Yangren and MacDonald 2010, 150–72.

Fowler, Loretta. 1982. *Arapahoe Politics, 1851–1978: Symbols in Crises of Authority*. Lincoln: University of Nebraska Press.

———. 2002. *Tribal Sovereignty and the Historical Imagination: Cheyenne-Arapaho Politics*. Lincoln: University of Nebraska Press.

———. 2010. *Wives and Husbands: Gender and Age in Southern Arapaho History*. Norman: University of Oklahoma Press.

French, Brigittine M. 2010. *Maya Ethnolinguistic Identity: Violence, Cultural Rights, and Modernity in Highland Guatemala*. Tucson: University of Arizona Press.

French, David H., and Kathrine S. French. 1996. "Personal Names." In I. Goddard 1996, 200–221.

Friedman, Jonathan. 2003. "Globalizing Languages: Ideologies and Realities of the Contemporary Global System." *American Anthropologist* 105 (4): 744–52.

Gal, Susan. 1998. "Multiplicity and Contention among Language Ideologies: A Commentary." In Schieffelin, Woolard, and Kroskrity 1998, 317–31.

Gatschet, Albert. Field Notes. Smithsonian Institution, National Anthropological Archives, MS 61, MS 231.

Gill, Sam D. 1982. *Native American Religions: An Introduction*. Belmont, Calif.: Wadsworth.

Glowacka, Maria, and Emory Sekaquaptewa. 2009. "The Metaphorical Dimensions of Hopi Ethics." *Journal of the Southwest* 51 (2): 165–86.

Godbout, Jacques. 1998. *The World of the Gift*. Translated by Donald Winker. Montreal: McGill-Queen's University Press.

Goddard, Cliff. 1992. "Traditional Yankunytjatjara Ways of Speaking—A Semantic Perspective." *Australian Journal of Linguistics* 12 (1): 93–122.

Goddard, Ives. 1984. "The Study of Native North American Ethnonymy." In Tooker 1984, 95–107.

———, ed. 1996. *Languages*. Vol. 17 of *Handbook of North American Indians*, edited by William Sturtevant. Washington, D.C.: Smithsonian Institution.

Godelier, Maurice. 1999. *The Enigma of the Gift*. Translated by Nora Scott. Chicago: University of Chicago Press.

Gómez de García, Jule, Melissa Axelrod, and Jordan Lachler. 2009. "English Is the Dead Language: Native Perspectives on Bilingualism." In Kroskrity and Field 2009, 99–122.

Goodman, Ronald. 1992. *Lakota Star Knowledge: Studies in Lakota Stellar Theology.* Mission, S.Dak.: Sinte Gleska University Press.

Grenoble, Lenore A., and Lindsay J. Whaley. 2006. *Saving Languages: An Introduction to Language Revitalization.* Cambridge: Cambridge University Press.

Greymorning, Stephen Neyooxet. 2001. "Reflections on the Arapaho Language Project; or, When Bambi Spoke Arapaho and Other Tales of Arapaho Language Revitalization Efforts." In *The Green Book of Language Revitalization in Practice*, edited by Kenneth Hale and Leanne Hinton, 287–97. New York: Academic Press.

———. 2003. "Hinono'eitiino'oowu' and the Work of Language Survival." In *A Will to Survive: Indigenous Essays on the Politics of Language, Culture, and Identity*, edited by Stephen Greymorning, 213–24. New York: McGraw-Hill.

Griffin-Pierce, Trudy. 2000. "The Continuous Renewal of Sacred Traditions: Navajo Religion." In Sullivan 2000, 121–41.

Grim, John A. 2000. "Traditional Ways and Contemporary Vitality: Absaroke/Crow." In Sullivan 2000, 53–84.

Gross, Feliks. 1951. "Language and Value Changes among the Arapaho." *International Journal of American Linguistics* 17 (1): 10–17.

Guilliford, Andrew. 2000. *Sacred Objects and Sacred Places: Preserving Tribal Traditions.* Boulder: University Press of Colorado.

Hanks, C. and B. Winter. 1986. "Local Knowledge and Ethnoarchaeology: An Approach to Dene Settlement Systems." *Current Anthropology* 27 (3): 272–75.

Harrison, David. 2007. *When Languages Die: The Extinction of the World's Languages and the Erosion of Human Knowledge.* Oxford: Oxford University Press.

Harrod, Howard L. 1987. *Renewing the World: Plains Indian Religion and Morality.* Tucson: University of Arizona Press.

Hickerson, Nancy Parrott. 1978. "The 'Natural Environment' as Object and Sign." *The Journal of the Linguistic Association of the Southwest* 3 (1): 33–44.

Hilger, M. Inez. 1952. *Arapaho Child Life and Its Cultural Background.* Smithsonian Institution Bureau of American Ethnology 148. Washington, D.C.: Smithsonian Institution.

Hill, Jane H. 1993. "Structure and Practice in Language Shift." In *Progression and Regression in Language: Sociocultural, Neuropsychological and Linguistic Perspectives*, edited by Kenneth Hyltenstam and Åke Viberg, 68–93. Cambridge: Cambridge University Press.

———. 1998. "'Today There is No Respect': Nostalgia, 'Respect,' and Oppositional Discourse in Mexicano (Nahuatl) Language Ideology." In Schieffelin, Woolard, and Kroskrity 1998, 68–86.

———. 2002. "'Expert Rhetorics' in Advocacy for Endangered Languages: Who Is Listening, and What Do They Hear?" *Journal of Linguistic Anthropology* 12 (2): 119–33.

Hill, Jane H., and Kenneth C. Hill. 1986. *Speaking Mexicano: Dynamics of Syncretic Language in Central Mexico.* Tucson: University of Arizona Press.

Hinton, Leanne, and Jocelyn Ahlers. 1999. "The Issue of 'Authenticity' in California Language Restoration." *Anthropology and Education Quarterly* 30 (1): 56–67.

Holland, Dorothy, and Naomi Quinn, eds. 1987. *Cultural Models in Language and Thought*. Cambridge: Cambridge University Press.

House, Deborah. 2002. *Language Shift among the Navajos: Identity Politics and Cultural Continuity*. Tucson: University of Arizona Press.

Ingham, Bruce. 2009. *Five Lakota Oral Discourses Translated and Transcribed: How an American Indian Nation Explains Its Philosophy of Life*. Lewiston, N.Y.: Edwin Mellen Press.

Ingold, Tim. 1987. *The Appropriate of Nature: Essays on Human Ecology and Social Relations*. Iowa City: University of Iowa Press.

Irvine, Judith T., and Susan Gal. 2000. "Language Ideology and Linguistic Differentiation." In Kroskrity 2000b, 35–83.

Irwin, Lee. 1994. *The Dream Seekers: Native American Visionary Traditions of the Great Plains*. Norman: University of Oklahoma Press.

Kari, James. 1989. "Some Principles of Alaskan Athabaskan Toponymic Knowledge." In *General and Amerindian Ethnolinguistics: In Remembrance of Stanley Newman*, edited by Mary Key and Henry Hoenigswald, 129–49. Berlin: Mouton de Gruyter.

Kelley, Klara Bonsack, and Harris Francis. 1994. *Navajo Sacred Places*. Bloomington: Indiana University Press.

———. 2005. "Traditional Navajo Maps and Wayfinding." *American Indian Culture and Research Journal* 29 (2): 85–111.

Kockelman, Paul. 2014. "Linguistic Anthropology and Critical Theory." In Enfield, Kockelman, and Sidnell 2014, 603–25.

Kroeber, Alfred. Field Notes. Smithsonian Institution, National Anthropological Archives, MS 2560.

———. (1902–7) 1983. *The Arapaho*. Lincoln: University of Nebraska Press.

Kroskrity, Paul V. 1998. "Arizona Tewa Kiva Speech as a Manifestation of a Dominant Language Ideology." In Schieffelin, Woolard, and Kroskrity 1998, 103–22.

———. 2000a. "Regimenting Languages: Language Ideological Perspectives." In Kroskrity 2000b, 1–34.

———, ed. 2000b. *Regimes of Language: Ideologies, Polities, Identities*. Santa Fe, N.Mex.: School of American Research Press.

———. 2009. "Embodying the Reversal of Language Shift: Agency, Incorporation, and Language Ideological Change in the Western Mono Community of Central California." In Kroskrity and Field 2009, 190–210.

———. 2012a. "Growing with Stories: Ideologies of Storytelling and the Narrative Reproduction of Arizona Tewa Identities." In Kroskrity 2012b, 151–83.

———, ed. 2012b. *Telling Stories in the Face of Danger: Language Renewal in Native American Communities*. Norman: University of Oklahoma Press.

Kroskrity, Paul V., and Margaret C. Field, eds. 2009. *Native American Language Ideologies: Beliefs, Practices, and Struggles in Indian Country*. Tucson: University of Arizona Press.

Kulick, Don. 1992. *Language Shift and Cultural Reproduction: Socialization, Self, and Syncretism in a Papua New Guinean Village*. Cambridge: Cambridge University Press.

Kun-hui, Ku. 2010. "'Who Is Your Name?' Naming Paiwan Identities in Contemporary Taiwan." In Yangren and MacDonald 2010, 197–223.

Lah, Ronald. 1980. "Ethnoaesthetics of Northern Arapaho Indian Music." PhD diss., Northwestern University.

Laird, Carobeth. 1976. *The Chemehuevis*. Banning, Calif.: Malki Museum Press.

Lakoff, George, and Mark Johnson. (1980) 2003. *Metaphors We Live By*. Chicago: University of Chicago Press.

Lakoff, George, and Zoltán Kövecses. 1987. "The Cognitive Model of Anger Inherent in American English." In Holland and Quinn 1987, 195–221.

Levinson, Stephen C. 1996. "Language and Space." *Annual Review of Anthropology* 25:353–82.

Lombard, Carol G. 2011. "The Sociological Significance of Niitsitapi Personal Names: An Ethnographic Analysis." *Names: A Journal of Onomastics* 59 (1): 42–51.

Maybury-Lewis, David. 1984. "Name, Person, and Ideology in Central Brazil." In Tooker 1984, 1–10.

McCarty, Teresa L. 2008. "Native American Languages as Heritage Mother Tongues." *Language, Culture and Curriculum* 21 (3): 201–25.

McCarty, Teresa L., Mary Eunice Romero, and Ofelia Zepeda. 2006. "Reclaiming the Gift: Indigenous Youth Counter-Narratives on Native Language Loss and Revitalization." *American Indian Quarterly* 30 (1–2): 28–48.

McCarty, Teresa L., and Lucille Watahomigie. 1999. "Indigenous Education and Grassroots Language Planning in the USA." *Practicing Anthropology* 21 (2): 5–11.

Meadows, William C. 2008. *Kiowa Ethnogeography*. Austin: University of Texas Press.

Meek, Barbra. 2009. "Language Ideology and Aboriginal Language Revitalization in Yukon, Canada." In Kroskrity and Field 2009, 151–71.

———. 2010. *We Are Our Language: An Ethnography of Language Revitalization in a Northern Athabaskan Community*. Tucson: University of Arizona Press.

———. 2014a. "Gender, Endangered Languages, and Revitalization." In *The Handbook of Language and Gender*, edited by Miriam Meyerhoff and Susan Ehrlich, 2nd ed., 549–66. New York: Wiley-Blackwell.

———. 2014b. "'She Can Do It in English Too': Acts of Intimacy and Boundary-Making in Language Revitalization." *Language & Communication* 38:73–82.

Mithun, Marianne. 1984. "Principles of Naming in Mohawk." In Tooker 1984, 40–54.

Mooney, James. (1896) 1973. *The Ghost-Dance Religion and Wounded Knee*. Mineola, N.Y.: Dover.

Moore, John. H. 1984. "Cheyenne Names and Cosmology." *American Ethnologist* 11 (2): 291–312.

Moore, Patrick. 2007. "Negotiated Identities: The Evolution of Dene Tha and Kaska Personal Naming Systems." *Anthropological Linguistics* 49 (3–4): 283–307.

Moore, Robert E. 1988. "Lexicalization versus Loss in Wasco-Wishram Language Obsolescence." *International Journal of American Linguistics* 54 (4): 453–68.

Muehlmann, Shaylih. 2014. "The Speech Community and Beyond: Language and the Nature of the Social Aggregate." In Enfield, Kockelman, and Sidnell 2014, 577–98.

Mühlhäusler, Peter. 1996. *Linguistic Ecology: Language Change and Linguistic Imperialism in the Pacific Region*. London: Routledge.

Neely, Amber A. 2012. "Tales of Tradition and Stories of Syncretism in Kiowa Language Revitalization." In Kroskrity 2012b, 90–114.

Neely, Amber A., and Gus Palmer Jr. 2009. "Which Way Is the Kiowa Way? Orthography Choices, Ideologies, and Language Renewal." In Kroskrity and Field 2009, 271–97.

Nettl, Bruno. 1951. "Musical Culture of the Arapaho." MA thesis, Indiana University.

Nevins, M. Eleanor. 2004. "Learning to Listen: Confronting Two Meanings of Language Loss in the Contemporary White Mountain Apache Speech Community." *Journal of Linguistic Anthropology* 14 (2): 269–88.

———. 2008. "'They Live in Lonesome Dove': Media and Contemporary Western Apache Place-Naming Practices." *Language and Society* 37 (2): 191–215.

———. 2010. "The Bible in Two Keys: Traditionalism and Evangelical Christianity on the Fort Apache Reservation." *Language & Communication* 30:19–32.

———. 2013. *Lessons from Fort Apache: Beyond Language Endangerment and Maintenance*. Chichester, UK: Wiley-Blackwell.

Nevins, M. Eleanor, and Thomas J. Nevins. 2012. "They Don't Know How to Ask: Pedagogy, Storytelling, and the Ironies of Language Endangerment on the White Mountain Apache Reservation." In Kroskrity 2012b, 129–50.

O'Neill, Sean. 2012. "The Politics of Storytelling in Northwestern California: Ideology, Identity, and Maintaining Narrative Distinction in the Face of Cultural Convergences." In Kroskrity 2012b, 60–89.

Ortner, Sherry. 2006. *Anthropology and Social Theory: Culture, Power, and the Acting Subject*. Durham, N.C.: Duke University Press.

Palmer, Gus, Jr. 2012. "Kiowa Stories Express Tribal Memory, Ideology, and Being." In Kroskrity 2012b, 23–43.

Pearce, Margaret Wickens, and Renee Pualani Louis. 2008. "Mapping Indigenous Depth of Place." *American Indian Culture and Research Journal* 32 (3): 107–26.

Perley, Bernard C. 2011. *Defying Maliseet Language Death: Emergent Vitalities of Language, Culture, and Identity in Eastern Canada*. Lincoln: University of Nebraska Press.

Powers, William K. 1986. *Sacred Language: The Nature of Supernatural Discourse in Lakota*. Norman: University of Oklahoma Press.

———. 2000. "Wiping the Tears: Lakota Religion in the Twenty-First Century." In Sullivan 2000, 104–20.

Preciado, Jenette A. 2010. "Arapaho Language Education: Language Ideologies in the Classroom." Senior honors thesis, University of Colorado Boulder.

Pye, Clifton. 1992. "Language Loss among the Chilcotin." *International Journal of the Sociology of Language* 93:75–86.

Quinn, Naomi, and Dorothy Holland. 1987. "Culture and Cognition." In Holland and Quinn 1987, 3–40.

Rajah, Ananda. 2010. "The Karen Naming System: Identity and Sociocultural Orientations." In Yangren and MacDonald 2010, 128–49.

Richland, Justin B. 2009. "'Language, Court, Constitution. It's All Tied Up into One': The (Meta)Pragmatics of Tradition in a Hopi Tribal Court Hearing." In Kroskrity and Field 2009, 77–98.

Sahlins, Marshall. 1985. *Islands of History*. Chicago: University of Chicago Press.

Salzmann, Zdenek. 1951. "Contrastive Field Experience with Language and Values of the Arapaho." *International Journal of American Linguistics* 17 (2): 98–101.

———. 1956. "Arapaho III: Additional Texts." *International Journal of American Linguistics* 22 (4): 266–72.

———. 1983. *Dictionary of Contemporary Arapaho Usage*. Wind River Reservation, Wyo.: Northern Arapaho Tribe.

Sammons, Olivia N. 2009. "Updating the Sauk Lexicon: Strategies and Implications for Language Revitalization." *Santa Barbara Papers in Linguistics* 20:46–59.

Samuels, David W. 2001. "Indeterminacy and History in Britton Goode's Western Apache Placenames: Ambiguous Identity on the San Carlos Apache Reservation." *American Ethnologist* 28 (2): 277–302.

———. 2004. *Putting a Story on Top of It: Expression and Identity on the San Carlos Apache Reservation*. Tucson: University of Arizona Press.

———. 2006. "Bible Translation and Medicine Man Talk: Missionaries, Indexicality, and the 'Language Expert' on the San Carlos Apache Reservation." *Language in Society* 35 (4): 529–57.

Sandoval, Rich A. 2016. "Gesture-Speech Bimodalism in Arapaho Grammar: An Interactional Approach." PhD diss., University of Colorado Boulder.

Schieffelin, Bambi B., Kathryn A. Woolard, and Paul V. Kroskrity, eds. 1998. *Language Ideologies: Theory and Practice*. New York: Oxford University Press.

Schreyer, Christine. 2006. "'What You See Is Where You Are': An Examination of Native North American Place Names." In *Space and Spatial Analysis in Archaeology*, edited by Elizabeth C. Robertson, Jeffrey D. Seibert, Deepika C. Fernandez, and Marc U. Zender, 227–32. Calgary, AB: University of Calgary Press.

Sekaquaptewa, Emory, and Dorothy Washburn. 2004. "They Go Along Singing: Reconstructing the Hopi Past from Ritual Metaphors in Song and Image." *American Antiquity* 69 (3): 457–86.

Shaul, David Leedom. 2014. *A Prehistory of Western North America: The Impact of Uto-Aztecan Languages*. Albuquerque: University of New Mexico Press.

Sillander, Kenneth. 2010. "Teknonymy, Name Avoidance, Solidarity, and Individuation among the Bentian of Indonesian Borneo." In Yangren and MacDonald 2010, 101–27.

Silverstein, Michael. 1979. "Language Structure and Linguistic Ideology." In *The Elements: A Parasession on Linguistic Units and Levels*, edited by Paul R. Cline, William F. Hanks, and Carol L. Hofbauer, 193–247. Chicago: Chicago Linguistic Society.

———. 1998. "Contemporary Transformations of Local Linguistic Communities." *Annual Review of Anthropology* 27:401–26.

Smith, Grant W. 1996. "Amerindian Place Names: A Typology Based on Meaning and Form." *Onomastica Canadiana* 78 (2): 53–64.

Smoak, Gregory E. 2006. *Ghost Dances and Identity: Prophetic Religion and American Indian Ethnogenesis in the Nineteenth Century.* Berkeley: University of California Press.

Spielmann, Roger. 1998. *"You're So Fat!": Exploring Ojibwe Discourse.* Toronto: University of Toronto Press.

Stoffe, Richard W., David B. Halmo, and Diane E. Austin. 1997. "Cultural Landscapes and Traditional Cultural Properties: A Southern Paiute View of the Grand Canyon." *American Indian Quarterly* 21 (2): 229–49.

Sullivan, Lawrence E., ed. 2000. *Native Religions and Cultures of North America: Anthropology of the Sacred.* New York: Continuum.

Thieberger, Nicholas. 2002. "Extinction in Whose Terms? Which Parts of a Language Constitute a Target for Language Maintenance Programmes?" In *Language Endangerment and Language Maintenance*, edited by David Bradley and Maya Bradley, 310–28. Curzon, N.Y.: Routledge.

Thompson, Chad. 1997. "Structure, Metaphor, and Iconicity in Koyukon Shamanistic Stories." *American Indian Quarterly* 21 (2): 146–69.

Toelken, Barre, and Tacheeni Scott. 1981. "Poetic Retranslations and the 'Pretty Languages' of Yellowman." In *Traditional Literatures of the American Indian: Texts and Interpretations*, edited by Karl Kroeber, 65–116. Lincoln: University of Nebraska Press.

Toll, Oliver W. 1962. *Arapaho Names and Trails: A Report of a 1914 Pack Trip.* Denver, Colo.: privately printed.

Tooker, Elisabeth, ed. 1984. *Naming Systems: The 1980 Proceedings of the American Ethnological Society.* Washington, D.C.: American Ethnological Society.

Trenholm, Virginia Cole. 1986. *The Arapahoes: Our People.* Norman: University of Oklahoma Press.

Vest, J. H. C. 2006. "Myth, Metaphor, and Meaning in 'The Boy Who Could Not Understand': A Study of Seneca Auto-Criticism." *American Indian Culture and Research Journal* 30 (4): 41–62.

Vom Bruck, Gabriele, and Barbara Bodenhorn, eds. 2006. *The Anthropology of Names and Naming.* Cambridge: Cambridge University Press.

Watahomigie, Lucille J. 1998. "The Native Language Is a Gift: A Hualapai Language Autobiography." *International Journal of the Sociology of Language* 132:5–7.

Weiner, Annette B. 1992. *Inalienable Possessions: The Paradox of Keeping-While-Giving.* Berkeley: University of California Press.

Weiner, James F. 1991. *The Empty Place: Poetry, Space, and Being among the Foi of Papua New Guinea.* Bloomington: Indiana University Press.

Wickwire, Wendy. 2007. "Stories from the Margins: Toward a More Inclusive British Columbia." In *Myth & Memory: Stories of Indigenous-European Contact*, edited by John Sutton Lutz, 118–39. Vancouver: University of British Columbia Press.

Wiles, Sara. 2002. "Interview with Richard Moss." Manuscript provided to Andrew Cowell.

———. 2011. *Arapaho Journeys: Photographs and Stories from the Wind River Reservation.* Norman: University of Oklahoma Press.

Wilkinson, Charles. 2005. *Blood Struggle: The Rise of Modern Indian Nations*. New York: Norton.

Wong, Laiana. 1999. "Authenticity and the Revitalization of Hawaiian." *Anthropology and Education Quarterly* 30 (1): 94–115.

Woolard, Kathryn. 1998. "Introduction: Language Ideology as a Field of Inquiry." In Schieffelin, Woolard, and Kroskrity 1998, 3–47.

Woolard, Kathryn, and Bambi B. Schieffelin. 1994. "Language Ideology." *Annual Review of Anthropology* 23:55–82.

Yangren, Zheng, and Charles J-J MacDonald, eds. 2010. *Personal Names in Asia: History, Culture and Identity*. Singapore: NUS Press.

INDEX

Anderson, Jeffrey D., 24, 50–51, 95, 179, 251, 282n8, 282–83n10
age-grade-society lodges, 16–17, 27–28, 37, 42, 106, 138, 181
agency, human: embedded in or expressed through folk etymologies, 190, 194; expressed in personal names, 132–33, 153, 155, 159; expressed in place names, 93–94, 98–102; in relation to paths, 60–61
analogical/symbolic thought, 82–83, 91–99, 116–17, 124–25, 172, 177–80, 204–8, 277n6. *See also* aural analogical/symbolic thought
announcing, formal, 44
Antelope, Howard, 198
ants: symbolic importance of, 96
Apache, Western, language and culture, 102, 113, 117–18, 234–36, 253–54
Arapahoe, WY, 117, 119–23, 164–65, 231–32, 237
Armajo, Hiram, 96
Athabaskan language and culture, 97
aural analogical/symbolic thought, 176–79, 185–86, 190, 196–98, 205–8

beadwork, 17, 47, 95, 106
Bear Butte, SD, 86, 107
Beaver Creek area, Wind River Reservation, WY, 109–11
Beaver Dodge, 110
Beesoowuunenno' people, 180–85, 189, 195–96, 280n5
Bighorn Mts, WY, 106
Black Hills, SD/WY, 106–7
Blackfoot language and culture, 10, 37–38, 61–62, 85–86, 131
Bluebird (legendary character), 193–94
borrowing, of words, 180, 202–4, 211–12, 227; language ideology related to, 170–71, 204, 207–8, 213–14
Boulder, CO, 169, 189
Bozeman, MT, 116
Brown, Francis, 139
buffalo, 88–89, 94, 107–8, 129
Buffalo Lodge, women's, 16

Canada: Arapaho speakers supposedly located in, 186
capital, symbolic, 12, 37, 40–41, 44–46, 106, 148–49, 154–55

casinos, 24–25, 29, 39, 42–43, 45, 145, 230, 232
caterpillars, Arapaho beliefs about and word for, 205
Casper, WY, 121
center/periphery, metaphor of, 50–55, 59, 61, 70, 73–74, 87–89, 96–97, 157, 211
Cheyenne language and culture, 173, 202–3, 281n4
chickadee: meanings and symbolics of the name, 205
Christianity, 27–28, 35–36, 39, 118, 173, 244–47, 250, 255, 264, 281n2, 281–82n4
clothing: terms for Euro-American items, 208, 211
code-mixing: grammar of, 226–27
code-switching, 30, 105, 213–15
community of practice (COP): definition of, 5, 242–43; list of primary COPs at Wind River Reservation, 31–32
cow: meanings and symbolics of the word, 180, 207, 211–12
Creation Story, Arapaho, 175–77, 187–88
Crispin, Tom, 90
crow: meanings and symbolics of the name, 206, 280n4
Crow Dance, 27, 32, 108

Denver, CO, 121–22, 169, 188, 226, 230, 276
design motifs, in Arapaho traditional artwork, 55, 60, 94–103, 106, 109, 205, 277n7, 278n14
Devil's Tower, WY, 107
dominant ideologies, of language usage, 19–22, 43–44, 260–61. *See also* language perfectionism, language purism, language transparency
Doris Duke Oral History Collection (University of Oklahoma), 179
drum, ceremonial Eagle, 38
Dubois, WY, 115–17, 123, 239

eagles, 87, 100–101, 107–9, 129, 134, 248, 250
elevation, and sacredness, 100–101
Endangered Languages Archive (ELAR), University of London, 8
erasure, 41–42, 53, 169, 224
Estes Park, CO, 96–97, 109, 279n7
Ethete, WY, 117, 119, 123, 163–65, 191, 228, 231–32, 237
ethnonyms: for other tribes, 185–89, 212; for Euro-Americans, 173–75, 179, 217; for Arapahoan sub-groups (*Beesoowuunenno'*), 180–85, 280n5; for Arapaho, 190–94

fog, Arapaho beliefs about and word for, 205
Ft. Fetterman, WY, 115
Ft. Laramie Treaty of 1851, 15
Four Old Men (Northern Arapaho ceremonial elders), 27, 137, 176
Fowler, Loretta, 251, 273n10, 283n10
fractal recursivity, 262
Friday, Ben, 104, 162, 254–65, 279n7

Gapun village, New Guinea, 31, 273n6, 273n8
gender roles, and changes in, over time, 16–17, 23, 26–29, 34, 146–47, 175, 255–62, 283n14; in personal names, 129, 132
Ghost Dance, 27, 32, 107–8, 264
ghosts and ghost stories, 56, 109–11, 177, 201, 206
gifts and gift theory, 98–99, 136–37, 148–49, 153–54, 254
Grand Lake, CO, 100
grandfathers, Sun Dance ceremonial, 16–17, 22, 27, 251, 279–80n4
Griswold, Gun, 90
Gros Ventre language and culture, 85–86, 116, 173, 185–89

Hannah, WY, 116
Hardin, MT, 116

homelanding: concept of, 60, 84–85, 87, 89, 98–99, 103, 114–15, 119–20, 124–26, 160; definition of, 84
Hudson, WY, 116
Hutchinson, Burton, 162

iconicity, syntactic, 93, 129–31, 133–34, 157
ideology of knowledge, traditional Arapaho: definition of, 18–19
immersion preschools, 64–66, 80, 163–65, 187–88, 193–94, 214, 222–23, 230–32, 237–38, 252–53, 258–60, 284n15
independent agency and existence: of the Arapaho language, 63, 65–72, 77, 261–62; of personal names, 132–33, 153–55, 159, 279n11
indigeneity: explicit discourses of, at Wind River, 36, 124, 248, 264, 281n2
introductions (formal), of self, in Arapaho, 81, 276n13

joking and humor, 239–40, 244, 249, 265–69; and folk etymologies, 174–75, 180, 196–99; and neologisms, 216–24, 238–39; and personal names, 142–47, 267–69; and place names, 115–18, 123–24, 166; institutionalized joking relationships, 23, 175

Kaska language and culture, 77–78, 157
killdeer: meanings and symbolics of the name, 205
Kiowa language and culture, 86
Kroeber, Alfred, 94–99, 102, 177–79, 206
Kumulipo, Hawaiian Creation Chant, 177–78

Lakota language and culture, 61–62, 130–31, 173, 206
Lander, WY, 121–23
language ideology: contextualized nature of, 8, 194; definition of, 3, 13

language perfectionism (in public performance): ideology of, 18–19, 43–44, 78–81, 260–62
language purism: ideology of, 30, 171, 204, 207–8, 212–14, 219, 232, 238, 262
language transparency: ideology of, 169–72, 177–78, 197–99, 225–26, 232, 238
Laramie, WY, 116
Little Popo Agie River, WY, 116
Little Wind River, WY, 3, 107, 117, 119–20
Littlebear, Dr. Richard, 239
Longs Peak, CO, 94
Lulu Pass, CO, 101

Maliseet language and culture, 124
master-apprentice relationships, 78–79, 139, 141–42, 145, 148, 163–64, 219–23, 232, 258
McCoy, Tim, 136
meadowlark: meanings and symbolics of name and calls, 206
Medicine Bow Mountains, CO/WY, 89, 100
Medicine Wheel (Bighorn Mts, WY), 87–89, 95–96, 98, 100, 108
Mississippi River, 86
Missoula, MT, 116
monkeys, words for, 174–75, 217
more-than-human (MTH) power: definition of, 9–11, 272n9
Moss, Paul, 51, 82–83, 87–89, 98, 100, 108, 114, 182, 264–65
motion verbs, in Arapaho, 55–60
Mount Meeker, CO, 94
Mummy Range, CO, 101

names and naming: definition of, 12–13
Navajo language and culture, 81
nicknames, 142, 147
nominalization, as a feature of endangered languages, 13–14, 70, 148, 236, 253–54
North Park, CO, 100
North Platte River, 85–86

Northern Arapaho Language and Culture Commission (NALCC), 227–28, 230, 232–33, 248, 252, 262
nostalgia, 23, 253, 274n12

onomatopoetic words, 205–7

path/journey, metaphor of, 55–70, 72–74, 76–77, 99–101, 275n6; connection to agency, 60–61; summary of, 61
per capita payments, 26, 29
peyote ceremony/Native American Church, 27–28, 32, 34–35, 39–40, 47, 108, 124, 243, 245
Pipe, Sacred, 16, 27, 34, 69–70, 77, 181, 189, 262
plant names and indigenous plant taxonomy, 208–11
Pleiades, 96
power, anthropological/theoretical: definition of, 11–12, 37–38
power, more-than-human, (indigenous): definition of, 9–10; as central focus of human inter-relationships, 10–11, 14, 37–38
powwows, 28, 34–35, 39–40, 47, 104, 122, 162, 189, 212, 243, 245
pulsed resources, 23, 26, 252, 273n4
Purgatoire River, CO, 168–69

quillwork, women's, 16–17, 19, 27, 94–95, 102, 106, 114, 191

Rabbit, Phillip, 179
Rabbit Lodge ceremony, 18, 27
raven: meanings and symbolics of the name, 205
reification, of the Arapaho language, 13–14, 64, 70–71, 76–78, 158, 253–54
resources, linguistic: definition of, 4, 271n3
respect: deeper ideologies and meanings of the term, 18, 23–25, 46, 74–75, 78–79, 111, 133–34, 139–42, 235–36, 251–55

Riverton, WY, 121–22
Rocky Mountain National Park, CO, 90–103, 278n14–15
Rocky Mountains, 85, 87, 89–90, 203–4, 208. *See also* Rocky Mountain National Park

sacredness of Arapaho language: ideology of, 9–11, 14, 30, 37–38, 55–56, 68–73, 74–80, 133–34, 178, 199, 254–55, 261–62, 265–66
Sage, Sherman, 90
Sand Creek CO and Sand Creek Masscre, 282n5
Sawtooth Mountain, CO, 101
schools and school-based language learning, 105–6, 138, 226–237, 258–59
screech owl: meanings and symbolics of the name, 206
semantic extensions, as a source of neologisms, 51–55, 62–70, 201–3, 208–11
semantic shifts, as a source of neologisms, 201–3
Sequoyah, 66
Shakespeare, Bill, 182
Shakespeare, Wes, 104–5
Shoshone Indians, 189
sign language, Plains Indian, 86, 212
slang, Arapaho, 175, 217–19, 221
snipe, Wilson's or common: meanings and symbolics of the name, 205
songs: sources of, 207
South Platte River, 85–86, 188
sovereignty, tribal, 29, 36, 40, 42, 247, 249
St. Stephens Mission, WY, 3, 121–22
streams and rivers: symbolic significance of, 60
student (high school and college) discourse, about the Arapaho language, 42–47, 70–76, 80–81, 247, 249, 262
sweat lodges/ceremonial sweating, 10, 27–28, 33, 35, 40, 47, 82–83, 106, 241, 243

ABOUT THE AUTHOR

Andrew Cowell is a professor of linguistic anthropology at the University of Colorado. His work focuses on language shift, documentation, maintenance, and revitalization, as well as topics in discourse, conversation, identity, and language ideology. He is the author or editor of several books, including *The Arapaho Language*.

Sun Dance, 10, 16–17, 22, 27–28, 32–33, 38, 47, 51, 61, 87, 124, 137, 166, 172, 175–76, 180, 182, 192, 212, 243, 245, 251, 265
symbolic language practices and ideologies: definition of, 8–9

Tangled Hair (legendary character), 96
teachers (Arapaho language teachers), 24, 65–68, 74, 76, 78–79, 138, 141–42, 163–64, 187–88, 193–94, 228–39, 249, 252, 258–62
television, 29–30, 53, 227
Thunderbird, 87, 96, 101
Toll, Oliver, 96–97
Tolowa language and culture, 118, 278n13
tracks, as metaphor for life in Arapaho, 59–60, 62, 99, 101
tribal colleges, 35, 39, 42–43, 81. *See also* Wind River Tribal College
Tribal Council, Northern Arapaho, 26, 247–48
Trickster (*Nih'oo3oo*), 60, 172–76, 178–79

turtles, 107–9, 114, 134, 175–76, 205–6, 250
Tyler, WY, 107

vision questing, 17, 33, 50–51, 87–88, 95, 97–100, 103, 109, 125, 132, 206

Warden, Cleaver, 179
Warden, Jim, 179, 192
Washakie, Chief (Shoshone), 189
Wheel, Sacred, 16, 69–70, 96
Whirlwind Woman (legendary character), 96
White Owl (legendary character), 96, 101
Willow, Edward, 139
Wind River Tribal College, 40, 43, 47, 70, 80–81, 103–4, 139, 143, 145, 164–65, 232–33, 247, 258, 262, 266, 268
World War II, 29–30

Yellow Calf, Chief, 164
Yellowstone area, 89
Yellowstone River, 86